TELEVISION
and the
AGGRESSIVE CHILD:
A Cross-National Comparison

COMMUNICATION

A series of volumes edited by:
Dolf Zillmann and Jennings Bryant

ZILLMANN and BRYANT • *Selective Exposure to Communication*

BEVILLE • *Audience Ratings: Radio, Television, and Cable*

BRYANT and ZILLMANN • *Perspectives on Media Effects*

GOLDSTEIN • *Reporting Science: The Case of Aggression*

ELLIS and DONOHUE • *Contemporary Issues in Language and Discourse Processes*

WINETT • *Information and Behavior: Systems of Influence*

HUESMANN and ERON • *Television and the Aggressive Child: A Cross-National Comparison*

GUNTER • *Poor Reception: Miscomprehension and Forgetting of Broadcast News*

RODDA and GROVE • *Language, Cognition, and Deafness*

TELEVISION
and the
AGGRESSIVE CHILD:
A Cross-National Comparison

edited by

L. ROWELL HUESMANN
LEONARD D. ERON
University of Illinois at Chicago

LAWRENCE ERLBAUM ASSOCIATES, PUBLISHERS
1986   Hillsdale, New Jersey   London

Lawrence Erlbaum Associates, Inc., Publishers
365 Broadway
Hillsdale, New Jersey 07642

Library of Congress Cataloging-in-Publication Data
Main entry under title:

Television and the aggressive child.

Includes bibliographies and index.
1. Television and children — Cross-cultural studies.
2. Violence in television — Cross-cultural studies.
3. Aggressiveness in children — Cross-cultural studies.
I. Huesmann, L. Rowell. II. Eron, Leonard D.
HQ784.T4T446   1986   305.2′3   85-24490
ISBN 0-89859-754-4

Printed in the United States of America
10 9 8 7 6 5 4 3 2

Contents

CONTRIBUTORS   ix

PREFACE   xi

1 THE DEVELOPMENT OF AGGRESSION IN CHILDREN OF
DIFFERENT CULTURES: PSYCHOLOGICAL PROCESSES
AND EXPOSURE TO VIOLENCE
L. Rowell Huesmann and Leonard D. Eron   1
Introduction   1
The Aims of the Study   23

2 THE CROSS-NATIONAL APPROACH TO RESEARCH ON
AGGRESSION: MEASURES AND PROCEDURES
Leonard D. Eron and L. Rowell Huesmann   29
Introduction   29

3 THE DEVELOPMENT OF AGGRESSION IN AMERICAN
CHILDREN AS A CONSEQUENCE OF TELEVISION
VIOLENCE VIEWING
L. Rowell Huesmann and Leonard D. Eron   45
Introduction   45
Method   49
Results   51
Discussion   76
Conclusion   78

4 *TELEVISION AND AGGRESSIVE BEHAVIOR AMONG*
FINNISH CHILDREN
Kirsti Lagerspetz and Vappu Viemerö 81
Introduction   81
Method   88
Results   92
Conclusion   110

5 *SOCIO-CULTURAL ENVIRONMENT, TELEVISION*
VIEWING, AND THE DEVELOPMENT OF AGGRESSION
AMONG CHILDREN IN POLAND
Adam Fraczek 119
Introduction   119
Method   127
Results   131
Discussion   152
Conclusion   155

6 *TELEVISION VIEWING AND ITS RELATION TO*
AGGRESSION AMONG CHILDREN IN AUSTRALIA
Peter W. Sheehan 161
Introduction   161
Comments on Literature   167
Analysis of the Content of Australian Television   171
Method   176
Results   178
Peer-Rated Aggression and Its Correlates   180
Discussion   189
Conclusion and Policy Implications   194

7 *THE DIFFERENTIAL EFFECT OF OBSERVATION OF*
VIOLENCE ON KIBBUTZ AND CITY CHILDREN IN ISRAEL
Riva S. Bachrach 201
Introduction   201
Method   212
Results   215
Discussion and Conclusion   234

8 *CROSS-NATIONAL COMMUNALITIES IN THE LEARNING OF*
AGGRESSION FROM MEDIA VIOLENCE
L. Rowell Huesmann 239
Summary   255

9 *INTERNATIONAL RESEARCH ON TELEVISION VIOLENCE: SYNOPSIS AND CRITIQUE*
Jo Groebel 259
Media Research in International Perspective 260
Methods of Cross-Cultural Research 262
Cross-National Comparison and Integration of the Results 275
A Cognitive Model of TV Violence Effects 278

APPENDIX I: INSTRUCTIONS FOR CLASSROOM PROCEDURES ... 283

APPENDIX II: COEFFICIENT ALPHAS FOR SELECTED
VARIABLES IN EACH COUNTRY..................................... 299

EPILOGUE 301

AUTHOR INDEX   303

SUBJECT INDEX   309

Contributors

Riva Bachrach
Ribbutz Child and
Family Clinic
Tel Aviv ISRAEL

Leonard D. Eron
Department of Psychology
University of Illinois at
Chicago
Chicago, IL 60680
USA

Adam Fraczek
Department of Psychology
Polish Academy of Sciences
Warsaw
POLAND

Jo Groebel
Department of
Communication
Psychology
Educational University
Rheinland-Pfalz
6470 Laundau
WEST GERMANY

L. Rowell Huesmann
Department of Psychology
University of Illinois at
Chicago
Chicago, IL 60680
USA

Kirsti Lagerspetz
Department of Psychology
University of Turku
SF-20 500 Turku
FINLAND

Peter Sheehan
Department of Psychology
University of Queensland
St. Lucia, Queensland
AUSTRALIA

Vappu Viemerö
Department of Psychology
Åbo Akademi
Turku
FINLAND

Preface

This book and the worldwide research program it summarizes had their conception in an airplane high above Lake Michigan in 1975. We were returning from a meeting in Toronto with our colleagues, Monroe Lefkowitz and Leopold Walder. At that meeting we had finished the draft of our previous book, *Growing Up To Be Violent*. While trapped in Chicago's usual air traffic congestion, we began discussing what direction our research should now take.

The Surgeon General's Report on Television and Social Behavior had been released just 3 years earlier amid an explosion of interest in the effects of media violence on aggression. Our 10-year follow-up study of over 800 children in New York State played a key role in that report. However, it was the impressive consistency (for psychological studies) of the entire body of emerging research literature, rather than any one study, that led the Surgeon General, Dr. Jesse Steinfeld, to issue his conclusion that "television violence, indeed, does have an adverse effect on certain members of our society." Fresh from integrating our results with the other research, we found it hard to believe that any reasonable scientist would doubt the Surgeon General's conclusion. More research linking media violence and the learning of aggression did not seem nearly as valuable to us as research that would pinpoint the psychological process through which media violence exerted its effect. Thus, we quickly set as our first goal a better understanding of the psychological processes involved in the media violence-aggression relation.

As it turns out, we were somewhat naive in assuming 10 years ago that the issue of whether media violence affects aggression had been solved. Yet one of the most important reasons as to why the controversy has persisted may be exactly the point we identified as our goal for future research. Without a psychological process model to explain how media violence affects aggression, it is very difficult to integrate the body of research literature into a coherent framework. Just as not every person who smokes cigarettes gets lung cancer, not every child who watches violence behaves more aggressively. Which child will be affected and why? What variables intervene in the process? What are the boundaries within which the effect occurs? For lung cancer, there is a physiological model that explains how the carcinogens released through smoking can engender cancer. This model makes the statistical evidence of a relation much more compelling than it would otherwise be. Without a comparable psychological model for the effects of media violence on aggression, the statistical evidence of a relation remains open to alternative explanations. It is no coincidence that among psychologists more familiar with the psychological processes involved in learning and personality development, the evidence that media violence engenders aggression is most readily accepted. Among other social scientists and statisticians who focus only on the descriptive data, skepticism is higher.

The second related conclusion we reached on that airplane flight was that media violence research must be integrated with other aggression research. Partially because the topic had initially attracted more communication researchers than aggression researchers, only a few scientists had attempted to place media violence within the framework of a general theory for the development of aggression. In analyzing our 10-year data, we had done exactly that, viewing TV actors as one of several models with which a child might identify. However, it had been a post-hoc approach. In fact, our original finding in 1960 of a relation between a boy's aggressive behavior and a boy's exposure to media violence had been mostly serendipitous. The questions about the child's television viewing habits had actually been "filler" items included only to space out the occurrence of items that might embarrass the child's parents. More longitudinal data were needed in which the role of media violence could be compared with the role of other hypothesized causes of aggression.

Finally, as our third goal, we wanted to extend the investigation of the TV violence-aggression effect beyond the North American environment. By 1975, television had become a major influence in virtually every developed country. Yet with a few exceptions, the entire body of research on TV violence and aggression had been obtained from North American samples. It was not only a question of whether the relatively uncontrolled round-the-clock programming available in the United States was necessary for media effects to be substantial. From a psychological perspective, the role of culture as an intervening variable was unknown. Cultural norms and programming differences might well interact with age and gender of children to produce quite different effects in different countries. One could hardly build a general psychological theory for how media violence engenders aggression based on only one culture and one programming system.

Given these goals, in late 1975 we proposed, as a first step, a 3-year longitudinal study to be carried out in the Chicago area. Huesmann took primary responsibility for designing the field study, obtaining funding for it, and implementing it. In 1976 the National Institute of Mental Health awarded a 3-year grant for the study, and data collection began in 1977. However, from the start our overall plan was to replicate this study in as many other countries as possible in as similar a manner as possible. Therefore, Eron began recruiting friends and collaborators who were willing to undertake the replications with little funding. In 1978, the University of Illinois generously provided Huesmann with a travel grant to visit most of the recruited collaborators and discuss the research plan with them. Without any guarantee of funds from us, most of them began data collection in that year or the next. However, in 1979 and 1980, NIMH awarded us two more grants — one to Eron for a 22-year follow-up of our original 1960 subjects in New York State and one to Huesmann specifically for the cross-national replications. Although little of the data from the 22-year follow-up are reported in this book, its results inevitably influenced our thinking. The grant for the cross-national research allowed us to complete our planned replications, and the last wave of data was obtained in 1983.

The results of the Chicago and cross-national research programs are the subjects of this book. We hope that this study of the television viewing habits and aggressive behaviors of children and their parents in five different countries (Australia, Finland, Israel, Poland, and the United States) demonstrates both the robustness of the causal connection between TV violence and aggression, as well as the limitations on it. What emerges is a psychological model in which TV violence viewing is both a precursor and a consequence of aggression.

As described in the book, the choice of countries participating in this program was purely adventitious, although as it turns out, these countries do cover a wide spectrum of cultural, economic and political systems, as well as a wide range in extent of governmental control of television programming. We also invited psychologists in a sixth country, The Netherlands, to participate in the research program. Although they agreed to join the study, they did not believe that the procedures used in the five other countries were suitable for The Netherlands. Therefore, they dropped some measures completely, shortened and adapted others and added a number of procedures of their own. Their data analyses also did not conform to those done in the other countries, and their monographic compendium of results was deemed unsuitable for this book. After much discussion, it was agreed that it would be best for them to publish their results independently. However, some of their already published results are compared and contrasted with the results of other countries in our summary chapters.

The book begins with two general chapters: an introductory chapter outlining the theoretical rationale, social importance, and historical background of the study, and a methods chapter that describes the common methodology adopted in all five countries. Where there are deviations from the common methodology because of local conditions, language difficulties and so on, these are taken up in detail in the chapter describing that country's results. As a matter of fact, however, the adaptations necessary were minimal. The third chapter describes the results in the United States, followed by chapters dealing with the findings in Finland, Poland, Australia, and Israel in that order. Each of these chapters is written by the individuals who carried out the research in the respective countries. All are seasoned investigators and distinguished psychologists: in Finland, Professor Kirsti Lagerspetz and Dr. Vappu Viemerö; in Poland, Professor Adam Fraczek; in Australia, Professor Peter Sheehan; and in Israel, Dr. Riva Bachrach. The results from the various countries are integrated, discussed, and contrasted with other research in chapter 8, which Huesmann has written. In chapter 9, Dr. Jo Groebel of the Department of Communication Psychology of the Educational University at Landau, West Germany has written a critique of the study from the prospective of an outside researcher. Finally, we have attempted to draw a few coherent conclusions in the brief epilogue.

In a project of such wide scope, there are many persons whose assistance has been invaluable and whose efforts in its behalf should be acknowledged. The individuals and organizations in each of the countries who were indispensable in carrying out the research there are mentioned in introductions or footnotes to those individual chapters. There are, however, some more general acknowledgments that should be made. We are deeply indebted to NIMH which, through grants MH-28280, MH-31866, and MH-38683, provided most of the funding for this project. Dr. David Pearl of NIMH was most helpful, and we appreciate his support and encouragement. The Research Board at the University of Illinois at Chicago provided preliminary funding including support of initial travel to contact foreign collaborators, and the Australian Research Grants Scheme co-funded the work in Australia. We are also grateful to Herr Konrad von Krosig, Director of the Werner Reimers Stiftung in Bad Homburg, West Germany for providing accommodations and facilities at that institution for a 5-day meeting of the collaborators from each country.

All of the major data analyses for every country were carried out under Huesmann's supervision on the University of Illinois at Chicago's time-sharing system. A number of individuals were instrumental in conducting these analyses. Dr. Pat Brice bore the brunt of the enormous amount of work involved in the initial data processing and early analyses. Dr Rebecca Mermelstein conducted many of the early psychometric analyses of the TV measures. Dr. Erica Rosenfeld developed the fantasy measure. Dr. Eric Dubow, Dr. Richard Romanoff, Evelynne Seebauer, and Patty Yarmel faithfully ran analysis after analysis for us over the years and assisted in the editing of the chapters. Gary Hudson and David Tulsky assisted in both the analyses and editing.

We are grateful to Dr. Elizabeth Feldman for her careful copyediting of the chapters from countries other than the United States and for her many suggestions for increasing the readability and comparability of the chapters. Laura Kavesh corrected the page proofs and constructed the indexes. Evelyn Diaz and Lisa Dryja worked countless hours typing and retyping various versions of the entire manuscript into our word processing systems. Joyce Rozwadowski was extremely helpful in facilitating mechanical details such as seeing that our research staff was appropriately paid, our foreign collaborators reimbursed, and our accounts correctly audited. Janet Garcia got our office organized when we started this study, and her sister, Diane Legac, flawlessly copied and organized the finished manuscript. And, of course, we could not have conducted this research at all without the support of our wives, Penny and Madeline, who put up with our strange hours and long absences from home. To all of these persons, as well as to those noted in the individual chapters, go our heartfelt thanks.

Rowell Huesmann
Leonard Eron
Rome, Italy

The Development of Aggression in Children of Different Cultures: Psychological Processes and Exposure to Violence

1

L. Rowell Huesmann
Leonard D. Eron
University of Illinois at Chicago

INTRODUCTION

It is arguable whether there is more or less interpersonal violence in the world today than at other times. Objective historical comparisons about violence are difficult to make because comparable statistics are seldom available in different areas of the world and for different historical periods. Furthermore, variations in levels of interpersonal violence between societies or even within segments of the same society have often exceeded variations across centuries. For example, how violent was Roman society? Certainly, violence was institutionalized in Roman society in ways that make us cringe today. Christians were thrown to the lions; gladiators routinely killed each other; criminals were regularly crucified. The Visigoths, Vandals, Huns, and other people whom the Romans called barbarians did themselves consider the institutionalized violence of the Romans cruel and uncivilized. However, at the height of Roman civilization, individual interpersonal violence was probably less than it has been in many socieities since then. Rome was a society of rule by law, and the laws and standards of the society limited interpersonal violence. As Rome declined in power, interpersonal violence seemed to increase. The lesson that has been repeated many times in history is that there is no necessary relation between institutionalized violence and individual interpersonal violence. Men who could never strike another man in anger can become instruments of violence toward multitudes in wars. Is the man in a missile silo who presses the button necessarily an aggressive man? Violent acts that a society would never condone if committed by an individual are accepted without qualm when ordered by the leaders of that society.

This book does not deal with the institutionalized aggression represented by wars and repressive governments (Singer, 1979, 1980). Rather, it deals with individual, interpersonal aggression and how certain facets of a society's structure may, perhaps unintentionally, promote such aggression.

What do we mean by aggression? For our purposes, an aggressive act is one that is intended to injure or irritate another person. However, past research has demonstrated that intentionality is difficult or impossible to measure, particularly in children (Eron, Walder, & Lefkowitz, 1971). Therefore, our operational definition of *aggression* is simply an act that injures or irritates another person. In the context of everyday life such an operational definition may fail to discriminate adequately between aggression and injurious acts that are accidental, e.g., an airplane crash, or done for the benefit of the individual, e.g., surgery. In studies with children, though, this operational definition has proved effective. One should note that, under either the everyday or operational definition of aggression, behaviors that many people might call aggressive (e.g., assertiveness, ambition, and striving) are excluded. The so-called "aggressive salesman" is only assertive by our definition. It is the antisocial aggressive act and its precursors that are under investigation here.

Concern with Aggression

Western societies are probably more concerned now about interpersonal aggression than ever before. Such heightened concerns about violent antisocial behavior are undoubtedly a product of many factors. Most notably, since World War II the levels of interpersonal violence as reflected in crime statistics have seemed to skyrocket in many countries. Between 1950 and 1981 the rate of homicides increased in the United States from 5.3 per 100,000 to 10.3 (U.S. Bureau of Census, 1982, p. 178). However, as Fig. 1.1 indicates, this increase was concentrated mostly in the years 1960 to 1974 with little increase before or after. If anything, recent data suggest that the homicide rates may be declining in the United States during the early 1980s (Uniform Crime Reports Booklet, 1983). Later in this chapter we present comparable data from the other countries. For now, it is sufficient to conclude that at least in the United States there was a substantial increase in violent crime during the 1960s.

Although many have attributed this increase to the disintegration of social institutions, other simpler explanations must also be considered. Many criminologists believe that the recent upsurge is a simple function of a bulge in the population of males between the ages of 16 and 25 (Hirschi & Gottfredson, 1983; Sagi & Wellford, 1968). These are the individuals who commit most crimes of violence. For example, in 1974 when the homicide rate was 10.2 per 100,000 for the whole population, the rate was over 31.2 per 100,000 for

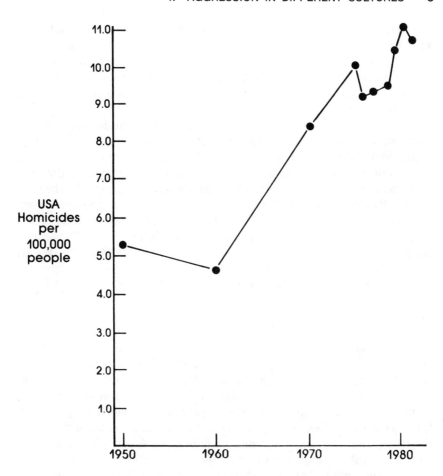

FIG. 1.1 Homicides per 100,000 people in the United States from 1950 to 1981.

males age 18 to 24 (Newman, 1979, p. 69–70). While the overall homicide rate in the United States doubled from 1950 to 1980, the rate among these young males tripled. At the same time, the percentage of 18-24-year-olds in the United States population was increasing. Thus, by the mid 1970s about 75% of all homicides were committed by young males (Newman, 1979). One might ask how much homicides would have increased over these years if the proportion of young males in the population had remained constant. Although no one can know the exact answer, when we correct statistically for the population changes, we find that about one quarter of the increase in homicides from 1950 to 1979 in the United States can be attributed entirely to the increase of young males in the population. According to this reasoning, crime rates should soon decline in the United States as the proportion of the population in the 15 to 24-year age range diminishes. Thus, although some governmental officials would like to attribute recent small declines in crime to the policies they have been promoting (e.g., 9% decrease in homicides from 1982 to 1983 according to the FBI's Uniform Crime Report Booklet, 1983), it is equally plausible that the decline is simply a function of the changing demographics.

Society's recent concern about violence may also stem in part from the communication and transportation revolutions of recent years. Expressways and rapid transit systems have opened the suburbs to the violence spawned by urban slums. Television graphically portrays violent crimes on dramatic shows and obsessively reports actual crimes on news programs. To the average middle-class person, violence must seem much closer and more threatening than in previous years. Finally, society's heightened concern about violent antisocial behavior may also reflect the evolution of most Western societies toward more collective responsibility for individual behavior. We are not as willing to let the possibilities for escaping the effects of violence depend on one's wealth, position, or place of residence.

The Causes of Aggression

Serious antisocial aggression clearly seems to be an overdetermined behavior—that is, a number of interrelated factors must converge for it to emerge (Eron, 1982). Genetic, physiological, and other constitutional factors undoubtedly play a role in many cases, but they cannot account for the extreme individual differences one finds in aggressive behavior among humans. It is the rare case of aggressiveness that can be traced to central nervous system (CNS) abnormalities. Hormonal variations, particularly in testosterone, may also explain some differences; but more differences remain unexplained. The truth is that no one factor by itself predicts aggressiveness very well in humans. The innate aggressive responses one finds in lower animals cannot usually be demonstrated in humans. Despite some ethologists' claims, there is little evidence to support the concept of an innate aggressive drive in man. Rather, the mounting evidence suggests that aggression is to a great extent learned. For most children, aggressiveness seems to be determined mostly by the extent to which their environment reinforces aggression, provides aggressive models, frustrates and victimizes the child, and instigates aggression. Thus, to understand the development of aggression, one must examine simultaneously a multiplicity of interrelated social, cultural, familial, and cognitive factors, each of which adds only a small increment to the totality of causation. It is unrealistic to expect that any one of these factors by itself can explain much about aggression. But in conjunction with each other they may explain a lot about aggression. Of course, to investigate the role of a set of these factors adequately, one must obtain substantial variations in them. For many factors, such variation can only be obtained by investigations of children that span the boundaries of culture, age, and gender. It was out of such thinking that the cross-national investigation reported in this book was initiated.

A Cross-National Approach to Aggression Research

The chapters in this book report on the results of a unique investigation of aggressive behavior in children carried out in five countries between 1977 and 1983. The countries participating in the study were Australia, Finland, Israel, Poland, and the United States. Originally, we had hoped this volume would include data from a sixth country, The Netherlands. However, the study that was eventually conducted by our collaborators in The Netherlands was unique in many essential design characteristics, and its authors decided to report its results separately. Nevertheless, where appropriate, we contrast results in the five participating countries with published results from The Netherlands study, and discuss any important differences.

In each country substantial samples of children and their parents were interviewed and tested repeatedly over 3 years. The reasons for the choice of these countries were primarily practical: collaborating researchers in these countries were interested in the project. However, this selection of countries also fortuitously provided us with substantial variations in aggressiveness of children and in other factors likely to be related to agressive behavior. But before the results can be described in later chapters, the goals, theories, and methods on which the investigation was based must be discussed.

Observed Violence and Violent Behavior

The major focus of this book is on the role that a child's exposure to violence plays in teaching him or her aggressive acts. Because violence appears on television to a much larger extent than in real life, the TV provides even more opportunities to experience violence than real life does. Evidence accumulated over the past 20 years from both laboratory and field studies has led most reviewers to conclude that aggressiveness and viewing violence are interdependent to some degree (Andison, 1977; Chaffee, 1972; Comstock, 1980; Eysenck & Nias, 1978, Hearold, 1979; Huesmann, 1982; Lefkowitz & Huesmann, 1980). More aggressive children watch more violent television. The relation is not strong by the standards used in the measurement of intellectual abilities, but the relation is highly significant statistically and is substantial by the usual standards of personality measurement with children. More importantly, the relation is highly replicable.

Although the relation between violence viewing and aggression is clear, the reason for the relation is not; nor has it been established that the relation goes in only one direction. Too often researchers have viewed the causal relation between violence viewing and aggression as an either/or proposition when, in fact, the causal effect may be bidirectional.

Does Television Violence Engender Aggressive Behavior?

There can be little doubt that in specific laboratory settings exposing children to violent behavior on film or TV increases the likelihood that they will behave aggressively immediately afterwards. In the typical paradigm, randomly selected children are shown either a violent or nonviolent short film and then are observed as they play with each other or with objects such as "Bobo dolls." The consistent finding is that the children who see the violent film clip behave more aggressively immediately afterwards. Many laboratory studies have demonstrated this effect (Comstock, 1980). It has usually been attributed to "observational learning" (Bandura, 1977; Bandura, Ross, & Ross, 1961, 1963a, 1963b) in which children imitate the behaviors of the models they observe. Just as they learn cognitive and social skills from watching parents, siblings, and peers, they can learn to behave aggressively from watching violent actors. Similarly, children can learn to be less aggressive by watching pro social models. For example, in Finland, Pitkänen-Pulkkinen (1979) showed that the aggressive behavior of 8-year-old boys could be reduced by their watching films depicting constructive solutions to conflicts that appear frequently in children's everyday life. The question is whether the positive correlations between violence viewing and aggressive behavior found in the laboratory generalize to the real world.

The first substantial evidence from a field setting implicating television violence as a cause of aggressive behavior was provided by the 10-year longitudinal study of Eron, Huesmann, Lefkowitz, and Walder (1972; Lefkowitz, Eron, Walder, & Huesmann, 1977). The results suggested that excessive violence viewing increases the likelihood that a boy behaves aggressively. Since the Lefkowitz et al. study, a number of other observational studies and field experiments have suggested that violence viewing is indeed a precursor of aggression (Belson, 1978; Granzberg & Steinbring, 1980; Hennigan, Del Rosario, Heath, Cook, Wharton, & Calder, 1982; Leyens, Parke, Camino, & Berkowitz, 1975; Loye, Gorney, & Steele, 1977; Parke, Berkowitz, Leyens, West, & Sebastian, 1977; Singer & Singer, 1981; Stein & Friedrich, 1972; Williams, 1978). However, the authors of one recent longitudinal study (Milavsky, Kessler, Stipp, & Rubens, 1982) have concluded that exposure to television violence does not affect aggressive behavior. Actually, as noted by Huesmann (1984), the results of the Milavsky study are not very different from those of other recent field studies. It is primarily Milavsky's interpretation of the findings that is different. For example, most of the regression coefficients Milavsky derives for predicting later aggression from earlier TV violence viewing are positive (12 of 15, which is well beyond chance). However, Milavsky focuses on the fact that only a few of these coefficients are significantly greater than zero. Cook, Kendzierski, and Thomas (1983) conclude that these data indicate a weak positive effect of TV violence on aggression. However, we believe such a conclusion understates the case. Milavsky and his colleagues approached the problem from an atheoretical perspective that provided little guidance for selecting appropriate analyses. As Huesmann (1984) has argued, hypotheses about psychological processes must be tested if one is to understand what the observed relations between variables signify. To the developmental psychologist familiar with how aggression is learned, Milavsky's conclusions seem unjustified.

Another argument sometimes leveled against the research linking television violence viewing by children to increased aggressiveness is that "real" aggression was not measured. Boisterousness, hyperactivity, and even some "nastiness" may be related to violence viewing, but these are not the same as the antisocial aggressive behavior of youths and adults that concerns society. Certainly, no one would argue that a fight among children can be equated with a fight among adults. However, the evidence indicates that these "childish" types of aggressive behaviors are the precursors of more serious antisocial aggressive behaviors of adults.

A rapidly accumulating body of data suggests that aggression, as a characteristic way of solving social problems, usually emerges early in life. Each individual seems to develop a characteristic level of aggressiveness early in life that remains relatively stable across time and situation. This does not mean that situational factors are unimportant. They can greatly influence the probability of occurrence of an aggressive act. Certain circumstances make aggression more likely for anyone, and at different ages different forms of aggression become most likely. The stability that we describe is a stability of relative position in the population. The more aggressive child very likely becomes the more aggressive adult. In his review of 16 separate studies with lags ranging from 6 months to 21 years, Olweus (1979) reported disattenuated stability coefficients ranging from .36 for Kagan and Moss' (1962) study of 36 five-year-olds who were followed for 18 years to over .95 for his own (1977) study of 85 thirteen-year-olds over 1 year.

Although these existing studies seem to establish quite clearly that aggression is not a transient behavior for most children, only a few studies have examined the extent to which childhood aggression is predictive of adult criminality and antisocial behavior. Yet, this is a critical issue for the media violence—aggression research. Most of that research has associated childhood aggression with childhood exposure to violence. But is such childhood aggression predictive of adult criminality?

Two recent studies suggest that the answer is yes. Roff and Wirt (1984) found that early aggression was predictive of later delinquency in males. Even more impressive evidence is provided by a recent study completed by

Huesmann, Eron, Lefkowitz, and Walder (1984). The subjects of this study were the 870 individuals who had been interviewed in 1960 as children in the Eron et al. (1971) study of aggression. Their parents had also been interviewed at that time. In 1981 we tracked down as many of the original subjects as possible. Their modal age was 30 at that time. We were able to locate and interview 295 of the original subjects in person and another 114 by mail and telephone for a total of 409 (198 males, 211 females). We were also successful in obtaining interviews with the spouses of 165 of the interviewed subjects and with 82 of the subjects' own children who at the time were approximately the same age as the subjects when first seen in 1960. In addition to the interviews, we obtained all available data from the New York State Divisions of Criminal Justice Services and Motor Vehicles about the subjects. We obtained at least some data from these archives on 542 of our original subjects. Coupled with the interview data, this gave us some 1981 follow-up data on 632 of our original subjects (358 males, 274 females).

Correlations between the early and later measures of aggression are shown in Table 1.1. As reported elsewhere (Huesmann et al., 1984), it is apparent that over 22 years there is good predictability from early aggression to later aggression, especially in the case of males. Also, the stability of aggression holds up across method, informant and situation as well as time. Especially

TABLE 1.1

Correlations of Peer-Nominated Aggression at Age 8 With Antisocial Aggression at Age 30

Age 30 Measures	Males Age 8 Aggression		Females Age 8 Aggression	
	N	r	N	r
Aggression				
MMPI Scales F + 4 + 9	290	.30***	209	.16*
				(.20**)
Spouse Abuse	88	.27**	74	—
Punishment of Child by Subject	63	.24*	96	.24**
Criminal Justice Convictions	335	.24***	207	—
				(.10)
Seriousness of Criminal Acts	332	.21***	207	—
				(.15**)
Moving Traffic Violations	322	.21***	201	—
Driving While Intoxicated	322	.29***	201	—
		(.24***)		
Self-rating of Physical Aggression	193	.25***	209	—
		(.29***)		

*p < .05   **p < .01   ***p < .001

Note: The correlations shown in parentheses are those that changed .04 or more when skew-correcting transformations were applied.

impressive is the correlation between aggression at age 8 and later encounters with the law as indicated by driving and criminal offenses. Structural models developed from these data to estimate the disattenuated stability of aggression revealed that the age 8 to age 30 stability for boys was about .50 and for girls was about .35 (Huesmann et al., 1984). Taken together, these data indicate that aggressive behavior is reasonably stable across time and situations and that peer-nominations of aggression at age 8 are predictive of serious antisocial behavior as an adult (Huesmann et al. 1984).

Such results convincingly counter the arguments some have made that childhood aggression as measured in most studies of media violence is not an important concern. The data suggest that aggressive habits are learned early in life and, once established, are resistant to change and are predictive of serious adult antisocial behavior. If a child's observation of violence promotes the learning of aggressive habits, it can have harmful lifelong consequences.

The Process of Learning Aggression from Violence Viewing

What are the psychological processes through which exposing a child to excessive media violence might engender aggressive behavior? Over much of the past 20 years, researchers' attentions have been focused primarily on three processes: (a) observational learning; (b) arousal processes; and (c) attitude change. Recently, however, following the emergence of information-processing models as a dominant force in cognitive psychology, a number of researchers (Berkowitz, 1974, 1984; Collins, 1973; Huesmann, 1982; Huesmann & Eron, 1984; Huesmann, Eron, Klein, Brice, & Fischer, 1983; Turner & Fenn, 1978) have turned toward information-processing models to explain the learning of aggression.

Observational Learning

According to advocates of observational learning, children learn to behave aggressively by imitating violent actors on television just as they learn cognitive and social skills by imitating parents, siblings, peers, and others. Since Bandura's original laboratory experiments (Bandura et al., 1961, 1963a, 1963b) suggested the validity of this thesis, a number of experiments and field studies attempted to test and elucidate the theory (Bandura, 1977). Although the research illuminated some of the conditions under which behaviors portrayed in the media are most likely to be imitated, the actual importance of observational learning in influencing the aggressiveness of children has not been determined.

Part of the problem has been that observational learning means different things to different people. Bandura's original definition was narrow and specifically behavioral. It has been expanded by some to include virtually any process by which an observed behavior influences a viewer. At the same time, many "purists" acted as if observational learning were a distinct process separated from a subject's other cognitive processes. In fact, until recently it was difficult to find evidence that many investigators of observational learning were aware of cognitive processes. This diversity of understandings of observational learning has hampered the formation of precise models and contributed to some important controversies. For example, the issue of whether children learn a generalized disinhibition of aggression or learn specific aggressive acts becomes less important when one casts these theories in information-processing terms. Current information-processing models of memory provide a perspective in which these theories can be complementary rather than competing.

The extent to which a child imitates an actor is greatly influenced by the reinforcements received by the actor. If the actor is seen being rewarded for aggressive behavior, the child is more likely to imitate that behavior (Bandura, 1965; Bandura et al., 1963a; Walters et al., 1963). If the actor is punished for a behavior, that behavior is less likely to be modeled (Bandura, 1965; Walters & Parke, 1964). This appears to be true for prosocial as well as for antisocial behavior (Morris, Marshall & Miller, 1973).

Although such vicarious reinforcements influence the probability of the child emitting the actor's behaviors, the persistence of the behavior seems to depend on the direct reinforcements the child receives. For some children, aggressive behavior may often produce inherently reinforcing consequences. Hayes, Rincover, and Volosin (1980) showed that even the reflexive movements of objects aggressed against can be reinforcing to the aggressor. These authors also found purely additive effects for imitation and reinforcement on aggression.

A number of researchers have attempted to determine the ages at which children are most susceptible to imitating observed behaviors. Eron et al. (1972) argued that once an individual has reached adolescence, behavioral predispositions and inhibitory controls have become crystallized to the extent that a child's aggressive habits would be difficult to change with modeling. More recent research has indicated that the period between 6 and 10 years is an especially sensitive one for learning by observation (Eron, Huesmann, Brice, Fischer, & Mermelstein, 1983). Collins (1973; Collins, Berndt, & Hess, 1974; Newcomb & Collins, 1979) consistently found that young children are less able to draw the relation between motives and aggression and therefore may be more prone to imitate inappropriate aggressive behaviors. Hearold's (1979) review generally supports these views but suggests that modeling might increase again among adolescent boys. Perhaps the more important question, however, is at how young an age children begin to imitate behaviors viewed on television. Experiments by McCall, Park, and Kavanaugh (1977) indicate that children as young as 2 years are facile at imitating televised behaviors and some imitation is observed in even younger children.

Another factor frequently hypothesized to be implicated in observational learning is the viewer's identification with the actor or actress being modeled. Within the existing literature, however, the evidence is ambiguous on the role that identification plays in observational learning. Bandura et al. (1963a, 1963b) found that boys and girls more readily imitated male rather than female models. One of the problems with using gender as a measure of identification with a television model is that aggression is highly correlated with sex-role orientation within genders (Lefkowitz et al., 1977). Girls who are aggressive may in fact identify more with male actors than with most female actors.

Studies measuring other types of identification besides sex role have also yielded ambiguous results. In studies comparing the race of the actor and viewer, black children have sometimes been found to imitate white models more than black models (e.g., Neely, Heckel, & Leichtman, 1973); and in some cases children have been found to imitate adults more than peers (Nicholas, McCarter, & Heckel, 1971) at least at a time long after viewing (Hicks, 1965). Even with two peer actors differing greatly in likability, no difference has been found in the propensity of the viewer to imitate either of the actors (Howitt & Cumberbatch, 1972). On the other hand, when subjects are asked to assume mentally the role of an actor who is aggressive, they are more likely to behave aggressively afterwards (Turner & Berkowitz, 1972). Although perceived similarity of interest between the model and child can enhance the likelihood of imitation (Rosekrans, 1967), the aforementioned findings suggest that a simplistic view of identification will not aid much in the understanding of observational learning. Rather, it appears that a child is most likely to imitate a model perceived to possess valued characteristics.

Attitude Change

Another way in which television violence exerts its influence on children is through the molding of children's attitudes. The more television a child watches, the more accepting is the child's attitude toward aggressive behavior (Dominick & Greenberg, 1972). Equally important, the more a person watches television, the more suspicious a person is, and the greater is the person's expectancy of being involved in real violence (Gerbner & Gross, 1974, 1980). Why? Again, from an information-processing standpoint, attitudes are attributions, rules, and explanations induced from observations of behavior. They serve as heuristics for future behavior. If a child's, or even an adult's major exposure to social interaction occurs through television, the conception of social reality would quite naturally be based on such observations. The attitudes toward aggression of heavy television viewers would be more positive because they perceive aggressive behavior to be the norm. Perhaps even the perception of what is an aggressive act changes. One problem with the evidence for such effects is the potential correlation of heavy violence viewing with other factors that could cause accepting attitudes toward aggression (e.g., social class and aggression in the environment). Doob and MacDonald (1979) found, for example, that the correlation between fear of victimization and violence viewing becomes insignificant when one controls for neighborhood. Despite such findings, the weight of evidence suggests that television violence can alter one's attitudes toward aggression and that one's attitudes in turn influence one's behavior.

One recent study that cleverly demonstrated the relation between television program material, viewer's attitudes, and viewer's later behaviors was performed in Georgia. Ryback and Connel (1978) examined the relative incidence of unruly behavior among white and black high school students in the weeks before, during, and after the broadcasting of *Roots*. Using a relatively objective dependent measure (number of after-school detentions), they found a significant increase for blacks during the weeks *Roots* was shown. Apparently, watching *Roots* changed the black students' attitudes about obedience. Another body of evidence has been provided by researchers investigating *desensitization* of viewers. This term, unfortunately, has been used to refer to two quite different processes: attitude change and arousal change. Here, we consider desensitization of attitudes. Although a fair amount of violence viewing might be required to affect an adult's attitudes, experiments by Drabman and Thomas (1974a, 1974b; Thomas & Drabman, 1975) revealed that young children's willingness to accept aggressive behavior in other children can be increased by even brief exposures to violent film scenes. Such accepting attitudes, in turn, make it more likely that the child may behave aggressively and perhaps make it more likely that the child will model aggressive acts. Meyer (1972) reported that whenever a subject observes violent acts perceived as justified, the probability increases that the subject will act aggressively. If one wishes to use the term *disinhibition,* it seems appropriate here. An attitude of acceptance toward aggression and violence can increase the likelihood of aggresson and violence being performed.

Another intriguing approach toward measuring the relation between television violence, viewer attitudes, and viewer behavior has been provided by the "mitigation" and "enhancement" studies. In these studies, researchers have attempted either to reduce or increase the effects of television programs on children by changing the children's attitudes. Friedrich-Cofer and her colleagues (Friedrich-Cofer, Huston-Stein, Kipnes, Susman, & Clevitt, 1979) demonstrated that the effects of prosocial television were greatly enhanced when it was coupled with other prosocial teaching. Hicks (1968) discovered that adults' comments about an aggressive scene only influenced the likelihood that a preschooler would imitate the scene so long as the adult was present, whereas Singer and Singer (1981) reported that a parent's presence, by itself, had no effect. On the other hand, Grusec (1973) found that with older children an adult's comments could have lasting influence.

One of the most dramatic demonstrations of how attitudes can mitigate the effect of violence viewing emerged from the current longitudinal study. After the first wave of measurements in the United States, children in the upper quartile on television violence viewing were selected and randomly divided into two groups—the experimental and placebo groups. Over the next 2 years, the experimental children were exposed to two treatments designed to mitigate the effects of television violence. First, at the beginning of the second year, they received three sessions in small groups during which the investigators attempted to teach them how unrealistic television violence was. The children were shown brief excerpts from violent shows and took part in a highly structured discussion of how unrealistic the actors' behaviors were and how their problems could have been solved without using aggression. The placebo group was shown nonviolent educational excerpts, followed by discussion of their content. Then, at the beginning of the third year, a more formal attitude-change procedure was used with the experimental subjects. Each of the experimental subjects was asked to write a paragraph on "why TV violence is unrealistic and why viewing too much of it is bad." Over the course of two sessions, the children in the experimental group wrote the paragraph, received suggestions and rewrote it, were videotaped reading the paragraph, and subsequently watched a television tape of themsevles and their classmates reading the paragraphs. The subjects were told that the tapes were going to be shown to the school children in Chicago. The placebo group also made a tape, but it was about "what you did last summer." The final wave of data on all the children in the study was collected 6 months after this intervention. Remarkably, the mean peer-nominated aggression score for the experimental group was now significantly lower than the score for the placebo group. Furthermore, the regression lines for predicting aggression were different within the two groups. Violence viewing was a much more important predictor in the placebo group. Because the children were randomly assigned to each condition, it would appear that changes in the children's attitudes brought on by the intervention engendered the difference in aggression. Indeed, it was determined by comparing before and after scores on a questionnaire about atitudes toward television, that those children whose aggressive behavior was not affected were those whose attitudes had not been changed by the intervention (Huesmann et al., 1983).

Arousal Process

One might designate the changes in attitudes brought about by frequent violence viewing as a cognitive desensitization to violence. Similarly, there is some evidence to indicate that a real physiological desensitization can occur. In a quasi-experimental field study (Cline, Croft, & Courrier, 1973), boys who regularly watched a heavy diet of television violence displayed less physiological arousal in response to new scenes of violence than did control subjects. Although these results have apparently been difficult to replicate in the field, Thomas, Horton, Lippincott, & Drabman, (1973) discovered similar short-term effects in laboratory studies of changes in skin conductance in response to violence. It should not be surprising that emotional and physiological responses to scenes of violence habituate as do responses to other stimuli. It is more difficult to make the case that such habituation would influence the future probability of aggressive behavior. On the one hand, one could argue that arousal heightens the propensity of the person to behave aggressively and television violence increases or perpetuates arousal. Studies by Geen and O'Neal (1969), Zillman (1971) and others demonstrate that increasing a subject's general arousal increases the probability of aggressive behavior. Although more recent experiments (Baron, 1977) placed limits on these results, it might follow that children who watched the least violence previously would be the most aroused by violence and the most likely to act aggressively afterward.

On the other hand, one could argue equally convincingly that the arousal fostered by television and film violence is an unpleasant consequence that serves as a negative reinforcer. In this case, the desensitized heavy violence viewers would be expected to behave more aggressively than those not desensitized. Confusion between these two processes is evident in the writings of communication researchers, some of whom argue that television is making children hyperactive by "overloading" them with stimulation (Halpern, 1975), whereas others claim television is anesthetizing children (Winn, 1977) by overloading them with stimulation. Still a third alternative is suggested by the recent research of Tannenbaum (1980) and Hayes et al. (1980) on the self-reinforcing properties of aggression. If we adopt the viewpoint that there is an optimal level of arousal that each individual finds most satisfying, then it follows that aggressive behavior might be used to generate desired levels of self-arousal. Because aggressive behavior of necessity produces heightened arousal, the desensitized violence viewer might behave more aggressively in order to achieve the desired level of arousal. Yet, once the higher level of arousal is achieved, the most likely behaviors to be emitted are those most readily retrievable from memory, i.e., the dominant responses (Zajonc, 1965). If these are aggressive responses, then aggression continues. Such a model provides a role for arousal both as a precursor and consequence of aggression.

An Information-Processing Model

One of the problems with evaluating any of the aforementioned theories is that the exact psychological processes involved often have been poorly specified. One way to surmount this problem is by adopting an information-processing model in which processes elaborated by cognitive psychologists are used to explain the learning of aggression. Recently, a number of researchers have adopted this approach (Berkowitz, 1974, 1984; Huesmann, 1982; Huesmann et al., 1983; Huesmann & Eron, 1984; Turner & Fenn, 1978). We have hypothesized that social behavior is controlled to a great extent by cognitive scripts, schemas, and strategies that have been stored in memory and are used as guides for behavior. These strategies must be encoded, rehearsed, stored, and retrieved in much the same way as are other strategies for intellectual behaviors. These strategies might be closely associated with specific cues in the encoding context, or might be abstractions unconnected to specific cues. By *encoding,* we mean the "formation of a representation of an external stimulus in the memory system" (Kintsch, 1977, p. 485). Under this view an aggressive strategy must be encoded, retained in memory, and retrieved later on in order to influence the child's behavior. A number of situational and interpersonal factors could influence each of these three processes. To encode an aggressive response, a child must attend to the behavior and must not reject the behavior as completely inappropriate. To maintain the encoded strategy in memory, the child must rehearse it. Through "elaborative" rehearsal the child may develop abstractions of the aggressive strategies. Finally, to retrieve the strategy, the child must be able to access it in memory. A child is constantly building and storing these algorithms for social problem solving in his or her memory. One source for the programs he or she constructs is the child's observation of problem-solving behaviors by others. A particular behavior that is observed may never be successfully encoded and stored; even if stored, it may become irretrievable. According to the encoding specificity principle, the retrievability will depend on the extent to which the specific cues present at encoding are also present at retrieval time. But what determines whether or not an algorithm is successfully stored? Certainly, from information-processing models of memory, one would predict that the more salient a scene and the more scene is rehearsed, the more likely it is to be stored.

Although only a few researchers have moved in this direction, there are data supporting this view. Turner and Fenn (1978) analyzed a number of case studies where juveniles imitated specific criminal acts portrayed on television (e.g., the Boston incident in which a gang burned a woman to death). In each case, they found that highly specific visual cues present in the television program (e.g., a woman carrying a bright red gasoline can) were present in the environment in which the imitated behavior was emitted. In one of the earliest studies of media comprehension, Holaday and Stoddard (1933) discovered that scenes with particularly salient visual and auditory cues were more likely to be recalled. More recently Calvert and Watkins (1979) confirmed these results. Of course, comprehension, recall, and recognition of television scenes improve with the viewer's age, but the errors young children make seem to be based on previously stored *scripts* for the situations (Newcomb & Collins, 1979). Cognitive researchers have found that scripts (expected behavior sequences) play an important role in guiding the recall of prose (Schank & Abelson, 1977; Bower, Black, & Turner, 1979); it is therefore not surprising that they should guide the recall of scenes viewed on television. How is a script formed? It may be based originally on what the child is told or the child's observations of his or her environment. But eventually, television programs themselves would influence scripts. A child who repeatedly watches television characters interacting violently may store a violent script for social interaction and store algorithms for behaving aggressively in social situations.

Based on this model, Huesmann and Eron (1984) have argued that fantasizing about specific aggressive acts observed on television could increase the probability that the aggressive acts would be performed. Fantasizing about aggression is viewed as a cognitive rehearsal of aggression that increases the likelihood that an aggressive script for social behavior will be recalled and used. This theory directly contradicts the notion of aggressive fantasies serving as a cathartic experience that reduces the likelihood of aggression. Despite the popularity of the notion of catharsis among some groups of psychologists, we have not been able to locate a single study indicating that engaging in aggressive fantasies reduces aggressive behavior.

This cognitive, information-processing interpretation of the learning of aggression might also explain why violent scenes perceived as unreal are not modeled as readily (Feshbach, 1976). The observer stores for later retrieval and rehearsal those scenes that have subjective utility as likely solutions to real social problems. Acts perceived as unreal would not fulfill this requirement and would not be stored.

The child's use of aggressive fantasies to rehearse aggressive behaviors should not be confused with the child's use of imaginative play and normal daydreaming. Singer and Singer (1981) found that children who engage in more imaginative play and fantasy in general are less aggressive. One reason may be that these children have rehearsed prosocial behaviors sufficiently for them to become dominant responses.

The foregoing approach has important implications for the controversy over whether television violence disinhibits general aggressive behavior or teaches observers specific aggressive acts. The research on observational learning and cognitive processes suggests how a generalized disinhibition of aggression might occur. Children who observe large numbers of aggressive behaviors on television could store and subsequently retrieve and perform those behaviors when the appropriate cues are present. Even seemingly irrelevant aspects of the scene (e.g., color) could serve as triggering cues. The recall of an aggressive behavior that provides a solution to a problem a child faces may lead to the evocation of that behavior. Although reinforcement of the behavior increases the likelihood that the child will emit that behavior again, it is not a prerequisite for the behavior. From this information-processing view, a certain type of disinhibition is plausible and builds on the learning of specific aggressive behaviors. Disinhibition could occur when the child forms an aggressive concept on the basis of his or her observation of numerous aggressive behaviors. If the aggressive concept becomes associated with successful social problem solving, new aggressive behaviors may emerge that are unrelated to the original observed behaviors.

The Cross-National Longitudinal Study

The aims of the current investigation are to understand better the process by which observation of violence promotes aggressive behavior and to establish the boundary conditions under which the effect occurs. As we have previously argued, it is quite probable that multiple processes are involved. It should be apparent from this discussion that one can hardly consider the boundary conditions under which media violence might influence a child's behavior without considering the child's culture, the child's age, and the child's gender. Although substantial differences in socio-cultural environments exist among the children of any country, many cultural factors remain relatively constant. Therefore, to obtain reasonable variation of these socio-cultural factors and test the generalizability of any model, one would like to study children from several countries simultaneously. Although a number of researchers have reported results from other countries comparable to those from the United States (e.g., Belson, 1978; Granzberg & Steinbring, 1980; Krebs & Groebel, 1977; Murray & Kippax, 1977; Williams, 1978), only a few have studied the effects of television violence with comparable methodologies in more than one country (e.g., Parke et al., 1977).

   If the relations demonstrated in one cultural setting do not hold in another setting, it is necessary to inquire into the ways in which the two settings differ. Such an investigation can often clarify the process by which one variable or set of variables causes or is antecedent to a specified outcome. However, before any difference in findings can be ascribed to the circumstances of the culture, it is essential to determine that the obtained difference is not a function of variation in the methodology used in the two settings. One cannot look to culture for an explanation of the difference in findings unless the methods of inquiry are precisely similar in both cultures. If the same questions are not asked or they are not asked in the same way, it is impossible to determine if any difference in findings is due to the variation in culture or the variation in method. Previous cross-national comparisons of the determinants and correlates of aggression (e.g., Goldstein & Segall, 1983) have not had the benefit of similar methodologies used across countries. In the cross-national study reported by the various authors in this volume, an effort was made to use identical methodologies in all the countries, and ultimately in each country, to ask the same questions of these data. Unfortunately, it was not possible to do this with all procedures in all countries. The deviations that occurred are noted in the appropriate chapters.

It is important that studies purporting to ascribe differences in behavior and personality among individuals to differences in the cultures in which these individuals have been socialized not be limited to comparisons between two countries, however different they appear to be. Lambert, Hamers, and Frasure-Smith (1979) point out in their cross-national study of child-rearing values how they had been misled by the statistically significant differences they found when comparing two national groups of parents, English Candians and French Canadians. When the comparisons were broadened to include another national group, Anglo-Americans from the United States, the original differences were no longer statistically reliable and none of the differences among the three groups was actually significant. This led the authors to the conclusion that there is a style of child-rearing values common to all three groups that might be termed a *North American Style*. Thus, as one's perspective broadens, differences noted in two nation comparisons disappear and a more general view is obtained. The authors state, "if we were to gradually increase the number of national samples in a comparison, we could get progressivly closer to making statements about humanity in general and any differences between pairs of nations that would otherwise be striking ones might, from a world view, be nothing more than local idiosyncracies" (p. 5).

With even the best designed cross-national study of behavior, one will always be on weak ground in ascribing differences in observed behavior to particular cultural differences. Is the United States' homicide rate higher than Poland's because the United States has a free market economy and Poland does not? Perhaps, or maybe that difference is irrelevant. One can never know with certainty from an observational field study what cultural difference is responsible for a difference in peoples' behaviors. One can conclude that differences in behavior are correlated with cultural differences, but that is all. For this reason, searching for similar relations among psychological variables appears to be a more valuable strategy for cross-cultural research than searching for differences in average scores. Is exposure to television violence related to aggressive behavior in each country? If comparable relations are found in each country, we will have greater confidence in the generalizability of the relations demonstrated. In this type of study such an outcome is probably the easiest to handle. However, if substantial differences in the relation are found across countries, then we must assume that the exceptions reflect real distinctiveness and impose limits on any generalization. Quite probably though, one will not be able to pin-point the cause of the distinctiveness.

In the current study, we have included five countries: Australia, Finland, Israel, Poland, and the United States. At the outset, we were aware that there were real differences among the selected countries in demographics as well as in the political/economic systems under which they function. Over and above these differences, however, in trying to establish the generality of a relation between viewing of television violence and the occurrence of violent behavior, it is important to sample from countries that have different rates of crime and also vary in the availability of television. These countries satisfy that requirement.

Crime in the Selected Countries

Earlier in this chapter the trend in homicide rates in the United States was shown to have increased substantially in the 1960s even when corrected for changing population demographics. Comparison of any crime statistic across countries is of questionable value because of the lack of common definitions of crimes and common procedures for collecting statistics. As Nettler (1984) points out, police discretion, judges' discretion, and researchers' discretion all can affect reported statistics dramatically. In addition, changing social norms (e.g., attitudes about rape) and changing laws may lead to more or fewer crimes being reported. Finally, because crime is a political issue, officials may deliberately distort statistics for their own purposes. This was dramatically illustrated in Chicago in the early 1980s. Politically inspired procedures for reclassifying crimes were revealed to have reduced officially tabulated violent crimes such as rape to almost 50% below their actual rate (Zeckman, 1982). Given these problems, any comparison across countries must be treated with caution. Probably the best approach is to compute trends over time rather than static rates and to utilize homicide rates that are the least susceptible to distortion.

In Fig. 1.2 the homicide rates in all five countries and The Netherlands are shown for the 1976 to 1981 periods (U.S. Bureau of Census, 1982, p. 79). These statistics were compiled by the World Health Organization based on each country's self-report. Although such statistics must be considered with caution, it seems apparent that the United States has 3 to 10 times more homicides than any other country in the study; that Poland has the lowest rates; and that Australia and Finland fall in between. Finland's rate is about one third the United States' and Australia's is about one fifth. Certainly, this represents substantial variation. The other clear conclusion is that homicide rates were not increasing much during the period of this study in any country. As Fig. 1.1 had illustrated, the largest increase in homicides in the United States occurred during the 1960s and early 70s. Landau (1984) has published some homicide data from the same period for four relevant countries: Israel, Finland, The Netherlands and United States. His data reveal increases in

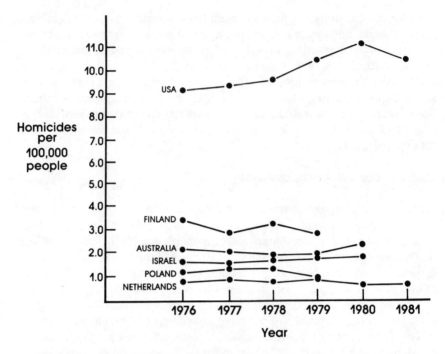

FIG. 1.2 Homicides per 100,000 people from 1976 to 1981 in the 5 countries studied and The Netherlands (U.S. Bureau of Census, 1982, p. 79).

Finland and The Netherlands during the late 60s and early 70s similar to those found in the United States. One might note, however, that Landau's data differ considerably from the data presented in Fig. 1.2. Such discrepencies are not unusual in this area.

Television in the Selected Countries

The five countries in the current study clearly vary substantially in frequency of antisocial aggression (if not in changes over time) as measured by homicides. How do they compare in television usage and programming? In Table 1.2 a number of statistics on television usage is presented for each country.

One can see that the United states is by far the largest consumer of television according to almost any statistic. The United States has over one and one half times more TV sets than any other country and almost three times the number of programming hours. To some extent, the usage statistics reflect economic considerations and the time that television was introduced in each country. For example, although many TV stations began broadcasting regularly in the United States shortly after World War II, Israel's first station was only established in 1968. Of course, government policies also affect broadcasting hours and content. In the United States and Australia, where most broadcasting is commercial, more hours are broadcast. In Finland, Poland, and Israel, television is state supported, with a corresponding increase in state control.

As with crime data, many statistics on television usage are notoriously unreliable. Different procedures and sources yield quite different numbers. The television violence statistics pressented in Table 1.2, for example, differ substantially from those of Gerbner and Gross (1980). The statistics in Table 1.2 were those that could be reliably computed given our resources. We examined the TV guide for one representative week during the study in each country and counted the number of programs shown that contained explicit scenes of interpersonal violence. As one can see, these data indicate that television usage and exposure to violence vary substantially across the six countries. Where available, Gerbner's statistics suggest the same conclusion. Absolute exposure to TV violence is by far the highest in the United States, though the percentage of programming hours devoted to violence is remarkably similar in all of the countries. In addition, violent shows from the United States frequently constitute a substantial portion of the violence broadcast in other countries. For example, *Charlie's Angels* was aired in every country in

TABLE 1.2
Television Usage and Programming Statistics in 1980 for the 5 Countries in the Current Study

	Country				
TV Statistics	*Australia*	*Finland*	*Israel*	*Poland*	*USA*
TV Sets/1000 population[a]	378	374	150	224	624
TV Channels in area	4	2	2[b]	2	8[d]
Hours per week in which at least one channel is available	119	60	62[e]	98	154
Estimated hours of programming per week	476	98	106[e]	154	1120
Estimated hours of programming per week with "significant violence"	61	14	11	10.5	188
Estimated % of programming hours with "significant[f] violence"	12.8%	14.3%	10.4%	6.8%	16.8%

[a]Source is U.S. Bureau of Census, 1982.
[b]One channel actually is based in Jordan.
[d]Excluding cable channels
[e]Excluding weekday educational TV
[f]"Significant violence" is defined as that which our raters assigned to the highest or second highest category on a 5 category scale.

our study at some time during the study. Of course, the impact of the same violent scene may be quite different for children living in another country than for the children in America.

These statistics indicate only the most obvious differences in television programming and usage in the six countries. Deeper differences in philosophies, policies, and programming exist. These are described in the individual chapters.

Sampling from the Population

As important as cultural differences among the samples are for a study like the current one, differences in age and gender are even more important. Without differences in age, one cannot determine the extent to which the psychological processes producing the observed relations are time limited or specific to a sensitive period in a child's development. Furthermore, if one does not examine the subjects longitudinally as they develop over a period of years, one cannot possibly disentangle cause and effect. Finally, without examining both boys and girls, one cannot determine whether observed processes are common to both genders.

An important finding in early field studies of aggression and television violence was that females were less affected by violence viewing than males (Bailyn, 1959; Eron, 1963). In our 10-year longitudinal study, conducted between 1960 and 1970, we found no correlation between a girl's violence viewing and her later aggressiveness (Eron et al., 1972). The explanations offered for the difference in results for boys and girls have been speculative but lead to some testable propositons. One hypothesis would be that observational learning was occurring for boys but not for girls because there were no aggressive females portrayed on TV. Since Bandura, Ross, and Ross (1963a, 1963b) and Hicks (1965) reported that both boys and girls more readily imitated male TV actors than female actors in laboratory studies, this explanation seems unlikely. However, the hypothesis can be tested by evaluating observed programs for male and female violence because both types of aggressors now appear on TV. A second hypothesis for gender differences is that females have been socialized so strongly to be non-aggressive that TV violence has little effect on them. Under this theory one might expect girls from cultures in which female aggressiveness is more acceptable to be more influenced by television violence. Thus, an effect might be found now in samples of American girls even though one was not found in the 1960s. Third, gender differences might be due to differences in the cognitive processes of boys and girls. For example, under several of the explanatory models, television violence would be more likely to elicit aggressive behavior if the violence depicted were perceived as a realistic response. Because there is evidence that girls think television violence is less realistic than boys do (Lefkowitz et al., 1977), under this theory one would expect them to be less affected than boys.

Finally, one cannot ignore the very important role a parent's behaviors and attitudes may play in the process through which a child learns aggression from television. How do parents' attitudes about television influence a child's reaction to it? Is the aggressiveness of a parent much more influential than the aggressiveness of the characters the child identifies with on TV? How do parents' child-rearing practices modify any effects television violence might have?

THE AIMS OF THE STUDY

In light of these considerations, the current longitudinal, cross-cultural field study was undertaken. Its objectives were to determine the boundary conditions under which the television violence/aggression relation obtains, to determine the relevant intervening variables, and to shed light on the process through which television violence viewing relates to aggression. Samples from five countries—the United States ($N = 758$), Australia ($N = 289$), Finland ($N = 220$), Israel ($N = 189$), and Poland ($N = 237$)—were included.

The study represents an attempt to formulate conclusions that span the boundries of age, gender, and culture about the psychological processes responsible for the relation between exposure to television violence and aggressive behavior. Our attempt was to use a common methodology and to approach the issues from a common theoretical position. However, the research was conducted by five independent teams of collaborators. Inevitably, as is apparent in later chapters, differences in theoretical perspectives and research approaches affected the outcome of the study in each country. What emerges is a body of research with some conclusions that are generalizable across countries and some that are specific to each country. Similarly, some conclusions represent a consensus of opinion among the researchers, while others represent the thinking of independent collaborators.

REFERENCES

Andison, F. S. (1977). TV violence and viewer aggression: A cumulation of study results 1956–1976. *Public Opinion Quarterly, 41,* 314–331.

Bailyn, L. (1959). Mass media and children: A study of exposure habits and cognitive effects. *Psychological Monographs, 73,* 1–48.

Bandura, A. (1965). Influence of models' reinforcement contingencies on the acquisition of imitative responses. *Journal of Personality and Social Psychology, 1,* 589–595.

Bandura, A. (1977). *Social learning theory*. Englewood Cliffs, NJ: Prentice-Hall.

Bandura, A., Ross, D., & Ross, S. A. (1961). Transmission of aggression through imitation of aggressive models. *Journal of Abnormal and Social Psychology, 63*, 575–582.

Bandura, A., Ross, D., & Ross, S. A. (1963a). Imitation of film-mediated aggressive models. *Journal of Abnormal and Social Psychology, 66*, 3–11.

Bandura, A., Ross, D., & Ross, S. A. (1963b). Vicarious reinforcement and imitative learning. *Journal of Abnormal and Social Psychology, 67*, 601–607.

Baron, R. A. (1977). *Human aggression*. New York: Plenum.

Belson, W. (1978). *Television violence and the adolescent boy*. Hempshire, England: Saxon House.

Berkowitz, L. (1974). Some determinants of impulsive aggression: The role of mediated associations with reinforcements for aggression. *Psychological Review, 81*, 165–176.

Berkowitz, L. (1984). Some effects of thoughts on anti- and prosocial influences of media events: A cognitive-neoassociation analysis. *Psychological Bulletin, 95(3)*, 410–427.

Bower, G. H., Black, J. B., & Turner, T. J. (1979). Scripts in memory for text. *Cognitive Psychology, 11*, 177–220.

Calvert, S. L., & Watkins, B. A. (1979). *Recall of television content as a function of content type and level of production feature use*. Paper presented at the meeting of the Society for Research in Child Development, San Francisco.

Chaffee, S. H. (1972). Television and adolescent aggressiveness (overview). In G. A. Comstock & E. A. Rubinstein (Eds.), *Television and social behavior* (Vol. 3). *Television and adolescent aggressiveness* (pp. 1–34). Washington, DC: U.S. Government Printing Office.

Cline, V. B., Croft, R. G., & Courrier, S. (1973). Desensitization of children to television violence. *Journal of Personality and Social Psychology, 27*, 360–365.

Collins, W. A. (1973). Effect of temporal separation between motivation, aggression, and consequences: A developmental study. *Developmental Psychology, 8*, 215–221.

Collins, W. A., Berndt, T. J., & Hess, V. L. (1974). Observational learning of motives and consequences for television aggression: A developmental study. *Child Development, 45*, 799–802.

Comstock, G. A. (1980). New emphases in research on the effects of televison and film violence. In E. L. Palmer & A. Dorr (Eds.), *Children and the faces of television: Teaching violence, selling* (pp. 129–148). New York: Academic Press.

Cook, T. D., Kendzierski, D. A., & Thomas, S. V. (1983). The implicit assumptions of television research: An analysis of the NIMH report on television and behavior. *Public Opinion Quarterly, 47*, 161–201.

Dominick, J. R., & Greenberg, B. S. (1972). Attitudes toward violence: The interaction of television exposure, family attitudes, and social class. In G. A. Comstock & E. A. Rubinstein (Eds.), *Television and social behavior* (Vol. 3) *Television and adolescent aggressiveness* (pp. 314–335). Washington, DC: U.S. Government Printing Office.

Doob, A. N., & MacDonald, G. E. (1979). Television viewing and fear of victimization: Is the relationship causal? *Journal of Personality and Social Psychology, 37*, 170–179.

Drabman, R. S., & Thomas, M. H. (1974a). Does media violence increase children's toleration of real-life aggression? *Developmental Psycholgoy, 10*, 418–421.

Drabman, R. S., & Thomas, M. H. (1974b). Exposure to filmed violence and children's tolerance of real life aggression. *Personality and Social Psychology Bulletin, 1*, 198–199.

Eron, L. D. (1963). The relationship of TV viewing habits and aggressive behavior in children. *Journal of Abnormal and Social Psychology, 67*, 193–196.

Eron, L. D. (1982). Parent–child interaction, television violence and aggression of children. *American Psychologist, 37*, 197–211.

Eron, L. D., Huesmann, L. R., Brice, P., Fischer, P., & Mermelstein, R. (1983). Age trends in the development of aggression and associated television habits. *Developmental Psychology, 19*, 71–77.

Eron, L. D., Huesmann, L. R., Lefkowitz, M. M., & Walder, L. O. (1972). Does television violence cause aggression? *American Psychologist, 27*, 253–263.

Eron, L. D., Walder, L. O., & Lefkowitz, M. M. (1971). *The learning of aggression in children.* Boston: Little, Brown, & Co.

Eysenck, H. J., & Nias, D. K. (1978). *Sex, violence and the media.* London: Maurice Temple Smith.

Feshbach, S. (1976). The role of fantasy in the response to television. *Journal of Social Issues, 32,* 71–85.

Friedrich-Cofer, L. K., Huston-Stein, A., Kipnes, D., Susman, E. J., & Clevitt, A. S. (1979). Environmental enhancement of prosocial television content: Effects on interpersonal behavior, imaginative play, and self-regulation in a natural setting. *Developmental Psychology, 15,* 637–646.

Geen, R. G., & O'Neal, E. C. (1969). Activation of cue-elicited aggression by general arousal. *Journal of Personality and Social Psychology, 11,* 289–292.

Gerbner, G., & Gross, L. P. (1974). *Violence profile no. 6: Trends in network television drama and viewer conceptions of social reality: 1967–1973.* Unpublished manuscript, Annenberg School of Communications, University of Pennsylvania.

Gerbner, G., & Gross, L. P. (1980). The violent face of television and its lessons. In E. Palmer & A. Door (Eds.), *Children and the faces of television: Teaching, violence, selling* (pp. 149–162). New York: Academic Press.

Goldstein, A., & Segall, M. (1983). *Aggression in global perspective.* New York: Pergamon.

Granzberg, G., & Steinbring, J. (1980). *Television and the Canadian Indian.* (Tech. Rep.). Winnipeg: Department of Anthropology, University of Winnipeg.

Grusec, J. E. (1973). Effects of co-observer evaluations on imitation: A developmental study. *Developmental Psychology, 8,* 141.

Halpern, W. I. (1975). Turned-on toddlers. *Journal of Communication, 25,* 66–70.

Hayes, S. C., Rincover, A., & Volosin, D. (1980). Variables influencing the acquisition and maintenance of aggressive behavior: Modeling versus sensory reinforcement. *Journal of Abnormal Psychology, 89,* 254–262.

Hearold, S. L. (1979). *Meta-analysis of the effects of television on social behavior.* Unpublished doctoral dissertation, University of Colorado.

Hennigan, K. M., Del Rosario, M. L., Heath, L., Cook, T. D., Wharton, J. D., & Calder, B. J. (1982). The impact of the introduction of television on crime in the United States. *Journal of Personality and Social Psychology, 42,* 461–477.

Hicks, D. J. (1965). Imitation and retention of film-mediated aggressive peer and adult models. *Journal of Personality and Social Psychology, 2,* 97–100.

Hicks, D. J. (1968). Effects of co-observers sanctions and adult presence in imitative aggression. *Child Development, 38,* 303–309.

Hirschi, T., & Gottfredson, M. R. (1983). Age and the explanation of crime. *American Journal of Sociology, 89*(3), 552–584.

Holaday, P., & Stoddard, G. (1933). *Getting ideas from the movies.* New York: Macmillan.

Howitt, D., & Cumberbatch, G. (1972). Affective feeling for a film character and evaluation of an anti-social act. *British Journal of Social and Clinical Psychology, 2,* 102–108.

Huesmann, L. R. (1982). Television violence and aggressive behavior. In D. Pearl, L. Bouthilet, & J. Lazar (Eds.), *Television and behavior: Ten years of scientific progress and implications for the eighties* (pp. 126–137). Washington, DC: U.S. Government Printing Office.

Huesmann, L. R. (1984). Television: Ally or enemy? *Contemporary Psychology, 29(4),* 283–285.

Huesmann, L. R., & Eron, L. D. (1984). Cognitive processes and the persistence of aggressive behavior. *Aggressive Behavior, 10,* 243–251.

Huesmann, L. R., Eron, L. D., Klein, R., Brice, P., & Fischer, P. (1983). Mitigating the imitation of aggressive behaviors by changing children's attitudes about media violence. *Journal of Personality and Social Psychology, 44,* 899–910.

Huesmann, L. R., Eron, L. D., Lefkowitz, M. M., & Walder, L. O. (1984). The stability of aggression over time and generations. *Developmental Psychology, 20* 1120–1134.

Kagan, J., & Moss, H. A. (1962). *Birth to maturity: A study in psychological development*. New York: Wiley.

Kintsch, W. (1977). *Memory and cognition*. New York: Wiley.

Krebs, D., & Groebel, J. (1977). *The effects of television violence on children (Tech. Rep.)*. Aachen, West Germany: Rheinish-Westfalischen Technischen Hochschule.

Lambert, W. E., Hamers, J. F., & Frasure-Smith, N. (1979). *Child-Rearing values: A cross-national study*. New York: Praeger.

Landau, S. (1984). Trends in violence: A cross-cultural analysis. *International Journal of Comparative Sociology, 20,* 133–158.

Lefkowitz, M. M., Eron, L. D. Walder, L. O., & Huesmann, L. R. (1977). *Growing up to be violent: a longitudinal study of the development of aggresson*. Elmsford, New York: Pergamon Press.

Lefkowitz, M. M. & Huesmann, L. R. (1980). Concomitants of television violence viewing in children. In E. L. Palmer & A. Dorr (Eds.), *Children and the faces of television: Teaching violence, selling* (pp. 163–181. New York: Academic Press.

Leyens, J. P., Parke, R. D., Camino, L., & Berkowitz, L. (1975). Effects of movie violence on aggression in a field setting as a function of group dominance and cohesion. *Journal of Personality and Social Psychology, 32,* 346–360.

Loye, D., Gorney, R., & Steele, G. (1977). An experimental field study. *Journal of Communication, 27,* 206–216.

McCall, R. B., Parke, R. D., & Kavanaugh, R. D. (1977). Imitation of live and televised models by children one to three years of age. *Monographs of the Society for Research in Child Development, 42,* 1–95.

Meyer, T. P. (1972). Effects of viewing justified and unjustified real film violence on aggressive behavior. *Journal of Personality and Social Psychology, 23,* 21–29.

Milavsky, J. R., Kessler, R. C., Stipp, H. H., & Rubens, W. S. (1982). *Television and aggression: A panel study*. New York: Academic Press.

Morris, W. N., Marshall, H. M., & Miller, R. S. (1973). The effect of vicarious punishment on prosocial behavior in children. *Journal of Experimental Child Psychology, 15,* 222–236.

Murray, J. P., & Kippax, S. (1977). Television diffusion and social behavior in three communities: A field experiment. *Australian Journal of Psychology, 39,* 31–43.

Neely, J. J., Heckel, R. V., & Leichtman, H. M. (1973). The effect of race of model and response consequences to the model on imitation in children. *Journal of Social Psychology, 89,* 225–231.

Nettler, G. (1984). *Explaining crime*. New York: McGraw-Hill.

Newcomb, A. F., & Collins, W. A. (1979). Children's comprehension of family role portrayals in televised dramas: Effects of socio-economic status, ethnicity, and age. *Development Psychology, 15,* 417–423.

Newman, G. (1979). *Understanding violence*. New York: Harper & Roe.

Nichols, K. B., McCarter, R. E., & Heckel, R. V. (1971). Imitation of adult and peer television models by white and negro children. *Journal of Social Psychology, 85,* 317–318.

Olweus, D. (1977). Aggression and peer acceptance in adolescent boys: Two shortterm longitudinal studies of ratings. *Child Development, 48,* 1301–1313.

Olweus, D. (1979). The stability of aggressive reaction patterns in human males: A review. *Psychological Bulletin, 85,* 852–875.

Parke, R. D., Berkowitz, L., Leyens, J. P., West, S., & Sebastian, R. S. (1977). Some effects of violent and nonviolent movies on the behavior of juvenile delinquents. In L. Berkowitz (Ed.), *Advances in Experimental Social Psychology* (Vol. 10, pp. 135–172). New York: Academic Press.

Pitkänen-Pulkkinen, L. (1979). Self-control as a prerequisite for constructive behavior. In S. Feshbach & A. Fraczek (Eds.). *Aggression and behavior change*. New York: Praeger, 250–270.

Roff, J. D., & Wirt, R. D. (1984). Childhood aggression and social adjustment as antecedents of delinquency. *Journal of Abnormal Child Psychology, 12,* 111-126.

Rosekrans, M. A. (1967). Imitation in children as a function of perceived similarities to a social model of vicarious reinforcement. *Journal of Personality and Social Psychology, 7,* 307-315.

Ryback, D., & Connel, R. H. (1978). Differential racial patterns of school discipline during the broadcasting of 'Roots'. *Psychological Reports, 42,* 514.

Sagi, P. C., & Wellford, C. F. (1968). Age composition and patterns of change in criminal statistics. *Journal of Criminal Law: Criminology and Police Science, 59,* 29-36.

Schank, R., & Abelson, R. P. (1977). *Scripts, plans, goals, and understanding.* Hillsdale, NJ: Lawrence Erlbaum Associates.

Singer, J. D. (1979). *The correlates of war: I. Research origins and rationale.* New York: Free Press.

Singer, J. D. (1980). *The correlates of war: II. Testing some realpolitik models.* New York: Free Press.

Singer, J. L., & Singer, D. G. (1981). *Television, imagination and aggression: A study of preschooler's play.* Hillsdale, NJ: Lawrence Erlbaum Associates.

Stein, A. H., & Friedrich, L. K. (1972). Television content and young children's behavior. In J. P. Murray, E. A. Rubinstein, & G. A. Comstock (Eds.), *Television and social behavior* (Vol. 2). *Television and social learning* (pp. 202-317). Washington, DC: U.S. Government Printing Office.

Tannenbaum, P. H. (1980). Entertainment as a vicarious emotional experience. In P. H. Tannenbaum (Ed.), *The entertainment functions of television* (pp. 107-131). Hillsdale, NJ: Lawrence Erlbaum Associates.

Thomas, M. H., & Drabman, R. S. (1975). Toleration of real life aggression as a function of exposure to televised violence and age of subject. *Merrill-Palmer Quarterly, 21,* 227-232.

Thomas, M. H., Horton, R. W., Lippincott, E. C., & Drabman, R. S. (1973). Desensitization to portrayals of real-life aggression as a function of exposure to television violence. *Journal of Personality and Social Psychology, 35,* 450-458.

Turner, C. W., & Berkowitz, L. (1972). Identification with film aggressor (covert role taking) and reations to film violence. *Journal of Personality and Social Psychology, 21,* 256-264.

Turner, C. W., & Fenn, M. R. (1978). *Effects of white noise and memory cues on verbal aggression.* Paper presented at the meeting of the International Society for Research on Aggression, Washington, DC.

Uniform Crime Reports Booklet (1983). *Crime in the United States: Uniform Crime Reports.* Washington, DC: U.S. Government Printing Office.

U.S. Bureau of Census (1982). *Statistical abstract of the United States.* Washington, DC: U.S. Government Printing Office.

Walters, R. H., & Parke, R. D. (1964). Influence of response consequences to a social model on resistance to deviation. *Journal of Experimental Child Psychology, 1,* 269-280.

Williams, T. M. (1978). *Differential impact of TV on children: A natural experiment in communities with and without TV.* Paper presented at the meeting of the International Society for Research on Aggression. Washington, DC.

Winn, M. (1977). *The plug-in drug.* New York: Viking.

Zajonc, R. B. (1965). Social facilitation. *Science, 149,* 269-274.

Zeckman, P. (1982, November). *Killing crime: A police cop out.* CBS News Special: Chicago, WBBM-TV.

Zillmann, D. (1971). Excitation transfer in communication-mediated aggressive behavior. *Journal of Experimental Social Psychology, 7,* 419-434.

2

The Cross-National Approach
to Research on Aggression:
Measures and Procedures

Leonard D. Eron
L. Rowell Huesmann
University of Illinois at Chicago

INTRODUCTION

As indicated in chapter 1, a perfect cross-national study would have used precisely identical procedures in all countries. Unfortunately, this was impossible in all of the countries in this study for a variety of reasons. Most important was the fact that the collaborating teams of investigators in the different countries consisted of seasoned, established investigators with their own investments in varying theoretical points of view and research agendas. This couldn't help but influence implementation of procedures to some degree. However, in most countries any modifications in the procedures were only minor, and it is felt that the benefits achieved by having indigenous investigators carry out the research in each country far outweighed the disadvantage of not having precisely an exact replication. Another limitation on exact replication was the difficulty of exact translation of the procedures from American English to the appropriate language for each country. There were also inevitable differences in subject availability and mobility, parental approval for participation in the study and differences in school routines. However, despite these differences, which are more fully described in the appropriate chapters, the goal of exact replication in five countries was largely realized. It was originally intended that data from a sixth country, The Netherlands, be included in this book. One of the major reasons why that became impossible was that our colleagues in that country did not believe it appropriate to use the same tests and procedures as collaborators in the other countries. As a result, their results require a monograph in itself for presentation.

In this chapter, we describe the methodology common to all five participating countries. Any deviations from the standard procedures described in this chapter are discussed by the individual investigators for their countries. Actually, as is apparent, there were very few alterations in the standard procedures.

General Procedure

The general design in all countries was that of a 3-year longitudinal field study of primary school children at two different ages. In most of the countries, data were collected from four sources — the child, the child's peers, the child's parents and the school.[1] In the initial year, data were obtained from all four sources; in the second, data were collected primarily from the subjects and their peers; in the third year data were collected again from the child, the child's peers, and the child's parents.

Data collection took place once a year for 3 years sometime in the middle of the academic year, so it could be fairly certain that the children in a particular class were well acquainted with one another and could serve as valid raters of their peers' behaviors. In each country, half of the subjects were first graders at the beginning of the study and half were third graders. Thus, we were able to trace the development of the relation between violence viewing and aggression from about age 6 to age 10, though there were some minor variations in age across countries. Further, this design, with the two cohorts overlapping at age 8, made it possible to differentiate to some degree cohort effects from real developmental effects and to test causal theories less equivocally. A more elaborate design with greater overlap might have been preferable, but would have been beyond the resources of the cross-national collaborators.

Most of the child and peer data were collected with paper-and-pencil procedures in the classroom situation. The data collection was completed in two sessions of approximately 40 minutes each. Booklets were distributed at the beginning of each session. Each page of the booklet contained a different question or set of questions that were read aloud by the examiner. Each page of the interview booklet was a different color so the monitors, by glancing around the room, could be sure children were attending to the correct page as they answered the questions. Further, each answer blank was denoted by a different picture of a familiar animal or object so that the children could readily keep their place. The one exception was with first-grade subjects who, it was felt, might not be able to read and write sufficiently well to cooperate in the group procedures. Therefore, the first-grade subjects were interviewed

---

[1]In Israel there were no parent interviews for reasons discussed in the chapter on Israeli findings.

individually in some of the countries. How each procedure was adapted for first-grade subjects is discussed with each of the measures to be described.

The parent data were obtained in individual, face-to-face interviews conducted either in the parents' homes or in a research office. Mothers and fathers were interviewed separately. Parents were generally interviewed in the first year of the study. In Australia, Finland, and the United States, an attempt was also made to interview at least some parents for a second time in the third year of the study. In Poland, there was only 1 year of parent interviews. School data were obtained from school records. Table 2.1 summarizes the differences in types of data collected in each country in each wave.

Child Measures

Aggression. Because the major focus of this study is on aggressive behavior, one must be particularly concerned with how it is measured. Two approaches were employed, one based on peer nominations and the other on self-ratings. For peer nominations, a slightly modified version of the Peer Rating Index of Aggression (Walder, Abelson, Eron, Banta, & Laulicht,

TABLE 2.1
The Data Collected In Each Country

Country Wave	Year of Interview	Age (Grade)			Data Collected		
		Younger Cohort		Older Cohort	Subject Interviews	Parent Interviews	IQ/Achievement Data
Australia							
Wave 1	1979	7	(1st)	9 (3rd)	291	569	—
Wave 2	1980	8	(2nd)	10 (4th)	262	—	—
Wave 3	1981	9	(3rd)	11 (5th)	225	425	—
Finland							
Wave 1	1978	7.5	(1st)	9.5 (3rd)	221	271	—
Wave 2	1979	8.5	(2nd)	10.5 (4th)	192	—	—
Wave 3	1980	9.5	(3rd)	11.5 (5th)	178	220	178
Israel							
Wave 1	1981	7	(1st)	9 (3rd)	186	—	186
Wave 2	1982	8	(2nd)	10 (4th)	162	—	—
Wave 3	1983	9	(3rd)	11 (5th)	158	—	—
Poland							
Wave 1	1979	7.8	(1st)	9.8 (3rd)	237	472	233
Wave 2	1980	8.8	(2nd)	10.8 (4th)	230	—	—
Wave 3	1981	9.8	(3rd)	11.8 (5th)	231	—	—
USA							
Wave 1	1977	7	(1st)	9 (3rd)	748	634	310[a]
Wave 2	1978	8	(2nd)	10 (4th)	607	135	—
Wave 3	1979	9	(3rd)	11 (5th)	505	306	—

Note: [a] Achievement test scores are available only for older cohort in the United States.

1961) was used. In this procedure, each child in the class nominates all other children in the class who engage in each of 10 specific aggressive behaviors. A child's aggression score is then computed by adding up the number of times he or she is named by his or her peers on all 10 items divided by the number of students in the class doing the ratings. These 10 items (e.g., "who pushes and shoves other children?") were selected from a much larger pool of items after extensive pretest and trial use. All items fit the definition of *aggression* as, "an act which injures or irritates another person." They are listed in Table 2.2. The scale possesses exceptional psychometric properties. In the current United States sample, its internal consistency (coefficient alpha) was .97 and its 1 month test–retest reliability, .91. Coefficient alphas for the other countries are shown in Appendix II. Over the course of 25 years, the Peer Rating Index of Aggression has been used in at least 10 countries in over 50 different studies with consistent success (e.g., Feshbach & Singer, 1971; Olweus, 1977; Pitkänen-Pulkkinen, 1979; Sand et al., 1975; Stroo, 1971). Its criterion validity has been established by numerous studies relating children's scores on it to their scores on other measures of overt aggression (Eron, Walder, & Lefkowitz, 1971). Construct validity of the measure has been established by its ability to predict differences that most theories of aggression predict (Eron & Huesmann, 1985; Eron et al., 1971; Huesmann, Lagerspetz, & Eron, 1984; Lefkowitz, Eron, Walder, & Huesmann, 1977). A slight modification of the original instructions was introduced for this study. Appendix I.1 contains instructions for the peer-nomination procedure. Subjects were instructed to consider only those behaviors that had occurred during the current school year. A more major modification for first graders in some countries was that, as previously mentioned, the procedure was administered individually. These children were asked to nominate their peers by pointing to their pictures on a class photograph containing individual pictures of each child in the class. Coefficient alpha and test–retest reliability for this modification in the United States were similar to the coefficients for the standard procedure.

TABLE 2.2
Items included in the Peer-Nomination Measure of Aggression

1.	Who does not obey the teacher?
2.	Who often says, "Give me that?"
3.	Who gives dirty looks or sticks out their tongue at other children?
4.	Who makes up stories and lies to get other children into trouble?
5.	Who does things that bother others?
6.	Who starts a fight over nothing?
7.	Who pushes or shoves children?
8.	Who is always getting into trouble?
9.	Who says mean things?
10.	Who takes other children's things without asking?

Self-ratings of aggression were also completed by the subjects. In previous studies when we had attempted to have primary school children rate themselves directly on the peer nomination items, we were singularly unsuccessful (Eron et al., 1971). However, for the current study, we used a format originally devised by Carl Rogers (1931) over 50 years ago for the Rogers Adjustment Inventory to encourage youngsters to give candid self-evaluations by rating their own similarity to fictional children (e.g., "John runs faster than anyone in his class. Am I just like John, a little bit like John or not at all like John?"). For purposes of this study, four aggressive behaviors similar to the ones in the peer-nomination index were presented in this format. Appendix I.2 contains the instructions used for these self-ratings, and Appendix II displays the coefficient alpha for each country. Although coefficient alpha was only .54 in the United States, self-ratings did correlate .38 with peer nominations. These correlations, although low by rigorous psychometric standards, were a substantial improvement over previous self-ratings with children of this age and were deemed to be sufficiently high for continued use.

Prosocial Behavior. There is reason to believe that prosocial behavior and aggression are antithetical (Eron & Huesmann, 1984). Children who respond with aggressive strategies in solving interpersonal problems have probably not developed appropriate social skills. A few measures of prosocial behavior were used, based on peer nominations. *Popularity* was evaluated with two items (i.e., "Who would you like to sit next to in class?" and "Who are the children you would like to have for your best friends?"). Coefficient alpha in the United States for the two items ($N = 748$) was .87 and 1 month test–retest reliability was .54. Criterion and construct validity for this measure have been well established in the studies just mentioned. *Avoidance of aggression* was assessed with two peer nomination items that tapped the extent of reluctance on the part of the subject to engage in fighting behavior with peers or incur the displeasure of peers. In the earlier study this measure was termed *aggression anxiety* and was presumed to inhibit aggressive responding. Coefficient alpha in the United States for this variable was .67 and 1 month test–retest reliability, .75. This measure relates in expected ways to aggression (Eron et al., 1971; Huesmann, Eron, Lefkowitz, & Walder, 1984) and to prosocial behavior (Eron & Huesmann, 1984), indicating very good construct validity for the measure. In Israel additional peer nomination items were used to assess affiliative and helping behaviors.

Television Viewing: Violence and Regularity. In the 1960 United States' study, (Eron et al., 1971), information about the subjects' TV habits was obtained from the parent interview. In that study, violence of preferred programs related significantly to aggression only for boys. In the current study, an effort was made to improve on the measures of frequency of TV viewing and amount of violence viewed. For one thing, the information was obtained from the subjects themselves, not their parents. In a review by Chaffee (1972), it was argued that children's own estimates seem to be more accurate than those of parents. Additionally, instead of having the subjects estimate their frequency of viewing, which children find very difficult to do, we had them estimate the regularity with which they watched their favorite programs.

In all countries in the current study regularity and violence viewing scores for children were obtained by presenting each child with several lists of programs. From each list they were asked to select the one or two programs they watched most. For the program selected, they then marked whether they watched it "once in a while," "a lot but not always," or "every time it's on." A child's regularity of TV viewing was computed as the sum of these responses for the selected programs. See Appendix I.3 for the instructions and lists of programs used in the first year of the study in the United States.

Violence of favorite television programs was determined from the same program selections. In each country at least two independent raters evaluated the amount of visually protrayed physical aggression on a 5-point scale from "not violent" to "very violent." Each rater received a paragraph giving detailed descriptions of what constituted violent behavior (e.g., graphically portrayed physical assaults). Raters were told to rate shows on the basis of visually portrayed physical aggression, ignoring verbal aggression, and to provide separate ratings for aggression by male actors, female actors, and overall aggression.[2] Interrater reliability was .75 in the United States and at comparable levels in the other countries. Previous analyses have shown (Lefkowitz et al., 1977) that this method yields ratings very comparable to

---

[2]The extract instructions given in the United States, Australia, Finland, Israel, and Poland were:

"Rate those TV shows you have seen for aggressive activity, using the following scale: 0 = definitely nonviolent, 2 = can't decide or unsure, 4 = definitely violent. 1 and 3 should be avoided if at all possible, but they indicate that the program is toward nonviolence or toward violence. Use the ratings 1, 2, or 3 only if you cannot possibly assign the show a 0 or 4 rating. Each program should get three ratings: one for overall violence, one for violence by female actors, and one for violence by male actors.

An aggressive act is one that is physical, intentional, interpersonal, and visually portrayed. This includes antisocial acts with the potential to do harm, but from which the victim escapes uninjured. For example, if someone intentionally tries to run down another individual with an automobile, whether or not he or she is successful, that is an aggressive act. On the other hand, if someone accidentally crashes into another automobile in which a person is injured, this is not an aggressive act (unless the person causing the accident was deliberately engaged in an antisocial act such as speeding or negligent driving). Another example of an aggressive act would be a person intentionally setting fire to a building, whether or not it resulted in injury to another individual."

those obtained from more objective content analyses (e.g., Signorelli, Gross, & Morgan, 1982). This was confirmed for the current procedure by our research colleagues in The Netherlands (Wiegman, Baarda, & Kuttschreuter, 1982). They used a more elaborate rating procedure but found that it yielded exactly the same results as our procedure. Thus, three TV viewing scores were available in most countries; a regularity of viewing score, a score for violence of favorite programs, and an overall TV violence viewing score computed by multiplying the violence score of each selected program by its regularity score. This overall score was the primary measure of TV violence viewing in most countries. To obtain a high score, a child would have to watch several very violent programs "every time it's on." The scale for violence ranged from 4 for "most violent" to 0 for "non-violent," whereas the scale for regularity ranged from 10 for "every time it's on" to 0 for "only once in a while."[3] In other words, a program that was viewed only once in a while did not contribute to a child's overall violence viewing score, no matter how violent the program was.

Realism of Television Programs. As mentioned previously, the major goal of this study was to determine the important mediating variables that affect the relation between violence viewing and aggressive behavior. On the basis of previous research, one might expect that an important mediating variable would be a child's ability to discriminate between fantasy and reality as portrayed on television. Violent scenes perceived as unrealistic by the child should be less likely to affect the child's behavior according to several models, and some evidence for such an outcome has been provided by Feshbach (1976). Also, previous research has indicated that young adults who believe television is realistic tend to be more aggressive (Lefkowitz et al., 1977). The measure used in the current study was adapted from research in which the subjects had been asked to estimate how realistic they thought one Western program, *Gunsmoke,* was in telling how life in the West really was and how true to life a crime show, *Mod Squad* was in telling what police work was really like. In the current study, the children rated how realistic they judged various programs to be. They were given a list of violent shows, including cartoons, and were asked, "How true do you think these programs are in telling what life is really like: Just like it is in real life, a little like it is in real life, or not at all like it is in real life." In the United States, for example, the list of shows during the first year included *Starsky and Hutch, The Six Million Dollar Man,* and *Road Runner* cartoons. The percentage of children saying these stories told about life just like it really is ranged from 53% for *Starsky and Hutch,* to 17% for *The Six Million Dollar Man,* to 11% for *Road Runner* car-

---

[3]The values used in all the countries were selected on the basis of regression analyses in order to maximize the prediction of aggression.

toons. The subject's total realism score was the sum of the ratings on the items. The instructions for administering the realism questions are contained in Appendix I.4. In the United States 1 month test–retest reliability was .74, whereas coefficient alpha was .72. Reliability coefficients for other countries are shown in Appendix II.

Identification with TV Characters. Although the weight of evidence from laboratory studies (Bandura, Ross, & Ross, 1963; Huesmann, 1982a) seems to indicate that all viewers are most likely to imitate an heroic, white male actor, individual differences should not be ignored. It may be that some children identify much more with some actors and this identification medi- ates the relation between violence viewing and aggressiveness. Such an identi- fication would be important not just in an observational learning model but also in a model that emphasizes norms or standards of behavior. The more the child identifies with the actors who are aggressors or victims, the more likely is the child to be influenced by the scene, believing that the behaviors are appropriate and to be expected. An identification score was derived from ratings made by the children to indicate how much they acted like certain adult television characters. In each country we tried to have the subjects rate eight characters: two aggressive males, two aggressive females, two un- aggressive males, and two unaggressive females. For example, in the United States, typical aggressive males were "The Six Million Dollar Man" and "Starsky," whereas typical unaggressive males were "Kotter" and "Donny Osmond." However, in some countries two examples of each could not be found. For each character the children were asked "How much do you act like or do things like the character?" Instructions for this measure are con- tained in Appendix I.5. The sum of these responses constituted a reliable measure of perceived similarity with TV characters. Coefficient alpha in the United States for the four aggressive characters was .71 and test–retest relia- bility over 1 month was .60. Coefficient alphas for other countries are shown in Appendix II. Although only perceived similarity was measured, we inter- pret the score to indicate identification with TV characters.

Sex Role and Aggression. Cultural expectations clearly play an impor- tant role in determining the differential aggressiveness of boys and girls. In each of the countries in this study, indeed as in most of the world, aggressive behavior is more acceptable for boys than girls. However, gender is not al- ways the best measure of preferred sex role. Girls who are aggressive might, for example, be more comfortable with the stereotypical male role than the female role. In an earlier study (Eron et al., 1971), preferred sex-role behav- ior was measured by a forced choice procedure with 10 "What would you rather do?" items. One choice was always a masculine game and the other was a feminine game. We found no significant relation between scores on this scale and aggression in boys although scores were related to other variables. The measure may have failed to correlate with aggression because feminine and masculine sex are not at opposite ends of a single dimension (i.e., high masculine sex-role preference does not necessarily imply low feminine sex-role preference for the same individual and vice versa). This is in line with more recent research on sex-role learning. (Bem, 1974; Spence, Helmreich, & Stapp, 1975).

Therefore, in the current study, it was decided to obtain three separate scores on the measure of prefrence for sex-typed activities (masculine preference, feminine preference, and neutral preference). The measure was designed so that a child was not forced to select either masculine or feminine items. It was adapted from a procedure used by Nadelman (1974) and comprised a booklet of four pages, each of which contained six pictures of children's activites. Two pictures in each set represented masculine, two feminine, and two neutral activities for the child's culture. The task for the children was to select the two activities they liked best on each page, and they received a score for the number of masculine, feminine, and neutral pictures they chose. The reason for including a neutral category was that, even though less masculine boys may not like traditionally feminine activities, they might prefer neutral over traditionally masculine ones. Similarly, for girls, we anticipated that those who did not prefer traditionally feminine activities might also eschew masculine activities but would subscribe to neutral ones. The sex-role measure's instructions are contained in Appendix I.6. In each country the activities and the gender classification of the activities were designated on the basis of ratings by university students of the gender appropriateness of the activities. Coefficient alpha is not the best measure of reliability for this scale because of the way subjects select items. However, 1 month test–retest reliabilities in the United States sample ranged between .55 and .60.

Fantasy.   Some theorists have argued that a child who reacts to television violence by fantasizing about aggressive acts might actually become less aggressive (Feshbach, 1964). However, no researcher has ever reported finding such a negative correlation in a field study. In fact, a more compelling argument exists that fantasizing about aggressive acts should lead to greater aggression by the child. From an information-processing perspective, the rehearsal of specific aggressive acts observed on TV through daydreaming or imaginative play should increase the probability of aggressive behavior. A Children's Fantasy Inventory was devised by Rosenfeld, Huesmann, Eron, & Torney-Purta (1982), containing 45 questions and 13 scales. Appendix I.7 contains instructions for administering the fantasy scales. In the current study, the most widely used scales were those that measured extent of *aggressive fantasy* and *active-heroic fantasy* (each with six items, e.g., "Do you sometimes have daydreams about hitting or hurting somebody you don't like," or "when you are daydreaming, do you think about being the winner in a game you like to play?"). Coefficient alphas for these scales in the United States were .64 and .61 respectively; 1 month test–retest reliabilities, .44 and .62.[4] Appendix II contains coefficient alphas for the other countries.

Intelligence.   It is important in any study that deals with the learning of aggression that the intellectual competence of the subjects be assessed. Conceivably, limited intellectual ability could serve as a frustrator instigating aggression in many situations. Further, the youngster with limited intellectual endowment is also limited in developing a repertoire of problem-solving skills and may be more likely to resort to aggressive responding than a youngster of more adequate intellectual ability. Also, overt aggressive behavior may interfere with intellectual development. In fact, data from our 22-year study (Huesmann, Eron, & Yarmel, in press) suggest that this is so. No single test (e.g., *WISC*) could be used to measure intellectual competence of each subject in each country. Rather, we were compelled to utilize whatever test scores or teacher evaluations were available in existing school records for an estimate of the child's intellectual level. In some countries, standardized intelligence tests were used; in some countries, achievement test scores were used; in others, teachers' ratings were used.

Parent Measures

The purpose of the parent interview was to obtain information about the parents' own behavior, including child-rearing practices, television habits, and characteristic aggressive level and style. Such data are essential in any attempt to understand how aggression is learned, whether from a reinforcement point of view, an observational learning stance, or from a more cognitive perspective. Also, parent characteristics may be important mediators in exacerbating or mitigating the effect of violence viewing on aggressive behavior of children.

Demographic Measures.   Just as intellectual functioning may affect aggressive behavior irrespective of cultural norms, so may the socioeconomic and demographic characteristics of a child's family. Information on demographic and socioeconomic characteristics was obtained primarily from school sources and parent interviews. In the parent interviews the subjects were asked questions about their own and their spouses' education, occupation, and income. In Israel, these data were obtained from school sources. In several countries, the father's occupation was used as an overall measure of family social class. In the United States, a technique developed by Warner,

---

[4]In Israel a measure of the child's *immature, fanciful fantasy* was also used. Coefficient alpha for the scale in the USA was .60 and its 1 month test reliability was .60.

Meeker, and Eels (1960) was used to scale father's occupation; however, it was difficult to apply this scale in all of the other countries. For example, the status accorded a steel worker may be quite different in the United States, Finland, and Poland. Information was also obtained from parent interviews and school sources where possible on the family's ethnic background, parent's age, child's birth order, other birth data, and residential mobility. Data about child-rearing practices were taken from the parent interview and included scales of nurturance, rejection, punitiveness, and mobility orientation. Most of these variables have been used in previous studies in the same way as in this study and their definitions, derivation, and psychometric properties have been discussed in reports of those studies (Eron et al., 1971; Lefkowitz et al., 1977). Some, however, were modifications of the previous measures.

Nurturance refers to the extent of concern the parent has for the child and how much the parent knows about the child. A low score on nurturance would be achieved by parents who do not know why their child cries, what upsets their child, who seldom try to figure out what their child fears, and who do not have time to talk to the child.

Rejection refers to whether the parent is satisfied with the child the way he or she is. A very high score on the rejection scale would represent a parent who complains that the child is too forgetful, has bad manners, does not read as well as expected, does not take care of his or her things, does not follow directions, and wastes too much time.

Punitiveness refers to how severely parents physically punish their children for doing bad things. A parent who scores high on punitiveness would be one who in the past year had spanked a child until the child cried, slapped a child in the face, beaten a child with a belt, and/or punched a child.

Mobility orientation of parents, which was hypothesized to affect the aggression level of the child, was assessed by a series of questions dealing with the respondents' willingness to disrupt their usual routine in order to improve their status in life, for example, "How willing would you be to give up friends in order to get ahead?" and "How willing would you be to move around the country a lot in order to get ahead?"

The reliability coefficients for these child-rearing scales are presented in Appendix II. Many of the coefficients are lower than what could be considered acceptable. However, these coefficients may be misleading. In each such case the scales have a few very low frequency items (e.g., the punishment item, "how many times have you washed out your child's mouth with soap?"). Deleting such items would increase coefficient alpha to more acceptable levels; but for the current study, focusing on television violence, we preferred to stay with the scale definitions formulated 25 years ago.

Parent Aggression.   It has sometimes been argued that the role of television violence in teaching a child aggression is minor compared with the role of an aggressive parent. It has been suggsted that only children of aggressive parents are influenced by aggressive characters on TV. To evaluate these hypotheses, it is important to examine the aggressiveness of the child's parents. The level of the parents' aggressive behavior was measured in a number of ways. Scales 4 and 9 of the MMPI, the sum of which is a valid and reliable indicator of aggression in young adults (Huesmann, Lefkowitz, & Eron, 1973) were placed at the end of the interview booklet. The parent read the questions and marked the answers while the interviewer waited.

Also administered to the parents were questions dealing with how often they had been the perpetrators, victims, or witnesses of certain physically aggressive acts (e.g., stabbing, punching, kicking, shooting). These questions had been used successfully in previous studies (Lefkowitz et al., 1977).

Parent Television Habits. As with children, a television violence viewing score was calculated for each parent interviewed. The violence viewing score was the sum of the violence ratings for the four programs the parents mentioned as their favorite shows, weighted by the regularity with which the parents reported watching them.

In addition, the parents estimated how many hours a week they watched TV. As a cross check on their children's self-reports the parents also were asked to name their children's four favorite programs and to estimate how many hours a week their children watched television. Also included was a measure of how regularly the parents watched the same programs their children did. This was done by asking them how often they watched the specific programs their children had already selected as their favorites. The parents were unaware of which programs their children had mentioned. Finally, a score for *Judged Realism of Television Violence* was derived and calculated in the same way as for the children.

Fantasy Behavior. Parents were asked a number of questions about their own and their child's fantasy behavior. They were asked how frequently they themselves engaged in aggressive fantasy, as described in Rosenfeld et al. (1982) and discussed for the child fantasy measure. For the purposes of this book only two scores are important: the parents' estimate of the frequency of their own daydreams of hurting somebody and their estimate of how often they read fairy tales to their young child.

Although a number of other parent and child variables were assessed in the data collection phase of this study, only the aforementioned variables are discussed in this book. As previously indicated, a few other variables were introduced by the collaborating investigators in conducting the study in their own countries. They are described in the individual chapters.

Data Analysis

Correlational analysis is the primary tool used in evaluating the data gathered in this cross-national investigation. Such analysis is necessitated by the nature of the study because there are no manipulations or random assignment to conditions. Further, comparison of mean scores among and between countries, although it is attempted for some variables, is inappropriate for many. For example, it is impossible to say that children in one country are more or less aggressive than children in another country because of a difference in mean scores on the peer nomination inventory. In some countries (e.g., Finland) the children are much less likely to nominate other children for any kind of behavior let alone aggression, than are children in other countries (e.g., Israel). Thus, a higher mean score in one country might signify nothing more than a greater tendency to nominate. As another example, in obtaining a measure of frequency of watching television programs children were asked if they watched the programs every time they were on. In the United States, the program might be broadcast three times a week, in Poland, once every other week. Thus, an American child watching the program every time it is on would actually be watching the program six times as frequently as the Polish child who also watched everytime it was on. They would both receive the same score, however. An even more dramatic example of the danger in comparing mean scores was revealed when mean scores on judged realism of television programs were compared. In Finland the subjects scored significantly higher than did the United States subjects. Further investigation revealed that the Finnish children were responding in terms of what they believed was realistic in America (these were American programs), but not necessarily in Finland. When asked to judge whether the programs were realistic for Finland, they scored much lower. Thus, an emphasis on relations between variables within a country (e.g., their correlations) and a comparison of these relations across countries is preferable to a comparison of mean scores across countries.

A caveat is in order when considering the correlational analyses and the size of the correlation coefficients. When the true upper limit of a correlation is 1.0, a correlation of .30 may not seem very high. It would explain only 9% of the variance in scores. However, the correlations reported in this volume, as well as correlations reported in most personality research (Block, 1963), have a limitation in maximum size that is considerably lower than 1.0. Attentuation in size results from the skewness of the measures used as well as from the unreliability of measurement, especially when different measures of the same construct are used at different times. For example, the correlation between aggression measured at age 8 and age 30 in one study (Huesmann et al., 1984), when uncorrected for attenuation was in the range of .30. However, when stability was estimated from a structural model involving a latent variable representing the "trait" of aggression, coefficients of stability over 22 years were .50 for males and .34 for females.

Although correlations are acceptable for measuring synchronous dependencies between variables, they possess deficiencies as measures of longitudinal relations between variables or as indicators of causal effects. In our previous longitudinal study, we had used cross-lagged correlations to demonstrate the plausibility of cause and effect relations. However, a number of inadequacies in this type of analysis have been reported (Huesmann, 1982b; Rogosa, 1980). Therefore, in the current study the decision was made to utilize multiple regression to test causal effects as well as to demonstrate longitudinal relations between and among variables. In order to interpret regression coefficients as causal coefficients, several conditions must be met. First the criterion (endogenous) variables must not cause any of the predictor (exogenous) variables in the proposed structural model. In the current case this condition was satisfied by using lagged observations on the predictor variables; so one knows they cannot have been caused by the criterion variable. Note that this does not rule out the possibility that the criterion variable could be causing the predictor variable's future values. Secondly, none of the unmeasured causes of the criterion variable can be causes of a predictor variable. This latter condition certainly is not satisfied in these analyses, though adding various third variables into the causal system can ameliorate the problem. Until such third variables are introduced, however, a plausible alternative hypothesis to a causal effect is a spurious relation due to the third variable. The third condition required is that the variables must be corrected for their measurement error (i.e., their unreliability) if inferences about causal relations among true scores are to be made. In the analyses presented in this book many of the variables are so highly reliable that the corrections make little difference. However, in some countries, both the corrected and uncorrected coefficients are presented. One should note that this analysis procedure is essentially equivalent to testing the parallel longitudinal structural model with a program for estimating structural coefficients, (e.g., LISREL; Joreskog, & Sorbom, 1981).

REFERENCES

Bandura, A., Ross, D., & Ross, S. A. (1963). Imitation of film mediated aggressive models. *Journal of Abnormal and Social Psychology, 66,* 3–11.

Bem, S. L. (1974). The measurement of psychological androgyny. *Journal of Consulting and Clinical Psychology, 42,* 155–162.

Block, J. (1963). The equivalence of measures and the corrections for attenuation. *Psycholoigcal Bulletin, 60,* 152–156.

Chaffee, S. H. (1972). Television and adolescent aggressiveness. In G. A. Comstock & E. A. Rubinstein (Eds.), *Television and social behavior, Vol. III: Television and adolescent aggressiveness* (pp. 149–172). Washington, DC: U.S. Government Printing Office.

Eron, L. D., & Huesmann, L. R. (1984). The relation of prosocial behavior to the development of aggression and psychopathology. *Aggressive Behavior, 10,* 201–211.

Eron, L. D., & Huesmann, L. R. (1985). The role of television in the development of prosocial and antisocial behavior. In D. Olweus, J. Block, & M. Radke-Yarrow (Eds.), *Development of antisocial and prosocial behavior* (pp. 285–314). New York: Academic Press.

Eron, L. D., Walder, L. O., & Lefkowitz, M. M. (1971). *Learning of aggression in children.* Boston: Little, Brown.

Feshbach, S. (1964). The function of aggression and the regulation of aggressive drive. *Psychological Review, 71,* 252–272.

Feshbach, S. (1976). The role of fantasy in the response to television. *Journal of Social Issues, 32,* 71–85.

Feshbach, S., & Singer, R. D. (1971). *Television and aggression: An experimental field study.* San Francisco: Jossey-Bass.

Huesmann, L. R. (1982a). Television violence and aggressive behavior. In D. Pearl, L. Bouthilet, & J. Lazar (Eds.), *Television and behavior: Ten years of scientific progress and implications for the eighties.* (Vol. 2, pp. 126–137). Washington, DC: U.S. Government Printing Office.

Huesmann, L. R. (1982b). Process models of social behavior. In N. Hirschberg (Ed.), *Multivariate methods in the social sciences: Applications* (pp. 261–288). Hillsdale, NJ: Lawrence Erlbaum Associates.

Huesmann, L. R., Eron, L. D., Lefkowitz, M. M., & Walder, L. O. (1984). The stability of aggression over time and generations. *Developmental Psychology, 20*(6), 1120–1134.

Huesmann, L. R., Eron, L. D., & Yarmel, P. W. (in press). Intellectual functioning and aggression. *Journal of Personality and Social Psychology: Personality Processes.*

Huesmann, L. R., Lagerspetz, K., & Eron, L. D. (1984). Intervening variables in the television violence-aggression relation: Evidence from two countries. *Developmental Psychology, 20,* 746–775.

Huesmann, L. R., Lefkowitz, M. M., & Eron, L. D. (1978). Sum of MMPI scales F, 4 and 9 as a measure of aggression. *Journal of Consulting and Clinical Psychology, 46,* 1071–1078.

Joreskog, K. D., & Sorbom, D. (1981). *LISREL 5 user's guide.* Mooresville, In: Scientific Software.

Lefkowitz, M. M., Eron, L. D., Walder, L. O., & Huesmann, L. R. (1977). *Growing up to be violent.* New York: Pergamon.

Nadelman, L. (1974). Sex identity in American children: Memory, knowledge and preference tests. *Developmental Psychology, 15,* 413–417.

Olweus, D. (1977). *Aggression in the schools: Bullies and whipping boys.* New York: Wiley.

Pitkänen-Pulkkinen, L. (1979). Self-control as a prerequisite for constructive behavior. In S. Feshbach & A. Franczek (Eds.), *Aggression and behavior change* (pp. 200–270). New York: Praeger, 200–270.

Rogers, C. (1931). *Test of personality adjustment ages 9–13.* New York: Association Press.

Rogosa, D. (1980). A critique of cross-lagged correlations. *Psychological Bulletin, 88,* 245–258.

Rosenfeld, E., Huesmann, L. R., Eron, L. D., & Torney-Purta, J. V. (1982). Measuring patterns of fantasy behavior in children. *Journal of Personality and Social Psychology, 42,* 347–366.

Sand, E. A., Emery-Hauzeur, C., Buki, H., Chauvin-Faures, C., Sand-Ghilain, J., & Smets, P. (1975). *L'Echec Scolaire Pre-Cole Variables Associes-prediction.* Bruxelles: Ministere de L'Education Nationale.

Signorelli, N., Gross, J., & Morgan, M. (1982). Violence in television programs 10 years later. In D. Pearl, L. Bouthilet, & J. Lazar (Eds.), *Television and behavior: Ten years of scientific progress and complications for the eighties. Vol. II, Technical reviews* (pp. 158–174). Washington, DC: U.S. Government Printing Office.

Spence, J. T., Helmreich, R., & Stapp, J. (1975). Ratings of self and peers on sex role attributes and their relation to self-esteem and conceptions of masculinity and femininity. *Journal of Personality and Social Psychology, 22,* 29–39.

Stroo, A. A. (1971). Het verband tussen agressief bij kinderen van ongeveen 8 jaar en opvoedingsvariabelen van moeders. Amsterdam: Vrije Universiteit, scriptie.

Walder, L. O., Abelson, R., Eron, L. D., Banta, T. J., Laulicht, J. H. (1961). Development of a peer rating measure of aggression. *Psychological Reports, 9,* 497–556, (monograph supplement 4–19).

Wiegman, O., Baarda, B., & Kuttschreuter, M. (1984). *The Dutch contribution to the cross-national study.* Paper presented at the conference on the Role of Culture and the Media in the Development of Aggressive Behavior, Werner-Reimers Stifting, Bad Hornburg, West Germany.

Warner, W. L., Meeker, M., & Eels, K. (1960). *Social class in America.* New York: Harcourt.

3 The Development of Aggression in American Children as a Consequence of Television Violence Viewing

L. Rowell Huesmann
Leonard D. Eron
University of Illinois at Chicago

INTRODUCTION

In the United States the question of whether television violence engenders aggressive behavior has been debated more vociferously, perhaps, than in any other country. For over 15 years the U.S. Congress, governmental administrators, police officials, the courts, health interest groups, parent groups, mental health professionals, and the violence purveyors themselves have been involved in round after round of studies, hearings, and reports (e.g., the Surgeon General's Report, the Pastore Hearings, the National Institute of Health reports). The reasons for such an abiding concern with media violence in the United States are not obscure.

Crime in the United States

The United States is generally viewed by its citizens as a society in which violent crimes have become more and more common. As documented in chapter 1, there has been a dramatic increase in violent crime in the United States since the Second World War. This increase has triggered a search for corresponding changes in the United States' social system that might be responsible. Regardless of the true causes, almost any substantial change in society during the same period has become suspect. Because the acceleration in the rate of violent crime occurred concomitantly with the entrance of television into most children's homes, it is not surprising that television has become suspect.

Television in the United States

The United States is the largest consumer of television programming in the world. In 1980 there were .624 television sets per capita in the United States compared with .471 in Canada which was second highest. In contrast, the figures for the other countries studied in this book were .378 for Australia, .374 for Finland, .150 for Israel, and .224 for Poland (U.S. Bureau of Census, 1982, pp. 882–883). In the Chicago metropolitan area in which the United States' part of this study was conducted, most homes (without cable connections) could receive five VHF channels and at least three UHF channels. Most of these stations broadcast at least 20 hours per day, 7 days per week. In other words, for over 80% of all hours, day or night, in a week, there were at least eight different programs being broadcast simultaneously. In a typical week of 168 hours, there would be over 1,120 hours of programs broadcast. Of course, with the advent of "cable" in the early 1980s, these numbers have become obsolete. For example, in suburban Chicago many viewers now have access to over 40 channels many of which broadcast 24 hours per day.

How much of this programming do American children watch? The answer is *a lot*! Data for the early 1970s collected by Comstock and his colleagues (Comstock, Chaffee, Katzman, McCombs, & Roberts, 1978) indicate that the average number of hours children watch increases from about 7 hours per week for 3-year-olds, to 17 hours per week for 7-year-olds, to 28 hours per week for 11-year-olds. Of course, there are substantial deviations from the average for individual children. Lyle and Hoffman (1972) reported that 10% of first graders do not watch any television on school days, but over 30% watch 4 or more hours. They also found that over 25% of sixth graders watch 40 or more hours per week. Viewing seems to peak at about age 10 or 11 and declines slightly after that perhaps because of the child's expanding social life at that age.

How much of this programming is violent? Although the exact answer to this question depends heavily on one's definition of violence, regardless of the definition, the general answer must again be *a lot*! According to Signorelli, Gross, and Morgan (1982), 81% of all programs in the United States contain violence, with an average of 5.2 violent acts per hour. The rates vary by time of day and are highest for weekends and daytime when children often are viewers (e.g., 94% violent programs and 5.8 violent acts per hour). It is difficult to compare these data, however carefully they were collected, with data from other countries because the same methodology has seldom been used in other countries. Sheehan (this volume) does report estimates for Australia computed in a comparable manner and these are substantially lower (i.e., 51% of programming hours contain violence). To compare violent programming across all our countries we adopted a different method as described in chapter 1. We examined the TV guide in each of the countries for one representative week during the study and counted the number of programs shown that contained explicit scenes of interpersonal violence. In the United States we found that there were about 188 hours of violent programming per week. This means that about 17% of all programming hours contained violence. The 188 hours of violence was by far the highest of the countries studied (see Table 1.2). Thus, regardless of how one measures violent programming, the United States seems to lead the world.

Another factor contributing to the passion of the arguments about media violence in the United States is the economic importance of media violence. Of the eight major channels operating in the Chicago area during this study, only one was non-commercial. The others depend almost entirely on revenue from advertising for income. Those shows attracting the largest audiences are most valuable because they demand the highest advertising rates. It is clear that media violence sells. Both children and adults are attracted to violent scenes though perhaps no more so than to other visually active scenes (Lesser, 1974). In the Spring of 1977, 24% of the 55 most popular shows for 6- to 11-year-olds in the United States contained significant violence. In other countries, where the income a television program generates does not depend on how many viewers watch it, the ability of violent scenes to attract viewers and rivet their attention on the show may not be as important. But in the United States, where a 1% increase in viewers can increase profits by millions of dollars, it cannot be ignored. Furthermore, violence is generally considered to be inexpensive to produce (Gerbner & Gross, 1980).One can get by with trite, mundane stories that are poorly acted when one has violence to attract viewers. On the other hand, successful dramatic stories that avoid gratuitous violence or sex generally require much more talent and cost correspondingly more. Interestingly, much of such quality drama that is shown on United States television is imported from other countries, whereas much of the violent television shown in other countries is exported from the United States. For example, of the violent programs evaluated in the first wave of the study in Finland, Poland, and Israel, about 60% had been imported from the United States.

Television in the United States differs from television in other countries in more than just violence content and hours of programming. Although formal mechanisms for government censorship of televison content exist in Australia, Finland, Israel, and Poland, none exists in the United States. At the same time, censorship by the commercial networks themselves in the United States is widespread. In addition, viewers can exert pressures that affect programming content by economic threats against sponsors, and the sponsors themselves, in anticipation of such problems, often attempt to control the content of TV programs. Commercials, regardless of content, also change the character of TV programming by forcing repeated interruptions in the action. Thus, the impact of the same program shown in the United

States, Australia, Finland, or The Netherlands, where at least some commercials are broadcast, may be different from Poland or Israel where there are no commercial interruptions.

The Diversity of American Society

An important goal of our study has been to compare the effects of television on aggressive behavior in the United States with its effects in other countries, yet one must realize that there may be as much variation in cultural norms about aggressive behavior within the United States as across countries. The United States is a pluralistic culture of diverse ethnic groups. Standards and norms for behavior differ across such groups and across geographic and socioeconomic boundaries. What may be acceptable behavior for a child in an Italian-American family in New York City may be unacceptable in a Japanese-American family in Southern California. What is acceptable for a child growing up in the mountains of Montana may be unacceptable for a child growing up in New Orleans. It is much more difficult, therefore, to characterize the culture of America than the cultures of the other countries studied. The United States is the most heterogenous of countries.

Are there any particularly notable characteristics that most sub-cultures in the United States share, but which the other countries in the study lack? Perhaps the only one is the very diversity of the environment previously described. More so than in any other country, the American child must deal with other children having different skin colors, speaking different languages, voicing different ideas, worshiping in different ways, and reaching for different goals.

TV Violence and Aggression in the USA

In the opening chapter of this book the evidence accumulated over more than 25 years of scientific research on media violence and aggression was summarized. The evidence seems compelling that more aggressive children watch more violent television. Furthermore, more aggressive children grow up to be more antisocially aggressive adults. These relations are not strong by the standards used in the measurement of intellectual abilities, but they are highly significant and substantial by the usual standards of personality measurement with children. Less compelling, but substantial nonetheless, is the evidence suggesting that violence viewing by children is a cause of their aggressive behavior. Why then, hasn't this body of research had more of an impact on viewing habits and programming policy in the United States? As argued in the introduction, perhaps the most important reason is that the psychological processes through which violence viewing affects aggressiveness have not been adequately identified and the boundary conditions on the

effects have not been determined. But in the United States, an equally important factor may have been the economic importance of media violence as previously described. Just as the tobacco companies have demanded virtually
unobtainably strong evidence that smoking causes lung cancer, so the television programmers have demanded impossibly strong evidence linking television violence to aggression. What probably most distinguishes the two areas
of research is that a physiological model exists to explain how smoking causes
cancer, whereas we do not yet have an adequate psychological model to explain the process by which television violence viewing engenders aggression.
The purpose of the current study is to provide the additional psychological
data needed to pinpoint these psychological processes.

To obtain this information, we interviewed and tested over 700 American
children between 1977 and 1980 about their TV viewing habits, their aggressiveness, and their psychosocial environment. As in the other countries, each
child was interviewed three times at 1-year intervals, and each child's parents
were interviewed once at the beginning of the 3 years and in many cases again
at the end of the 3 years.

METHOD

The USA Sample

The original group of subjects in the United States was comprised of 672
children in the public schools of Oak Park, Illinois, an economically and socially heterogenous suburb of Chicago, and 86 children from two inner-city
parochial schools in Chicago. The pool from which these subjects were
drawn consisted of all the children in the first and third grades of these
schools in 1977. The parochial schools were added in order to increase the
ethnic and socioeconomic heterogenity of the sample, although Oak Park is
by no means uniformly middle class. In 1977 it ranked 110 in median family
income ($19,820) among Chicago's 201 largest suburbs. Minority enrollment
in the public schools ranged from 5% to 18%, with an average of 14% per
school. Of the two parochial schools, one included a predominantly lower
middle-class Hispanic population and the other, a predominantly lower
middle-class black population. One of the Oak Park schools was dropped
from the study before any data were collected because the principal felt the
study would be too disruptive.

Having selected the schools, we compiled class lists of all first- and third-
grade children and solicited their parents' permission for them to participate
in the study. Through repeated written and personal contacts, we raised the
final permission rate to 76%. Of the remaining children, 14.8% declined to
participate, while 9.2% never responded. The response rates were similar in

all schools. This procedure yielded a final pool of 841 children from which samples could be selected. Eighty-three children were used for pilot testing, leaving a sample of 758 for the study.[1]

Of the 758 subjects who thus constituted the United States sample at the start of the study in 1977, 384 were girls (207 first graders and 177 third graders) and 374 were boys (194 first graders and 180 third graders). In 1978 for the second wave, 607 children remained in the sample, and in 1979 for the third wave, there were 505. Almost all of the subject attrition was attributed to children leaving the school systems.

During the first and second waves of data collection in the United States, parents of 591 children were interviewed (177 with both mother and father, 378 mother only, and 36 father only for a total of 768 interviews). About two thirds were interviewed during the first wave and one third during the second. After the third wave, one of the parents was reinterviewed for 300 children (285 mother-only, 15 father-only) whose parents had been interviewed in the first wave. An attempt was made to interview at least one parent of every child, and those not interviewed represented the more reluctant parents. Thus, the United States parent sample is somewhat biased and excludes less cooperative parents. The effect of this bias is examined in the results section.

Procedure

In the United States the children were initially interviewed and tested during the Spring of 1977. They were retested at the same time of the year in 1978 and 1979. The testing procedures were described in chapter 2. The only major change in procedure over the three waves of child interviews occurred between the first and second grades. Each first-grade child received the peer-nomination procedure and the television viewing questions in an individual 30-minute session. The other measures were administered in group sessions. For the second and higher grades, however, both sessions were group sessions. The individual sessions for first graders were necessitated by their low reading level.

Each group session was conducted by at least two experimenters and contained no more than 25 children. The teacher and children not participating in the study were not present except during peer-nomination in split grade classes. In these classes the non-participating children, except for those whose parents had denied permission, were also included as raters to obtain enough nominators for valid scores.

---

[1]The response rate to our original letter sent in the mail was 55%. Telephone follow-ups only raised the rate to about 65%. Then, a few days before testing was to begin, we gave a prize to each child for whom a letter had been returned regardless of the decision of the letter. The other children were given another copy of the permission letter to take home and were told that they would receive the same prize if they returned the letter on the next day, no matter how it was signed. This procedure raised our final response rate to about 91% and our permission rate to 76%.

The parent interviews were conducted individually by research assistants. Some were conducted in a field office and some in the parent's home. In either case, only the parent and interviewer were present in the room while the questions were being asked. For the most part, the interviewer read the questions and recorded the parent's answers. However, the MMPI and a few other sensitive questions were placed at the end of the booklet, and the parent read those questions and marked the answers while the interviewer waited. Parents who traveled to the field office for interviews were paid their travel expenses.

Measures

Most of the tests and questionnaires employed have been described in chapter 2 of this book. However, the exact measures for evaluating a child's TV habits differed somewhat in each country. In the United States eight lists of 10 programs each were used to obtain regularity of television viewing and violence viewing scores. The 80 shows used were those most popular for children ages 6–11 during the current year (1977, 1978 or 1979) according to Nielsen ratings. The programs were arranged into lists; so that each list had equally popular violent and non-violent programs. Additionally, an attempt was made to equate each list for average time of day and week when the programs were shown. Two psychology graduate students, who themselves had small children, rated all programs for the amount of visually portrayed physical aggression on a 5-point scale from "not violent" to "very violent." Interrater reliability was .75. Some examples of shows rated "very violent" are *Starsky and Hutch,* the *Six Million Dollar Man, Road Runner,* and *Barretta.* Some examples of non-violent shows are *Bob Newhart, The Waltons, Donny and Marie, Flipper,* and *The Brady Bunch.* On each list, the children were asked to select the one program they watched the most. For the program selected, they then marked whether they watched it "once in a while" (1), "a lot but not always" (2), or "every time it's on" (3). A child's regularity of TV viewing and TV violence viewing scores were computed from these selections as described in chapter 2.

In the United States a child's judgment of TV realism was based on evaluation of 10 programs and a child's identification with TV characters was based on the child's self-rated similarity to eight characters.

RESULTS

The Effects of Age and Gender on Aggression and Violence Viewing

Figure 3.1 shows how peer-nominated aggression changed for boys and girls over the course of the 3 years. One can see that in the United States the occurrence of peer-nominated aggressive behavior increased from first to fifth

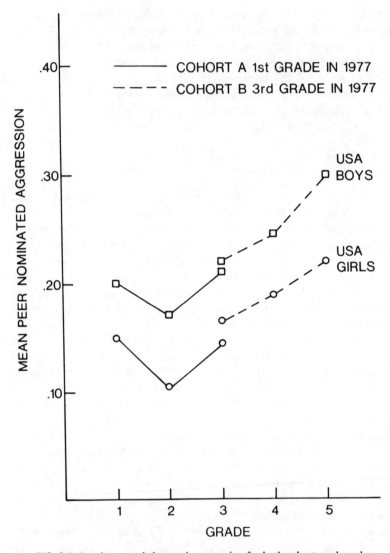

FIG. 3.1 Developmental changes in aggression for both cohorts and genders.

grades as has been reported previously (Eron, Huesmann, Brice, Fischer, & Mermelstein, 1983). To give this graph more substantive meaning, one should remember that an aggression score of .20 indicates that a child was nominated on aggression questions 20% of all possible times. The dip in average peer-nominated aggression between the first and second grade is perhaps due to the change in nomination procedure between the grades. In the first grade, children pointed to pictures. In all other grades they circled names.

Within the United States, the amount of violence shown on television did not change to an appreciable extent over the course of the three years (Signorelli, et al., 1982). Furthermore, during each year approximately the same number of violent shows was included in the 80 programs from which the children made their selections (i.e., 25% of them were violent). Thus, any changes in average TV violence viewing scores over the 3 years represent changes in viewing behavior, not changes in programming. As Fig. 3.2 indicates and as has been reported previously (Eron et al., 1983), average TV violence viewing in the United States sample peaked in the third grade. This suggests that the third-grade time period might be particularly important in the television violence-aggression association.

Violence viewing scores are more difficult to interpret than are aggression scores. Because each score represents the product of the amount of violence

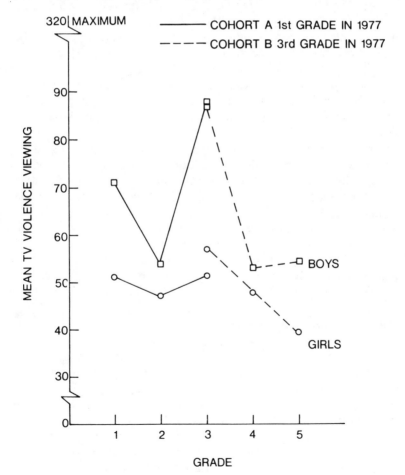

FIG. 3.2 Developmental changes in TV violence viewing for both cohorts and genders.

occurring on the selected shows times the self-reported viewing regularity, the same score can have somewhat different meanings. For example, a score of 80 (the mean score for third-grade boys) could be obtained if the child reported watching two of the most violent programs every time they were on, or if the child reported watching four of the moderately violent shows every time they were on, or if the child reported watching eight of the slightly violent shows every time they were on. Nevertheless, no child in the United States sample scored in the upper quartile on violence viewing unless he or she watched at least five highly violent shows regularly.

Because of the overlapping longitudinal design, we could separate out (at least partially) the effects of gender, grade, and cohort on aggression and television violence viewing. A gender by cohort by wave repeated measures analysis of variance confirmed that boys were consistently more aggressive than girls [$F(1,486) = 24.3, p < .001$] and watched more television violence than girls [$F(1,420) = 26.1, p < .001$]. In addition, as suggested by Fig. 3.1, aggression increased significantly with age as indicated by the significant main effects for both wave [$F(2,972) = 34.6, p < .001$] and cohort [$F(1,486) = 22.83, p < .001$]. The main effect for cohort, however, cannot be taken as evidence of a "cohort effect," because it is confounded with age. Rather, one must examine the contrast between the two cohorts' aggression in the overlapping grade (i.e., the third grade). This difference was not significant.

Because of the gender differences in aggression and TV viewing, all of the remaining analyses were conducted separately for boys and girls. In addition, for longitudinal analyses either grade was entered as a covariate, data were averaged over waves, or correlations were averaged over grades. This latter procedure usually yields lower correlations than using the entire sample together. For example, the correlation between television violence and aggression among all subjects in the first wave was .221, whereas the average of the correlations for the four grade-gender subsets in the first wave was .185. The overall correlation is enhanced because boys and older children both act more aggressively and watch more violence than girls and younger children.

Television Viewing and Aggression

As Table 3.1 reveals, positive correlations were found between overall television violence viewing and peer-nominated aggression in all grades in the United States. Unlike our previous results, which were significant only for boys (Eron, 1963; Eron, Huesmann, Lefkowitz, & Walder, 1972), positive correlations were obtained for both boys and girls. In fact, on the average the correlations were somewhat higher for girls. The correlations also increased slightly with age. Even the correlations for first graders were significant; so it appears that the child may be at risk for learning aggression from television

TABLE 3.1
Correlations Between Television Violence Viewing and Peer-Nominated Aggression
in the United States

Cohort	Grade	Males		Females	
		Correlation	N	Correlation	N
First Grade	1	.16*	188	.22**	201
	2	.20*	144	.25*	158
	3	.15	114	.28***	124
Third Grade	3	.24**	167	.13+	168
	4	.18*	131	.26***	138
	5	.20*	99	.29***	107

$+p<.10.$ $*p<.05.$ $**p<.01.$ $***p<.001.$
Note. All probabilities are two-tailed.

TABLE 3.2
Correlations between Aggression Averaged over Wave and Average Scores on TV
Viewing Measures

Child's Television Viewing	Child's Aggression	
	Boys (N = 200)	Girls (N = 221)
Regularity of TV Viewing	.21**	.35***
TV Violence Viewing	.25***	.29***
TV Violence Viewing (Female Violence)	.26***	.23***
TV Violence Viewing (Male Violence)	.26***	.30***
Identification with TV Characters	.24***	—
Identification with Aggressive TV Characters	.22**	—
Product of Violence Viewing and Identification	.29***	.15*
Judgment of Realism of TV Violence	.22**	—
Product of Violence Viewing and Realism	.28***	.27***

$*p<.05.$ $**p<.01.$ $***p<.001.$

as early as age 6. In fact, recent research by Singer and Singer (1981) suggests that the period of vulnerability extends even earlier—down to age 3 or younger.

The relations between aggressiveness and the major television variables averaged over waves are summarized in Table 3.2. The correlations between self-reported regularity of television viewing (regardless of violence) and peer-nominated aggression were positive and significant for both boys and girls in the United States averaged over waves and also for 11 of the 12 grade gender samples. In fact, the self-reported TV regularity score for girls averaged over waves correlated substantially more with aggression than did violence viewing (.35 vs. .29). Thus, the relation between violence viewing and aggression seems to depend strongly on the regularity of exposure. Regular exposure to mild violence is more highly associated with aggression than is infrequent exposure to severe violence.

Gender of Viewers and of Observed Character

As maintained in the introduction, a possible explanation for differential effects of violence on boys and girls might be that they respond differently to observing male and female aggressors. Unlike previous studies, in the current study, as just noted, we found a relation between violence viewing and aggression in girls. Such a relation had not existed in the 1960s. Perhaps girls learn aggressive behaviors more readily from female models who are now appearing more frequently on TV, (e.g., *Charlie's Angels, Wonder Woman,* and *Police Woman*). To test the hypothesis that girls would be affected more by violent programs depicting female aggressors, we scored television programs separately for the amount of violence perpetrated by males and females. These scores were highly correlated, $r = .85$, because most shows with female aggressors also had male aggressors. However, we found that for girls there were slightly higher correlations between their aggressiveness and their viewing of a *male* character's violence than between their aggressiveness and their viewing of a female character's violence. In the United States the average correlation of a girl's average aggression with female aggressor violence was .23 compared to .30 with male aggressor violence (see Table 3.2). Thus, it does not seem reasonable to attribute the recent emergence of a relation between violence viewing and aggression in the United States girls to the more frequent appearance of aggressive female models on TV.

One of the problems with using gender as a measure of identification with a television model is that aggression is highly correlated with sex-role orientation (Eron & Huesmann, 1980; Lefkowitz, Eron, Walder, & Huesmann, 1977). Girls who are aggressive may in fact identify more with male actors than with most female actors. More important than the sex of the model may be the behaviors the model is performing. If masculine activities are intrinsically more appealing to some subjects of either sex, then these subjects could be more likely to attend to male characters and be influenced most by their behaviors. In the current study, as described in chapter 2, we measured sex-role orientation by having children select the activities they preferred most from pictures representing stereotypic male, female, and neutral activities. The correlations of these variables with aggression and TV habits are shown in Table 3.3.

The most consistent significant finding about sex role and aggression seems to be that a preference for neutral activities (non sex-typed) is associated with lower aggression in both boys and girls. The boys' overall correlation for scores averaged over years was $- .24$ ($p < .001$) with an average correla-

TABLE 3.3
Correlations of Child's Preference for Sex-Typed Activities With Aggression and TV
Viewing Averaged Over 3 Years of Measurements

Aggression and TV Measures	Boys (N = 186) Type of Preferred Activity			Girls (N = 205) Type of Preferred Activity		
	Male	Female	Neutral	Male	Female	Neutral
Aggression	.24***	—	−.24***	—	.16*	−.25***
Aggressive Fantasy	.26***	—	−.27***	.19**	—	—
Active-Heroic Fantasy	.17*	—	−.17*	—	—	−.20**
Regularity of TV Viewing	.26***	−.19*	−.22**	.17*	—	−.19**
TV Violence Viewing	.20**	—	−.17*	—	—	−.15*
Identification with TV Characters	—	—	—	−.20**	.27***	−.17*
Judgment of Realism of TV Violence	.16*	—	−.15+	−.25**	.18*	—
Intellectual Achievement	−.19	.18	.14	—	—	.20
Popularity	—	—	—	—	—	—

$+p<.10.$ $*p<.05.$ $**p<.01.$ $***p<.001.$

tion of $-.15$ in the six age-cohort subsamples (3 of 6 significant). For girls the overall correlation was $-.25$ ($p<.001$) with an average correlation of $-.16$ in the six age-cohort subsamples (3 of 6 significant). It may be that a preference for neutral activities is indicative of a greater cognitive flexibility on the part of the child that promotes non-aggressive solutions to interpersonal problems. Although a child's sex-role orientation was not related to parental education or occupation, it did relate somewhat to intellectual achievement. More achieving girls, in particular, preferred more neutral activities. Besides being less aggressive, boys and girls with a stronger neutral orientation fantasized less about heroic and aggressive acts, watched TV less intensely, watched less TV violence, and either identified less with TV characters (girls) or thought TV violence was less realistic (boys).

The results of analyses of variance with these variables, however, did not support the hypothesis that a child's preference for stereotypic male, female, or neutral activities interacted with television violence viewing to affect aggression. Similarly, the correlation between TV violence and aggression did not change substantially when the sex-role scores were partialed out. Nevertheless, when we divided girls into those who scored high and low on preference for stereotypic male activities, we found a greater correlation between violence viewing and aggression among the "high male," girls ($r = .30$, $N = 110$, $p<.001$) than among the "low male" girls ($r = .15$, $N = 130$, $p<.09$). This later finding suggests that the emergence of a positive correlation between violence viewing and aggression in girls at this time as opposed to previous times (e.g., Eron, 1963) might be explained to some extent by the shift toward acceptance of more traditionally masculine behaviors that seems to have occurred for females over this period.

Identification with TV characters

Gender and sex-typed activity preferences tap only one dimension of similarity between a child and a TV character. More specific individual differences were measured by asking the child how much he or she acts "like" specific TV characters. As Table 3.2 shows, the extent to which boys thought they act "like" TV characters was significantly positively correlated with the boy's aggressiveness in most age-gender groups. Interestingly, the correlations are just about the same for "identification with aggressive characters" as they are for "identification with all characters" (the two variables correlated with each other .87). Children seem to see themselves either as acting like most TV characters or as acting like no character. Children who identify most are also those who watch the most TV violence (overall $r = .37$, $p < .002$ for boys; overall $r = .32$, $p < .001$ for girls).

As Table 3.2 shows, for boys the correlation between identification with aggressive TV characters and aggression was .22 ($p < .01$). This compares with a correlation of .25 ($p < .001$) for TV violence viewing and aggression. However, one can see that the multiplicative product of these two variables, identification and TV violence viewing, correlates even higher with aggression ($r = .29$, $p < .001$) than either variable alone. Later in the chapter we show that for boys, a strong identification with TV characters seems to exacerbate the effect of violence viewing on aggression. Boys who both view excessive violence and identify strongly with characters seem to be the ones most at risk for developing aggression.

Judgment of TV Realism

The children's perception of television violence as realistic declined significantly with age (Eron et al., 1983) but remained substantial in every grade, as Fig. 3.3 illustrates. For example, 45% of first graders thought *Charlie's Angels* showed life "just like it really is," as did 29% of third graders and 7% of fifth graders. In the earlier 10-year longitudinal study (Lefkowitz et al., 1977) it was found that girls thought television was significantly less realistic than boys did. It was hypothesized that this might be one of the reasons for the lack, at that time, of a significant longitudinal relation between girls' violence viewing and their aggression. In accordance with this hypothesis, American girls and boys, whose behaviors in the current study are more equally affected by TV violence, now also perceive television violence to be equally realistic (see Fig. 3.3). Furthermore, though the correlation between aggression and believing TV is realistic in Table 3.2 is much higher for boys than for

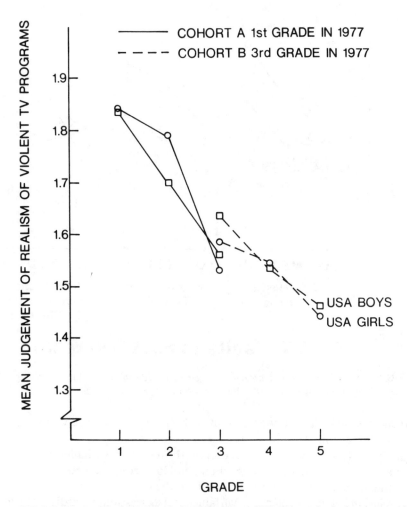

FIG. 3.3 Developmental changes in judged realism of TV violence for both cohorts and genders.

girls, there were significant positive correlations between aggression and believing TV is realistic in 4 of the 6 subsamples of girls (as there were in 4 of the 6 for boys). Similarly, for both genders, believing that TV violence is realistic was correlated within subsamples with violence viewing (average $r = .29$, 6 of 6 significant for boys; average $r = .30$, 5 of 6 significant for girls). As was the case with identification and violence viewing, for boys the product of realism and violence viewing correlated higher with aggression than either variable alone ($r = .28$, $p < .001$). Although no interactive effect of realism and violence viewing on aggression could be detected with regression analyses, the previous correlations demonstrate that perception of TV

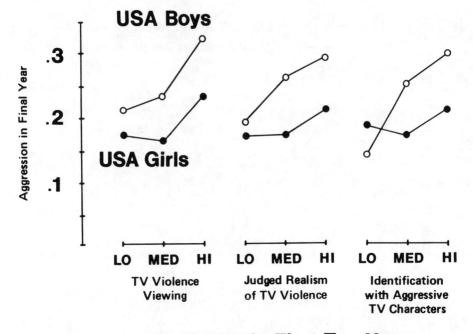

TV Habits in First Two Years

FIG. 3.4 The relation between the children's aggression in the third year of the study and their television viewing habits and attitudes in the first 2 years.

violence as realistic is a concomitant of both higher violence viewing and greater aggression.

In Fig. 3.4, the main effects for each of the television variables on aggression are summarized. The high, medium, and low groups represent the upper quartile, middle 50%, and lower quartile of the sample in each case. The direct relation between each of the variables and aggression, regardless of gender, is clear.

The Causal Connection Between Violence Viewing and Aggression

Observational data can never provide as firm a basis for causal inferences as data from experiments in which one variable is manipulated and another observed. However, with longitudinal observational data such as we obtained in this study, some causal inferences can be drawn with appropriate analyses (as outlined in chapter 2).

Table 3.4 contains a multiple regression analysis indicating the effect of television violence viewing on later aggression while controlling for earlier aggression. Under our information-processing model of the learning of aggression, it is most appropriate to examine the cumulative effect of violence over time. Therefore, the major predictor variable in the regression analysis is total violence viewing over the first 2 years of the study and the criterion variable is aggresssion in the final wave. Aggression in the first wave is included as a predictor to control for initial level of aggressiveness. The analysis reveals a significant positive effect of television violence viewing on later aggression for United States girls but only a marginal effect for United States boys.

The means in Table 3.6 illustrate these results for girls. No matter what the initial level of aggression of girls, those who watch more television violence are likely to become more aggressive than those who watch less. However, the data do not support a conclusion of undirectional causality. Regressions in Table 3.4 predicting TV violence viewing revealed that children who are more aggressive also are more likely to become heavier violence viewers regardless of their initial level of violence viewing. The bidirectionality of the

TABLE 3.4

Multiple Regressions Relating Aggression to TV Violence Viewing Controlling for Initial Level of the Dependent Variable

Dependent Variable	Predictors	Standardized Regression Coefficients	
		Girls (N = 221)	Boys (N = 191)
3rd Wave Aggression			
	Grade	.251*** (.253)	.132** (.132)
	1st Wave Aggression	.526*** (.526)	.695*** (.714)
	TV Violence Viewing in 1st & 2nd Waves	.135** (.152)	.079 (.086)
		$R2 = .407,$ $F (3,217) = 49.7,$ $p < .001$	$R2 = .547,$ $F (3,187) = 75.3,$ $p < .001$
3rd Wave TV Violence Viewing			
	Grade	−.216*** (−.249)	−.364*** (−.429)
	1st Wave TV Violence Viewing	.293*** (.298)	.190*** (.257)
	Aggression in 1st & 2nd Waves	.257*** (.294)	.165* (.178)
		$R2 = .191,$ $F (3,217) = 17.1,$ $p < .001$	$R2 = .170,$ $F (3,187) = 12.7,$ $p < .001$

Note: The numbers in parentheses are the regression coefficients corrected for the unreliability of the measures.

effect suggests that a simple observational learning model is not sufficient to explain the correlation between violence viewing and aggression.

These regressions also reveal that aggression is a reasonably stable behavior for both boys and girls in the age range studied. The corresponding 3-year stabilities were .72 for boys' aggression and .57 for girls' aggression. On the other hand, TV violence viewing is not very stable over the 3 years for either boys (.19) or girls (.31). This difference in stability is reflected in the higher multiple correlation obtained in Table 3.4 for predicting aggression as compared with predicting violence viewing.

The regressions in Table 3.4 do not reveal much of a longitudinal effect for violence viewing by itself on aggressiveness in boys. However, as described earlier, the product of violence viewing and identification with TV characters correlated more highly with aggressiveness in boys than either variable by itself. Therefore, the longitudinal regressions predicting aggression for boys were repeated with the product of violence viewing and identification with aggressive characters as the predictor variable.[2] These regressions, shown in Table 3.5, reveal a significant regression coefficient for early TV viewing to later aggression. Because of the differing reliabilities of the variables, the coefficients of a "true score" regression analysis are indicated in parentheses in Table 3.5. These coefficients are even more significant. On the basis of the significant regression coefficient for the product, it can be concluded that those boys who watched violent television and identified with aggressive TV characters became more aggressive 2 years later, regardless of their initial level of aggressiveness. When these regressions were calculated separately for the two cohorts of boys, we found that the causal effect was somewhat stronger in the older cohort, where the regression coefficient was .19 ($p < .011$), than in the younger cohort, where the coefficient was .13 ($p < .07$). Thus, particularly for older boys, identification with aggressive characters seems to act like a catalyst, increasing the effect of television violence. Identification with aggressive TV characters by itself is a good predictor of aggression, but not as significant a predictor as its product with television violence viewing.

These effects of TV violence viewing and identification with TV characters are illustrated by the means for boys in Table 3.6. Regardless of his initial level of aggressiveness, the boy who watches more violence and identifies with the violent character is likely to increase more in aggression over 3 years. Again, however, as Table 3.5 shows, this relation is bidirectional, although aggression is not nearly as good a predictor of these two TV variables as the TV variables are of aggression. It should be noted that these effects only ob-

---

[2]Such a product captures the linear effects of TV violence and identification with TV character as well as their interaction. By itself the interactive effect was not significant when the main effects were partialed out.

TABLE 3.5
Multiple Regressions Relating Boys' Aggression to a Multiplicative Composite of
TV Violence Viewing and Identification with Aggressive TV Characters Controlling
for Initial Level of the Dependent Variable

		Standardized Regression Coefficients	
Dependent Variable	Predictors	Boys (N = 191)	
3rd Wave Aggression			
	Grade	.151***	(.160)
	1st Wave Aggression	.679***	(.677)
	Product of TV Violence Viewing and Identification with Aggressive Characters in 1st & 2nd Waves	.152**	(.199)
		$R^2 = .563, F (3,187) = 80.3, p < .001$	
Product of TV Violence Viewing and Identification with Aggressive TV Characters in 3rd Wave			
	Grade	−.236***	(−.267)
	Product of TV Violence Viewing and Identification with Aggressive Characters in 1st Wave	.384***	(.612)
	Aggression in 1st & 2nd Waves	.102	(.059)
		$R^2 = .232, F (3,187) = 18.9 p < .001$	

$**p < .01.$ $***p < .001.$
Note: The numbers in parentheses are the regression coefficients corrected for the unreliability of the measures.

tain for boys. For girls there is a positive correlation between aggression and the product of violence viewing and identification, but the identification variable does not add to the power of the violence viewing variable in predicting a girl's aggression.

It is particularly interesting that this effect is equally as strong when one uses the variable "identification with all characters" instead of "identification with aggressive characters." Of course, the two variables are correlated. Still, the results show that even the child who believes he is like non-violent TV characters is more likely to increase in aggressiveness after regular violence viewing.

TABLE 3.6
USA Girls' and Boys' Mean Peer-Nominated Aggression in the Third Wave
as a Function of Their Earlier TV Viewing and Aggression

Initial Peer-Nominated Aggression	Boys		Girls	
	Product of TV Violence Viewing and Identification with Aggressive TV Characters for First Two Waves		TV Violence Viewing for First Two Waves	
	Lo	Hi	Lo	Hi
Hi	.419 ($N = 25$)	.427 ($N = 49$)	.284 ($N = 21$)	.334 ($N = 42$)
Med	.195 ($N = 38$)	.214 ($N = 35$)	.131 ($N = 63$)	.167 ($N = 56$)
Lo	.098 ($N = 46$)	.148 ($N = 27$)	.096 ($N = 37$)	.115 ($N = 24$)
	.206 ($N = 109$)	.292 ($N = 111$)	.147 ($N = 121$)	.214 ($N = 122$)

Note: Standard deviations ranged from .08 to .28 and are correlated with means.

Aggressive Predispositions

An oft-repeated claim about the relation between TV violence and aggression is that "only those predisposed to be aggressive are affected." In fact, the evidence from this field study directly contradicts such a statement. In analyzing each variable, we controlled for previous level of aggression and still obtained significant results. Table 3.6 shows that television violence can affect any child, regardless of his or her initial level of aggression. None of the theories proposed to explain the aggression-television violence relation has provided a compelling mechanism by which previous level of aggression would interact with TV violence viewing, and no evidence of such an interaction was found in this study. Thus, the claim only makes sense at the more general level—that is, in order for aggression to become a serious problem, it is necessary that a number of factors be present to increase a child's aggression. No one factor would probably be sufficient.

Regularity of Viewing and Violence Viewing

TV violence viewing correlates .74 with regularity of viewing for boys and .71 for girls. This is not surprising because the violence viewing scores were obtained by multiplying violence ratings of programs by how regularly they were watched. Given these correlations, we were not surprised to discover that the regression predicting aggression from regularity looked very similar to the regressions predicting aggression from violence viewing. However, the key regression coefficients were higher for both boys and girls when violence viewing was used as the predictor.

Aggressive Fantasy

Although some catharsis theorists might expect aggressive fantasizing to be negatively related to peer-nominated aggression, we had hypothesized a positive relation under the assumption that fantasizing about aggression would serve as a cognitive rehearsal for aggressive acts. In fact, fantasizing about aggressive acts and heroic acts, as Table 3.7 shows, correlated positively with peer-nominated aggression, especially in the older cohort. The overall correlation for boys was .23 ($p < .001$) between aggressive fantasy and aggression and for girls was .20 ($p < .001$). Use of aggressive fantasy did not correlate significantly with TV violence viewing, but use of active-heroic fantasy did correlate significantly with violence viewing for United States girls (overall $r = .18, p < .01$; average $r = .15$, 3 of 6 significant). Furthermore, as Table 3.7 shows, both kinds of fantasy correlated very highly with identification with TV characters and significantly with regularity of TV viewing. This suggests that children who watch TV regularly and identify with aggressive TV heroes rehearse heroic and aggressive acts more. However, we could find no evidence that high fantasizers were more affected by television violence than were low fantasizers (i.e., there was no interactive effect of violence viewing and extent of aggressive fantasy on peer-nominated aggression).

Popularity

Popularity was negatively correlated with aggression in every grade among both boys (average $r = -.347$, 6 of 6 significant) and girls (average $r = -.295$, 5 of 6 significant). The overall correlations were even stronger, $-.46$ ($p < .001$) for boys and $-.41$ ($p < .001$) for girls. Longitudinal regressions, similar to those used with TV violence and aggression, demonstrated that earlier aggression was predictive of later unpopularity even after initial popularity was partialed out ($b = -.19, p < .001$ for girls; $b = -.14, p < .02$ for boys). At the same time, earlier unpopularity was found to be predictive of later aggression ($b = -.10, p < .08$ for girls; $b = -.14, p < .01$ for boys). Thus, aggression seems to lead to unpopularity and unpopularity to aggression.

Although unpopularity did not interact with violence viewing to affect aggression, it was correlated with higher levels of violence viewing and increased regularity of viewing, particularly for girls as Table 3.7 shows. Fur-

TABLE 3.7

Correlations of the Children's Aggression and TV Habits Averaged Over the First Two Years with Their Popularity, School Achievement, and Type of Fantasy

	Boys (N = 287)				Girls (N = 307)			
	Aggres. Fan.	Heroic Fan.	Pop-ularity	School Achiev.	Aggres. Fan.	Heroic Fan.	Pop-ularity	School Achiev.
Aggression	.23***	.17**	−.46***	−.40***	.20***	.16**	−.41***	−.38***
Regularity of TV Viewing	.20**	.17**	−.12*	−.27**	.15**	.18**	−.17**	−.17*
TV Violence Viewing	—	—	−.11+	−.25**	—	.18**	−.18**	−.11
Identification with TV Characters	.14*	.41**	−.11+	−.19*	.19***	.42***	—	—
Judgment of Realism of TV Violence	—	.34***	−.22***	−.39***	—	.25***	—	−.21*
Aggressive Fantasy	1.00	.50***	—	−.19*	1.00	.53***	—	−.14
Heroic Fantasy	.50***	1.00	—	−.11	.53***	1.00	—	—
Popularity	—	—	1.00	.47***	—	—	1.00	.31***
School Achievement	−.19*	−.11	.47***	1.00	−.14	—	.31***	1.00

+$p<.10.$ *$p<.05.$ **$p<.01.$ ***$p<.001.$

thermore, a longitudinal regression analysis revealed that for both genders unpopularity led to an increase in television violence viewing over the 2 years ($b = -.11$, $p < .02$), but television violence viewing did not lead to a decrease in popularity ($b = -.02$, n.s.).

Academic Achievement

Although the child's intelligence was not measured directly, academic achievement was measured during the first wave of the study for the older cohort in the United States. Academic achievement was measured by the California Achievement Test (Tiegs & Clark, 1970). The correlations of achievement with aggression and television violence viewing are also shown in Table 3.7. One can see that academic achievement was significantly inversely related to both the child's aggression and violence viewing. The lower the child's academic performance, the greater was the child's aggression, the more violence the child watched, and the more the child thought that television violence was like real life. The correlation between achievement and aggression in the United States ($r = -.40$ for boys; $r = -.38$ for girls) was one of the highest correlations obtained for aggression. Low achievement may be both a frustrator, instigating aggressive responses, and a marker of a reduced capacity to deal intelligently with difficult social situations. The low-achieving child may turn to television violence to obtain vicariously the successes that he or she cannot obtain in school. In turn, increased television viewing and the aggression it spawns may contribute to a further decline in academic achievement. Recent evidence from a 22-year developmental study suggests that in the long run, aggressive behavior may be more of a cause of diminished intellectual performance than diminished intellectual capacity is a cause of aggressive behavior (Huesmann, Eron, Lefkowitz, & Walder, 1984).

In considering such speculations, however, one must remember that low achievement is correlated with lower socioeconomic status ($r = .25$, $N = 268$, $p < .001$) and with lower parental education ($r = .35$, $N = 258$, $p < .001$). Thus, the relation between achievement and aggression in this study is confounded with the relation between social class and aggression. One must also wonder whether the significant longitudinal relation between TV violence viewing and later aggression might be explained by the fact that lower class and less intelligent children watch more TV violence and behave more aggressively. At least in the United States, such an hypothesis can be dismissed, as the analyses shown in Table 3.10 will confirm. But first, some comments must be made about parental influences in general.

Parental Influences

The analysis of the role of the parents in the aggression-television violence relation must be preceded by a discussion of certain biases in these data introduced by incomplete sampling of parents. In the United States there were 167 children (22%) for whom there were no parent interviews. An attempt was made to interview all parents; so those not interviewed were, by definition, those more likely to be absent from the home, or less cooperative, and/or less interested in their children. Therefore, it was not surprising to discover that the children of these parents differed in a number of ways from the children whose parents were interviewed (Huesmann, Lagerspetz, & Eron, 1984). The children of the uninterviewed parents were significantly more aggressive, scored significantly higher on television violence viewing and frequency of television viewing, and were marginally less popular. They thought television violence was significantly more like real life than did the other children, and they identified much more with aggressive characters. In other words, due to self-selection, the parent sample is biased in favor of parents of the better adjusted children. This introduces two problems. First, one could expect observed relations between parent variables and child variables to have been attenuated from the true relations because of the restrictions in range that the sampling produced. Second, one must be concerned whether any relation discovered is representative of all children or only of the better adjusted children. A comparison of the within-child correlations in the two samples provides some assurance with regard to this latter concern. For example, in the United States the overall first-wave correlation between violence viewing and aggression among children whose parents were interviewed was .255 compared to .237 for children whose parents were not interviewed. Of course it is impossible to know whether the same consistency would hold for correlations with parent variables.

One might also be concerned that the children who dropped out of the study during the course of 3 years were significantly different from the children who remained. However, there was no significant difference in TV violence viewing or aggression between those children who completed the study and those who dropped out; although the dropouts did score significantly higher on identification with TV characters and judgment of TV realism.

Parents' Aggression.   It will be recalled that our measure of parent aggression was the sum of scales 4 and 9 on the MMPI (Huesmann, Lefkowitz, & Eron, 1978). Table 3.8 shows the relations between this measure of parental aggression and TV habits. Sons of more aggressive parents are significantly more aggressive, identify more with TV characters, and believe that TV violence is realistic. Perhaps the violence they see on TV matches more closely what these boys observe at home. This is not true of girls, and there are differences for mothers and fathers as well. The mother's influence seems greater. For boys in the United States we found a significant relation of peer-nominated aggression with mother's aggression (MMPI) scores ($r = .245$, $N = 248$, $p < .001$) but not with father's. For girls the correlations between mother's and father's MMPI and aggression were positive but not significant.

TABLE 3.8
The Correlations Between Parent and Child TV Habits and
Aggression Averaged Over Waves

Child Measures	Parent Measures			
	Aggression (MMPI49)	Frequency of TV Viewing	TV Violence Viewing	Judged Realism of TV Violence
Boys (N = 145)				
Aggression	.18*	—	—	—
TV Violence Viewing	—	.20*	—	.24**
Regularity of TV Viewing	—	.21*	—	.26**
Judged Realism of TV Violence	.29**	.12	−.13	.29***
Identification with TV Characters	.19*	—	.17+	.13
Identification with Aggressive TV Characters	.25**	—	—	.22*
Girls (N = 139)				
Aggression	—	.14+	—	—
TV Violence Viewing	—	—	.17+	—
Regularity of TV Viewing	—	.15+	—	—
Judged Realism of TV Violence	—	.19*	.12	.20*
Identification with TV Characters	—	—	.18*	—
Identification with Aggressive TV Characters	—	—	.14	—

$+p<.10.$ $*p<.05.$ $**p<.01.$ $***p<.001.$

The positive relation between the mother's score on scales 4 and 9 of the MMPI and her son's aggression is particularly notable because the two scores came from different sources. The mother's aggression is based on her self-report of her attitudes, opinions, and behavior, whereas the child's aggression score is based on peer observations. A multiple regression analysis over the 3 years of data did not yield a significant regression coefficient from early mother's aggression to later child aggression once early child aggression was partialed out. It may be that the effect of mother personality on child aggression exerts itself when the child is younger. Therefore, although the overall level of aggression of a 6- to 11-year-old child would correlate with mother's aggressiveness, changes in aggression during these ages would not.

Although mother's and son's aggression were correlated, we found no evidence that the parents' aggression either exacerbated or mitigated the effect of TV violence on their children. Neither parent's aggressiveness was significantly correlated with the child's violence viewing, and no significant interactive effect was found for parent aggression and child TV violence viewing on child aggression. Nevertheless, as sons of more aggressive parents do believe TV violence is more realistic and do identify more with TV characters, one cannot positively rule out a mediating role for parental aggression.

Parents' Television Viewing. As described earlier, a parent's report of child's violence viewing correlated significantly with the child's report, lending validity to the measures. However, the parent's own self-reported violence viewing, as Table 3.8 reveals, was uncorrelated with their son's self-reported violence viewing and only slightly correlated with their daughter's. This was somewhat surprising because one might expect the entire family to be watching the same programs. In fact, the parents' own self-reported hours of TV viewing did correlate positively with their estimates of their child's hours ($r = .38, N = 582, p < .001$) and, as Table 3.8 shows, with the child's regularity as estimated by the child. Also the more the parents reported watching the child's programs themselves, the greater were their estimates of their child's hours of viewing ($r = .30, N = 556, p < .001$) and the greater was the child's self-reported regularity of viewing ($r = .17, N = 556, p < .001$). Finally, again from Table 3.8, the more the parents believed that violent shows tell about life "just like it really is," the more the child believed it (average $r = .29, p < .001$ for boys, average $r = .20, p < .05$ for girls). Given these correlations between parent and child viewing habits, the lack of correlation between parent and child TV violence scores is puzzling. Violent programs may be treated differently than other programs by many families; so the adults watch them, whereas the children do not. Further evidence in support of this hypothesis is developed in the section on social class. Despite these modest relations between parent and child viewing, no significant correlations between parent viewing and child aggression were discovered.

Parents' Education and Social Status. Correlations of the parents' education and social status with child aggression and TV viewing are displayed in Table 3.9. One can see that there are consistent effects of both social status and parent education on both the child's television viewing and aggression. In the United States, socioeconomic status of the family was defined for the study by the father's occupation. As Table 3.9 indicates, the lower the parents' education and socioeconomic status, the more aggressive was the child,

TABLE 3.9
The Correlation of the Parents' Social Status and Parents' Education
with the Child's and Parents' Aggression and TV Viewing Habits

	Social Status	Parents' Education
Social Status	1.0	—
Parents' Education	.59***	1.0
Child's Achievement	.24***	.34***
Child's:		
Aggression	− .17***	− .09*
TV Violence Viewing	− .11*	− .15***
Regularity of TV Viewing	− .14**	− .16***
Judged Realism of TV Violence	− .21***	− .28***
Identification with TV Characters	− .21***	− .23***
Parents':		
Mother's Aggression	− .12**	− .09*
Father's Aggression	− .16*	—
TV Violence Viewing	—	.09*
Frequency of TV Viewing	− .27***	− .31***
Judged Realism of TV Violence	− .11**	− .13**
Watch Child's Favorite Programs	− .25***	− .27***
Estimate of Child's Viewing Frequency	− .24***	− .27***

$*p<.05.$ $**p<.01.$ $***p<.001.$
Note: Social status was recoded from father's occupation so a high score means higher socioeconomic status. Achievement was measured by scores on the California Achievement Test.

the more the child watched television and television violence, the more the child believed the violent shows "tell about life like it is," and the more the child identified with TV characters. Similarly, the lower the parents' education and social status, the more aggressive were the parents, the more the parents watched TV, and the more the parents believed TV violence was realistic. However, one can also see from Table 3.9 that the more highly educated and higher status parents watched slightly more TV violence and less of their children's programs than the more poorly educated and lower status parents. Higher status parents watch a lot less TV, but slightly more of what they watch is violent. Finally, an examination of the mother's working status revealed that on the average, the daughters of working mothers watch marginally more television ($t = 1.53$, $p<.13$) and behave more aggressively ($t = 3.13$, $p<.01$), and the sons of working mothers behave more aggressively ($t = 2.91$, $p<.01$). Although this was not true of children whose mothers had high-status occupations, nevertheless it suggests that at least some children of working mothers might be more at risk for learning aggression from television.

More educated and higher status parents watch less TV but prefer more violent shows. Similarly, the parents of children with higher achievement scores prefer more violent shows (overall $r = .16, p < .01$). At the same time, higher achieving children and children of more educated parents themselves watch less violence and watch TV less regularly than other children. These results are consistent with the earlier reported fact that parental violence viewing is uncorrelated with child violence viewing in our population. Together, these results suggest that violent shows are treated differently than other shows by many families. It may be that on the average violent shows appeal more to more educated adults than the usual alternative (e.g., situation comedies). These more highly educated adults eschew the type of shows their children watch. At the same time, these adults, concerned about the violence, discourage their children from viewing the programs. Of course, such a hypothesis cannot be tested with the current data, and there are probably alternative explanations.

In order to test whether education, socioeconomic status, and intelligence might account completely for the relation between violence viewing and aggression, these variables were added to the multiple regression equations predicting later aggression from earlier violence viewing (and for boys from earlier identification with TV characters). In Table 3.10 both the raw regressions and the regressions corrected for the unrealiability of the measures are shown. Unfortunately, because of the incomplete survey of parents and school achievement records, the samples were greatly reduced in size for these analyses. However, the regression coefficients for the reduced sample were approximately the same as for the total sample before the covariates were introduced, and the introduction of achievement, education, and social class did not change them much. Thus, the relation of early violence viewing to later aggression cannot be attributed solely to the effect of the child's intellect, the parents' education, or the family's social class.

Child-Rearing Styles. Four measures of a parent's child-rearing behaviors were collected during the interview: upward mobility orientation (e.g. willingness to sacrifice to get ahead), rejection (e.g. dissatisfaction with the child), nurturance (e.g. concern about the child), and severity of punishment of the child. The correlations between these measures and the child's aggression and TV habits are shown in Table 3.11. More aggressive boys are punished more and rejected more by their parents and have parents who are somewhat less nurturant and more willing to sacrifice to get ahead. More aggressive girls are also rejected more. For boys, greater rejection and punishment by their parents are also associated with more regular TV viewing, more violence viewing, more identification with TV characters, and a stronger belief in the realism of TV violence. For girls, the only significant finding was that daughters of parents with a stronger upward mobility orientation watched more TV violence.

TABLE 3.10
Multiple Regressions Showing Effects of SocioEconomic Variables and Academic
Achievement on the Relation Between TV Violence Viewing and Aggression

Dependent Variable	Predictors	Standardized Regression Coefficients	
		Girls (N = 89)	Boys (N = 84)
3rd Wave Aggression	1st Wave Aggression	.341*** (.318)	.731*** (.782)
	TV Violence Viewing for Girls in 1st & 2nd Waves	.169* (.193)	
	Product of TV Violence Viewing and Identification with Aggressive TV Characters for Boys in 1st & 2nd Waves		.188* (.292)
	Parents' SocioEconomic Status	.059 (.165)	.034 (.036)
	Parents' Educational Status	.080 (.175)	−.031 (.012)
	Child's Academic Achievement	−.340*** (−.375)	.045 (.121)
		$R2 = .342$, $F (5,83) = 8.63$, $p < .001$	$R2 = .593$, $F (5,78) = 22.7$, $p < .001$

$*p < .05.$ $***p < .001.$
Note: The numbers in parentheses are the regression coefficients corrected for the unreliability of the measures. Because achievement data was only available for third grade subjects, grade was not included as a predictor.

The substantial relations between rejection and aggression and, for boys, between punishment and aggression are open to several interpretations. Aggressiveness in children in school may be indicative of aggressiveness at home and may breed rejection and punishment by the parents. Alternatively, rejection and punishment at home may frustrate the child, as well as provide models of aggressive behavior for the child to imitate. In an attempt to distinguish between these possibilities, we calculated regression predictions of later aggression from early rejection and punishment controlling for early aggression, and we calculated predictions of later rejection and punishment from early aggression controlling for early rejection and punishment. For boys we found that early aggression was a significant predictor of later rejection and punishment even after the effects of the parents' early rejection and punishment were partialed out. However, the converse was not true. Early rejection and punishment were not predictive of later aggression once initial aggression was partialed out. Thus, parental rejection and punishment seem to be more a response to aggression than a cause of aggression.

TABLE 3.11

The Correlations Between Parents' Child Rearing Styles Averaged Over Waves and Their Child's Aggression and TV Viewing Averaged Over Waves

Child Measures	Parent Measures			
	Upward Mobility	Rejection	Nurturance	Punishment
Boys (N = 154)				
Aggression	.14$^+$	.31***	−.17*	.31***
TV Violence Viewing	—	.31***	—	.16$^+$
Regularity of TV Viewing	.13	.18*	—	.11
Judged Realism of TV Violence	−.19*	.28***	−.11	.11
Identification with TV Characters	—	.22*	—	.17$^+$
Identification with Aggressive TV Characters	—	.22*	—	.20*
Girls (N = 143)				
Aggression	—	.30***	—	—
TV Violence Viewing	.18*	.14	—	—
Regularity of TV Violence	.13	—	—	−.13
Judged Realism of TV Violence	.12	—	−.12	—
Identification with TV Characters	—	—	—	—
Identification with Aggressive TV Characters	.12	—	—	.10

$^+p<.10.$ $*p<.05.$ $***p<.001.$

Finally, in Table 3.12, we have examined the effect of TV violence viewing on later aggression when we control for all parent variables. Surprisingly, for girls, TV violence viewing was a better predictor of later aggressiveness than any of the parent variables, whose effects are only marginal. For boys, however, parental rejection and punishment were significant predictors of aggression, and their inclusion in the equation diminished the utility of TV violence viewing in predicting aggression. Rejection of the child by the parent, severe punishment of the child, TV violence viewing, and aggression by the

TABLE 3.12

Multiple Regressions Showing Effects of SocioEconomic Variables, Parent Behaviors, and Parent Child Rearing Practices on the Relations Between TV Violence Viewing and Aggression

Dependent Variable	Predictors	Standardized Regression Coefficients	
		USA Girls (N = 194)	USA Boys (N = 178)
3rd Wave Aggression	Cohort	.254***	.219**
	TV Violence Viewing for Girls	.215**	
	Product of TV Violence Viewing and Identification with Aggressive Characters for Boys		.103
	Parents' Socioeconomic Status	—	—
	Parents' Educational Status	—	—
	Parents' Mobility Orientation	−.103	.125+
	Parents' Aggressiveness	—	—
	Parents' Aggressive Fantasy	—	—
	Parents' TV Violence Viewing	—	—
	Parents' TV Frequency	.112	—
	Parents' Nurturance of Child	—	—
	Parents' Rejection of Child	.100	.163*
	Parents' Punishment of Child	—	.188***
		$R2 = .205$ $F(12,181) = 3.88$ $p < .001$	$R2 = .193$ $F(12,165) = 3.30$ $p < .001$

+$p < .10$.   *$p < .05$.   **$p < .01$.   ***$p < .001$.

75

child all correlate positively. However, as the separate analyses of rejection and punishment revealed, they appear to be responses to aggression, whereas TV violence viewing appears to be both a precursor of aggression and a response to aggression.

DISCUSSION

Reciprocal Processes in the Relation Between TV Violence and Aggression

The data presented thus far have confirmed and elaborated what the multitude of previous laboratory and field studies on media violence and aggression have suggested. At certain periods in a child's development extensive exposure to television violence promotes aggressive behavior on the part of the child. Children ages 6–11 seem to fall in this critical age range. As outlined in chapter 1, aggressive habits that are established during this time are resistant to extinction and often persist into adulthood (Huesmann, Eron, Lefkowitz, & Walder, 1984). The current data indicate that, at least in the United States, both boys and girls are affected by excessive exposure to media violence. For boys who identify strongly with TV characters the effect is strongest and more unidirectional than it is for girls. For all children, however, the effect seems to be bidirectional to at least some extent. More aggressive children watch more violence, and that viewing seems to engender more aggression.

What mediating variables play a role in this cycle? We have already seen that, of the TV variables, only the child's identification with TV characters interacts directly with violence viewing to affect aggression in boys. However, a number of other child characteristics are correlated both with violence viewing and aggression. We hypothesize that three of these characteristics play a particularly important role in maintaining the violence viewing–aggression relation. These are the child's intellectual achievement, the child's social popularity, and the child's fantasizing about aggression.

As described earlier and as shown in Table 3.7, children who have poorer academic skills behave more aggressively, watch TV more regularly, watch more TV violence, and believe that the violent programs they watch are telling about life as it really is. This is particularly true for boys but also true for girls. Longitudinal regressions to estimate causal coefficients could not be calculated on these data, because intellectual achievement was only measured once during the first year of the study. However, recent data reported by Huesmann, Eron, and Yarmel (in press) indicate that aggressiveness in an 8-year-old child interferes with intellectual development as much or more than intellectual failures frustrate and stimulate aggression. Perhaps aggressiveness interferes with the social interactions with teachers and peers that a child needs in order to develop his or her academic potential. For popularity, as described earlier, longitudinal regressions also suggested a bidirectional relation with aggression. Furthermore, early unpopularity was predictive of later increased TV viewing.

Taken together, these relations suggest a reciprocal process through which aggression and violence viewing perpetuate themselves and each other. Children who are heavy viewers of television violence regularly observe characters behaving aggressively to solve interpersonal problems. To the extent that the children (particularly boys) identify with the aggressive characters, the children may encode in memory the aggressive solutions they observe. We hypothesize that social behavior is controlled to a great extent by cognitive scripts, schemas, and strategies that the child observes, stores in memory, and uses as a guide for behavior. The child who is constantly exposed to violence is more likely to develop and maintain cognitive scripts emphasizing aggressive solutions to social problems. These violent scenes may also stimulate aggresive fantasies in which the encoded aggressive scripts are rehearsed making them more likely to be recalled and utilized in the future. If the aggressive behaviors are emitted in the appropriate situations, the aggressive behaviors may be reinforced with desirable outcomes, making their future occurrence more likely. However, as the aggression becomes habitual, it must eventually interfere with both social and academic success. The more aggressive child becomes the less popular child and the poorer academic achiever in school. These academic and social failures may become frustrators instigating more aggressive responses. In addition, however, the children who are less successful in school and less popular become the more regular television viewers. Perhaps they can obtain the satisfactions vicariously from television that they are denied in school and in their social lives. These less popular, less intellectually able children watch more television violence, identify more with TV characters, and believe that the violence they observe on television reflects real life. All these conditions promote the learning of new aggressive schemas from television and the reinforcement of old ones. Because these children's intellectual capacities are more limited, the easy aggressive solutions they observe may be incorporated more readily into their behavioral repertoires. The heavy viewing isolates them from their peers and gives them less time to work toward academic success. The violence they see on television may reassure them that their own behavior is appropriate or teach them new coercive techniques, which they then attempt to use in their interactions with others. Thus, they behave more aggressively, which in turn makes them even less popular and drives them back to television. The cycle continues with aggression, academic failure, social failure, violence viewing, and fantasizing about aggression mutually facilitating each other.

A number of the other variables may have similar circular relations with television violence viewing and aggression. Although none of these interacted significantly with violence viewing to affect aggression, they correlated with both variables. For example, it was found that the more a parent believes television violence is realistic, the more the child believes it is realistic; and the more a child believes this, the more the child views violence and acts aggressively. The violence the child views and the aggression the child commits may combine to increase the child's belief in the appropriateness of violent solutions to interpersonal problems that, in turn, would increase the likelihood of the child behaving aggressively.

CONCLUSION

Antisocial aggressive behavior in children is most often the result of the convergence of a number of predisposing and precipitating factors. This convergence provides a learning environment within which aggressive responding can become habitual. Although no single factor can make a child aggressive, each contributes something. In the current study, we have examined the conditions under which exposure to media violence is most likely to lead to heightened aggressiveness.

A sample of 758 children in the United States was interviewed and tested in each of 3 years in an overlapping longitudinal design spanning grades 1 to 5. For girls and boys, television violence viewing was significantly related to concurrent aggression and significantly predicted future changes in aggression. The strength of the relation depended as much on the regularity with which violence was viewed as on the seriousness of the violence. For boys the effect was exacerbated by the degree to which the boy identified with TV characters. Longitudinal regression analyses suggested a bidirectional causal effect in which violence viewing engenders aggression and aggression leads to violence viewing. No evidence was found that those children predisposed to aggression or those with aggressive parents are more strongly affected by TV violence. However, a number of other variables were found to be correlates of both aggression and violence viewing. The child most likely to be aggressive would be one who watches violent programs most of the time they are on, who believes these shows portray life "just like it is," who identifies strongly with the aggressive characters in the shows, who frequently has aggressive fantasies, and who, if a girl, prefers boys' activities. In addition, such a child is likely to have a more aggressive mother who works at a low-status job, to have parents with lower education and social status, to be performing poorly in school, and to be unpopular with peers.

A plausible model to explain these findings seems to be a multi-process, reciprocal action model, in which violence viewing and aggression mutually facilitate each other, contribute to academic and social failure, and are engendered by such failure. Imitation of specific aggressive acts undoubtedly plays a role, but such imitation may be no more important than the attitude changes TV violence produces, the justification for aggressive behavior TV violence provides, the scripts for aggressive behavior it teaches, the cues for aggressive problem solving it furnishes, or the social and intellectual isolation it encourages.

ACKNOWLEDGMENTS

This research was supported in part by grants MH-28280, MH-31886, and MH-38683 from the National Institute of Mental Health to the first author. A large number of people assisted in the collection and analysis of the data in the United States including Pat Brice, Eric Dubow, Paulette Fischer, Gary Hudson, Patricia Jones, Esther Kaplan-Shain, Rosemary Klein, Rebecca Mermelstein, Susan Moloney, Sharon Morikawa, Vita Musonis, Richard Romanoff, Erica Rosenfeld, Evelyne Seebauer, James Stewart, Ann Washington, Linda White, and Patty Yarmel. Portions of this chapter have appeared previously in Huesmann, Lagerspetz, and Eron (1984).

REFERENCES

Comstock, G., Chaffee, S., Katzman, N., McCombs, M., & Roberts, D. (1978). *Television and human behavior.* New York: Columbia University Press.

Eron, L. D. (1963). Relationship of TV viewing habits and aggressive behavior in children. *Journal of Abnormal and Social Psychology, 67,* 193–196.

Eron, L. D., & Huesmann, L. R. (1980). Adolescent aggression and television. *Annals of New York Academy of Sciences, 347,* 319–331.

Eron, L. D., Huesmann, L. R., Brice, P., Fischer, P., & Mermelstein, R. (1983). Age trends in the development of aggression and associated television habits. *Developmental Psychology, 19,* 71–77.

Eron, L. D., Huesmann, L. R., Lefkowitz, M. M., & Walder, L. O. (1972). Does television violence cause aggression? *American Psychologist, 27,* 253–263.

Gerbner, G., & Gross, L. P. (1980). The violent face of television and its lessons. In E. Palmer & A. Dorr (Eds.), *Children and the faces of television: Teaching, violence, selling* (pp. 149–162). New York: Academic Press.

Huesmann, L. R., Eron, L. D., Lefkowitz, M. M., & Walder, L. O. (1984). The stability of aggression over time and generations. *Developmental Psychology, 20,* 1120–1134.

Huesmann, L. R., Eron, L. D., & Yarmel, P. (in press). Intellectual functioning and aggression. *Journal of Personality and Social Psychology.*

Huesmann, L. R., Lagerspetz, K., & Eron, L. D. (1984). Intervening variables in the television violence-aggression relation: A binational study. *Developmental Psychology, 20,* 746–775.

Huesmann, L. R., Lefkowitz, M. M., & Eron, L. D. (1978). Sum of MMPI Scales F, 4 and 9 as a measure of aggression. *Journal of Consulting and Clinical Psychology, 46,* 1071–1078.

Lefkowitz, M. M., Eron, L. D., Walder, L. O., & Huesmann, L. R. (1977). *Growing up to be violent: A longitudinal study of the development of aggression.* New York: Pergamon.

Lesser, G. (1974). *Children and television: Lessons from "Sesame Street."* New York: Vintage Books.

Lyle, J., & Hoffman, H. R. (1972). Children's use of television and other media. In E. A. Rubinstein, G. A. Comstock, & J. Murray (Eds.), *Television and social behavior (Vol. 4), Television in day-to-day life: Patterns of use* (pp. 129–256). Washington, DC: U.S. Government Printing Office.

Signorelli, N., Gross, L., & Morgan, M. (1982). Violence in television programs 10 years later. In D. Pearl, L. Bouthilet, & J. Lazar (Eds.), *Television and behavior: Ten years of scientific progress and implications for the eighties. Vol. II, Technical reviews* (pp. 158–174). Washington, DC: U.S. Government Printing Office.

Singer, J. L., & Singer, D. G. (1981). *Television, imagination and aggression: A study of preschoolers play.* Hillsdale, NJ: Lawrence Erlbaum Associates.

Tiegs, E. W., & Clark, W. W. (1970). *California Achievement Test.* Ne York: McGraw-Hill.

U.S. Bureau of the Census (1982). *Statistical Abstract of the United States: 103rd Edition.* Washington DC.

4

Television and Aggressive Behavior Among Finnish Children

Kirsti Lagerspetz
Vappu Viemerö
Åbo Akademi, Turku, Finland

INTRODUCTION

Finland and Turku

Although the republic of Finland is quite large geographically, 338,145 sq-km, its population is only about 4.9 million. It has a free-market economy, a high national income and standard of living, and lively social and cultural exchanges with Western countries. Finland also has active trade, travel, and information exchanges with the Soviet Union, though these are formally restricted. Finland's economic and cultural relations with both the Western Alliance and the Soviet Union, plus its geographical position on the east side of the Baltic and close to the Arctic make its position unique in Western Europe. Language also contributes to Finland's isolation. Finnish belongs to the Feno-Ugric language group, which is not related to the Indo-European languages. It differs both in structure and vocabulary so that English is more like Russian than Finnish is like either language. Finland's neighbors, that is Sweden, Norway, and the Soviet Union, all have Indo-European languages.

The Finnish people, however, try hard to compensate for their geographical and linguistic situation. They are enthusiastic travelers, follow world politics and cultural events through an active press, have much literature translated into Finnish, and import many programs for cinemas and television, especially from Western countries.

The population of Finland is Caucasian. Social class differences, as calculated by income, are relatively small. Political and cultural life and social class structure are similar to the Scandinavian countries with which Finland has been closely connected during its historical development. Recently, Finland has shifted from a predominantly agricultural society to an urban one. The change has been rapid. At present, 60% of the population lives in urban areas, whereas in 1950 the percentage was only 32. There are no very big cities in Finland. Helsinki, which is the capital and largest city, has about 500,000 inhabitants. The former capital, Turku, is its third largest city. It has about 170,000 inhabitants and was chosen as the site for this study. As Finland's "gate to the West," Turku is a port with ship-building, food, and textile industries. It is also an educational center with two universities. In existence before 1229, Turku has the longest cultural tradition in Finland.

It can be asked whether a sample from Turku would be representative of the whole of Finland. It would, of course, have been preferable if all countries had collected data from both rural and urban communities. Nevertheless, results from Turku are likely to be typical for Finland as a whole, as Finnish society has a rather homogenous ethnic background, schooling, and standard of living. Furthermore, when the way of life and use of time was studied in Finnish families, no great differences were found between rural and urban communities (Takala, 1984). These findings may be explained, in part, by the recent migration from rural areas to urban areas and, in part, by the effective communication possible in a country with a relatively small population. Therefore, samples taken from Turku are likely to produce results that are not very different from what might be obtained from other areas in Finland. Nevertheless, because of the restricted sample, some caution is necessary when interpreting results.

The Family in Finland

Some social and cultural features of Finnish families are relevant. The marriage rate in Finland has increased during this century. During the first 3 decades, it was economically more difficult to support a family, especially in urban areas. Thus, the proportion of people who never married was higher than it is at present (Jallinoja & Haavio-Mannila, 1983). The marriage rate increased after World War II. In 1969, 60.9% of the population aged 15 years or older lived with their spouses. The divorce rate in Finland has increased recently, although it is still lower than in many other developed countries (Lindgren & Pulkkinen, 1984). In 1970, there were 1.31 divorces per 1,000 persons, whereas in 1982, the corresponding figure was 2.02. The number of unmarried couples living together also has increased rapidly. In 1968, the percentage of couples living in consensual union was 0.7, whereas in 1982, it was 10.9 (Jaakkola, Aromaa, & Cantell, 1984). It seems that consensual unions before marriage have become more acceptable. If both marriages and consensual unions are considered, 63.4% of the population aged 15–64 years lived as couples in 1982. It seems this unusually high percentage may be accounted for by the loneliness experienced by those who have become victims of Finland's rapid urbanization and who have consequently lost contact with relatives and former friends (Jaakkola et al., 1984).

Most children in Finland live in small family units. Nuclear families have become increasingly common compared to extended families including relatives or "outsiders" such as servants or lodgers. In 1980, reflecting the rising divorce rate, 14.7% of the families were one-parent families (*Yearbook of Population Research in Finland, XXII,* 1984). Also, the average number of children per family has decreased recently. In 1975, the average number of children under 18 years in Finnish families was 1.69 in urban and 1.93 in rural areas.

In Finland, the proportion of married women in the labor force is among the highest in Western Europe. In 1975, 67% of mothers in families that included both parents and at least one child under 18 were employed. This statistic suggests that children in Finland are likely to grow up in families in which the mother is working.

In many respects, women in Finland have been equal to men for longer than women in other countries. For example, in 1906, women became eligible to vote, making Finland the second country in the world (after New Zealand) to extend voting rights to women. Among the Scandinavian countries, Finland has proportionately more women studying at universities, employed outside the home, and elected to the parliament (Haavio-Mannila, 1968; Naisten tutkijanuran ongelmat ja esteet, 1982). Finland has a long tradition of educating women. In the academic year 1964–1965, the number of female students exceeded males in Finnish universities (Riihinen, Pulkkinen, Ritamies, Penttinen, 1983). Men, however, still take higher professional and graduate university degrees more often than do women.

Although women in Finland are legally free to act independently, attitudes regarding social roles for men and women have been found to be rather conservative when compared to the other Scandinavian countries (Haavio-Mannila, 1968). It has been said that Finnish society encourages women to work and take on social responsibilities but still requires that they fulfill the traditional womanly role at home. For instance, if both spouses in a family with children are employed, the wife carries out approximately two thirds of the domestic work (Takala, 1984). The amount of the husband's participation in household work increases only slightly when family situations change, but the number of children significantly influences how much time the wife spends in domestic work (Säntti & Väliaho, 1982). Although participation of husbands in household work has increased during the last 20 years (Takala, 1979), women still have greater domestic responsibilities than do men in Finnish families.

In summary, the average Finnish child grows up in a small family, sometimes with divorced or remarried parents. The parents or family may have moved to the city from the countryside. The child's mother is most probably working full time. There may be problems with alcoholism and drunken behavior in the family or in the neighborhood (Jallinoja & Haavio-Mannila, 1983). The standard of living is good and the educational level of the parents is rather high. The children in Finland are physically well taken care of, which is reflected, for instance, by the death rate of infants under one year, one of the lowest in the world. As the urban lifestyle is not as well developed as in many other European societies, the child does not live in a very big city. The family is likely to have one or two TV sets. They may also have a car, although, except for Poland, this is less likely than in other countries participating in the present study. In Finland, the family often has a house for vacations in the countryside. Thus, the average Finnish child is rather privileged, at least in material respects.

Criminal Violence in Finland

Children's aggression, which is the main theme of the book, differs from adult criminality, which is perhaps more dependent on economics, demographics, politics, public control, and other social conditions than child aggression.

There is some evidence for the relation of early aggression to violent and other offenses in adulthood (Huesmann, Eron, Lefkowitz, & Walder, 1984; Pulkkinen, 1982). The relation of aggression to homicides has recently been discussed by Turner, Cole, and Cerro (1984) who reviewed the literature and concluded that impulsive aggression is likely to play a role with homicides, whereas violence in connection with robberies is more often motivated by material incentives. Reacting with impulsive aggression may be more likely when the prevailing social environment condones or supports such behavior for solving interpersonal problems. Among Scandinavians, the Finns have had a reputation for being violent and using knives, especially when drunk. The frequencies of crimes against life (both homicides and suicides) have been higher in Finland than in other Scandinavian countries or in central European countries (Aromaa, 1983; Verkko, 1951). Violent behavior has been attributed to the Finnish "national character." It is possible that certain impulsive aggressive acts have been more tolerated by Finns than by other nationalities. Furthermore, around 80% of assaults, batteries, and homicides in Finland occur under the influence of alcohol. Alcoholism and drunken behavior are recognized as a national problem in Finland, although the yearly consumption of alcohol is not particularly high. In 1981, it was 6.5 liters of 100% ethanol per inhabitant. The corresponding figures available for other countries in the present study are Australia 10.0, United States 8.3, and Poland 6.5.

At present, criminal violence in Finland is approximately at the same level as in Sweden. In 1979, it was 3.0 homicides per 100,000 inhabitants. Comparisons of violence rates should, however, be viewed with caution. Slight differences in reporting practices in different countries and at different times in the same country can alter the statistics noticeably. Furthermore, reported criminality is always only a part of actual criminality.

Television in Finland

Regular TV broadcasting began in Finland in 1955. By 1981, TV networks covered 99.9% of the country and reached 98.8% of the population. In 1979, 94% of the households in Finland had at least one television set (Sinkko, 1980). In 1980, the frequency of TV sets per capita in Finland was the ninth highest in the world, 374 sets per 1,000 persons.

Radio and TV broadcasting in Finland is controlled by a share-holding company in which the government owns 99.9% of the shares and different organizations own the remaining 0.1%. The basically government-owned National Broadcasting Company leases broadcasting time to a commercial broadcasting company, MTV, which broadcasts about 20% of the programs, typically films, series, and general entertainment. Finnish TV broadcasts on two channels for about 6 hours per channel daily beginning around 5:30 p.m. and ending before midnight. In addition, there are school TV programs during the day on week days.

During the year 1981–1982, 40% of all programs were imported. Domestic production included some series and films, many educational programs, most informational features, and all newscasts. In 1981–1982, 91% of the series were imported, most frequently from the United States, the United Kingdom, France, and Sweden (Sarkkinen, 1983). Because TV broadcasting in Finland is governmentally controlled, programs can be selected for their educational impact and artistic quality. Compared to films available on videotape and to some films shown at cinemas, the violence allowed on TV in Finland is relatively mild. Most of it occurs in the American imports, which consist mostly of series and fiction films. During a 3-week survey in 1974, 12 out of 34 American programs shown contained violence. Corresponding figures were 4 out of 28 for English, 4 out of 9 for French, and 0 out of 15 for Swedish films (Ruusala, 1975).

Because drama series depicting violence are almost exclusively imported and never dubbed, the people shown in them speak a language that children (and many adults) do not understand. Furthermore, the imported programs also show remote places, types of clothing, ways of behaving, and human races that Finnish children never or very seldom see in real life. Moreover, unless they can read the subtitles, they would find it difficult to follow the plots. Thus, it is likely that violent drama series seem more unreal to the Finnish than to the American child. Also, it might be easier to idealize the behavior of characters populating such a "fairy land."

Gerbner (1972) has studied the so-called "TV population," that is, the fictional characters and their lifestyles that appear on TV. According to Gerbner, there are more upper and middle-class characters on TV than in the real population, more men than women, more physicians but fewer individuals who are chronically ill or dying, and so on. For people in Finland (and other small countries), TV characters have one more important characteristic: They are foreigners.

Because the content of TV programs is controlled and only a few are chosen for commercial purposes, viewers in Finland are less exposed to violence on TV than are viewers in the United States. In addition, at the time of our investigation, only two channels were available in the Turku area, and neither of them showed much violent material. Therefore, a person in Finland cannot choose to look at violent programming at any time or on any day as can be done in most parts of the United States. Thus, the maximum exposure to violence on TV cannot become as high for a child in Turku as it can for a child living in the Chicago area.

At the time the data were collected, the children did not have many opportunities to view programs other than those shown on Finnish TV. Films shown in the cinemas were the other possibility. Among these were some more violent than any shown on TV. Since then, home videotape equipment has become increasingly common in Finland. In the near future, more programs will become available through foreign satellite TV. In addition, some urban areas in Finland, including Turku, have acquired cable TV.

Observations of Violence on the Finnish TV

We monitored the two TV channels in Finland for the occurrence of violence on two occasions: In 1981, during the week between May 17 and May 23; and in 1983, during the last week in October. Using a technique developed by Gerbner (1972), we counted acts of physical injury toward other persons or animals on all the TV programs shown during the observation period. Table 4.1 indicates the amount of violence found in each program category. The average amounts were 0.61 acts per hour in 1981 and 1.14 acts per hour in 1983. In contrast, Gerbner and Gross (1981) found 5 acts per prime time hour and 18 acts per weekend daytime hour. In Finland, the two observations produced slightly different results, the later period having a somewhat higher frequency than the earlier one. The observation week in 1981, however, was Easter week, and it is possible that less violent programs had been selected for showing.

TABLE 4.1
Indices of Perceived Violence for Different Program Categories

Program Category	Number of Programs	Number of Hours	Percent of Programs Violent	Percent of Hours of Programs Containing Violence	Number of Violent Episodes per Program	Number of Violent Episodes per Hour
CARTOONS	7	2.6	71.4	76.9	5.1	13.9
CHILDREN'S PROGRAMS	10	6.4	20.0	10.3	0.7	1.1
FICTION	26	24.2	57.7	65.2	1.7	1.9
Crime	5	4.4	100.0	100.0	3.4	3.9
Western	–	–	–	–	–	–
Action	14	15.5	57.1	63.1	1.9	1.7
Comedy	7	4.3	28.6	35.3	0.3	0.5
NON-FICTION	117	52.8	5.9	5.8	0.1	0.2
Variety	17	11.2	0.0	0.0	0.0	0.0
Documentary	70	25.8	8.6	8.7	0.1	0.3
Educational	23	11.7	4.4	7.1	0.1	0.3
Sports	7	4.1	0.0	0.0	0.0	0.0
TOTAL	160	85.9	18.1	25.0	0.6	1.1

Analysis of the programs from the 1983 observation period indicated that 25% of the programs contained violence. As described in chapter 1, such statistics are difficult to compare across countries. Certainly, the absolute number of broadcast hours in Finland that contain significant violence is substantially less than in the United States or Australia.

METHOD

The Sample

In the Spring of 1978, 1979, and 1980, 220 first- and third-grade pupils from two schools in Turku were interviewed. Of the pupils, 115 were girls (64 first graders and 51 third graders) and 105 were boys (56 first graders and 49 third graders). In 1979, for the second wave, 191 children remained in the sample, and in 1980, for the third wave, there were 178 who remained. The parents of the children were interviewed twice, in the first and the third year. One of the schools investigated was situated in the center of the city, whereas the other was in a suburb. Both schools were public schools as are almost all schools in Finland, and there were no obvious social class differences between the schools. After the municipal school board and the directors of the schools had given their permission, five first-grade classrooms and four third-grade classrooms were chosen by lot. Parents' permission was requested by a letter. Of the parents, 16.3% refused to permit their child to participate. Of the parents who did not refuse their permission, 16.8% did not want to be interviewed themselves. Table 4.2 summarizes the number of subjects tested.

The children in the nine initial classes were followed for 3 years. In 1980, they were in 12 different classes. The children of the younger cohort had chosen to study different languages and thus were in different classrooms. A small dropout occurred because some children had gone to music classes at the time of the testing. These were not included because of practical difficulties. The greatest dropout of subjects, however, was due to mobility of the families. Nevertheless, the Finnish sample's dropout rate of 19% was lower than that of the United States, 33%. The difference may perhaps reflect the greater mobility of the United States' population. Finland is a small

TABLE 4.2
Number of Subjects Participating in the Study in Finland

Year	Subjects	Parents
1978	220	337 (191 mothers, 146 fathers)
1979	191	
1980	178	220 (132 mothers, 88 fathers)

country; moreover, Finnish people do not move outside Finland to any very great extent, primarily because of language difficulties.

In Finland, children start school during the year of their seventh birthday. Thus, the children in the Finnish sample were on average 9 months older than those of the United States sample, because the younger cohort in all samples consisted of children who had started school in the fall.

The Measures

To obtain comparable results, we tried to alter the protocols as little as possible from those of the Chicago study. In cross-cultural comparisons, items are sometimes adapted to suit prevailing cultural conditions. In principle, this is a good way to proceed. In reality, it is not possible to know whether an item has been changed enough or too much to mean relatively the same thing in the second culture as it meant in the first. Furthermore, after an item has been changed, differences in responses to it can no longer be explained on the basis of the different meanings that the item holds for the two cultures. Thus, we retained the items in their original form as far as possible and risked that later we might have to interpret discrepant results as reflecting differences in culture. An example of such an item concerned how realistic the children experienced TV programs to be. As we point out, this question obviously had a different meaning for Finnish and United States children.

We did make some minor changes in the items. We collected normative data on the sex-role identification pictures by asking 58 college students to rate the pictures and made changes accordingly. For instance, the picture of the baseball in the sex-role identification test was changed to a football (soccer ball), which was familiar to Finnish children.

However, the reactions of the children in the testing situations made us question how appropriate some of the items were for measuring behavior and attitudes in Finnish children. Therefore, in 1983, 3 years after the study reported here had been completed, we reformulated a version of the peer-rating questionnaire of aggression. The aims of altering the items were to: (a) make aggressive act in question more like the way Finnish children behave or express themselves. For instance, the original question, "Who is always getting into trouble?" was changed to "Who always quarrels with other people?" In addition, the word "child" was changed to "pupil" or "people." (b) Make the aggressive act sound more justified and therefore more likely to occur. For example, the question "Who starts a fight over nothing?" was changed to "Who usually starts a fight?" (c) Ask about issues we felt were important when discussing aggression but were omitted in the original version. For instance, instead of asking "Who does things that bother others?" we asked "Who likes to tease other people?" Exactly the same wording was retained only in one item. A sample of 51 sixth graders, approximately 12 years old, were tested first with the original peer-rating questionnaire and then retested 4½ months later with the modified version. For this sample, coefficient alpha of the original test was .949 and that of the modified version was .947.

These data suggest that, although the wording of the original items used in the study may have seemed somewhat awkward, the results would probably not have been different if the altered version of the nomination questions had been used.

The items of the parent inverviews were also altered as little as possible from the Chicago study. Some stability coefficients for the Finnish parent variables over 2 years are presented in Table 4.3. Among the attitude and personality variables, self-rated aggression in both fathers and mothers and punitiveness have the highest stability coefficient (about .60). Nurturance, however, has low stability (coefficient about .29). Even TV viewing frequency of the mothers seems to be unstable (about .41).

It is interesting that not even the socioeconomic variables correlate perfectly between the years. According to mothers' reports, even family income seems to fluctuate. It seems that many mothers have either given different information about their own occupation in the two interviews or changed occupations during the 2-year period.

The TV Programs

All drama series shown on Finnish TV during the spring school terms when data were collected were included in the study regardless of the time of day when they were shown. The requirement that programs be series was adhered to as far as possible so that each child would have the opportunity to see at least one episode in the series. The five lists presented to the Finnish children contained 7 series each, whereas in the Chicago study, there were eight lists of 10 TV programs. The total number of series each year was 35, much less than the 80 series appearing in the Chicago investigation. The smaller choice of

TABLE 4.3
Stability Coefficients Over 2 Years for Some Parent Variables

	Father	Mother
Education	.838	.849
Occupation	.773	.305
Income	.791	.453
Rejection	.646	.637
Nurturance	.347	.233
Punishment	.443	.601
Parent's self-rated aggression	.608	.597
Parent's self-rated TV-frequency	.539	.412
Parent's rating of child's TV-frequency	.239	.519

programs might have different consequences for the analysis: results may be more dependent on the qualities of individual episodes. Moreover, because a smaller total number of aggressive films was included, it is not possible for Finnish children to choose to view as many aggressive films as the American children can. The programs were rated for aggression by two psychology students. The scale was the same as in the Chicago study. The inter-rater reliability was .85. Acts had to be intentional in order to be considered aggressive; accidents and unintentional injury were not taken into account. Clearly intended acts of physical aggression, however, were included even when they proved unsuccessful and no damage was caused. (Note that this was not the definition of aggression in the study of the children or their parents.) We found that approximately 43% of the series rated contained at least one aggressive act.

The TV series included in the study were, to some extent, the same from country to country. In 1978, 14.3% of the programs in the Finnish study had been included in the Chicago study. In 1979 and 1980, the corresponding percentage was 17.4%. Of the films used in our study, 40% were American and 19.4% were British. The rest consisted of 4–5% each from German, French, Swedish, Polish, and Czech productions. Of the films, 15.2% were Finnish, mostly consisting of child programs. It is apparent that speed of international communications has increased tremendously. One indication of this is the rapid spread of commercial TV films to other parts of the world.

The Procedure

The children were interviewed twice each spring. The time between the two interviews ranged from a few days to 1 week. Group interviews with the whole class were used except for the younger cohort. During the first wave, the younger children were interviewed individually because we could not be sure that they were able to read and write. Questionnaires were similar to those used in the Chicago study. In the individual interviews, first graders were shown a class photograph to help them recall their classmates.

By the last wave, third graders had been separated into several different classrooms and had to be interviewed there. Thus, to get the peer ratings for our subjects, all pupils in the respective classes had to be tested. After completing the peer-rating items, the other children were dismissed, and the subjects completed the rest of the questionnaire.

Parents were interviewed individually. The interviewer filled out the booklet, except for the MMPI scales that the parents filled in themselves. Not all the parents agreed to participate; therefore, the sample might be somewhat biased as parents who were less interested in their children or less cooperative might have dropped out.

Information was obtained from the parents about their education, occupation, and income. The "social class" of the family was estimated on basis of the father's occupation only.

RESULTS

Level of Aggressiveness

Aggressive behavior of the subjects was measured in two ways, by self-ratings and by ratings made by the peers.

Figure 4.1 shows the means of peer-nominated aggression for the boys and the girls in Finland in the different grades and in the two cohorts.

In general, peer-nominated aggression is higher for the older than for the younger children both for boys and for girls. Analysis of variance showed significant main effects for both years of analysis [F (2.348) = 8.40, $p < .001$] and for cohort [$F(1.174) = 4.45, pp < .04$]. There was, however, a

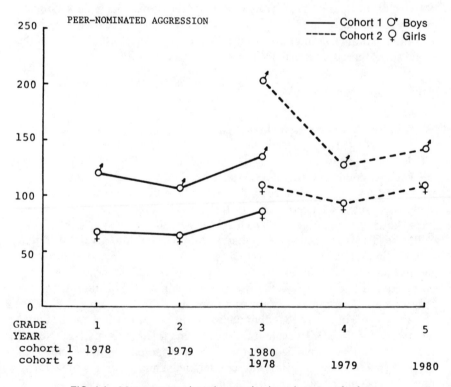

FIG. 4.1 Mean peer-nominated aggression in each wave and cohort.

significant difference between the two overlapping third-grade groups tested in 1978 and in 1980. The aggression of the 1978 third graders was significantly higher. One possible explanation for these results might be that the younger cohort was tired of testing by the third grade and therefore gave few answers. Because the older cohort was tested for the first time in the third grade, they might have been more eager to participate in this novel experience and thus responded with more positive identifications on the peer nomination for aggression. This interpretation is supported by evidence that the older cohort also scores highly on the other variables during the first trial.

Out of 47 variables measured, boys scored higher on 22 and girls on 17 variables. These variables included viewing of violent programs, looking at male aggression (for boys), identification with several types of TV figures (male, aggressive, non-aggressive; in boys), considering TV as realistic (for boys), aggressive fantasy (for boys), and peer-nominated popularity (for boys). All these are variables that would be susceptible to having scores inflated by impulsive responding. Furthermore, the same trend was observed in the Chicago results. Even there, the cohort that started in the third grade had higher values on several variables. The increasing scores on peer-nominated aggression over the years was also observable in the results from some of the other countries, especially the United States.

The low scores of the Finnish children in comparison with scores in other countries could, of course, indicate a hesitation to nominate others for unfavorable charcteristics. It was also the case, however, that the Finnish children scored lower than children from other countries on aggressive fantasy and self-rated aggression. The same scales were used in all countries for the measurement of these variables. Therefore, these means are more comparable than are the means for nomination variables. Thus, it is conceivable that the results reflect some lower habitual aggression in the Finnish sample.

Aggression in Boys and Girls

The level of peer-nominated aggression was higher for boys than for girls in all countries, Finland included. In most research, girls have been found to be less aggressive (Maccoby & Jacklin, 1974). Moreover, in most cultures, the socialization of girls includes an inhibition of aggressive impulses. At least physical aggression is not encouraged, so girls may be more likely to express aggression verbally.

The present study also found that boys' aggression was more stable over the years than girls' aggression. (In Finland, the stability for boys over 3 years was .74 and for girls it was .62; $p < .001$.) Because girls' aggressiveness is more likely to be inhibited by society, it is possible that it is expressed through more varied outlets than the aggressiveness of boys. Even among highly aggressive girls, straightforward hitting and shoving is displayed only occasionally, whereas more subtle ways to harm others may be invented for different occasions. This may be why girls' aggression looks more "state dependent." In addition, Whiting and Edwards (1973) found that boys are more likely than girls to initiate aggressive acts, whereas no differences exist in defensive (retaliatory) aggression.

In studies by Kagan and Moss (1962) and Block (1971), adult aggression was predicted by adolescent aggression with higher probability for males than for females. Puberty, however, makes the predictability lower for both males and females (Pitkänen-Pulkkinen, 1981). Because girls reach puberty earlier than boys, it might be that the girls in our older cohort had reached puberty during the follow-up period, whereas the boys had not yet reached that stage.

The concepts of homotypic and heterotypic continuity of traits (Kagan, 1980) are also useful for attempting to understand the apparently lower stability of girls' aggressiveness. In homotypic continuity, the same type of behavior continues. In heterotypic continuity, the same motivations and needs persist, but overt expression changes depending on time and situation. Because overt aggressive behavior is not supported for girls, their aggressiveness may be expressed in more varied ways, which would result in lower correlations when aggression is repeatedly measured with the same instrument.

There was still another peculiarity in the comparison of girls' and boys' aggression. For the boys, peer-nominated aggression correlated significantly with their own perception of their aggression. In the successive years, the correlations were .253, .245, and .389. A comparable result was found in the follow-up study by Lefkowitz, Eron, Walder, and Huesmann (1977) as described in the introductory chapter to this volume. In Finland, Pulkkinen (1982) reported positive significant correlations between several types of self-rated aggression and peer-nominated aggression for boys at age 8 and age 14.

For girls in Finland, however, this relation did not hold. The correlations between peer-ratings and self-ratings of aggression for the girls were significant only in the last year. This failure to find correlations also may be explained by the attitude of society toward aggression in girls. Because girls feel that their aggressiveness is not valued, they may try to avoid rating themselves as very aggressive. Thus, there might be more "faking" in the girls' responses, which then might lower the correlations.

This interpretation is supported by some results by Björkqvist, Ekman, and Lagerspetz (1982) on bullying behavior in the 12 to 14-year-old Finnish school children. The authors studied bullies and their victims both in their overt behavior and their self-images. Children were asked how they thought their behavior corresponded to the norms of the society. Girls in this study felt that society's norms required less dominance from them than boys felt for themselves. Furthermore, those girls that had been rated as bullies by their peers said that they wanted to be less dominant than they felt themselves to be. The boy bullies, on the other hand, wanted to be even more dominant than they felt themselves to be. This implies that the girl bullies were dominant as if "against their ideal." These results are relevant to a discussion of the greater state dependence of girls' aggression. It seems that aggression in girls is not as much an expression of a positive attitude to aggression as it is in males. Aggressive behavior in females thus seems to be a situational reaction rather than the expression of a pervasive attitude. Consequently, it can take different forms in accordance with different situations.

TV Viewing

Frequency of viewing favorite TV programs, hereafter called *regularity,* showed a general rising trend over the years and grades. This was similar to results obtained in the United States. In Finland, however, overall viewing fluctuated so that the highest scores were obtained both by the older and the younger cohort in 1979. Because there are few programs on Finnish TV, changes in programming strongly influence viewing frequencies and no doubt produced the fluctuation in frequency for 1979. Possibly because fewer programms are available, Finnish children (according to mothers' reports) viewed less TV (10.12 hours per week in the older cohort) than did the United States children (14.99 hours per week). Viewing of violence on TV also increased with age for the children in Finland. This can be seen in Fig. 4.2. At every age, boys watched significantly more violent programs than did the girls [$F (1.174) = 43.5, p < .001$]. Finnish boys even watched programs with female aggressors more than did Finnish girls.

Identification With the TV Characters

If young boys and girls perceived themselves as being "like" an actor, they are said to identify with the actor. In a later study, which we carried out in Finland in 1983 partly with the same subjects, we found that those who identified with TV characters were also more likely to imitate them. For instance, boys' imitation correlated with identification with aggressive masculine charcters .28 ($p < .001$, $N = 193$) and girls' imitation correlated with identification with feminine characters .28 ($p < .001$, $N = 202$). Therefore, a child's own perceived similarity (identification) with TV characters was measured each year. As described in chapter 2, the children in this study were asked if they felt that they acted like the characters on their favorite TV programs.

The boys felt they acted more like the male TV characters than the girls did (mean for boys, 3.1; mean for girls, 1.31), and the girls identified more with female characters than the boys did (mean for boys, 1.32; mean for girls, 1.69). This seems logical and is in accordance with previous findings (e.g.,

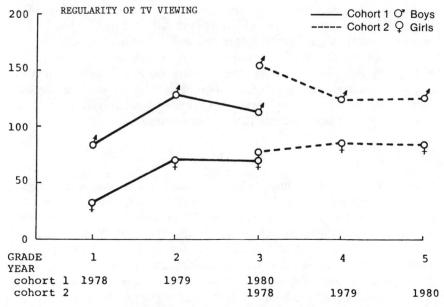

FIG. 4.2 Mean regularity of TV viewing in each wave and cohort.

Maccoby and Wilson, 1957, found that children remembered acts from films better when they were performed by persons of their own sex). The girls in the present study, however, did not think they acted more like female than male charcters, but stated that they acted similarly to both male and female characters. This corresponds to results from studies of imitation (e.g., Hicks, 1965), which show that both boys and girls attend to male models more than female models, but, in addition, girls imitate females more than boys do. Such results could be interpreted to suggest that although what the males do on TV is important for boys and girls, what females do has more significance for girls than for boys. Thus, an increase of female aggression on TV might be more likely to influence the behavior of girls than of boys.

Regularity of TV Viewing and Aggression

Regularity of TV viewing did not correlate significantly with peer-nominated aggression in Finland although it did in most groups in the United States. This difference may be attributed, perhaps, to lower frequency of TV programs and particularly violent programs on TV in Finland. American children who watch their favorite shows "every time they're on" are likely to be watching more TV and seeing more TV violence than comparable Finnish children. Thus, the lack of a correlation in Finland suggests that the correlation between regularity of viewing and aggression in the United States may be an artifact of the higher frequency of violence on TV series in the United States.

TV Violence Viewing and Aggression

The amount of television violence a child watched did correlate positively with a child's aggression in the Finnish sample. Although correlations were significant in the 2 last years of the study, they were generally not as high as in the United States sample as Table 4.4 reveals. The correlations between average TV violence viewing and average aggression over the 3 years were .21 (*p* < .05) for boys and .16 (n.s.) for girls. It is interesting that positive correlations with aggression were found in Finland where the amount of violence on TV is relatively limited. The correlations in Finland are approximately the same as those in Poland. For girls in Finland, however, the correlations between TV violence viewing and aggression are not as high as for boys. Girls' correlations reached statistical significance only in the older cohort of the first wave. In the United States, there was no such difference between the genders. In the previous study in the United States, (Lefkowitz, et al., 1977), however, girls failed to show a positive correlation between aggression and TV violence viewing. Finnish girls apparently resemble American girls of 10 years ago. A similar result was also found for the Australian girls in the present study.

Aggression and Identification With TV Characters

Identification with TV characters as measured by perceived similarity was the variable that correlated most consistently with peer-nominated aggression in the Finnish sample. Table 4.5 shows the correlations between peer-nominated aggression and identification with aggressive TV characters. It is interesting that identification with all TV characters, not only aggressive ones, correlated with aggression. It is possible that children who do not have appropriate normative models for identification in their everyday life tend to seek identification objects from the TV. Often these may be children from

TABLE 4.4
Correlations Between Television Violence Viewing and Peer-Nominated Aggression

	Boys	*Girls*	*All Subjects*
Cohort 1			
Grade 1	.03	.14	.14
Grade 2	.27*	.02	.26**
Grade 3	.09	.33**	.20*
Cohort 2			
Grade 3	.04	.05	.16
Grade 4	.38***	−.16	.23*
Grade 5	.28*	.04	.22*

*p < .05.   **p < .01.   ***p < .001.

TABLE 4.5
Correlations of Peer-Nominated Aggression with Perceived Identification with
Aggressive TV Characters

	Boys (N = 105)	Girls (N = 115)
Cohort 1		
grade 1	.061	.063
grade 2	.357**	.156
grade 3	.223	.592***
Cohort 2		
grade 3	.248*	.258*
grade 4	.280*	.036
grade 5	.182	.208

*p < .05.   **p < .01.   ***p < .001.

"problem families" who are likely to adopt aggressive ways of behavior in their social interactions (Groebel & Krebs, 1983).

Table 4.6 contains the correlations between mean aggression and TV habits over the 3 years. The correlations for boys are generally higher than for girls, but even the girls show significant relations between identification with aggressive TV characters and aggression.

Identification with aggressive characters may have correlated higher with aggression than overall violence viewing in Finland because of the low frequency of violence on TV. Identification is more independent of the availability and frequency of violence on the TV than other TV variables. Even if children seldom have the opportunity to see the object of identification on the screen, they can still identify strongly. Such an effect can emerge even in a country like Finland where the amount of violence on the screen is limited.

Predicting Later Aggression from Earlier TV Habits

Table 4.7 depicts the correlations of aggression in the third year with some TV habits averaged over the first 2 years. There is some justification for regarding these as reflecting the effects of previous experience with TV viewing on later aggression. A comparison of the correlations in the two tables, 4.6 and 4.7, contains some evidence for a different kind of effect in boys than in girls. For the boys, the correlations are very similar in both tables. For girls, however, significant correlations disappeared when TV measures were lagged behind the aggression measure in time (Table 4.7). Neither early violence viewing nor early identification with TV characters correlated with later aggression although concurrent measurements did.

How should this difference between the genders be explained? We noted previously that there was some evidence that girls did not idealize aggressive behavior as much as boys did. We pointed out that the aggression in girls may be more tied to situational demands, whereas boys' aggression related to their idealizing and accepting attitude toward aggression. The aggression-enhancing effect of violent films is often considered dependent on a change of attitudes toward more acceptance of aggression (e.g., Huesmann, Eron, Klein, Brice, & Fisher, 1983). In girls, however, this kind of change is opposed by socialization experiences (i.e., aggression is not considered appropriate for girls). Therefore, a change of attitudes stimulated by mass media is not likely to be as effective for girls as it is for boys. Thus previous violence viewing may not have long-lasting effects on later aggression in girls.

The longitudinal relations for boys from early TV violence viewing and identification with TV characters to later aggression suggest that violent television may be teaching aggressive habits to boys in Finland. The plausibility of such a model can best be tested by examining the multiple regression analyses shown in Table 4.8. In the first analysis, later aggression is predicted for the boys from both their early aggression and the product of their early violence viewing and identification with TV characters. The significant effect for TV indicates that viewing more violence and identifying more with TV characters is predictive of increases in aggression for boys regardless of their initial level of aggression. Thus, television violence seems to be a cause of aggression among boys in Finland.

At the same time, the second analysis reveals that a boy's viewing of TV is also influenced by his previous aggression. More aggressive boys seem to increase their violence viewing and identification with TV characters. Thus, among Finnish boys, there seems to be a circular process involving exposure to media violence and aggression. Changes in one seem to be predictive of

TABLE 4.6
Correlations of TV Variables and Peer-Nominated Aggression Over 3 Years

TV Variables	Average peer rated aggression over 3 years	
	Boys	Girls
Average TV violence viewing over 3 years	.21* ($N = 93$)	.16 ($N = 85$)
Average violence of preferred programs over 3 years	.18[+] ($N = 93$)	.23* ($N = 85$)
Average identification with characters over 3 years	.43*** ($N = 76$)	.28* ($N = 64$)
Average identification with aggressive TV characters over 3 years	.35** ($N = 80$)	.27* ($N = 66$)
Average identification with TV characters times average TV violence viewing	.37*** ($N = 76$)	.19 ($N = 64$)

[+]$p<.10.$ *$p<.05.$ **$p<.01.$ ***$p<.001.$

TABLE 4.7
Correlations of Early TV Violence Viewing and Perceived Similarity to TV Characters
with Later Aggression

| TV Variables | Peer rated aggression for 3rd year | |
	Boys	Girls
Average TV violence viewing for first 2 years	.17$^+$ (N = 93)	—
Average violence of preferred programs for first 2 years	.25* (N = 93)	—
Average identification with TV characters for first 2 years	.43*** (N = 84)	.13 (N = 68)
Average identification with aggressive TV characters for first 2 years	.38*** (N = 89)	.16 (N = 71)
Average identification with TV characters times average TV violence for first 2 years	.35*** (N = 84)	—

$^+p<.10.$ *$p<.05.$ ***$p<.001.$

changes in the other. Boys who increase their violence viewing increase in aggression. These increases in aggression in turn lead to increased violence viewing. This pattern was not seen in the Finnish girls although it was in both boys and girls in the United States. Although there were correlations between concurrent TV violence viewing and aggression for the girls, lasting effects over 3 years were not detected.

TV Realism

The effects of TV violence on viewers' aggression previously has been found to depend on how realistically the viewer thinks that the film depicts life (Lefkowitz et al., 1977). Weak but significant positive correlations between child's aggression and how much the child believed violent shows realistically portray life also were found in the current study. In Finland, the correlations for all subjects ranged from .254 ($p<.001$) in 1979 to .092 (n.s.) in 1980. There was no systematic difference between boys and girls. In Finland, realism did not interact significantly with TV violence viewing to affect the aggression measure.

Children in Finland perceived television as significantly more realistic than did their contemporaries in the United States [$F(1.580) = 135.9, p<.0001$]. High realism scores for some groups were also obtained in Poland and in Israel. The lowest scores were obtained in the United States. We found the relatively high realism ratings of the Finnish children puzzling, especially because the Finnish children did not score higher when asked about how realistically newspapers and certain fairy tales describe life. However, the violent programs on Finnish TV were almost exclusively imported. In the present study, all the violent programs watched by the children were produced outside Finland. It occurred to us that perhaps the children thought that the programs depicted life realistically for the foreign countries where the films had been made, but not for Finland. The language, the settings, and even the actor's behavior seem more unfamiliar, unintelligible, and culturally alien to the Finnish than to the American child. Children from the United States may evaluate the violence they see on how likely it is to occur in their "own backyard," but Finnish children probably evaluate the violence they see on its likelihood of occurring in exotic places.

To test this hypothesis, we reexamined a subsample of 190 Finnish children, some of whom were in our original study, in the Fall of 1981. They were

TABLE 4.8

Multiple Regressions Predicting a Boy's Aggression from His Earlier TV Violence Viewing and Identification with Aggressive TV Characters While Controlling for His Initial Aggressiveness

Dependent Variable	Predictors	Standardized Regression Coefficients Finn Boys (N = 80)	
3rd wave aggression	Cohort	−.174	(−.202)
	1st wave aggression	.747***	(.754)
	Product of TV violence viewing and identification with aggressive characters in 1st and 2nd waves	.205***	(.271)
		$R^2 = .604$, $F(3,76) = 38.6$, $p < .001$	
Product of TV violence viewing and identification with aggressive characters in 3rd wave	Cohort	−.080	(−.186)
	Product of TV violence viewing and identification with aggressive characters in 1st wave	.319***	(.528)
	Aggression in 1st and 2nd waves	.178	(.213)
		$R^2 = .129$, $F(3,76) = 3.74$, $p < .01$	

***$p < .001$

Note: The numbers in parentheses are the regression coefficients corrected for the unreliability of the measures.

asked two questions about violent programs that had been shown on TV in Finland the preceding spring:

1. "How accurately does the program depict life in Finland?"
2. "How accurately does the program depict life in the country of origin?" (USA, England, or Germany).

These data showed that children did indeed think that the series depicted life as it really was in the foreign countries but not in Finland. The realism scores of the Finnish children for Finland (1.65) did not differ significantly from the American children's mean realism judgments for United States programs (1.51). Thus, the impact of the "foreignness" of imported programming on viewers should be considered when the influence of TV violence on viewers is studied.

One may ask how observing TV violence only in foreign productions affects the relation between TV violence and the aggressive behavior of viewers. According to Feshbach (1976), anything that increases one's belief in the realism of the film would be expected to increase imitation of aggression in the film. At the same time, identification with film characters was found in the present study to be related to aggression in the viewers. Although we did not collect data on whether children identify more with exotic and foreign characters or with familiar ones on the screen, it seems plausible that foreign circumstances and languages would tend to make identification with the film actors more difficult and would decrease imitation. Still a third factor to consider are the attitudes about the country in which the film is set. Although foreign cultures and values are often somewhat disliked, foreign lifestyles are also admired and imitated. These conflicting attitudes are especially apparent toward the big Western countries like the United States, Britain, France, and West Germany which have produced most of the violent films shown on Finnish TV. Thus, admiration might facilitate more identification, which would in turn increase the influence of the films and the possibility that aggressive acts in the films might be copied.

As in most countries, the girls in Finland perceived televison violence as significantly less realistic than did the boys [$F (1.157) = 10.24, p < .002$]. The belief that violence on TV reflects life accurately also decreased with age. It is easy to understand that older children might be more critical evaluators of TV programs than younger ones. But why should girls see the programs as less realistic than boys? It is possible that during the ages studied, girls matured more quickly than boys. Their greater maturity could be reflected both in their assessment of TV reality as well as their relative disinclination to imitate violence on TV. As just described, girls' aggression measures did not correlate significantly with violence viewing. Finally, a more detached critical attitude toward mass media and other products of technology may be more typical for females. For example, Simone de Beauvoir describes women as "the spectators of the culture" in *La Deuxieme Sexe.*

Sex Roles

Gender identification and the learning of appropriate roles are exceedingly important variables in development (Maccoby & Jacklin, 1974). In the present study, sex typing was investigated by asking the children to choose pictures of playthings that had been rated as typically "masculine," "feminine," and "neutral." In Finland, as in other countries, boys choose the masculine playthings more often, and girls choose the feminine ones. This is, perhaps. trivial information but supports the validity of the test for determining the masculine or feminine orientation of the subjects. The neutral playthings, however, were chosen significantly more often by girls than by boys, suggesting that these items were not neutral but somewhat more feminine.

The mean scores in Finland show that no dramatic changes in masculine and feminine sex roles occurred during the years of the study. However, boys decreased their selection of feminine playthings while girls increased their selection of masculine items. These trends are similar to results observed in Israel and the United States. It may be that as children become older, boys learn they should not play with feminine things because they will be labeled "sissies," while girls become aware of the "modern" trend to encourage masculine interests for girls.

There was also a cohort effect for these variables, perhaps indicating a change in the cultural climate during this period. Masculine interests seem to have become increasingly appropriate for girls and feminine interests for boys $[F(1,173); = 17.3, p < .001; F(1,173) = 29.6, p < .001]$. No cohort effect appeared in the Finnish data for the neutral sex-role preference, although there was a small increase with increasing age $[F(2,356) = 11.95, p < .001]$ in both sexes. This perhaps can be interpreted as a diminished dependence on sex-appropriate choices with increasing age.

It was expected that masculine sex-role identification would increase the effects of TV violence on aggression because aggression is generally considered a masculine characteristic. In fact, the Finnish data did show a positive correlation between peer-nominated aggression and masculine sex-role identification both for boys $(.24, p < .01)$ and girls $(.26, p < .01)$. Aggressive children were more likely to be more interested in masculine than feminine activities.

Although choosing female-type activities did not correlate significantly with aggression in the Finnish data, choosing neutral play activities did correlate negatively with peer-nominated aggression. The correlation was highly significant for the boys $(-.33, p < .001)$ and approached significance for the girls $(-.20, p < .10)$. This is not unlike the United States results. If aggression is part of a masculine orientation, one would expect that avoiding typically male activities would be related to non-aggression.

Popularity

Peer-nominated popularity and aggression were negatively correlated in at least some subgroups as they were in several countries (e.g., United States, Israel). In Finland, however, the most popular children were in the middle range of aggressiveness. It is conceivable that some optimal degree of aggression is needed to make a child "interesting" and popular in the eyes of their peers in Scandinavian cultures. Some previous findings would support this assumption. When studying the bullying behavior in Swedish schools, Olweus (1978) found that bullies were almost as popular among their peers as children in the control group but that victims of bullying were the most unpopular. In a comparable study of 12- to 14-year-old children in Finland, Lagerspetz, Björkqvist, Berts, and King (1982) also found bullies to be more popular than their victims, although children rated well-adjusted by their teachers were the most popular.

Parental Behavior and Child Aggression

Environmental characteristics, especially the child's family, often have been found to influence both the child's aggression and TV viewing habits. In Sweden, for example, Sonesson (1979) found that children whose environment offers too few or too contradictory standards for behavior are likely to turn to the mass media for direction. She also found that mothers with the least amount of schooling had children who were the most frequent TV viewers. In another Swedish study, Olweus (1978) found that aggressive children had less strong and less positive ties to their parents.

In the present study, parents were interviewed to obtain information about their personality, education, TV viewing habits, and some socioeconomic background so that these data might be related to the children's behavior.

TV Viewing of the Parents

Some TV habits of family members were significantly correlated, e.g., the amount of time spent watching TV by fathers and their children correlated .37 ($p < .001$), and by fathers and mothers correlated .27 ($p < .001$). Parents' viewing of violence, however, did not show any significant correlation with their children's viewing of violence as Table 4.9 reveals.

It was expected that parents who watch TV frequently might stimulate their children's interest in TV characters and thus enhance their perceived similarity with these characters. This prediction was not strongly supported,

TABLE 4.9
The Correlations Between Parent and Child TV Habits Averaged Over Three Waves

	Parent Measures		
Child Measures	Frequency of TV Viewing	TV Violence Viewing	Judged Realism of TV Violence
Boys (N = 93)			
Aggression	.25*	—	
TV Violence Viewing	.13	—	—
Regularity of TV Viewing	—	.13	—
Judged Realism of TV Violence	—	—	—
Identification with TV Characters	.17	—	—
Girls (N = 100)			
Aggression	.22*	.13	—
TV Violence Viewing	—	—	—
Regularity of TV Viewing	.13	.12	—
Judged Realism of TV Violence	.21⁺	—	.21⁺
Identification with TV Characters	.24⁺	.18	.13

$^+p<.10.$ $^*p<.05.$

although correlations between parents' TV viewing frequency and children's identification with TV characters were consistently positive. Only for girls was the correlation near significance (.24, $p<.10$).

In Finland, parents' TV viewing frequency did correlate significantly with their sons' and daughters' peer-nominated aggression. For sons the correlation was .25 ($p<.05$), while for daughters the correlation was .22 ($p<.05$). Other research in Finland (Pitkänen-Pulkkinen, 1981) also has found that parents of aggressive children watch TV more than the parents of non-aggressive children. One explanation has been that the parents who watch a lot of TV do not have time and attention left for their children and, consequently, the children become frustrated and aggressive. On the other hand, watching TV is one of the primary activities that children and parents do together (Takala, 1984), and there are other possible explanations for correlations between parents' TV viewing and children's aggression. One would be that if parents are very absorbed in and influenced by the "television world" (Gerbner, 1972), they might develop unrealistic expectations and ideals for life and their children. The discrepancy between reality and the television world may be frustating and could influence their interactions with their children. Another explanation is that children watch more TV because their parents watch more and therefore are exposed more to aggressive models.

Child-Rearing Practices

The correlations of the parents' aggression and child-rearing practices with the child's aggression and TV habits are shown in Table 4.10.

Rejection. Eron, Walder, and Lefkowitz (1971) found that parents in the United States who held rejecting attitudes toward their children had more aggressive children. In Sweden, Olweus (1980) found rejection by parents was the second best predictor of a child's aggression after mothers' positive attitude toward aggression. As could be expected from these results, parental rejection in Finland also showed positive relations with aggression. From Table 4.10 one can see that parental rejection correlated significantly with child

TABLE 4.10
The Correlations of Parent Aggressiveness and Child-rearing Methods with
Child Aggression and TV Habits Averaged Over Three Waves

Child Measures	Parent Measures			
	Aggression (MMPI-4 + 9)	Rejection	Nurturance	Punishment
Boys (N = 93)				
Aggression	—	.36***	—	.20+
TV Violence Viewing	.19+	—	—	—
Regularity of TV Viewing	.16	—	—	—
Judged Realism of TV Violence	—	—	—	—
Identification with TV Characters	.29*	.16	.20+	—
Girls (N = 100)				
Aggression	—	.26*	—	.38***
TV Violence Viewing	—	—	−.16	—
Regularity of TV Viewing	—	—	−.19+	.16
Judged Realism of TV Violence	—	—	—	—
Identification with TV Characters	−.20	—	—	—

+p < .10.   *p < .05.   ***p < .001.

aggression particularly for boys. When rejection by mothers and fathers was examined separately, it was found that rejection by mothers correlated slightly higher with aggression. Because a mother traditionally offers empathy, support, and physically expressed affection to the child, her rejection may be more influential than the father's.

When the rejection scores for parents of high, medium and low aggressive boys and girls are compared, a significant effect for boys also obtains. The most aggressive boys had mothers who scored highest on rejection (11.9), mid-range boys had less rejecting mothers (9.6), and the low aggressive boys had the least rejecting ones (9.3; $F = 5.6, p < .005$). Fathers' rejection scores did not show a similar pattern, but aggressive boys did have the most rejecting fathers. Data for girls showed a similar trend but were not significant. It is possible that rejecting attitudes by parents affect girls less than boys. Of course, it is also possible that rejection by parents is simply a response to the child's aggression. To test this hypothesis, we compared regression coefficients for predicting aggression from rejection with coefficients for predicting rejection from aggression. As in the United States (see chapter 3) we found that rejection was more predictable from aggression than vice-versa, suggesting that rejection of children by their parents is more a response to aggression than an instigation to aggression.

Punishment.   The use of physical punishment by parents frequently has been found to be correlated with children's aggression. Carroll (1977) showed that criminally violent behavior of fathers and sons could be traced through three generations. Pitkänen-Pulkkinen (1981) found that parents of aggressive children endorsed corporal punishment more often than did the parents of other children. Parents of the aggressive children also had more inconsistent disciplinary methods. A connection between use of physical punishment and children's aggression has also been found by Eron et al. (1971), McCord, McCord, and Howard (1961), Sears, Maccoby, and Levin (1957), George and Main (1979), and Olweus (1980).

In this study, as Table 4.10 illustrates, parental punitiveness also showed positive relations with children's aggression. The correlation between the parents' punishment style and their daughters' aggression was quite significant, but the relation was only marginal with sons' aggression.

An examination of the unique punishment preferences of each parent helps to clarify these relations. When children were separated into the highest 25%, the middle 50%, and the lowest 25% on aggression, we found that the most aggressive girls had mothers who used harsher punishments than did the girls with medium or low aggression scores. Similarly, fathers of the highly aggressive girls used physical punishment more often than fathers of the other girls, though the difference was not significant. For boys, maternal punitiveness was also more closely related to aggression ($p < .01$) than parental punitiveness, but the boys' results were not as clear as the girls'. It seems plausible that severe punishment by the mother is more likely to teach a girl aggressive habits than a boy. Children usually identify more with the parent of their own gender and are more likely to imitate that parent's behavior. The alternative hypothesis that punishment differences are mostly a response to aggression must also be considered, of course. Multiple regression analyses revealed that parental punishment in the last wave of the study was more predictable from early aggression than aggression in the last wave was from early punishment. Thus, as with rejection, parental punishment in Finland must be considered as much a response to aggression as an instigator of aggression.

The items on the punishment scale reflected primarily severe physical punishments. Fathers generally reported they punished more severely than mothers did. However, the mean of the parents' punitiveness scores was lower in Finland than in any other country (1.85 for boys compared to 5.06 in Poland, 4.61 in Australia, and 3.42 in the United States). Currently, the use of physical punishment is not much favored in Finland. In fact, parliament passed a law in 1983 that prohibits corporal punishment of children.

Punitiveness also correlated with rejection in both parents. The correlation was .26 ($p < .05$) for mothers and .31 for fathers ($p < .01$). This correlation is certainly at least partially due to the fact that more aggressive children are both punished more and rejected more. Punitiveness of fathers correlated negatively with age ($-.21$, $p < .01$) so that younger fathers were somewhat more punitive toward their children than the older ones. Aggressive fantasies by parents also correlated with their punitiveness in this study. This result conflicts with the theory that aggressive fantasies are cathartic. During the first wave, a similar result was obtained for the subjects themselves. Girls who had aggressive fantasies were more aggressive than the other girls.

Nurturance.   The nurturance of fathers and mothers correlated significantly (.22, $p < .01$), although fathers were on the average less nurturant than mothers. But, as Table 4.10 shows, nurturance scores of parents did not correlate with the aggression of their children. Because nurturance had low stability coefficients, further results for this variable are not reported.

Aggressiveness of the Parents

As Table 4.10 reveals, aggressiveness of parents and children did not correlate significantly with each other in Finland. The parents' aggression also did not correlate with socioeconomic variables. This also occurred in most of the other countries in the study. It is possible that parental aggression as measured by our self-rating procedure was not sufficiently salient in the parents' overt behavior to provide a model of aggressive behavior. Self-rated aggression of parents did correlate significantly with their rejection of their child. This variable, in turn, correlated with aggression in children. Furthermore, significant correlations were obtained between aggression and aggressive fantasies in parents that in turn correlated with punishment preferences. Such individual differences suggest that punishment and rejection by parents are not just responses to child aggression but reflect characteristic differences in the parents that may influence the development of aggression in their children.

Socioeconomic Variables

In many previous studies the socioeconomic background of children has been found to correlate negatively with their level of aggressiveness. More aggressive children typically had parents who were less educated, had lower income levels, and belonged to lower social classes. Our colleagues in Australia, Poland, and the United States have reported such relations in their chapters. However, in Finland there was no relation between socioeconomic status and aggression in boys and only a very slight trend for girls from lower class families to be more aggressive. In most other countries, a child's TV habits were also related to the family's socioeconomic status, but in Finland a significant relation was discovered only for boys. The product of their TV violence viewing and identification with TV characters correlated $-.28$ ($p < .02$) with their father's occupational status (i.e., lower class boys watched more TV violence).

It may be that the educational practices and parental attitudes of various socioeconomic groups in Finland are not so very different from each other. We found only a few significant correlations between parents' socioeconomic or educational background and their child-rearing practices. Punitiveness of fathers correlated with income in both waves ($-.22, p < .007, -.17, p < .06$, respectively). For mothers, there was a slight correlation between punitiveness and education ($-.22, p < .006$), while both parents' rejection of their son correlated marginally with the son's later aggression ($r = .21, p < .07$). The TV viewing frequency of fathers showed some correlations with occupation, education and income, but only in the last wave of parent interviews. Other parental variables like mother's TV viewing, parents' self-rated aggression, rejection, and nurturance were not related to socioeconomic variables.

Thus, the aggressiveness of Finnish children may not vary along with socioeconomic background because these factors do not create great differences in the emotional climate and educational practices of Finnish families. There were differences, as can be seen from the correlations mentioned previously, but not as many as in other countries.

In Sweden, Olweus (1978) also failed to find a relation between aggression in boys and socioeconomic variables. It is possible that in small, developed, democratic countries with an effective communication network, a uniform system of education as well as ethnic and linguistic homogeneity, socioeconomic factors are less likely to create differences in socialization practices and thus in the aggressiveness of children.

Explaining the Effect of TV Violence

The longitudinal effect of TV violence and identification with TV characters on increased aggression in Finnish boys might be attributed to many third factors instead of a learning effect. However, as the regressions in Tables 4.11 and 4.12 reveal, none of the third variables that we have measured explains away the effects. Although many third variables are related to aggression or TV viewing, the effect of TV on the development of aggression remains independent of those variables. From Table 4.11, one can see that the effect cannot be explained away as an artifact of a boy's social class or intellectual competence. From Table 4.12, one can see that the effect cannot be explained away as an artifact of parents' aggression, TV viewing, or child-rearing practices. Furthermore, one should note that partialling of the effects of these variables actually increases the magnitude of the regression coefficients for the TV violence variable. The significant coefficients for socioeconomic status deserve comment. For girls, the marginal negative coefficient for SES reflects the fact that lower class girls are slightly more aggressive. For boys the interpretation of the very significant positive coefficient is more complex. A boy's social class is uncorrelated with his aggression and negatively correlated with his TV violence viewing and his rejection by his parents. TV violence viewing and rejection, in turn, are positively related to aggression. Therefore, the positive regression coefficient for social status in predicting aggression represents a classical suppression effect. The variations in a boy's TV violence viewing and rejction that predict aggression must be mostly independent of the variations in violence viewing and rejection that are predicted by social class. The direct positive coefficient of social class on aggression balances the indirect negative effect of social class through decreased TV violence viewing and rejection to yield no overall effect.

CONCLUSION

Our study in Finland can be taken to corroborate the previously obtained results that the amount of aggressive behavior in children is related to their viewing of violence on TV. This was more typical for boys than for girls, which also is a finding obtained in many previous studies, such as Eron (1963) and Lefkowitz et al,, (1977).

TABLE 4.11
Multiple Regressions Showing Effects of Socioeconomic Variables and Academic Achievement on the Relation Between TV Violence Viewing and Aggression

Dependent Variable	Predictors	Standardized Regression Coefficients	
		Girls (N = 76)	Boys (N = 81)
3rd Wave Aggression	Cohort	−.094 (−.105)	−.140 (−.138)
	1st Wave Aggression	.650*** (.667)	.673*** (.665)
	TV Violence Viewing for Girls in 1st & 2nd Waves	.049 (.057)	
	Product of TV Violence Viewing and Identification with Aggressive TV Characters for Boys in 1st & 2nd Waves		.210** (.303)
	Father's Occupational Status	−.154 (−.210)	.166 (.282)
	Parents' Educational Status	−.022 (.021)	−.087 (−.145)
	Child's Academic Achievement	.059 (.081)	−.129 (−.152)
		$R2 = .432$, $F (6,69) = 8.75$, $p < .001$	$R2 = .564$, $F 6,74) = 16.0$, $p < .001$

$**p < .01.$ $***p < .001.$
Note: The numbers in parentheses are the regression coefficients corrected for the unreliability of the measures.

TABLE 4.12

Multiple Regressions Showing Effects of Socioeconomic Variables, Parent Behaviors, and Parent Child Rearing Practices on the Relations Between TV Violence Viewing and Aggression

Dependent Variable	Predictors	Standardized Regression Coefficients	
		Girls (N = 71)	Boys (N = 80)
3rd Wave Aggression	Cohort	$.218^+$	—
	TV Violence Viewing for Girls in 1st & 2nd Waves	.160	
	Product of TV Violence Viewing and Identification with Aggressive Character for Boys in 1st & 2nd Waves		.294**
	Father's Occupational Status	−.208	.392**
	Parents' Educational Status	—	—
	Parents' Mobility Orientation	.181	—
	Parents' Aggressiveness	−.133	—
	Parents' Aggressive Fantasy	−.169	—
	Parents' TV Violence Viewing	—	—
	Parents' TV Frequency	.188	—
	Parents' Lack of Nurturance for Child	—	—
	Parents' Rejection of Child	—	.358**
	Parents' Punishment of Child	.438***	—
		$R2 = .388$	$R2 = .291$
		$F\,(12,58) = 3.06$**	$F\,(12,63) = 2.16$*

$^+p<.10.$ *$p<.05.$ **$p<.01.$ ***$p<.001.$

In Finland, perceived similarity with TV characters correlated positively with aggression in the two cohorts and the different age groups. These correlations were more consistent than those of aggression with violence viewing or with regularity of viewing. When TV has a limited number of violent programs, as in Finland, children cannot choose to watch much violence. Therefore, children's interest in TV and its impact on them may be revealed more by how much they identify with TV charactres. Given the measures used in the present study, the relation between TV viewing and aggression is best indicated by the correlation of aggression with perceived similarity with characters on TV.

The best predictor of subsequent aggression in boys was viewing of violent content coupled with perceived similarity with a character in the program. This relation was apparent even when the initial level of aggressiveness at the outset of the follow-up was partialed out. Subsequent TV variables could not be predicted from previous aggression in a comparable way. This can be taken as support for the causal effect of violence viewing on aggression and does not support a bidirectional effect.

For girls in Finland, the same relation did not hold, although the simultaneous correlation of aggression with violence viewing and perceived similarity with the characters was significant. Girls' results differed from boys' in other ways as well. For instance, the girls thought that the violent films were less realistic than the boys did. Perceiving TV programs as realistic correlated, in turn, with the level of peer-nominated aggression. The boys in Finland showed significantly more aggression than the girls. This was also the case in all the countries involved in the present cross-national study.

Our investigation of the children's perceptions of the realism of violent programs revealed that the children in Finland thought the programs showed life as it really was in the country of program origin, although they did not think that life was like that in Finland. This opens new possibilities for studying the effects of imported films in countries with different customs, languages, and ways of life. Perceiving programs as realistic previously has been established as enhancing imitation. But what does it imply if the realism is only an imaginary one? American children who lived in the country of origin of the films did not perceive them as realistic. Our guess is that the effect on imitation is largely dependent on the reputation and status of the culture from which the films come.

The educational and socioeconomic background of parents were found to bear little relation to the aggression and TV viewing of children. On the other hand, punitiveness and a rejecting attitude on the part of the parents were found to correlate with aggression in the children. The amount of time the parents spent watching television was positively correlated with both TV watching and aggression in their child. Nevertheless, when the effects of both child-rearing and socioeconomic variables are partialed out, the instigating effect of early television on later aggression remained and even increased for boys. In Finland, boys who are exposed more to TV violence and who identify more with TV characters seem to become more aggressive regardless of family background and parental child-rearing practices. The most plausible explanation would seem to be that they are learning to be more aggressive from viewing the TV violence.

Cross-National Differences

In different contexts, we have tried to look at results from Finland in comparison with other participating countries. One conspicious feature was that peer-nominated aggression was lowest in Finland. Because nomination variables are susceptible to differences in willingness to nominate others for positive and/or negative characteristics, this result perhaps should not be taken at face value. Nevertheless, self-rated aggression was also lowest in Finland, although the means differed significantly only from those in some of the other countries. Still, according to the results of the present study, it is conceivable that Finnish children are not particularly aggressive, although that cannot be stated definitively given the design of the current study. Parental punishment also was significantly lower in Finland than it was in any other country, which may conceivably bear some relation to the low aggression of the children.

Another conspicuous result was that socioeconomic variables did not show the negative correlations with children's aggression, which were found in most of the other countries. We suggested that this feature might be attributed to the uniformity of the culture in a small country, especially because the educational attitudes of the parents were not related to their economic and educational status to any great extent.

In cross-cultural comparisons of psychological variables, similarities are easier to interpret than differences. The similarities can be seen as reflections of general invariances, typical for human nature. There were many such similarities in the present investigation. Most important, aggression was positively related to television violence viewing for both girls and boys in Finland as they were for girls and boys in most other countries. Moreover, for boys in Finland, as for boys in the United States, violence viewing coupled with identification with TV characters seemed to predict future aggression better than they were predicted by previous aggression. These similar results lend validity to the conclusion that a common psychological process is operating in different cultures that causes children who watch extensive media violence to behave more aggressively.

ACKNOWLEDGMENTS

This research has been supported by The Council of Social Sciences, Academy of Finland. Thanks are due to the following persons for assistance in collecting and analyzing data: Birgitta Hägg, Raija-Leena Holmberg, Liisa Kärkkäinen, and Bo Lillkåll.

REFERENCES

Aromaa, K. (1983). *Causes of criminal violence in Finland.* Presentation at the Polish-Finnish Symposium on Aggression in Warsaw.

Björkqvist, K., Ekman, K., & Lagerspetz, K. M. J. (1982). Bullies and victims: Their ego picture, ideal ego picture, and normative ego picture. *Scandinavian Journal of Psychology, 23,* 281–290.

Block, J. (1971). *Lives through time.* Berkeley, CA: Bancroft Books.

Carroll, J. C. (1977). The intergenerational transmission of family violence. The long-term effects of aggressive behavior. *Aggressive Behavior, 3,* 289–299.

Eron, L. D. (1963). Relationship of TV viewing habits and aggressive behavior in children. *Journal of Abnormal and Social Psychology, 67,* 193–196.

Eron, L. D., Walder, L. O., & Lefkowitz, M. M. (1971). *Learning of aggression in children.* Boston: Little, Brown.

Feshbach, S. (1976). Children and the perceived reality of television. In J. P. Murray, E. A. Rubinstein, & G. A. Comstock (Eds.), *Television and social behavior* (Vol. 2). Washington, DC: U.S. Government Printing Office.

George, C., & Main, M. (1979). Social interactions of young abused children: Approach, avoidance, and aggression. *Child Development, 50,* 306–318.

Gerbner, G. (1972). Violence in television drama: Trends and symbolic functions. In G. A. Comstock & E. A. Rubinstein (Eds.), *Television and social behavior* (Vol. 1). Washington, DC: U.S. Government Printing Office.

Gerbner, G., & Gross, L. (1981). The violent face of television and its lessons. In E. L. Palmer & A. Dorr (Eds.), *Children and the faces of television: Teaching, violence, selling.* New York: Academic Press.

Groebel, J., & Krebs, D. (1983). A study of the effects of television on anxiety. In C. D. Speilberger & H. Diaz-Guerrero (Eds.), *Cross cultural anxiety* (Vol. 2, 89–98). Washington, NY: Hemisphere/McGraw Hill.

Haavio-Mannila, E. (1968). *Suomalainen nainen ja mies.* (The Finnish man and woman.) Helsinki: Werner Söderström Oy.

Hicks, D. J. (1965). Imitation and retention of film mediated aggressive peer and adult models. *Journal of Personality and Social Psychology, 2,* 97–100.

Huesmann, L. R., Eron, L., Klein, R., Brice, P., & Fischer, P. (1983). Mitigating the imitation of aggressive behaviors by changing children's attitudes about media violence. *Journal of Personality and Social Psychology, 44,* 899–910.

Huesmann, L. R., Eron, L. D., Lefkowitz, M. M., & Walder, L. O. (1984). The stability of aggression over time and generations. *Developmental Psychology, 20,* 1120–1124.

Jaakkola, R., Aromaa, K., & Cantell, I. (1984). The diffusion of consensual unions in Finland in the 1970s. *Yearbook of population research in Finland, XXII* (pp. 15–25). The Population Research Institute, Helsinki.

Jallinoja, R., & Haavio-Mannila, E. (1983). State intervention and privatization of family life. *Yearbook of Population Research in Finland, XXI* (pp. 7–25). The Population Research Institute, Helsinki.

Kagan, J. (1980). Perspectives on continuity. In O. G. Brim, Jr. & J. Kagan (Eds.), *Constancy and change in human development.* Cambridge, MA: Harvard University Press.

Kagan, J., & Moss, H. A. (1962). *Birth to maturity. A study in psychological development.* New Haven and London: Yale University Press.

Lagerspetz, K. M. J., Björkqvist, K., Berts, M., & King, E. (1982). Group aggression among school children in three schools. *The Scandinavian Journal of Psychology, 23,* 45–52.

Lefkowitz, M. M., Eron, L. D., Walder, L. O., & Huesmann, L. R. (1977). *Growing up to be violent. A longitudinal study of the development of aggression.* New York: Pergamon Press.

Lindgren, J., & Pulkkinen, A. (1984). *Avioerot 1950–1980 avioliittokohorteittain* (pp. 1–11). (The divorces in Finland in relation to marriage cohorts.) The Population Research Institute, Helsinki.

Maccoby, E., & Wilson, W. (1957). Identification and observational learning from films. *Journal of Abnormal and Social Psychology, 55,* 76–87.

Maccoby, E. E., & Jacklin, C. N. (1974). *The psychology of sex differences.* Stanford, CA: Stanford University Press.

McCord, W., McCord, J., & Howard, A. (1961). Familial correlates of aggression in nondelinquent male children. *Journal of Abnormal and Social Psychology, 62,* 79–93.

Naisten tutkijanuran ongelmat ja esteet. Opetusministeriön asettaman työryhmän mietintö (1982). (The problems and obstacles of female research carriers) Helsinki: Valtion painatuskeskus (Government Printing Office).

Olweus, D. (1978). *Aggression in the schools: Bullies and whipping boys.* New York: Wiley.

Olweus, D. (1980). Familial and temperamental determinants of aggresssive behavior in adolescent boys: A causal analysis. *Developmental Psychology, 16,* 644–660.

Pitkänen, K. (1983). Infant mortality decline in a changing society. *Yearbook of population research in Finland, XXI* (pp. 46–74). The Population Research Institute, Helsinki.

Pitkänen-Pulkkinen, L. (1981). Long-term studies of the characteristics of aggressive and non-aggressive juveniles. In P. Brain & D. Benton (Eds.), *Multidisciplinary approaches to aggression research* (pp. 225–243). Amsterdam: Elsevier.

Pulkkinen, L. (1982). Search for alternatives to aggression in Finland. In A. P. Goldstein, & M. Segall (Eds.), *Aggression in global perspective.* New York: Pergamon Press.

Riihinen, O., Pulkkinen, A., Ritamies, M., & Penttinen, H. (1983). Education, work, and number of children. *Yearbook of population research in Finland, XXI* (pp. 142–158). The Population Research Institute, Helsinki.

Ruusala, R. (1975). *Televisio ja Väkivalta.* Teoreettis empiirinen selvitys väkivallasta televisiossa. (Television and violence). Helsinki: Oy Tleisradio Ab.

Säntti, R., & Väliaho, H. (1982). Miesten, naisten ja lasten työpanos palkattomassa kotityössä. (The unpaid homework by men, women and children.) *Kotityötutkimus, X. SVT,* XXXII: 78, Helsinki.

Sarkkinen, R. (1983). *Televisio-ohjelmiston rakenne ohjelmatyypeittäin ja alkuperämaittain toimintavuosina 1980/81 ja 1981/82.* (The structure of the television programs during the operation years 1980/81 and 1981/82). Oy Yleisradio Ab., Suunnittelu- ja tutkimusjaosto, Series B 2/1983, Helsinki.

Sears, R. R., Maccoby, E., & Levin, H. (1957). *Patterns of child rearing.* Evanston, IL: Row & Peterson.

Sinkko, R. (Ed.). (1980). *Televisio ja Suomalainen.* (Television and the Finnish people). Espoo: Weilin & Göös.

Sonesson, I. (1979). *Förskolebarn och TV.* (The pre-schooler and the TV.) Malmö: Esselte Studium.

Takala, M. (1979). *Family's way of life, parental awareness of parenthood, and children's development.* (In Finnish.) (Rep. No. 219), Department of Psychology, University of Jyväskylä.

Takala, M. (1984). Family life and interaction patterns. In W. Doise & A. Palmonari (Eds.), *Social interaction* (pp. 42–62). Cambridge: Cambridge University Press.

Turner, C. W., Cole, A. M., & Cerro, D. S. (1984). Contributions of aversive experiences to robbery and homicide: A demographic analysis. In R. M. Kaplan, V. J. Konecni, & R. W. Novaco (Eds.), *Aggression in children and youth.* The Hague: Martinus Nijhoff.

Verkko, V. (1951). *Homicides and suicides in Finland and their dependence on national character.* Copenhagen, G. E. C. Gads Forlag.

Whiting, B. B., & Edwards, C. P. (1973). A cross-cultural analysis of sex differences in the behavior of children aged three through eleven. *Journal of Personality and Social Psychology, 91,* 171–188.

Yearbook of Population Research in Finland, XXII. (1984). The Population Research Institute, Helsinki.

5 Socio-Cultural Environment, Television Viewing, and the Development of Aggression Among Children in Poland

Adam Frączek
Polish Academy of Sciences, Warsaw, Poland

INTRODUCTION

In Poland, as in the other countries discussed in this volume, one cannot examine the relation between children's interpersonal aggression and their contact with TV violence without considering the children's overall socialization experiences. Numerous sociological and psychological variables, connected with either the children and/or their parents, could have significance for explaining aggression and must be considered.

Some Aspects of Polish Society

During the period of our investigation (1979–1981), and especially in the second half of 1980 and the first half of 1981, the whole social and political fabric in Poland underwent very distinct changes. The social upheavals of the time and the formation of the country-wide social movement "Solidarity" brought about widespread social–political involvement in both national issues and specific problems. The active participation of many people in public life and socio-political activities must have had important effects on family lifestyles as well as on the functioning of social institutions, including television and schools.

Although there is no empirical evidence indicating the impact of these factors on our variables, especially those pertaining to the social functioning of school children, it seems worthwhile to note some results of public opinion polls from February to May 1981. On the one hand, respondents clearly indicated their awareness of a decline in the country's economic functioning as well as of a worsening of people's material situation. On the other hand, very high indices of so-called social optimism were obtained from the same respondents (i.e., they expected that the bad situation would improve soon and believed that the changes observed in various spheres of life were important and would solve many of the country's problems).

Leaving aside the question of the relation between socio-political dynamics and children's interpersonal functioning, let us examine three more specific socialization issues in Polish society: (a) the evidence of aggression in social life; (b) the way the family fulfills its socialization functions; and (c) the functioning of Polish television.

Crime and Attitudes Toward Aggression

Criminological and statistical data are the basic sources of information concerning social manifestation of aggression. For the purposes of this chapter, we have investigated specific types of crimes (i.e., those that are very highly physically aggressive). Assigned to this class were murder, serious bodily injury, other bodily injury, participation in a fight or beating, and mistreatment of family members. The crime index is expressed in terms of the number of legally valid sentences passed.[1] Table 5.1 gives a detailed overview of the relevant data.

Several points concerning the general picture of criminality in Poland during 1979–1981 can be made. The total number of sentences decreased during this period, especially in 1981. There is a possibility that our data for 1981 (see Table 5.1) reflect the more general social situation in Poland that interfered with the legal proceedings. Also, it can be seen that the proportion of sentences for aggressive offenses to the total number of sentences did not change much during this period (fluctuating around 15%), and the most drastic forms of interpersonal aggression (i.e., murders or serious bodily injuries) had a steady, very low rate of occurrence.

The data in Table 5.1 illustrate criminality among the adult population. However, similar trends have been found for this period in Poland for criminality in younger (i.e., below 17 years) age groups. The decline in criminality in the younger age groups is all the more surprising because, in most countries, records show little change in criminality among those groups for the comparable period of time.

To complete the picture of criminality in Poland, we add data on the relation between criminal offenses and alcohol abuse (Jarosz, 1979, 1982). Ac-

---

[1]In crime statistics, the number of sentences in a given period of time is higher than the number of persons found guilty, as the same person may be found guilty for more than one criminal act. At the same time, it is lower than the number of crimes reported or revealed to police, as some cases do not appear in court for various reasons.

TABLE 5.1

Number of Criminal Justice Convictions for Adult Polish Population (over 17) in 1979–1981

| Categories of offenses | N of sentences in: | | | | | | | | |
| | 1979 | | | 1980 | | | 1981 | | |
	N	%	Index	N	%	Index	N	%	Index
Total number of sentences	153,030	100	60	151,960	100	58	126,400	100	49
For aggressive type of offenses	22,763	14.8	.90	23,251	15.3	.90	20,751	16.3	.70
Murder	313	.20	.01	320	.20	.01	332	.30	.01
Serious bodily injury	496	.30	.02	482	.30	.02	414	.30	.01
Other bodily injury	6,086	4.0	.20	6,334	4.20	.25	5,512	4.3	.20
Taking part in a fight or beating	5,806	3.8	.20	6,028	4.0	.25	5,167	4.1	.19
Rape	1,037	.80	.04	1,060	.70	.05	.913	.70	.04
Mistreatment of family member	9,025	5.7	.35	9,027	5.9	.31	8,419	6.4	.28

N = number of criminal justice convictions
% = percentage of the total number of criminal justice convictions
Index = rate per 10,000 persons in the adult population (over 17)

cording to police records, alcohol is implicated in about 28% of all crimes. This proportion increased dramatically for such crimes as maltreatment of family members (where almost 72% of offenders were intoxicated), murder (68%), and severe bodily injury (about 56%). Although this evidence emphasizes the links between alcohol abuse and crime in Poland, it also shows clearly that alcohol abuse is one of the most serious social problems in Poland (Jarosz, 1982). The problem, however, cannot be reduced to the amount of alcohol consumed; in this respect many other countries exceed Poland. Far more important are alcohol preferences. In Poland people drink liquors with high alcohol content (vodka) and the amounts consumed rapidly lead to inebriation. The criminogenic role of alcohol appears to stem from its facilitating effect on impulsive and uncontrolled aggressive behaviors most frequently directed toward family members. Alcohol abuse and resulting dysfunctions lead to conflicts and acts of violence in the immediate environment, (i.e., victimizing family members; Jarosz, 1979, 1982).

Unfortunately, it is difficult to compare these outlined trends for criminality in Poland with crime records from other countries as comparative evidence is lacking. Moreover, criminological comparisons are fraught with many problems originating from differences in legal systems, differences in the definitions of crimes and sentences classifications, reliability of statistics, and so forth (Jasinski, 1975). Nonetheless, according to data on serious aggressive crimes (i.e., murder and severe bodily injury) published periodically by Interpol as well as by some U.N. agencies, Poland belongs to the group of European countries with lowest crime rates. As noted in chapter 1, among the countries in the current studies, Poland had the lowest reported homicide rates.

The role of aggression in social life is also reflected in social attitudes toward crime and criminals as well as in moral approval of acts of aggression. These attitudes are evidenced by the degree to which individuals feel threatened by crime and fearful of becoming a victim of an act of violence. According to data collected by the Public Opinion Research Center, at the end of the 1970s a majority of the Polish population found that the possibility of being beaten up, robbed, and so forth was rather low. About 75% of the respondents said they did not worry about these dangers, and 80% said they were opposed to guns for self-defense.

Despite a relatively low incidence of severe aggressive crimes and a rather low sense of threat, Polish society is traditionally punitive toward deviant behaviors, including criminal acts (Kwasniewski, 1983; Podgorecki, 1964; Podgorecki, Kurczewski, Kwasniewski, & Los, 1971). A variety of research shows that for many years, including the late 1970s, about 45% of respondents were against the abolition of capital punishment, whereas 67% were convinced that crimes such as murder deserved capital punishment.

In this context, a comparative Polish-Finnish study on moral approval of various forms of interpersonal aggression (Fraczek, 1985; Lagerspetz & Westman, 1980), showed very similar patterns in both Polish and Finnish samples. Poles and Finns share the same moral standards with respect to aggression (i.e., that aggression — if it occurs at all — should serve as an effective means of interpersonal control and should be used either to protect oneself against attack or to benefit others). The Polish sample did reveal greater approval for some forms of aggressive interactions. These results might stem either from various social factors at the time of investigation or from a higher tolerance for aggressive interactions in social life.

Both aggressive crimes and attitudes toward acts of violence and aggressive behaviors may be regarded as significant contributions to the social-psychological environment that affects the development of aggressive tendencies in children.

The Polish Family: Its Characteristics and How it Functions

The organization and functioning of the family is one of the essential constituents of the socio-cultural background of the current research. Overall, the structure and functioning of the Polish family is similar to that noted in other countries (Duval, 1971; Tyszka, 1982). This seems especially true for urban families. Because our sample was drawn from the urban community, we describe this group only. The main recent change has been a decrease in family size. Joint or extended families have been replaced by so called nuclear ones, planned parenthood has become the norm, and urban families generally expect to have two, less frequently three, children. Studies on familial duties within the family (Markowska, 1980) indicate that urban families tend to set an egalitarian model. However, about 33% of the families interviewed still speak of a traditional division of duties between wife and husband (i.e., the husband does not engage in such traditionally female activities as cooking meals, dishwashing, and cleaning up).

In urban families (Markowska, 1980), a "democratic" pattern of contacts with children is decidedly endorsed, at least in the realm of beliefs. However, other research (Bogunia, 1980) describes how parents actually behave and what techniques they employ in raising their children. In answering how parents should act when children transgress, only 9% of the parents sampled thought that punishment was not appropriate. The remainder stated that in such conditions one should prohibit (about 38%), punish corporally in conjunction with other punishment (about 13%), or use some other kinds of "negative reinforcement." Families aspirations are decidedly high for their children in education. About 75% (Markowska, 1980) expect, or at least wish, both sons and daughters to have some kind of a higher education (college, university). Parents declare that they wish their children to achieve a successful family life, satisfaction with a profession, a stable life, and financial prosperity. Even if this reported pattern of values is mostly a reflection of stereotypes, it gives us some ideas about the socio-cultural background of child-rearing practices in Poland.

In characterizing the family's function in Poland we cannot bypass the religious factor. This has significance not only because the everyday life of most families is subjected to some form of direct or intermediate contact with the Catholic Church but also because Polish culture, value systems, and customs are historically linked with Catholicism. In a sample tested in Poland (Darczewska, 1982), about 86% of the adult subjects declared they were believers whereas only about 7% clearly declared themselves nonbelievers and opponents of religion. Of particular interest is the fact that although nonbelievers usually do not participate in Church ceremonies, many conform to Church rules and make various material offerings to the Church when taking part in family events such as weddings, christenings, and funerals. This conformist orientation in nonbelievers is also manifested in the need for and assignment of value to religious education. Children's religious education is valued not so much for purely religious reasons (only about 15% of parents give such a justification) as for giving the child a broader ethical background, transmitting the cultural-normative traditions, and so forth. Also, some parents are motivated by pressure from the social environment to send children for religious instruction. Last but not least, in certain social circles in Poland (e.g., disenchanted youth and political dissidents) manifesting connections with the Church may be an expression of political orientation rather than an indication of a traditional religiosity. Thus, presently in Poland relations among religious factors and the family's socializing and cultural functions have a more complex character than in other European countries with an equally long tradition of catholicism.

The social functioning of the family is also expressed in cultural values and participation in cultural events (Tyszka, 1982). Watching television is both the most common everday recreational activity and the most common source of contact with such performing arts as films and theatrical productions. The second main source of contact with culture is radio broadcasting, although the radio is often used as a verbal-musical background that accompanies various tasks performed at home or at work. In cities, the daily newspapers, mainly local, are fairly systematically read, or at least skimmed, by about 90% of the population. Participation in more formal cultural events outside the home as well as the frequency with which such activities are undertaken are related to educational level and family traditions. Outside the home, the most popular cultural activity in cities is frequenting the cinema. It is worth noting that spouses usually participate together in cultural events outside the home, such as the cinema and theater.

Let us consider some social-demographic phenomena that are not specifically familial characteristics but that affect family functioning in several ways. First, professional activity among the Polish female population is rather high (Tymowski, 1982). In several areas, such as medicine (including physicians), teaching, and commerce, the proportion of women in the labor force is over 70%. Under an amendment to the Social Security Act, it became possible for mothers who take care of their babies to leave the labor force for a 3-year period (the so-called "care-taking" leave allowed until the baby is 3 years old). However, particularly since the economic upheaval of the early 1980s, the financial support offered by the state has been barely sufficient to cover family expenses and thus has blocked the availability of these leaves. Work outside the home becomes necessary to fulfill basic economic needs. Furthermore, the birth rate in Poland has been stable for many years and is among the highest in Europe. In the last 10 years the birth rate was 9.2 for urban populations. Surprisingly, perhaps, this rate was not diminished by the social upheavals in Poland in the early 1980s. This relatively high rate creates problems for social services, (e.g., nursery schools and kindergartens), especially for child care in households where both parents work.

Organization and Functioning of TV in Poland

Much importance is attached to TV and radio broadcasts in Poland both by the government and by the political leadership of the country. Therefore, this institution has, on the one hand, considerable autonomy in the matter of management, whereas, on the other hand, various aspects of its functioning are managed directly from a central authority. The statuatory role of the Committee for Radio and TV is to broadcast information and to shape public opinion. The institution is headed by its chairman who holds the rank of Cabinet Minister and is appointed by the Prime Minister. Radio and television in Poland have a decidedly centralized organizational structure and broadcasting format. The same materials are broadcast all over the country, except for a few local programs.

Polish TV broadcasts programs on two channels. Programs are shown on TV from late morning until late evening, on average 14 hours a day, with small variations on different weekdays. In the morning, educational programs as well as feature films are broadcast for various age groups. In the afternoon, programs for young audiences predominate. Informative, educational, and documentary programs including news are broadcast as well. Occasionally, coverage of sports events that arouse wide public interest is provided. News and comments are broadcast at 7:30 p.m. Feature films, theatrical plays, and documentaries either for the general audience or for adults only follow. TV 2 usually broadcasts only in the afternoon and evenings, on average about 9 hours a day. Generally speaking, TV 2 specializes in programs on cultural issues, on popular sciences, or for specific audiences. As a rule Polish TV does not broadcast advertisements, although from time to time short broadcasts about various goods serve as informative guides rather than commercials in the sense of United States TV.

Availability of TV reception depends on the area of residence and the economic status of the family. It can be assumed that in urban environments every family owns a TV set. This holds true even for families with low economic status, because a TV set is preferred over other household equipment. Even among those who are well-off, it is very rare to have more than one TV set in the household. Although many programs are broadcast in color, relatively few families can afford a color TV set. Thus, black and white television still prevailed in Poland during the period covered by our study.

There is no available evidence on the contents of programs broadcast by Polish TV comparable to that reported by Gerbner and Gross (1976) on TV in the United States. For the purposes of the present study, we have evaluated the occurrence of aggressive episodes on Polish TV. Estimates of the proportion of broadcasting time containing aggressive episodes to total broadcasting time were calculated on the basis of systematic viewings during selected weeks in 1979, 1980, and 1981. A wide range of programs was identified as presenting aggressive episodes, for example, sports events (soccer, hockey, boxing, and so forth); film and theater pieces both for adult and child audiences (cartoons included) that portray conflicts resolved by violence; detective stories; and war films. For instance, during 1 week in the spring of 1981, total broadcasting time for the two channels was 154 hours, of which 10.5 hours were found to depict aggressive episodes of different types. Thus, aggressive episodes appeared in 6.8% of the total broadcasting time. Similar trends were found for other periods of time. Although our indices of probability of exposure to aggressive episodes on TV may shift depending on programming, we can be reasonably sure that this procedure gives an accurate enough notion of the aggressive content of our TV programs.

Production and presentation of entertainment shows and educational as well as cultural programs for children are organized by the Children's Programs Department and by the Television Theater for Children of the Polish TV. The repertory includes games to develop music appreciation, puppet shows, animated cartoons, feature films, dramatizations of children's literature, and programs advocating hobbies. Certain requirements must be met by programs for children.

This pertains not only to the contents of these programs but also to details concerning their broadcasting. A special committee selects appropriate sources for a given program and evaluates the final output prior to broadcast. Members of such a committee are mostly TV professionals and government representatives responsible for broadcasting, as well as psychologists or educational specialists from scientific centers.

In the majority of children's programs produced by Polish TV, such behavior patterns as friendship, solidarity, cooperation, and intellectual curiosity are emphasized, whereas aggressive scenes are infrequent and usually negatively evaluated. However, in war movies, which are rather frequent on Polish TV and often watched by children, scenes of violence and physical assault usually involve larger groups, and seldom present violent actions of individuals. In these films individual violence is not exhibited and emphasis is laid on a "positive hero" (i.e., a character who defends important social values or acts for important social reasons). Hence, these films may provide models for generalized attitudes and values rather than for individual brutality and aggressive behavior. Personal violence, assault, and aggressive behavior are most frequent in crime-detective and Western movies. Due to the fact that most of these movies are produced in the United States or Western Europe, their settings are quite alien to Polish reality (at least as adults perceive them). It can be assumed that the behaviors they present are also quite different from those observed in the children's immediate environment.

The majority of the programs for children are usually broadcast once a week at a regular hour. However, these are not serials or "soap operas" as shown on television in the United States. Programs with many aggressive episodes and much brutality are not readily available to children due to late broadcasting hours and the possibility of parental control as there is usually only one TV set in the household. Nonetheless, Polish children do have some contact with media violence.

We are well aware of the fact that our discussion provides a rather limited picture of those processes constituting the so-called social-cultural milieu and influence both the development of children and the social functioning of adults. Lack of space makes it impossible to discuss more general issues such as national experience, historical traditions, economic factors, or such organizations as the educational system. Although this list may be easily extended, we believe that the information provided will help us to better understand our empirical data.

METHOD

In collecting data in Poland for the current cross-national project, our aims were twofold. First, we wanted to provide data on children's television habits and aggression that could be compared with data from other countries. Second, we wanted to understand the effects that the Polish child's unique environment might have on the development of aggression. In line with these aims, an attempt was made to match procedures in the Polish sample to those used elsewhere. The specific techniques prepared and used earlier in the United States (see chapter 2, this volume) were adapted for Polish subjects. Methodological problems of comparative, cross-cultural research have been discussed elsewhere (Fraczek & Szustrowa, 1980).

Child Sample

Children from two Warsaw schools in two city districts were studied.[2] A rough preview of the children's social background revealed no noteworthy differences in the two districts. Organization of schoolwork and school facilities were also similar. According to the research strategy, our subjects were all first-graders from one school and third-graders from the other who had received written consent from their parents to participate. The procedure for collecting consents comprised two stages. First, we sought the approval of the district school authorities and school headmaster. Next, school authorities addressed letters to the parents of each child. This letter explained the aims of the study and the school's support of the project. Parents were asked whether they would permit their children to participate and whether they would volunteer their own participation. Of the parents, 95% consented to their children's participation and 79% agreed to participate themselves. Table 5.2 presents data pertinent to the characteristics of the sample: boys and girls from whom we received complete sets of data in the subsequent years of the investigation. Drop-out from the initial sample was negligible; 11% in the younger and 8% in the older age group, mostly unpromoted pupils, had to be excluded from the final analyses.

Table 5.2 also shows the estimated average age of children tested in subsequent years. In Poland, children begin to attend school when they are 7 years old. Moreover, our investigation started several months after the beginning of the school year. Our sample was somewhat older than those studied in other countries (with the exception of Finland). Thus, two cohorts were formed: cohort 1 comprised children who were followed from grades 1 through 3 (approximately 7.8 to 9.8 years), whereas the older cohort comprised children followed from grades 3 to 5 (approximately from 9.8 to 11.8 years).

Because the variables, procedures, and design have been presented earlier in this volume (see chapter 2), we discuss modifications introduced for the present study.

---

[2] The author wishes to express his gratitude to the parents of the children participating in the study, to the children, and to the school district authorities and school teachers for their cooperation and help in the realization of the project.

TABLE 5.2
Number of Children Over 3 Years of the Study and Mean Age of Children
in the Polish Sample

| | | N of Subjects | | | | |
Cohort	Grade/Year	Boys	Girls	Overall	% of Dropout	Mean Age
Younger	1/1979	65	56	121	–	7.8
	2/1980	62	52	115	5%	8.8
	3/1981	59	49	108	11%	9.8
Older	3/1979	76	63	139	–	9.8
	4/1980	74	61	135	3%	10.8
	5/1981	70	59	129	8%	11.8

Measures

Some changes were introduced in techniques used to rate sex-role identification. For cultural reasons, some drawings had to be replaced (e.g., boys in Poland play soccer and not football). Of course, Polish words were introduced in the drawings if needed. These changes, however, do not undermine the basic assumptions of the technique. Moreover, in our opinion, these changes are a good example of a situation in which the nature of a variable is clear and cultural modifications increase validity. The materials were evaluated by a psychologist, a teacher and a housewife. They were asked to sort the drawings into three groups representing games "most characteristic of boys," games "most characteristic of girls," and games not clearly identified with either of the sex roles. The interrater reliability was .97.

To measure intelligence, we used Choynowski's (1980) Short Intelligence Scale, known in Poland as KSI, which is essentially a preliminary selection technique based on the American E-G-Y principle (Kent, 1950). The KSI is used to measure intelligence in 6- to 14-year-olds and correlates with the Polish adaptation of the WISC ($r = .78$ for the Verbal IQ and $r = .76$ for the Full scale IQ).

Procedure

The research procedure was the same as in the United States. Subjects from grade 1 were tested first individually and next in groups, whereas grade 3 subjects were tested twice in groups. Tests were administered during classes (in the absence of teachers) and testing sessions were carried out by trained examiners. Children whose parents did not agree to their participation elsewhere with their teachers. Every year, each child received a small gift as a pencil, toy, or sweets.

Selection of the TV Programs for the Study

Given the organization and functioning of Polish TV, selection of programs that would be similar to those used in the United States was not an easy task. Polish TV broadcasts three categories of films viewed by children: cartoons, feature serials produced for children and youth, and films intended for adults. We found that the number of programs that at least partially fulfilled the criteria of popularity and seriality was so scanty that practically all programs had to be included in the project. Because there was no choice, popularity of the programs could not be checked systematically. Selected films had been serialized to various extents; the number of installments ranged from 3 to 12 in the 3-month period, and intervals between installments had varied from 1 week to over two weeks.

Using the same procedure as in the United States, we tried to identify aggressive content during the 3 months preceding each stage of the study (1979, 1980, 1981). Two judges viewed selected films at least twice and then evaluated them on three 5-point scales for violence content: one for the total load of violence in the film, and one each for the aggressiveness of male and female heroes. Finally, three sets of four programs each were selected and presented to children: four from six feature serials intended for adults but often viewed by children. Examples of our list include such titles as *Huckleberry Hound* and *Pixie and Dixie,* cartoons from the United States evaluated as aggressive, *Curro Jimenez* from Spain and *The Return of the Saint* and *Charlie's Angels* from the United States, all evaluated as highly aggressive, and *Rexie* and *Bolek and Lolek* from Poland, which were non-aggressive cartoons. In contrast to the Chicago study in which about 80 programs were chosen from a larger pool, we were able to list only 12 programs in Warsaw, of which not all met the criteria perfectly.

Parent Sample

In 1979, during the first stage of our study, parents of children from both cohorts were interviewed. In 181 families, both parents participated in the research unless one of them was not available for the interview. We also interviewed 16 single mothers. The mothers' mean age was 34.1 (ranging from 24 to 47) and the fathers' mean age was 37.5 (28 to 53). Our social-demographic records show that, in general, both parents were well educated (as a rule, at the college level) and held higher status, "white collar" professions. Thus, in our sample the so-called intelligentsia" were well represented, whereas workers with unskilled jobs or lower occupational status constituted a negligible portion of the sample.

Interviews were conducted by trained staff at homes and at a time convenient for parents. No payment was offered for participation. Just as for children, the procedure was a replication of the United States research project. However, two issues need further clarification.

Only minor changes were made in the Polish translation of the United States questionnaire to eliminate some cultural misunderstandings. However, many parents were very reluctant to answer questions about punishment of children as well as questions about their own marital life. They found some of these questions too personal, and despite their initial consent, respondents sometimes refused to continue answering when the interview was already under way. Hence, the responding sample may be somewhat biased. We also encountered serious difficulties when coding parent's social status. The United States researchers assumed that income is an indirect index not only of the economic status of occupations but also of their prestige. However, in Poland there is frequently a discrepancy between the social prestige of occupations and income. For instance, the highest social prestige is ascribed to university professors, priests, state administration authorities, and so forth, even if their income is lower than that of craftsmen. Differentiation by group was necessary for the present study, but our example shows the disadvantages of using income as a criterion. In Poland, special criteria for social status were developed from sociological studies (Reszke, 1982). Under these circumstances, virtually every finding in the analysis of relations between the social position of parents and the effects of TV violence on behavior in children should be interpreted cautiously when compared cross-nationally.

RESULTS

Though the empirical data reflect many phenomena, our report is confined to data most pertinent to the main factors and to their interplay.[3]

---

[3]The empirical evidence from the Polish studies as well as data from the cross-cultural investigation were presented on several occasions: Frączek A., Szustrowa, T., *Cross-cultural study of media violence and aggression among children: Comments on assumption and methodology,* Proceedings of the XXII International Congress of Psychology, Leipzig, GDR, 1980; Frączek, A., *TV violence and development of aggresion - Polish sample,* Paper read at the ISRA Meeting, Mexico City, Mexico, 1982; Frączek, A., *Mass media violence and development of aggression in Polish children,* Paper read at the Audiovisual Communication and Mental Health Congress, Helsinki, Finland, 1983; Frączek, A., Kirwil, L., *Sex-role identification and aggression among children: Cross-cultural comparison,* Paper read at the ISRA Meeting, Turku, Finland, 1984. With the publisher's permission, we include the data already reported in A. Frączek, Age and gender related trends in patterns of TV violence viewing and interpersonal aggression in children, *Polish Psychological Bulletin,* 1983, *14,* 25–38. All statistical analyses of data presented in this chapter and in other presentations were carried out under L. R. Huesmann's supervision at the Department of Psychology, UIC, USA.

Developmental Trends in TV Viewing and Attitudes Toward Programs

Table 5.3 summarizes the parent's reports of how many hours their children spent watching TV during an average week in the spring of 1979. Mothers reported that their children devoted smaller amounts of time to TV viewing than did fathers. This holds for all the children, irrespective of age and sex. Mothers' estimates, however, seem more likely to be accurate as mothers are typically home more than fathers. According to parents, boys spend more time viewing TV than girls do, and differences are systematic. Older boys watch more TV than younger ones, whereas there is a reverse tendency among girls. Finally, Polish children spent the least time watching TV, especially in comparison to United States and Australian children.

Violence viewing among Polish children was measured by the sum of the violence ratings for the child's favorite programs weighted by the child's self-reported regularity of viewing these programs. Generally speaking, the data on violence viewing reported in Fig. 5.1 show that boys scored significantly higher than girls across all age groups and at all stages [$F (1,192) = 18.8$, $p < .001$]. Violence viewing scores increased with age both for boys and girls [$F (2,384) = 21.3$, $p < .001$]. The same trends were observed for American and Finnish children (Huesmann, Lagerspetz, & Eron, 1984; see also chapters 3 and 4, this volume).

The realism score reflected how similar to real life the children believed violent TV programs were. These scores were about the same for all children, irrespective of age and gender, although there were some fluctuations related to grade and wave of the study. The Polish children attributed a higher degree of realism to violent TV programs than did Australian, Finnish, Israeli, or American children. A study by Lagerspetz (Huesmann, Lagerspetz, & Eron, 1984; see also chapter 4, this volume) found that the Finnish children's judgments of the reality of selected programs were based on a belief that the programs accurately depicted life in the country of origin and not necessarily in the children's own country. The same explanation seems plausible for Polish children. Our data, however, reflects more generalized attitudes of children toward TV. In Poland, children watch many programs that feature ordinary daily activities and social events (e.g., programs on harvest, manufacturing goods, methods of production) and hence may be inclined to consider other TV programs as depicting reality as well.

The next behaviors that concern us are the child's fantasizing about TV programs and the child's identification with aggressive TV characters. The amount of fantasy related to TV programs was slightly higher for boys than for girls, but this difference was not statistically significant. Fantasizing associated with TV programs was also slightly greater in the younger cohort (grades 1 through 3), whereas the older cohort (grades 3 through 5) showed ir-

TABLE 5.3

Mean Hours per Week Polish Children Watch TV as Evaluated by Parents

Cohort	Grade/Year	Mother's Report		Father's Report		Both Parents' Report	
		Boys	Girls	Boys	Girls	Boys	Girls
Younger	1/1979	8.86	8.83	11.27	9.02	10.06	8.62
		(N = 61)	(N = 50)	(N = 55)	(N = 46)	(N = 61)	(N = 50)
Older	3/1979	10.07	7.84	11.70	8.23	10.80	8.03
		(N = 73)	(N = 60)	(N = 68)	(N = 56)	(N = 73)	(N = 60)

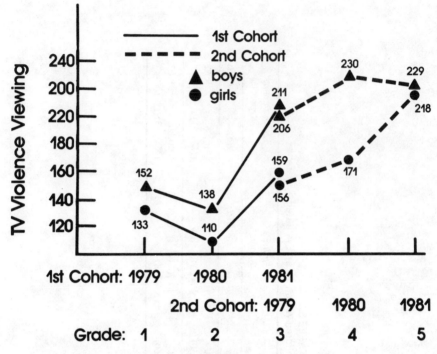

FIG. 5.1   Trends in overall TV violence viewing among Polish children.

regular fluctuations. Identification with TV characters was measured by asking children how much they acted like TV characters. As Fig 5.2 shows, boys
identified aggressive TV characters significantly more than did girls [F
$(1,186 = 32.3, p < .001$]. Among the boys in both cohorts, the level of identification decreased in the successive stages of the study. A different pattern of
identification was found for girls. Generally, they not only scored lower than
the boys did, but also showed no decrease over time [$F (2,372) = 15.3$,
$p < .001$ for the year by sex interaction].

Data on age and gender related trends for TV viewing and attitudes toward
TV programs in the sample of Polish children can be summarized as follows:
(a) as boys became older, they watched more TV than girls did, although the
viewing of violent programs increased significantly with age for both boys
and girls. (b) in both cohorts there was a significant decrease in boys' identification with aggressive TV characters across successive stages of the study,
whereas girls, for whom the identification level was significantly lower,
showed no decrease in identification scores from grades 1 through 4; and (c)
no distinct gender differences emerged for judgments of the realism of
violent programs nor did they for fantasizing about TV programs.

Intercorrelations of TV Habits

Most of the measures of TV viewing behavior were positively correlated for both boys and girls. Overall TV violence viewing correlated with regularity of watching of favorite programs (for boys $r = .82, p < .001, N = 101$). This was to be expected because overall violence viewing represents the regularity with which the child watches violent programs. Of greater interest, overall TV violence viewing correlated with identification with all TV characters (for boys $r = .24, p < .01, N = 123$; for girls $r = .25, p < .01, N = 101$) and with identification with aggressive TV characters (for boys $r = .25, p < .01, N = 123$; for girls $r = .21, p < .01, N = 101$).

Developmental Trends in Aggression

Three forms of aggression were measured in our sample. First, as described in chapter 2, interpersonal aggression was identified by the peer-nomination procedure. Second, the child rated his or her own aggression by estimating his or her similarity to hypothetical aggressive children. Third, the intensity of aggressive fantasy was evaluated through a structured interview with each child.

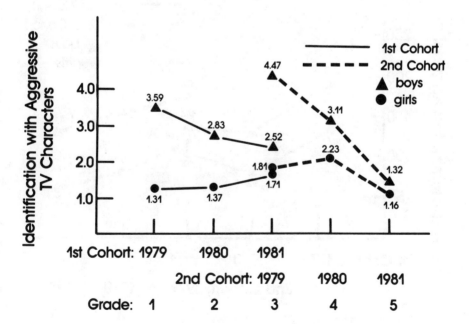

FIG. 5.2 Trends in identification with aggressive TV characters among Polish children.

As the data in Fig. 5.3 show, peer-nominated aggression scores are higher for boys than for girls, which was confirmed by the analysis of variance [F (1,210) = 10.2, $p < .005$;bc. This pattern has been widely reported in other studies as well as in all countries in the current research. Aggression also decreased significantly with age [F (2,420) = 34.8, $p < .001$], but the decrease may be due, at least partially, to the longitudinal research design.

In the younger cohort a pronounced decrease in aggression level between grades 1 and 2 seems to result primarily from changes introduced in the procedure. In grade 1, a set of snapshots was used for peer nomination, and the child pointed to pictures of classmates who behaved in a particular way. In grade 2, a list of names without photographs was used on the assumption that all children knew classmates and were able to recognize their names. Our explanation of this finding is corroborated by the fact that a similar trend (i.e., a decrease in peer-nominated aggression between grades 1 and 2) was found in both the United States and Finnish studies.

In the older cohort of the Polish sample, there was a consistent and statistically significant decrease in the level of peer-nominated aggression across stages. At least three hypotheses may be formulated to explain the changes. First, despite time intervals between measurements, the decreased scores may

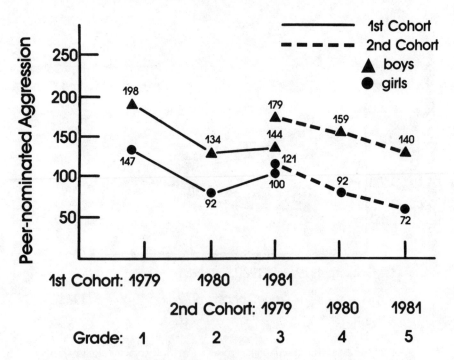

FIG. 5.3 Trends in peer-nominated aggression among Polish children.

be due to repeated use of the peer-nomination procedure with the same group. However, this explanation does not embrace changes reported for the younger cohort, in which the change in peer-nominated aggression, although marginal, was in the opposite direction. Second, this aggression measure may be identifying a genuine decline in these behavioral patterns among older children. For the time being, the origins of this change (i.e., the underlying social and psychological factors) remain obscure. Finally, our data may reflect changes in attitudes toward aggression as well as changes in willingness to attribute these behaviors to others. Following this line of reasoning, the decrease in aggression may be explained by specific characteristics of moral norms related to aggression or by situational activation of norms prohibiting the attribution of aggressive behaviors to others. The reported decline is all the more remarkable considering that it is not duplicated by the United States and Finnish studies.

Analyses of changes in self-rated aggression (see Fig. 5.4) and in aggressive fantasy (see Fig. 5.5) supplement these findings. Again, boys scored higher than girls on self-rated aggression [$F (1,198) = 62.3, p < .001$]. Thus, level of aggression for boys is higher than for girls not only as rated by peers, but also as rated by oneself. Self-rated aggression remained relatively stable

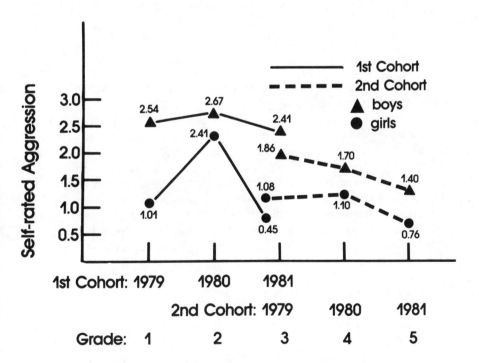

FIG 5.4 Trends in self-rated aggression among Polish children.

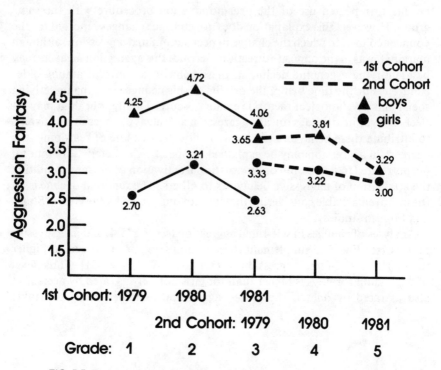

FIG. 5.5 Trends in frequency of aggressive fantasy among Polish children.

throughout the investigation, except for the older cohort boys, for whom scores decreased markedly with age. This outcome corresponds with the pattern of changes in peer-nominated aggression. The interpretation of data on aggression in girls is more complex. Although in the younger cohort, scores for subsequent years shift markedly, initial levels of aggression in the older cohort are stable and drop significantly in the last stage of the investigation. In general, however, the main finding indicated by the analysis of variance is that self-rated aggression decreases $[F(2,396) = 4.7, p < .01]$.

Differences between boys and girls were also found for aggressive fantasy. Just as for the two other measures of aggression, boys scored higher than girls $[F(1,192 = 16.7, p < .001]$, and there was a decrease in aggressive fantasy with increasing age $[F(2,384) = 5.0, p < .01]$.

Intercorrelations of Aggression Measures

We examined relations among the separate measures of aggression for our sample. Because the detailed analysis of these data is beyond the scope of this chapter, our discussion is confined to the main findings. Average scores on the two self-report measures of aggression (aggressive fantasy and perceived similarity to hypothetical aggressive children) were highly related for both boys ($r = .50, n = 102, p < .001$) and girls ($r = .45, n = 93, p < .001$). In addition, both boys and girls who scored higher on the peer nominations of aggression scored higher on the similarity with aggressor measure ($r = .23, n = 104, p < .02$ for boys; $r = .30, n = 98, p < .004$ for girls). However, only girls who scored higher on peer-nominated aggression fantasized significantly more about aggression ($r = .20, n = 95, p < .05$ for girls; $r = .12, n = 108$, n.s. for boys). This outcome suggests that aggressive fantasy may play different roles for girls and boys.

In summary, a number of age and gender-related trends emerge from our data for the three measures of aggression: (a) On each of the three measures, boys scored higher than girls, (b) Peer-nominated aggression scores decreased markedly with age both for boys and girls. Similar trends were found for self-rated aggression and aggressive fantasy, but these two measures depended on cohort as well as on gender factors. (c) While there was a correlation between peer-nominated and self-reported aggression, correlations between aggressive fantasy and each of the two other measures varied with age and gender.

TV Violence Viewing and Aggression in Children

The correlations between overall TV violence viewing and peer-nominated aggression for the separate subgroups and years of the investigation are shown in Table 5.4.

It is evident from this data that the highest correlation coefficients were obtained from the younger boys in grade 1 and the older girls in grade 5. The data indicate a general positive relation between the two variables even though some shifts occur. We have noted earlier that the Polish sample showed a pronounced decrease in peer-nominated aggression across successive years of the study together with increased TV violence viewing. This may

TABLE 5.4
Correlations Between Overall TV Violence Viewing and Peer-Nominated Aggression in the Polish Sample

Cohort	Grade/Year	Boys		Girls	
Younger	1/1979	.30*	($N = 59$)	—	
	2/1980	.17	($N = 59$)	.18	($N = 46$)
	3/1981	—		—	
Older	3/1979	.26*	($N = 70$)	.24+	($N = 59$)
	4/1980	.18	($N = 68$)	.13	($N = 59$)
	5/1981	—		.28*	($N = 57$)

$^+p < .10.$ $^*p < .05.$

explain the reduced correlations for boys in the third stage of the study. In addition, the Polish subjects, being older than those in other countries, were approaching puberty at the time, which probably introduces error variance that might result in differences in the aggression measures.

Generally speaking, there is a positive relation between a child's identification with aggressive TV characters (as measured by self-reported similarity) and the degree of the child's interpersonal aggression. The correlations for the whole sample were .24 ($p < .01$) for the first year, .17 ($p. < .05$) for the second year, and .23 ($p < .01$) for the third year. However, this relation was much stronger for boys (five coefficients out of six were statistically significant) than for girls (only one coefficient reached the level of statistical significance, see Table 5.5). One reason for these sex differences is undoubtedly the predominance of aggressive male characters on Polish TV. Due to the negligible proporton of female aggressive characters in TV programs viewed by our sample, data could not be analyzed separately by character's gender. However, there is also a possibility that the function of identification with aggressive models differs for boys and girls.

In Table 5.6 the subjects' average TV viewing scores over the 3 years of the study are correlated with average peer-nominated aggression. Because we averaged the data over 3 years, the results in Table 5.6 delineate the more stable trends and exclude transitory shifts. It is very clear from this table that higher levels of interpersonal aggression are found in those children who had relatively more contacts with TV violence, preferred aggressive programs, and identified themselves to a greater extent with TV characters in particular. Even though this general trend was similar for boys and girls, the relations among these variables consistently reached higher levels of statistical significance for boys. Such variables as frequency of TV violence viewing and judgment of realism of TV violence did not correlate with peer-nominated aggression in these subjects.

TABLE 5.5
Correlations Between Identification with Aggressive TV Characters and
Peer-Nominated Aggression in the Polish Sample

Cohort	Grade/Year	Boys		Girls	
Younger	1/1979	.35**	($N = 59$)	.14	($N = 49$)
	2/1980	—		.13	($N = 46$)
	3/1981	.24$^+$	($N = 57$)	.45**	($N = 49$)
Older	1/1979	.37**	($N = 70$)	.10	($N = 59$)
	2/1980	.25*	($N = 68$)	.14	($N = 59$)
	3/1981	.20$^+$	($N = 64$)	—	

$^+p < .10.$ $*p < .05.$ $**p < .01.$

TABLE 5.6
Correlation of Average Scores on TV Viewing Measures over 3 Years and Average
Peer-Nominated Aggression over 3 Years in the Polish Sample

TV viewing variables	Peer-nominated aggression	
	Boys	Girls
Overall TV violence viewing	.17^{+}	.17^{+}
	(N = 107)	(N = 96)
Regularity of TV violence viewing	—	—
Violence of preferred shows	.26**	.16
	(N = 107)	(N = 96)
Identification with all TV characters	.31***	.23*
	(N = 102)	(N = 90)
Identification with aggressive TV characters	.35***	.25*
	(N = 105)	(N = 85)
Overall TV violence × identification with aggressive TV characters	.38***	.21*
	(N = 105)	(N = 85)
Violence of preferred shows × identification with aggressive TV characters	.41***	.23*
	(N = 105)	(N = 85)

$^{+}p<.10.$ $^{*}p<.05.$ $^{**}p<.0$. $^{***}p<.001.$

From this review three conclusions emerge: (a) tendencies to watch violent TV programs and to identify with TV characters are associated with higher levels of interpersonal aggression among children in Poland; (b) relations among the variables that characterize TV violence viewing and peer-nominated aggression are both more consistent and stronger for boys than girls; and (c) gender-related differences may originate from the fact that boys watch more TV and more violent programs than girls; from programming that provides more aggressive male than female models; and, finally, from the possibility that watching violent programs may have different functions for boys and girls.

Other Child Characteristics and Aggression

In our sample, negative correlations were consistently found between popularity in the classroom and interpersonal aggression (see Table 5.7). These results are comparable to those obtained for the American children and kibbutz children in Israel (see chapters 3 and 7). Low scores on the popularity scale indicate poor relationships with peers. These poor relationships probably reflect social isolation and rejection by peers. Although it seems reasonable to assume that aggression may lead to isolation and rejection, low

TABLE 5.7

Correlations Between Average Scores on Selected Children's Measures over 3 Years and Average Aggression and TV Viewing over 3 Years in the Polish Sample

| | Children's Variables | | | | | |
| | Peer-Nominated Aggression | | TV Violence Viewing | | Identification With TV Char | |
Children's Variables	Boys	Girls	Boys	Girls	Boys	Girls
Popularity	-.46*** (N = 113)	- .42*** (N = 101)	—	—	-.19* (N = 102)	—
IQ (measured only in 1979)	-.17+ (N = 111)	-.13 (N = 99)	.17+ (N1 = 106)	.22* (N = 99)	-.19* (N = 102)	—
Preferences for male activities	.18+ (N = 106)	—	—	—	.25*** (N = 99)	—
Preferences for female activities	—	.19+ (N = 99)	—	—	—	—
Preference for neutral activities	-.14 (N = 106)	- .23* (N = 99)	—	—	-.29** (N = 99)	—
Aggressive fantasy	-.12 (N = 108)	.20* (N = 95)	—	—	- .24* (N = 102)	.29** (N = 89)
Active-heroic fantasy	.14 (N = 108)	.21* (N = 95)	—	—	.57*** (N = 102)	.33*** (N = 89)

+p < .10.   *p < .05.   **p < .01.   ***p < .001.

popularity may also engender aggressive behavior. Also, it has been reported (Lefkowitz, Eron, Walder, & Huesmann, 1977) that children who are not popular with their peers spend more time watching TV and therefore may watch more violence on TV. However, our data on the relations among popularity and various TV viewing measures did not support this hypothesis.

The relation between general mental ability (IQ) and interpersonal aggression in children has been studied by many authors, and several hypotheses have been advanced (Feshbach & Price, 1984; Huesmann & Eron, 1984; Huesmann, Eron, & Yarmel, in press). There is evidence that IQ mediates the relation between violence watching and the development of aggression and that aggression affects later intellectual development. In the Polish sample, our analysis of the relation between IQ (measured once at the beginning of our investigation) and peer-nominated aggression averaged over 3 years, indicated that the relation between these two variables was negative but almost negligible (see Table 5.7). There was a positive relation between IQ and popularity ($r = .14, p < .05$ for boys and $r = .16, p < .10$ for girls). But just as for peer-nominated aggression, the effect of IQ was very limited.

We have also found rather interesting relations between IQ and various TV viewing measures. Children with higher IQs have more frequent contacts with TV violence (the correlation coefficients between IQ and TV violence viewing were $r = .17, p < .10$ for boys and $r = .21, p < .05$ for girls); watch their favorite shows regularly ($r = .13$, n.s. for boys and $r = .21, p < .05$ for girls); and prefer more aggressive programs ($r = .11$, n.s. for boys and $r = .29, p < .01$ for girls). Thus, the more intelligent girls from our sample had significantly more intense contacts with TV violence. These results are completely dissimilar from any found in other countries. In fact, in most other countries there was a tendency for TV viewing to be negatively correlated with IQ. Considering the difference, it is relevant to note that measurement of IQ in children is at least partially an indirect measure of their social, cultural, and psychological milieu.

Research on gender differences in behavior (Eagly, 1983; Froddi, Macaulay, & Thome, 1977) and on correlates of sex-role identification has led to questions about the effect of sex-role identification on interpersonal aggression. One may expect that preference for gender-determined roles are related to the forms and intensity of aggression in children. We took up this problem in our study and we report the most important findings (Frączek & Kirwil, in press).

Two interesting facts emerged from the analysis of identification with a prescribed sex role. First, identification with sex roles was very stable for boys and girls in all age groups. This implies that social-cultural conditions promote a relatively early identification with social sex roles and insure that no marked shifts occur. Second, same-sex identification is significantly higher for boys than for girls. Assuming that the finding was not an artifact of measurement (i.e., resulting from pictures that were less ambiguous for boys than girls), it might be suggested that social-cultural conditions allow girls to deviate more from traditional roles than boys.

Concerning the relation between all measures of sex-role identification and peer-nominated aggression (see Table 5.7), we have found a positive (albeit marginal) correlation between same-sex identification and intensity of interpersonal aggression for boys and girls ($r = .18$ and $.19$). We also found a negative correlation between the so-called neutral sex-role preferences and aggression for boys and girls, although the correlation coefficient reached statistical significance only for girls ($r = -.23, p < .05$). The data are apparently at odds with a common-sense cultural stereotype that associates interpersonal aggression with masculininty and the lack of interpersonal aggression with femininity. For the whole sample and especially for girls, however, the so-called neutral or nonsex-typed identification was negatively correlated with aggressive behavior. These latter results parallel those found in the United States. The measurement of neutral identification did not force children to choose less "active" games. This category includes such activities as seesawing and cycling as well as parlor games that demand higher intellectual involvement. It seems possible that these activities give much less opportunity to display and practice aggression. This line of reasoning might be of interest for educational and socialization purposes.

Family Background and Family Influences

Interviews provided the information about the parents' social status (e.g., educational level, incomes), their TV habits (e.g., frequency of TV viewing), their child-rearing methods (e.g., punitiveness), as well as some cognitive behaviors (e.g., aggressiveness of fantasies).

Considering that social stratification in Poland is not reflected in either residential or school locations (which is especially true of urban communities) it might be assumed that social status in our sample would be highly varied. Because our population lived in Warsaw, we may reasonably assume that our sample included mainly parents having middle educational status and "white collar" occupations. This group roughly approximates the American middle class. Of the socio-economic variables measured (education, occupation, and income) only educational status of the two parents were correlated ($r = .55, p < .001, N = 176$). The occupational status and the income of each of the parents did not correlate with each other. This suggests that education may be the best measure of a family's social status in Poland.

The mother's and father's responses to the questions on TV habits, self-reported aggression, and child-rearing methods tend to be similar. Mother's and father's frequencies of TV watching correlated $.27$ ($p < .001, N = 176$). Their evaluations of the realism of violent programs correlated $.25$ ($p < .001$,

$N = 176$), and their self-reported fequencies of watching their child's favorite programs were correlated .18 ($p < .01$, $N = 176$). There were also similarities between the two parents with respect to child rearing. Correlations were found between measures of rejection ($r = .56$, $p < .001$, $N = 176$), punitiveness ($r = .22$, $p < .01$, $N = 179$), and nurturance $r = .42$, $p < .01$, $N = 176$). Moreover, our data indicated that self-reported indices of aggression in parents were correlated as well ($r = .19$, $p < .01$, $N = 176$).

Socioeconomic status (SES), as measured by education, correlated with a number of other parent variables. Mothers with higher education levels reported that TV programs with aggressive episodes were less realistic than other TV programs ($r = -.23$, $p < .01$, $N = 180$). For the fathers, we found that a higher educational level was associated with a higher mobility orientation ($r = .19$, $p < .05$). For mothers, a higher educational level correlated with slightly more rejection of the child ($r = .14$, $p < .05$, $N = 194$), and at the same time, with less punitiveness ($r = -.13$, $p < .05$, $N = 194$).

As Table 5.8 illustrates, girls who watch more TV violence have parents of lower educational status and fathers of lower occupational status who watch more TV violence themselves and believe it is more realistic. In addition, girls who identify more with TV characters have parents who fantasize more. For boys, more frequent contact with TV violence was positively related to parents' aggressiveness and punishment, whereas the boy's identification with TV characters was positively related to parents' evaluations of TV programs' realism and the parents' rejection of the child. Although this correlational data did not allow formulation of clearcut conclusions, the evidence fosters an impression that variables related to parental characteristics have greater impact on girls' contacts with and perception of TV programs.

Relation of Parent Characteristics to a Child's Aggression

In Table 5.8 parent characteristics are correlated with child behaviors measured simultaneously. Because of the social changes in Poland in 1980 and 1981, it was decided not to correlate 1979 parent characteristics with later child behavior. These correlations suggest that children from lower SES families displayed slightly more interpersonal aggression. In addition, aggression, both in girls and in boys, is positively and significantly related to parental rejection. This last finding fits well with the data reported in the literature (cf. Feshbach, 1974; Lefkowitz et al., 1977; Olweus, 1977, 1978; Sears, Maccoby, & Levin, 1957). Similarly, a significant negative relation between interpersonal aggression in girls and parents' nurturance corroborates the results reported by other investigators. However, we have not found this relation in boys. Even more suprising are our data on the relation between parental punitiveness and aggression in boys. Although for girls punishment increases as aggression increases, there was no significant relation for boys.

TABLE 5.8
Correlations of Selected Parent Variables with Aggression and TV Viewing Measures Among Children in Poland

	Children's Variables in 1979					
	Peer-Nominated Aggression		TV Violence Viewing		Identification With TV Char	
Parent Variables in 1979	Boys	Girls	Boys	Girls	Boys	Girls
Education	—	-.14 (N = 90)	—	-.20* (N = 90)	—	—
Father's occupational status	—	—	—	-.20* (N = 90)	—	—
Income	-.18+ (N = 107)	-.17+ (N = 90)	—	—	—	—
Overall TV violence viewing	—	—	—	.25** (N = 90)	—	—
Realism of TV violence	.20* (N = 103)	.15 (N = 87)	—	.15 (N = 87)	.21* (N = 102)	—

Rejection	.43*** (N = 107)	—	—	.23* (N 106)	—
Punishment	.37*** (N = 90)	.35*** (N = 90)	.14 (N = 107)	—	—
Nurturance	—	-.24* (N = 90)	—	—	—
Intensity of fantasizing	—	—	—	—	.23* (N = 88)
Parents' aggressive fantasy	—	—	—	—	—
Parents' self-reported physical aggression	—	—	.30 (N = 107)	—	.17 (N = 88)
Parents' aggression on MMPI 4 + 9	.18+ (N = 93)	—	—	—	.15 (N = 79)

$+ p < .10.$ $* p < .05.$ $** p < .01.$ $***$

Note: Correlations are between measurements in 1979.

TABLE 5.9
Correlations Between Children's Aggression and Their Parents' Rejection and
Punishment of Them

| | Parent Variables | | | |
| | Boys | | Girls | |
Children's Variables	Reject	Punish	Reject	Punish
Peer-nominated aggression	.43***	—	.37***	.35***
Aggressive Fantasy	—	.23*	.25*	—
Self-reported Aggression	—	—	—	.23*

*p < .05.   ***p < .001.
Note: Correlations are between measurements in 1979.

The correlations of all three measures of child aggression with rejection and punishment of the child by the parents are shown in Table 5.9. For girls, parental rejection correlates with both overt aggression and fantasy aggression, but parental punishment of the girl correlates only with overt aggression (and perceived similarity to aggressors). For boys, rejection correlates only with overt aggression and punishment correlates only with fantasy aggression. This pattern suggests that girls and boys may respond differently to parental rejection and punishment, and that parents may respond differently to the same types of aggression in boys and girls.

Predicting Aggression in Children

The data reported thus far clearly indicate that more aggressive children in Poland have been exposed to more TV violence. Aggression and TV habits are related to numerous other child and parent variables as well. The question is whether there is a causal link among the variables under consideration and aggressive behavior in children, and which of these variables may be considered as predictors of interpersonal aggression in children.

Multiple regressions were used to evaluate the causal effect of selected variables on peer-nominated aggression in children.[4] In Table 5.10, a child's aggression in the final year of the study is predicted from aggression in the first year and preference for violent shows in the first 2 years. First, early aggression is a very significant predictor of later aggression. Though our investigation covered a relatively short period of time (3 years) and involved a relatively small and homogeneous sample, the data fit well with what is known

---

[4]Because the rationale, conditions, and limitations of regression analysis applied to data of this type are presented elsewhere (see Huesmann and Eron, this volume), we shall not repeat this information here.

about the stability and consistency of aggression: The level of aggression in early life is the best predictor of later aggression (Crains & Crains, 1984; Huesmann, Eron, Lefkowitz, & Walder, 1984; Olweus, 1980). However, both the nature and the origins of these internal "stabilizers" of aggression remain obscure. Most important, however, the results in Table 5.10 indicate that an early preference for watching TV programs that contain interpersonal violence is a good predictor of later interpersonal aggression. It will be recalled that the regression coefficient for TV violence indicates the effect of TV violence viewing on later aggression while controlling for earlier aggression. Thus, the results are suggestive of a causal effect of violence viewing on aggression for both boys and girls. Unlike some other countries (see chapters 3 and 4 for examples), the reverse regressions predicting TV violence viewing from aggression were not significant in Poland. Thus, a bidirectional causal model does not seem plausible in Poland.

The relations demonstrated by these regressions are illustrated in Fig. 5.6. As the data in Fig. 5.6 show, the final level of aggression was mainly a function of initial aggression, whereas exposure to TV violence was of lesser importance. This relation was found both for boys (despite their higher overall aggression) and for girls. At this point, our tentative conclusion is that the watching of violence stimulates the development of aggression but other variables may be more important.

Our final set of analyses, shown in Tables 5.11 and 5.12, are multiple regression analyses relating a child's aggression in the final wave to a number of social class and parent variables. The results showed, first, that the effect of TV violence viewing on child aggression cannot be attributed to social class, IQ, or parent characteristics. In fact, the effect of TV violence is slightly

TABLE 5.10

Multiple Regressions Relating Aggression in Final Wave to Initial Level of Aggression and TV Violence Viewing in the Polish Sample

	Standardized regression coefficients		
Predictor variables	Boys (N = 95)	Girls (N = 84)	Overall (N = 179)
Gender (Male = +)			.09*
Cohort	−.06	−.07	−.05
Initial aggression	.82***	.72***	.76***
Violence of preferred shows in 1st and 2nd waves	.14*	.14+	.14**
R2 =	.73	.56	.69
df =	3,91	3,80	4,174
F =	83.8	34.2	97.8

$^+p<.10$. $^*p<.05$. $^{**}p<.01$. $^{***}p<.001$.

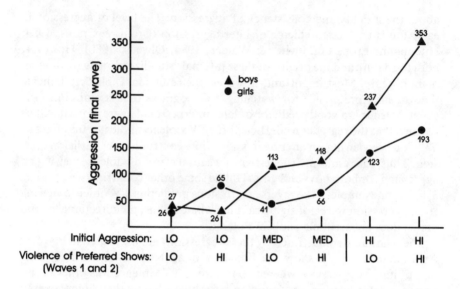

FIG. 5.6 Level of peer-nominated aggression in final wave as a function of initial aggression and mean TV violence viewing in the first two waves.

TABLE 5.11

Multiple Regressions Showing Effects of Socio-Economic Variables and Academic Achievement on the Relation Between TV Violence Viewing and Aggression in Poland

		Standardized Regression Coefficients	
		Boys	Girls
Dependent Variable	*Predictors*	*(N = 95)*	*(N = 84)*
3rd Wave Aggression			
	Cohort	—	—
	1st Wave Aggression	.81***	.70***
	Preference for Violent TV in 1st & 2nd Waves	.15*	.12
	Father's Occupational Status	—	—
	Parents' Education	—	—
	Parents' Income	—	−.15
	Child's IQ	—	—
	R2 =	.75	.58
	df =	7,87	7,76
	F =	36.8***	14.9***

*$p < .05$.   ***$p < .001$.

150

TABLE 5.12

Multiple Regressions Showing Effects of Socio-Economic Variables, Parent Behaviors, and Parent Child-Rearing Practices on the Relations Between TV Violence Viewing and Aggression in Poland

Dependent Variable	Predictors	Standardized Regression Coefficients		
		Boys (N = 84)	Girls (N = 78)	All (N = 162)
3rd Wave Aggression				
	Gender(Male = +)			.11
	Cohort	−.16	−.16	−.16*
	Preference for Violent TV in 1st & 2nd Waves	.32**	.26*	.31***
	Parents' Educational Status	−.21	−	−.13
	Parents' Income	−	−.25*	−.12
	Parents' Self-reported Physical Aggression	−	−.15	−
	Parents' Aggression from MMPI Scales 4 + 9	−	−	−
	Parents' Aggressive Fantasy	−	−	−
	Parents' TV Violence Viewing	−	−	−
	Parents' TV Frequency	−	−	−
	Parents' Nurturance of Child	−	−.19+	−
	Parents' Rejection of Child	.32**	.30*	.32***
	Parents' Punishment of Child	−	.20+	−
	R2 =	.28	.43	.32
	df =	12,71	12,65	13,148
	F =	2.25*	4.11***	5.38***

$^+p<.10.$ $^*p<.05.$ $^{**}p<.01.$ $^{***}p<.001.$

stronger for boys when all these variables are partialed out. As already mentioned, an interesting relation has been found between punishment and the intensity of aggression. Bivariate correlations indicated that the magnitude of this relation was different for boys as compared with girls: More frequent punishment correlated significantly with higher aggression in girls but only slightly with aggression in boys. However, as Table 5.12 illustrates, when the data were submitted to multiple regression analysis, punishment was not a significant predictor of aggression. Rejection was a very significant predictor of later aggression for both boys and girls. From these results it appears most plausible that parental punishment is more a reaction to a child's aggression than an instigator, whereas rejection is as much an instigator as a reaction. This finding conforms to the concept of the role of rejection in the development of aggressive behavior. Our evidence points to the role of rejection not only as a correlate of aggression in children but also as a predictor of later aggressive behavior (Bandura & Walters, 1959; Eron, Walder, & Lefkowitz,

1971; Feshbach, 1974; Olweus, 1978; Sears, Maccoby, Levin, 1957). Nevertheless, once early aggression was partialed out from the prediction, neither punishment nor rejection were significant predictors of later aggression in this sample. The same was true in the United States (see chapter 3), but in Australia (see chapter 6) rejection did predict later aggression even after early aggression was partialed out. This finding emphasizes the necessity for a more complex investigation of the role of punishment and rejection in children as well as expanding the study to tie this variable to other interpersonal and psychological factors.

A summary of the evidence presented in this section is as follows: (a) Our data, collected over a 3-year-period, indicated that the initial level of expressed aggression in children is the main predictor of their later aggressive behavior. There is a remarkable stability of aggressive behavior in children. We have found, however, that expressed aggression drops with age and with promotion to higher school classes. (b) Parents' rejection played an important role in shaping aggression in children. Our data pointed out the role of rejection that both correlated with and predicted interpersonal aggression in children. (c) We also found that there was a higher probability of aggression in children from families having lower economic status. (d) A child's exposure to violence on TV seemed to affect the development of aggression. A greater preference for violence viewing was predictive of greater aggression. Nevertheless, the effects are not large and must be treated cautiously.

DISCUSSION

Brief summaries of our empirical findings were presented earlier. In order to avoid repetitions, we focus here on more general theoretical and methodological problems that emerged from the study. We also examine some aspects of the psychological theory of development of interpersonal aggression.

On the Specificity of the Polish Results

During the 3 years of the study, aggression decreased both for boys and girls on all three measures of aggression (i.e., peer-nominated aggression, self-report, and aggressive fantasy). The dynamics of the observed changes, together with the fact that all three measures of aggression indicate a common general trend, suggest that this phenomenon cannot be ascribed to the repetition of measurements. However, our data do not provide sufficient grounds to determine whether the children who participated in our study actually had less aggressive interactions and fantasies in the subsequent stages. The possibility remains that only attributing these behaviors to others as well as reporting one's own aggressive behavior were inhibited.

The hypothesis that less frequent exposure to TV violence played a role in the decrease in aggression should be rejected. We have shown that over a 3-year period there were no shifts in the "load of aggressiveness" of TV programs in Poland. Moreover, overall TV violence viewing and related measures increased systematically during this period.

Our tentative hypothesis for the reduction in aggression is that this phenomenon relates to the development of moral norms. When a society exhibits punitiveness and rigorism toward "offenses" and when religious education enhances critical evaluations of undesirable behaviors, developing children should become more and more reticent about both their own and others' aggression. An alternative explanation is that the decrease in expressed aggression is associated with socio-psychological conditions that control social behavior. A "social climate" that involves many people in public life and encourages optimism could have influenced to some extent the schools' functioning and relations among both adults and children. These factors might have produced changes in parental attitudes, e.g., more kindness, benevolence, and support (unfortunately we lack evidence on changes in child-rearing procedures in the subsequent years of the study). Those general, unspecific changes together with specifics change in attitudes toward children might have led to the decrease in the expression of aggression.

The second point of interest is the gender-related differences in Poland. Obviously, we do not refer here to the fact that boys score higher on aggression. Similar results were reported for children brought up in different countries, and this finding was not surprising. What seems more intriguing, however, is the fact that the relation between the three measures of aggression were different for the two sexes. In girls, there was a positive relation among these three expressions or types of aggression. In the light of these data, aggressive fantasy appears to serve girls as rehearsal for interpersonal aggression. In boys, peer-nominated aggression was positively related to self-reported aggression, which correlated with aggressive fantasy. But there was no correspondence between peer-nominated aggression and aggressive fantasy. Thus, although our data indicate the effect of gender on aggressive fantasy, they also bolster the hypothesis that boys use aggressive fantasy as a substitute for interpersonal aggression.

Several other measures disclosed interesting differences with respect to the socialization of aggression in boys and girls. Parental punitiveness was significantly positively related to aggression in girls but only slightly related to overt aggression in boys. Boys who were punished more fantasized more about aggression. Both boys and girls who were rejected more behaved more aggressively, but only the girls also fantasized more about aggression. Gender-related differences also were found for patterns of TV viewing. As boys became older they watched more television and scored higher on identification with TV characters. The relation between intensity of aggression and various aspects of TV violence viewing were stronger for boys than girls. Thus, both the exploration of the origins of aggression and the investigation of the development of aggression would be incomplete without consideration of gender-related specificity (Parke & Slaby, 1983).

Excessive parental rejection may be a key factor in the development of aggression in children. Our data point out that this variable is the direct, clear, and positive predictor of a later aggression in children. Moreover, rejection is related to other variables that are also predictors of aggression. Thus, parental rejection is positively related to a girl's intensity of aggressive fantasy, to a boy's identification with TV characters (and, in particular, with the aggressive TV characters). Not only does rejection produce tendencies to react aggressively but it also creates supplementary psychological conditions that facilitate both the acquisition and consolidation of aggressive patterns of behavior.

Finally, we found that a preference for TV violence was predictive of later aggression. Even though the socio-cultural background and TV programming in Poland were very different from the United States, we obtained evidence of a causal effect.

Psychological and Socio-Cultural Factors in the Development of Aggression

It is widely recognized that various environmental and educational influences together with already formed individual psychological features and biological potentialities control the development of both aggressive behavior and its psychological mechanisms (Frączek, 1979; Huesmman & Eron, this volume; Malak & Frączek, in press).

Longitudinal and cross-situational stability of aggression is very high (Huesmann, Eron, Lefkowitz, & Walder, 1984; Olweus, 1980). In order to explain this behavior pattern, an assumption is made that intrinsic habitual tendencies (intrinsic motivation, personality variables, traits, and so on) that regulate aggressive behavior are stable (Berkowitz, 1962; Huesmann, Eron, Lefkowitz, and Walder, 1984; Kornadt, 1982, 1984; Olweus, 1980; Reykowski, 1979). However, this assumption generates two problems: What is the nature of these intrinsic "stabilizers" of interpersonal aggression and on what do they depend?

Despite many differences, explanatory models of aggression share several common ideas. The analysis of psychological regulation of aggression should take into account two complementary mechanisms: One is responsible for the arousal of aggressive tendencies (aggressive motivation, readiness to agress, and so forth), whereas the other is responsible for the arousal of aggression inhibiting tendencies (cf. Berkowitz, 1962; Dollard, Doob, Miller, Mowrer, & Sears, 1939; Eron, Walder & Lefkowitz, 1971; Kornadt, 1982,

1984). In principle, the mechanisms of aggression arousal and inhibition are formed in the course of personal experiences (Eron et al., 1971; Kornadt, 1982; Lefkowitz et al., 1977) and are affected by constitutional factors (sex and temperament). The second source of differences is individual personality dispositions formed in the course of development (Frączek, 1986a; Zumkley, 1984).

In order to explain the longitudinal stability and cross-sectional consistency of aggressive acts, the interaction between intrinsic structures (tendencies, features, traits) and situational influences (situational cues, aggressive activation values of the situation, and so forth) has been considered (Berkowitz, 1981, 1984; Frączek, 1979; Kornadt, 1984). Cognitive appraisal of the situation plays a pivotal role in this interaction (Frączek & Geller, 1981; Huesmann, 1982; Huesmann & Eron, 1984; Kornadt, 1983). Finally there is widespread opinion that the term *aggressive behavior* applies to heterogenous phenomena, both when the analysis is focused on its expression as well as — or even more so — when analysis focuses on the determinants of psychological regulation of aggression. For instance, in some cases the significance of emotional reactivity should be considered first, whereas in other cases generalized hostile attitudes and perceptions of threats gain importance and should be taken into account (Frączek, 1981; Leyens, & Frączek, 1984). Thus, both longitudinal and cross-sectional stability of interpersonal aggression should be explained in relation to the specific forms of aggressive behavior (i.e., by indicating those mechanisms that control the given type of interpersonal aggression).

CONCLUSION

These observations are considered the cornerstone of a psychological model for the development and operation of interpersonal aggression. In our study, empirical evidence and theoretical analysis point out that social experiences gained in the family are a key factor both in the generation and development of aggression in children. These experiences originate in the family's general life situation (its economic and social status, settlement in a broader sociocultural environment) and in nurturant interactions with the child. By now, this thesis is rather well established (Lefkowitz et al., 1977; Olweus, 1980; Pitkanen-Pulkkinen, 1981; Sears, Maccoby, & Levin, 1957), although more accurate explication of some problems is still needed. For instance, research has yet to yield conclusive findings on the impact of general social functioning and mood on the parent's attitudes toward a child. We must know whether the family ideological and religious attitudes — which seem essential to us — do indeed affect the social development of children (Eron et al., 1971).

It appears that at least some role in the process of shaping psychological mechanisms for aggressive behavior may be ascribed to TV viewing. Violence presented on TV not only directly provides certain behavior patterns that may be acquired through observational learning but also provides certain norms related to aggression and affects the emotional sensitivity of a growing child (Eron, 1982). According to Huesmann (1982), four different psychological processes should be taken into account to explain this relation. They are observational learning, attitude change, emotional and physiological arousal, and self-justification. The effects of TV violence viewing on children's aggression may depend heavily on the social-educational circumstances under which the child watches TV, e.g., whether or not the program meets with parents' and/or peers' approval (Dorr, 1981).

Considering the role of TV in the social development of children and in the development of aggression, we must realize that socialization through TV does not work in a social and ecological vacuum; (Bronfenbrenner, 1979; Eron, 1982; Malak & Frączek, in press). TV is a part of a more complex socio-cultural context, and its role may vary. When speaking about the factors that control the impact of TV on the social development of children, we have to consider: (a) whether TV viewing limits or eliminates other forms of activity in children, which may produce both positive and negative effects; (b) the extent to which parents employ TV in child rearing or whether banning of TV viewing serves to punish the child (Dorr, 1976); (c) to what extent TV programming and functioning mirror the ideological and social attitudes and values of a given society; and (d) whether ideological and moral norms are used to justify TV violence (Birnbacher, 1984; Geen, 1984).

We cannot think of a better way to end this chapter than to draw attention to the fact that the development of aggression in children can be considered a particular issue within a wide range of studies aimed at the analysis of social influences and socialization mechanisms that underlie the formation of personality. A theoretical model for such research should include various levels of relations between children and their social and ecological environment so that parental as well as TV influences would be recognized both as a product of a given socio-cultural system and as carriers of the socialization process.

ACKNOWLEDGMENTS

The part of the project conducted in Poland was supported by grant 11.8 from IFiS PAN, Poland, in 1979–1980, and grant MR-111-18 from MNSzWIT, Poland in 1981–1984, to A. Fraczek. The cross-cultural research project was supported by grants MH-28280 and MH-31886 from NIMH, USA, to L. R. Huesmann and L. Eron. The author wishes to acknowledge the assistance of Dr. Teresa Szustrowa, Dr. Wanda Ciarkowska, Ms. Krystyna Jankowska, and students from the Department of Psychology, University of Warsaw, in collecting the data in Poland.

REFERENCES

Bandura, A., & Walters, R. H. (1959). *Adolescent aggression.* New York: Ronald Press.

Berkowitz, L. (1962). *Aggression: A social psychological analysis.* New York: McGraw-Hill.

Berkowitz, L. (1981). The concept of aggression. In P. F. Brain & D. Benton (Eds.), *Multidisciplinary approaches to aggression research* (pp. 3–15). Amsterdam: Elsevier/North Holland Biomedical Press.

Berkowitz, L. (1984) Some effects of thoughts on anti and pro social influences of media events: A cognitive neoassociationist analysis. *Psychological Bulletin, 95,* 410–427.

Birnbacher, D. (1984). Social justice and the legitimation of aggressive behavior. In A. Mummendey (Ed.), *Social psychology of aggression* (pp. 157–170). Berlin: Springer-Verlag.

Bogunia, L. (1980). Akceptowane i negowane przez rodzicow reakcje na pierwsze przejawy demoralizacji nieletnich [Accepted and denied parental responses to first symptoms of demoralization in adolescents]. In *Patologia spoleczna-zapobieganie* [Social pathology prevention] (pp. 17–34). Warsaw: Wydawnictwo Prawnicze.

Bronfenbrenner, U. (1979). *The ecology of human development.* Boston: Harvard University Press.

Choynowski, M. (1980). Podrecznik do "Krotkiej Skali Inteligencji" [A manual to "The Brief Scale of Intelligence"]. In *Testy psychologiczne w poradnictwie wychowawczo-zawodowym* [Psychological tests in occupational counseling] (2nd ed., pp. 8–99). Warsaw: PWN.

Crains, R. B., & Crains, B. D. (1984). Predicting aggressive patterns in girls and boys: A developmental study. *Aggressive Behavior, 10,* 227–242.

Darczewska, K. (1982). Rodzina i postawy religijne [The family and religious attitudes]. In M. Jarosz (Ed.), *Rodzina polska lat siedemdziesiatych* [The Polish family in the 1970's] (pp. 197–217). Warsaw: PWN.

Dollard, J., Doob, L., Miller, N., Mowrer, O., & Sears, R. (1939). *Frustration and aggression.* New Haven: Yale University Press.

Dorr, A. (1976). Research on the socialization influence of television in the United States. In *Television and socialization processes in the family* (pp. 26–53). Munich: Verlag Dokumentation.

Dorr, A. (1981). Interpersonal factors mediating viewing and effects. In G. V. Coelho (Ed.), *Television as a teacher* (pp. 61–92). Rockville, MD: National Institute of Mental Health.

Duval, E. M. (1971). *Family development.* New York: J. B. Lippincott.

Eagly, A. H. (1983). Gender and social influences: A sociopsychological analysis. *American Psychologist, 38,* 971–981.

Eron, L. D. (1982). Parent–child interaction, television violence and aggression of children. *American Psychologist, 27,* 197–211.

Eron, L. D., Walder, L. O., & Lefkowitz, M. M. (1971). *Learning of aggression in children.* Boston: Little and Brown.

Feshbach, N. (1974). The relation of the child-rearing factors to children's aggression, empathy and related positive and negative social behavior. In J. DeWit & W. W. Hartup (Eds.), *Determinants and origins of aggressive behavior* (pp. 26–53). The Hague: Mounton.

Feshbach, S., & Price, J. (1984). Cognitive competencies and aggressive behavior: A developmental study. *Aggressive Behavior, 10,* 185–200.

Fraczek, A. (1979). Functions of emotional and cognitive mechanisms in the regulation and aggressive behavior. In S. Feshbach & A. Frączek (Eds.), *Aggression and behavior change: Biological and social processes* (pp. 139–157). New York: Praeger.

Fraczek, A. (1981). Possibilities and limitations of experimental social psychology in aggression research. In P. F. Brain & D. Benton (Eds.), *Multidisciplinary approach to aggression research* (pp. 101–111). Amsterdam: Elsevier/North Holland Biomedical Press.

Fraczek, A. (1983a). Age and gender related trends in patterns of TV violence viewing and interpersonal aggression in children. *Polish Psychological Bulletin, 14,* 25–38.

Fraczek, A. (1986b). *Temperament and regulation of interpersonal aggression.* Polish psychological bulletin (accepted for publication).

Fraczek, A. (1985). Moral approval of aggressive acts: A Polish-Finnish comparative study. *Journal of Cross-Cultural Psychology, 16,* 41–54.

Fraczek, A., & Geller, S. (1981). Die kognitive regulation der interpersonal aggression [The cognitive regulation of interpersonal aggression]. In T. Tomaszewski (Ed.), *Zur Psychologie der Tatigkeit* [The psychology of action]. Berlin: VEB.

Fraczek, A., & Kirwil, L. (in press). Identyfikacja ze spolecznymi wzorcami pici a agresja u dzieci [Identification with social patterns of sex role and aggression in children]. In A. Fraczek (Ed.), *Studia nad uwarunkowaniami i regulacia agresji interpersonalnej* [Studies on determinants and regulation of interpersonal aggression]. Wroclaw: Ossolineum.

Fraczek, A., & Szustrowa, T. (1980). Cross-cultural study of media violence and aggression among children: Comments on assumptions and methodology. *Proceedings of the XXII International Congress of Psychology.* Leipzig, GDR.

Froddi, A., Macaulay, J., & Thome, P. (1977). Are men more aggressive than women? A review of the experimental literature. *Psychological Bulletin, 84,* 634–660.

Gerbner, G., & Gross, L. (1976). Living with television: The violence profile. *Journal of Communication, 26,* 173–199.

Geen, R. G. (1984). Aggression and television violence. In R. G. Geen & E. I. Donnerstein (Eds.), *Aggression: Theoretical and empirical reviews,* (Vol. 2, pp. 103–125). New York: Academic Press.

Huesmann, L. R. (1982). Television violence and aggressive behavior. In D. Pearl, L. Bouthilet, & J. Lazar (Eds.), *Television and behavior: Ten years of scientific progress and implications for the eighties* (pp. 126–137). Rockville, MD: National Institute of Mental Health.

Huesmann, L. R., & Eron, L. D. (1984). Cognitive processes and the persistence of aggressive behavior. *Aggressive Behavior, 10,* 243–251.

Huesmann, L. R., Eron, L. D., Lefkowitz, M. M., & Walder, L. (1984). The stability of aggression over time and generations. *Developmental Psychology, 20,* 1120–1124.

Huesmann, L. R., Eron, L. D., & Yarmel, P. W. (in press). Intellectual functioning and aggression. *Journal of Personality and Social Psychology. Personality Processes and Individual Differences.*

Huesmann, L. R., Lagerspetz, K., & Eron, L. D. (1984). Intervening variables in the television violence-aggression relation: A binational study. *Developmental Psychology, 20,* 746–775.

Jasinski, J. (Ed.), (1975). *Zagadnienia przestepczosci w Polsce* [The problem of delinquency in Poland]. Warsaw: Wydawnictwo Prawnicze.

Jarosz, M. (1979). *Problemy dezorganizacji rodziny* [The problems of disorganization of the family]. Warsaw: PWN.

Jarosz, M. (1982). Rodziny dysfunkcjonalne [Dysfunctional families]. In M. Jarosz (Ed.), *Rodzina polska lat siedemdziesiatych* [The Polish family in the 1970's] (pp. 153–197). Warsaw: PWN.

Kent, G. H. (1950). *Mental tests in clinics for children.* New York: Van Nostrand.

Kirwil, L. (in press). Zmiany rozwojowe agresji interpersonalej u dzieci [Developmental changes of interpersonal aggression in children]. In A. Fraczek (Ed.). *Studia nad uwarunkowaniami i regulacja agresji interpersonalnej* [Studies on determinants and regulation of interpersonal aggression]. Wroclaw: Ossolineum.

Kornadt, H. J. (1982). *Aggression Motiv and Aggression Hemmung* [The Motivation and Inhibition of Aggression]. (Vol. 1). Bern: Verlag Hans Huber.

Kornadt, H. J. (1984). Motivation theory of aggression and its relation to social psychological approaches. In A. Mummendey (Ed.), *Social psychology of aggression* (pp. 21–34). Berlin: Springer-Verlag.

Kwasniewski, J. (1983). *Spoleczenstwo wobec dewiacji* [Social Attitudes towards deviations]. Warsaw: Wydawnictwo UW.

Lagerspetz, K., & Westman, M. (1980). Moral approval of aggressive acts: A preliminary investigation. *Aggressive Behavior, 6,* 119–130.

Lefkowitz, M. M., Eron, L. D., Walder, L. O., & Huesmann, L. R. (1977). *Growing up to be violent.* New York: Pergamon Press.

Leyens, J. P., & Fraczek, A. (1984). Aggression as an interpersonal phenomenon. In H. Tajfel (Ed.), *Social dimensions* (pp. 184–203). Cambridge: Cambridge University Press.

Malak, B., & Fraczek, A. (in press). Zjawiska i mechanizmy socjalizacyjne a formowanie agresji interpersonalnej [Phenomena and mechanisms of socialization and the development of interpersonal aggression]. In A. Fraczek (Ed.), *Studia nad uwarunkowaniami i regulacja agresji interpersonalnej* [Studies on determinants and regulation of interpersonal aggression]. Wroclaw: Ossolineum.

Markowska, D. (1980). Kultura dnia codziennego miejskich rodzin pracowniczych w Polsce [The daily life culture in Polish urban families]. Unpublished manuscript.

Olweus, D. (1977). Aggression and peer-acceptance in adolescent boys: Two short-term longitudinal studies of ratings. *Child Development, 48,* 1301–1313.

Olweus, D. (1978). *Aggression in the school: Bullies and whipping boys.* Washington, DC: Hemisphere.

Olweus, D. (1980). Familial and temperamental determinants of aggressive behavior in adolescent boys: A causal analysis. *Developmental Psychology, 6,* 644–660.

Parke, R., & Slaby, R. G. (1983). The development of aggression. In P. H. Mussen (Ed.), US Handbook of child psychology (Vol. 4, pp. 547–641). New York: Wiley.

Pitkanen-Pulkkinen, L. (1981). Long-term studies of the characteristics of aggressive and non-aggressive juveniles. In P. Brain & D. Benton (Eds.), *Multidisciplinary approaches to aggression research* (pp. 225–243). Amsterdam: Elsevier/North Holland Biomedical Press.

Podgorecki, A. (1964). *Zjawiska prawne w opini publicznej* [Legal phenomena in public opinion]. Warsaw: Wydawnictwo Prawnicze.

Podgorecki, A., Kurczewski, J., Kwasniewski, J., & Los, M. (1971). *Poglady spoleczenstwa polskiego na moralnosc i prawo* [Polish society views on morality and law]. Warsaw: KiW.

Reszke, I. (1982). Kryteria prestizu zawodow [Criteria of social status of various occupations]. *Studia Socjologiczne* [Sociological Studies], *86/87,* 173–194.

Reykowski, J. (1979). Intrinsic motivation and intrinsic inhibition of aggressive behavior. In S. Feshbach & A. Fraczek (Eds.), *Aggression and behavior change: Biological and social processes* (pp. 158–182). New York: Praeger.

Sears, R. R., Maccoby, E., & Levin, H. (1957). *Patterns of child rearing.* Evanston, Illinois: Row and Peterson.

Tymowski, A. (1982). Dylematy rodzinnych i zawodowych obowiazkow wspolczesnej kobiety [Dilemmas of familial and occupational responsibilities of modern women]. In M. Jarosz (Ed.), *Rodzina polska lat siedemdziesiatych* [The Polish family in the 1970's] (pp. 139–153). Warsaw: PWN.

Tyszka, Z. (1982). *Rodziny wspolczesne w Polsce* [The contemporary family in Poland]. Warsaw: Instytut Wydawniczy ZZ.

Zumkley, H. (1984) Individual differences and aggressive interactions. In A. Mummendey (Ed.), *Social psychology of aggression* (pp. 33–49). Berlin: Springer-Verlag.

6 Television Viewing and Its Relation to Aggression Among Children in Australia

Peter W. Sheehan
University of Queensland, Australia

INTRODUCTION

Aggression is stated by many to be a primary trait influencing human behavior, and argument can be made that it reflects a major personal attribute that renders responses across different situations relatively consistent. Situations also impose constraints on behavior so that the context in which aggressive behavior occurs and the personal attributes of the person involved interact. These interactions are the focus for analysis of societal effects on the display of aggression. Media presentation of violent events is one way in which aggression is displayed readily and frequently. Thus, the prevalence of television watching in a particular society raises important questions about how the presentation of aggression on TV is related to aggressive behavior, which factors mediate that association, and what responsibility the medium has to the public.

In the current study, the aggression content of Australian TV was systematically evaluated and the relation between TV watching and aggression among Australian schoolchildren was explored. This chapter provides an overview of the importance of TV and the structure of the industry in Australia. It also presents characteristics of Australian society related to aggression and criminality. Further, some processes said to explain observed relations are considered. Finally, empirical data from the study are presented, evaluated, and discussed.

Television Viewing in Australia

Television watching is the dominant leisure-time activity in Australia, especially for children. The statistics on the use of television in Australia make compelling reading. A survey of 400 children in the 10- 12-year age group conducted recently by the Australian Broadcasting Tribunal (ABT: see its Research Report, 1979a) tapped children's and parents' reactions to the medium in several major Australian cities. Results demonstrated that television watching occupies almost all of children's time after school. Of the children who were surveyed, 56% watched an average of 3 hours or more television each day. A comparable proportion (57%) said they watched television at least some of the time while doing homework (55%) and having supper (60%). In most cases (70%), prohibitions were ineffective. Further, 44% of the children reported more than one television set in their home. For these Australian children, viewing time was extensive and often underestimated by parents. United States comedy, cartoons, and science fiction were the most popular programs with children. Children reported humor and action were major reasons for liking programs and boredom was the principal reason for disliking programs. Summaries of other surveys (see Murray & Kippax, 1979, for review) suggest that age-related patterns of viewing are consistent cross-culturally and comparable to Australian findings. Frequency of viewing tends to rise gradually, peak in early adolescence, and then decline.

The Structure of the TV Industry

Television arrived in Australia relatively late in comparison with other countries. It was not until June 1949, that the Australian Government decided to introduce a national television service into the Commonwealth. The first permanent television station offering regular transmission in Australia was established in September 1956. The years up to 1968 yielded a steady increase in the number of new stations coming on air. By that time all of the largest population centers were covered by a national television and a commercial service (ABT Report, 1980). The commercial system is operated under licenses given by the Australian Broadcasting Tribunal, which exerts a strong influence on operation and policy. As of June 1981, commercial service consisted of 50 stations. Of these, 15 were in capital cities, 33 in country areas, and 2 in the Territories. About 90% of the population receive at least one commercial channel (Stewart, 1983).

Children form the bulk of the television audience up to 10 a.m. and resume that status from 4 to 5 p.m. Thereafter, adults form the main audience in the peak viewing hours after 6 p.m. There is some seasonal fluctuation in viewing time, but in Brisbane, where the Australian data were collected, this variation is minimal. There are, on the average, some four major television stations in capital cities; and Brisbane, capital of Queensland, has three commercial and one nationalized service. Differences in programming between the commercial and national services are clear-cut. National television broadcasts less drama and light entertainment than commercial stations and has a much heavier commitment to daytime educational programs. Program content is changing, however. National television has begun to give more attention to informational and children's programs (ABT Report, 1980). Both commercial and national services make consistent use of cinema films.

Comments on Australian Society

Much has been written about the characteristics of Australians and Australian society. Published work includes historical analyses, sociological essays, infrequent empirical studies, and copious impressionistic observations. Much of the material has been critical. Australians have been criticized at one time or another for their easy-going, laissez-faire attitude (Horne, 1965), their lack of relative independence from the influence of other larger nations (McGregor, 1966), and their inherent belligerence (King, 1978).

About 15.2 million people live in Australia (1981 Census). Most of them are located around the perimeter of the continent with the heaviest concentration on the eastern side of the country. Seventy percent live in six capital cities. Australia has been involved in 11 major skirmishes (including two world wars) with a loss of approximately 100,000 lives (King, 1978). It is also one of the most urbanized countries in the world. Increased immigration has loosened its early ties with Britain, and the country appears to be achieving a greater sense of national independence. It is, however, heavily influenced by American consumerism.

In 1974 a Royal Commission on Human Relationships was established and reported on the influence of family relationships on the behavior of Australian children as well as other national social issues. Among its findings, the Commission (1977) reported that punishment was practiced by many Australian parents as a form of disciplinary control, which seems likely to affect child aggression as measured in the present study. The Commission also found that males and females are quite firmly differentiated in their sex roles, and the current study bears on this issue as well. Furthermore, the Commission reported that the family unit was strong, and that the country experienced neither the depths of poverty nor the extravagant wealth evident elsewhere (for example, in the United States). Significant social problems, however, were increasing and included difficulties (e.g., alcoholism) frequently associated with antisocial behavior. Brisbane, the site of the present study, was not unrepresentative of the populations from which the Commission data were drawn. For example, Brisbane is reporting, as are other Australian population centers, an increasing incidence of child abuse.

Relatively few empirical studies have reported extensive psychological data bearing on the national identity. For the most part, data offered have been impressionistic. Oeser and Hammond (1954), however, undertook a community study of both adults and children in Melbourne, one of

Australia's most populous cities. Most relevant for the present research, Oeser and Hammond observed 129 sixth grade children in an Australian urban environment similar to the location of the current study. Their findings were relatively consistent with data from other sources (Broom & Lancaster-Jones, 1976). Currently, the overall picture indicates that Australia is a relatively stratified society; has been ethnically homogenous, though rising immigration rates are changing this pattern; subscribes to middle-class attitudes; and has the highest level of home ownership in the world.

That Australians are satisfied with their material well-being is widely acknowledged (Conway, 1978; Horne, 1965; Oeser & Hammond, 1954). For some, material comforts seem to take the sting out of Australians' hostility toward their compatriots. For others (e.g., King, 1978), aggression among Australians seems to be an ingrained and inevitable consequence of the country's convict beginnings. However, aggression did not appear to be a particularly relevant trait in a longitudinal study of the personality development of Australian men followed through time (Oeser & Hammond, 1954). Extraversion and its variants were more evident. These data lie closer to an image of the Australian as someone who lives in a lucky country and is strongly motivated to search for companionship (Horne, 1965). In Australia, leisure time is valued especially highly. Television watching and sport constitute the most significant components of free time activity. In Brisbane, sport is a major community activity and TV usage is typically extensive. (See previous discussion of statistics on television viewing in Australia.)

Differential taxation and the basic wage keep the range of individual incomes somewhat narrow so that there are relatively few very rich and very poor. In Australia, Henderson, Harcourt, and Harper (1970) found that the poor constituted a much smaller proportion of the population than in Britain and the United States. An even distribution of earnings also helps to explain the high rate of middle-class identification among Australians (Broom & Lancaster-Jones, 1976).

Education in Australia

There is also a strong drive to attain status and mobility through education in Australia (Royal Commission Report, 1977). Children are pressured to do well at school, and the country has a lengthy history of compulsory education. Typically, the pattern of progression through the school system is at least 8 years.

Though the sample used by Oeser and Hammond (1954) was taken from a single urban setting and the research was done some time ago, their data remain informative about children in the Australian school system. Most children start school at the age of 5 or 6. The majority of children, particularly from lower income groups, go to State schools, which for the most part, emphasize obedience or conformity to authority. The child mixes with a large group of children. Though children must often fend for themselves, physical aggression is checked by adults. Oeser and Hammond (1954) report that by 9 years of age children begin to reject those who are unduly aggressive and those who behave in ways that are known to be forbidden. Aggressive children without compensatory capacities such as the ability to invent games are unpopular with their peers. At school, physical punishment is used and considered a reliable control by parents (Human Relationships Report, 1977).

The curriculum in Australian schools is heavily sex biased. Even at preschool age, males have been found to have more status (Dixon, 1976). For 5 year olds, schooling is likely to consist of play, which includes both same and mixed gender groups. In play involving boys and girls, a girl may sometimes be the leader. But in many games (particularly outdoor ones), girls frequently adopt a subordinate position to boys. Boys tend to be regarded as sissies if they are still playing with dolls by the age of 9. Additionally, a comparison of age groups suggests greater differentiation of sex role with increasing age. From her study of 1,214 secondary school students in Victoria, Edgar (1975) reported that schools perpetuated and reinforced stereotyped sex-role behavior so that future occupational decisions were influenced. She also showed that girls were more self-deprecating than boys and significantly lower in self-esteem.

Parents expect their children to avoid "bad" company, particularly those children whom they consider "tough." Parents give praise much less frequently to older than to younger children. Oeser and Hammond's data further suggest parents pressure girls more than boys to develop what they consider desirable qualities. Also, boys appear to be encouraged to adopt certain behavior patterns, whereas girls seem to be encouraged to accept particular moral values or attitudes. Finally, parental pressure is usually directed more toward behavior in the family than toward participation in broader social situations.

Crime Data in Australia

Despite the notion that Australians are characteristically violent and becoming more so with time, close analysis shows no real data to support this contention. Nevertheless, claims persist that Australia is violent. King (1978), for example, argued that Australia is basically a violent nation, as one in 14 citizens are victimized each year. Biles (1977), highlighted a 67% increase over 7 years in serious crime (e.g., rape, homicide, robbery, assault, and forgery) with the population growth of 11.5% during the same period. As Biles also acknowledged, the most appropriate question to ask is not whether crime is increasing in Australia, but rather which crimes and jurisdictions are increasing during what time periods. Clearly, the nature of the crime requires close scrutiny. In particular, statistics on crimes involving persons suggest the need for reassessment. Offenses against persons are the substance of interpersonal aggression, but statistics show that this type of offense has actually remained constant during the period 1900–1976. The rate of offenses against persons was about 2% in 1900 as it was in 1976. The significant increase in the total number of crimes can be substantially accounted for by increases in petty offenses. Crimes involving property show dramatic growth but crimes involving persons do not. The Australian justice system is overloaded with minor offenses such as drunkenness and traffic violations. In a comparison of five countries (Mukherjee, 1981), Australia reported the second lowest crime rate for all four crime categories (homicide, robbery, rape, and burglary). In 1978, approximately the time of commencement of testing in this study, the number of offenses reported per 100,000 total population in Australia was 4.0 homicides (vs. 9.0 in the United States), 24.9 robberies (vs. 191.3 in the United States), 5.9 rapes (vs. 30.8 in the United States) and 1,120.7 burglaries (vs. 1,423.7 in the United States). During the 14-year period analyzed, the Australian-reported homicide rate varied only between 4.4 and 5.7 per 100,000 population aged 10 years and older. (Editor's note: These rates are somewhat higher than those reported in chapter 1 [2 to 2.5], perhaps because they are based only on the population aged 10 and higher. Also, according to chapter 1, Australia's homicide rate was lower than Finland's, but higher than Poland's or Israel's).

Some researchers have observed an increase in Australia's crime rate for females. Biles (1977), for example, reported that in 1964, females comprised 7.6% of the total persons involved in serious crime. By 1972, this had risen to 12.1%. However, Mukherjee (1981) argues that the rate of increase for offenses against persons actually has been rising much more markedly for males than for females since the mid 1930s. Further, the magnitude of the rate of change for males is far larger than for females. Offenses against property, however, show a higher rate of increase for females, and the number of property offenses committed by females is now particularly high.

In summary then, analyses of statistics on Australian crime, based on data provided from the country's criminal justice system, suggest that major crimes against the person are not appreciably increasing overall. Crimes against persons are not increasing nearly as much for women as for men. Property crimes, especially burglary, are rising. Explanation of these statistics is difficult. Crime and aggression have been reliably linked with socioeconomic conditions such as poverty and unemployment (for review, see Royal Commission Report, 1977), but theories have not worn well in explaining the intricacies of the data (see Naffin, 1981).

The Role of the Media

The relation of the media to levels of aggression as indexed by crime in Australia is complex. From a survey conducted in three major Australian cities, Wilson and Brown (1973) demonstrated that most Australians feel crime is increasing but may have unrealistic perceptions of its prevalence. Wilson and Brown argue that the problem is not as acute as it is in the United States and that much public concern and fear about crime appears to be unjustified. Nevertheless, people across Australia appear to be modifying their personal and social behavior. Half of Wilson and Brown's sample said they avoided talking to strangers, being on the streets after dark, and being out alone. Mukherjee (1981) concluded that the media are fostering the public's perception of a growing crime rate. Australian TV focuses on rare incidents and sensationalizes the treatment of vivid and gruesome events so that community fears are reinforced or produced. Crimes against persons dominate the TV screen. On the other hand, crimes against property, (for example, corporate misdemeanors and felonies or consumer fraud), receive far less attention on TV but are far more prevalent.

Data indicate that, although Australian TV depicts the bulk of population inaccurately, it reflects more accurately the activities of those who shape the culture (Stewart, 1983). It focuses, for example, on middle-aged, middle-class, Anglo-Saxon males who comprise a small minority of Australians but who dominate the power structure of the society. The media, like the schools, treat males and females in stereotypic ways that support the status quo (Edgar, 1975).

Conclusions

In conclusion, it appears that Australia is not a very aggressive society. Study of the personal characteristics of its citizens does not highlight aggressiveness. Although crime is definitely increasing, our statistics do not emphasize crimes against persons, which typify aggression in its most direct form. It seems likely, however, that patterns of adult criminality would relate positively to child aggression and that significant societal problems (alcoholism and poverty, for example) would mediate the nature of that association.

The Australian media reflect criminal aggression inaccurately. The media distort the incidence of crime, for example, and appear to reinforce attitudes of fear and mistrust. As suggested elsewhere (Goldstein & Segall, 1983), it may well be that because of the unrelenting display of televised aggression, TV is a major contributor to the acquisition of aggressive behavior as well as the instigation of its enactment.

COMMENTS ON THE LITERATURE

Drawing together data from field and experimental studies on the relation between television viewing and aggressive behavior (see Huesmann, 1982; Murray & Kippax, 1979 for review), a vast network of variables emerges as relevant. The data tell us that we need to consider the significance the viewer attributes to events, the alternatives for behavior, the interactions between the content of the television programs and the viewers' perception of that content, and the influence of various social and demographic characteristics. Situational factors such as family viewing patterns and the way programs are discussed, as well as personality factors such as the viewer's frustration tolerance and predisposition to aggression are also potentially relevant. Television may yield its influence directly (e.g., through imitation or modeling) or indirectly by modifying values, attitudes, or perceptions so that violent solutions to problems seem legitimate or acceptable. Age and sex are relevant. Further, the actual regularity of viewing is important. A positive relation between number of hours of television watched and self-reports of aggression (Robinson & Bachman, 1972) has been identified. Moreover, frequent TV viewers have been found to be more likely to perceive television portrayals as real, and the effects are stronger for younger children (Greenberg & Reeves, 1976).

The general literature is reviewed in detail elsewhere in this book. In summary, all those reviewing the field (see Comstock, Chaffee, Katzman, McCombs, & Roberts, 1978; Huesmann, 1982; Murray & Kippax, 1979; Noble, 1975; Rubinstein, 1976) acknowledge that violence on the TV screen can increase aggressive behavior but that this effect is not uniform across groups of children. The real argument concerns the conditions under which television viewing is likely to exert an influence. Though Schramm, Lyle, and Parker (1961) claimed that most television was neither particularly beneficial nor harmful for most children under most conditions, they concluded that "For *some* children, under *some* conditions, *some* television is harmful. For *other* children under the same conditions, or for the same children under *other* conditions, it may be beneficial" (p. 1). Their conclusion still seems tenable today.

Australian Research

Four major themes have emerged in Australian television research. These are the impact of television on aggressive behavior and attitudes, the use of television by the viewer, the frequency of television watching, and (most recently) the relevance of the family context to television watching and its effects. Australian researchers uniformly acknowledge that increased aggressive behavior is related to television viewing under particular circumstances. The nature of those circumstances, however, varies according to the type of factors investigated. In a series of comprehensive reviews (Murray, 1980; Murray & Kippax, 1979), Murray outlined the range of variables involved. Australian data indicate, as do cross cultural data, that televised violence is one factor in the maintenance and production of aggressive behavior.

Despite such agreement, theorists do differ. Edgar (1977a) and Noble (1975) assert that television does not make an appreciable contribution to aggressive behavior in children. According to Edgar, television presents the viewer with a particular account of the world that may not be accurate, so that TV reality may not necessarily be children's reality. The critical factor for Edgar is whether what is being shown or portrayed fits existing social norms. Violent TV programs are less likely to affect viewers if they do not reflect the social realities of the viewers' everyday environment. This important notion relates to Gerbner's (1972) work on the extent to which the television world can influence or even supplant a viewer's external reality and normative orientations. Edgar's research draws needed attention to socialization processes at work in the television situation. It is important to ask, for instance, how children select from different social definitions of reality and how this relates to their experience. If violent television has an impact, the effect may be greater when external reality seems to parallel closely what is shown on the screen. Research in this international study (see chapter 4 by Lagerspetz and Viemero for Finland; and chapter 5 by Fraczek for Poland) demonstrates the relevance of taking at least some account both of societal norms and of the cognitive "fit" of televised events with children's cultural environment. The present work emphasizes the impact of situational as well as cognitive influences on the child.

Noble (1975) challenges, more directly than does Edgar, the notion that television has pervasive negative effects. He argues that negative effects depend on the type of televised violence being portrayed and on the aggressiveness of the viewer. According to Noble, we should ask not what the televised program does to the child but what the child does with the televised aggression. Noble contends that the catharsis model fits the data better than a strict modeling theory. He found, for instance, that children played more imaginatively after viewing a war film than a puppet film, and that stylized aggression helped free aggressive boys for more imaginative play. Noble claims that certain types of films will have adverse effects on child viewers but that such effects depend on the nature of the aggression (whether or not it is stylized), the characteristics of the viewer (whether or not the child is aggressive) and the opportunity for fantasy release. The preponderance of studies in the United States provides evidence that contradicts the catharsis hypothesis.

Although the work of Edgar and Noble has had the greatest impact in Australia, many other studies have attempted to relate televised aggression or film aggression to perception of violence and aggressive attitudes (e.g., Lovibond, 1967). Lovibond found that Australian children who showed a preference for aggressive content in the media (including television) were rated as more antisocial or aggressive. Nevertheless, none of these studies that have investigated the correlates of televised aggression and child behavior has been conducted cross culturally.

Use of television by the viewer was investigated by Kippax and Murray (1977, 1980). Initially they found support for a relation between television watching and need gratification (Kippax & Murray, 1977). Selection of television programs was related to viewer's needs, and the needs themselves were related to situational and social characteristics of the viewer. Television was perceived as best meeting escape or entertainment and information needs, and was used as an actual source of gratification. Subsequently, they found that selection of television programming (and broadcasts in other media) could not be easily predicted from viewers' needs, though television was perceived as fitting various needs (Kippax & Murray, 1980).

The third theme relates to statistics describing daily TV watching. Australian research has focused on this issue in some detail. Comparative viewing patterns have been well analysed (ABT, 1979a; Tindall & Reid, 1975; Tindall, Reid, & Goodwin, 1977). Television watching has been related to variables such as self-esteem of the viewer (Edgar, 1977b) and aggressiveness of the viewer (Langham & Stewart, 1981). One of the most comprehensive analyses of TV viewing habits was the research conducted by the ABT (1979a). Statistics from that study have already been reviewed in the introduction to this chapter and indicate the extent to which television is a major leisure-time activity in Australia for both adults and children.

The fourth theme relates to the relevance of the family milieu and is illustrated by a range of studies including the portrayal of family life on prime time television (Stewart, 1983), the analysis of parental lifestyles in relation to children's television viewing (Holman & Braithwaite, 1982), and parental communication style as related to children's television behavior (Evatt, 1980). Stewart postulates that children construct an image of reality shown by the media and react differently depending on how their parents and peers mediate the content of what is shown. Holman and Braithwaite (1982) found that children's viewing was associated with parental attitudes. Frequent viewers had parents who were less concerned about the negative effects of TV and who saw less need to control it. Evatt found that mothers primarily determined or influenced the way in which television was viewed by children.

Other research issues have interested Australian investigators as well. This review only samples the research and does not do justice to the variety of research that is conducted overall.[1] Investigators have examined neurophysiological effects of television on chidren (showing no effects), the production aspects of children's programs, and the nature of viewers' program preferences and opinions about television content (see ABT, 1983). Research spon-

---

[1]In this review, certain research pursuits not germane to the main concerns of this chapter have been excluded. One theme, for example, is the isolation of those program characteristics that engage children's attention and encourage their response to specific kinds of television presentations (see Noble & Sinclair, 1983).

sored by the ABT and by investigators whose work has been reviewed was also placed before the Australian Parliamentary Senate in 1978. This inquiry into children's television expressed concern about the level of violence on Australian television and its effects, and the matter is again under debate by the Senate Select Committee on video material that was formed by the Australian Government in 1984, but has not yet been reported.

Consistent with the thrust of this report, Australian research essentially agrees with the conclusion that television produces negative effects for some children in some circumstances, especially when particular programs are considered. The strength of the assertion of a link between televised violence and aggressive behavior, however, varies across theories and depends on factors isolated for analysis. For some (e.g., Edgar) the relation between the world constructed on TV and the children's personal conception of the real-world environment is important, whereas for others, the relevant factor is the nature of aggression being displayed and the viewer's level of aptitude for aggression. Australian research as a whole cannot be easily placed in any one theoretical camp (e.g., modeling or catharsis theory) and suggests most obviously the multiple causality of the link between TV violence and aggression.

Viewed within a cross-cultural context, the focus for the present study is fourfold. First, the study aims to closely analyze the content of Australian TV in relation to aggression, as aggressive content differs across countries. Second, it aims to establish the boundary conditions for determining the relation between television viewing and aggressiveness in Australian children. Third, it comments on possible mediational variables relevant to this relation. And fourth, it attempts to draw policy implications suitable for Australia in relation to the data that emerged from the study. Because the research discussed in this chapter is part of the larger cross-cultural research program reported in this book, comment at times is made on data gathered in other countries, especially the United States.

ANALYSIS OF THE CONTENT OF AUSTRALIAN TELEVISION

Only preliminary research that systematically analyzes the aggressive content of television programs has been conducted in Australia. Nevertheless, concern about the possible negative effects of TV has been most typically expressed around programming content. Extensive analysis of foreign programs (which Australia imports heavily) shows that commercial entertainment emphasizes violence and aggression more than any other single theme. One of the major content analyses conducted to date examined the portrayal of family life in prime time television as part of an international project on television and the family (Stewart, 1983). Stewart showed that violence within the family, as displayed on TV, was relatively uncommon and that physical violence was portrayed only between family members and outsiders. Although this study did not analyze aggressive episodes in formal detail, it nevertheless highlighted the dependence of Australian TV on imported programs. Data indicated that a third of the programs reviewed were imported from the United States and one fifth from Britain. This dependence on foreign programs was also highlighted by Haines (1983).

The most broadly based analyses of the content of Australian TV are provided by the Chairman of the Australian Broadcasting Tribunal in annual reports to the Minister for Communications on the activities of the Tribunal. In its 1982-1983 report for instance, regulations that exist for controlling the kinds of programs children watch during the peak viewing hour (4-5 p.m.) after school are discussed. This control is introduced through the Children's Program Committee. The Tribunal also lays down requirements that specify the proportion of time to be devoted to programs with Australian content. Since July 1980, television stations have been required to broadcast not less than 5 hours (per week) of programs suitable for children between 4 p.m. and 5 p.m. Stations were also obliged to televise 30 minutes each weekday before 4 p.m. of shows designed especially for pre-school children. Standards have also been updated (ABT, 1984). Thus the Australian position is quite different from the United States, for instance, where no regulations require commercial networks to show children's programming (Edgar, 1983). Not surprisingly, educational programming received the smallest percentage of time allotted to various types of programs by commercial television stations in Australia. The United States program, *Knight Rider,* was the most popular imported program for 1982-1983, and there is an especially heavy following among Australian television watchers for locally produced drama shows.

Method and Procedures for Content Analysis

This analysis focused directly on the issue of the aggressive content of children's television viewing. Eighty television programs, used as part of the wider study, were subjected to a detailed rating analysis using the Message System Analysis developed by Gerbner, Gross, Morgan, and Signorielli (1980). This methodology allows orderly and reliable observations of programming content. The list was composed of popular programs available for children during a normal viewing week and included a range of characters differing in sex roles and display of physical aggression. Programs also spanned a range of content and included cartoons, fiction (crime, western and action/adventure, and domestic comedy), and nonfiction (variety and quiz programs, documentary and current affairs programs, and educational shows). Features movies, sports, and religious programs were not included. It should be noted that this method of measuring violence of TV programs was not the one used to classify programs in this study either in Australia or the other countries.

Programs were broadcast over the period May through July 1981 and were sampled from all four Brisbane TV channels (commercial and national). All programs were broadcast during the time third-grade children (age 8) would be available for viewing. This involved broadcast time before 8:30 a.m. and between 3:00 p.m. and 11:30 p.m. on weekdays with hours extended to midnight on Friday. Programs were taken from the full broadcasting day on Saturday from 6:00 a.m. to 8:30 p.m. on Sunday.

The primary focus of the study was on the display of violence, defined as "the overt expression of physical force (with or without a weapon, against self or other), compelling action against one's will on pain of being hurt or killed, or actually killing or hurting" (Gerbner et al., 1980, p. 2).[2] The major unit of violence was the violent episode that was formally defined as a scene illustrating violence restricted to the same participants. A change in characters involved meant another episode was defined. Three types of units were classified: The program was rated as a whole; specific violent actions were judged; and particular classes of characters were identified. The tone of the program (comic, mixed, or serious), the time frame (past, present, or future) and the location of events (urban, rural, uninhabited/mobile) were analyzed. Characters were also evaluated by dramatic role, gender, and their positions as heroes, villains, or both. The data are reported in detail elsewhere (McCann & Sheehan, 1985) and were analyzed by the prevalence, frequency, and rate of violent episodes. Prevalence consisted of the percent of programs in any sample or sub-sample containing violence and was calculated for both the percent of program hours containing violence and the percent of programs containing violence. The frequency of violent action was calculated for the rate of violent episodes per program per hour. Two raters, using Gerbner's methodology and trained in rating procedures, watched and rated one episode for each of the 80 nominated programs. Both raters observed a sample of programs in order to provide reliability estimates for their judgments. The reliability estimate for this common sample of programs with respect to number of violent episodes was .91.

Results and Discussion

Analysis of the programs indicated that 51.3% of programs and 53% of program hours contained violence. This is lower than estimates based on United States data (80.3% reported by Gerbner et al., 1980) and Japanese

---

[2]It should be noted that there are some differences in the definition of aggression adopted by Gerbner et al. (1980) and the definition used by researchers in this international study. Both definitions, however, clearly overlap.

data (81% reported by Iwao, de Soola Pool, & Hajiwana, 1981). Fiction shows contained a heavy proportion of violence. Those found to be especially violent were cartoons (85.7%), crime shows (96.7%), and action/ adventure programs (73.7%). Data are presented in Table 6.1

Analysis of the intensity of violence broadcasting (columns 4 and 5 in Table 6.1) indicated an overall rate of 4.0 violent episodes per program and 5.4 violent episodes per broadcast hour. This estimate ranks comparably with New Zealand data (Haines, 1983), is higher than Canadian rates with two violent episodes per hour (Haines, 1983), but is below the rate per hour in Japan (7.0; Iwao et al., 1981) and the United States (8.1; Haines, 1983). Data also indicated a particularly high proportion of weapon use in fictional programs and a substantial proportion of fictional programs (48%) in which violence was significant to the plot. A significant proportion (20%) of the weapon use was associated with violence considered gratuitous to plot development.

The content of programs showed a clear sex bias. Males commit 90% of the violence, which is comparable to estimates in the United States (82.7%) and Britain (83%; Halloran & Croll, 1972). Male characters also constituted 76.1% of victims and 90.3% of the characters killed. Thus, Australian television depicts males as both aggressors and victims. The data also indicate, however, that when females are present on Australian TV, they are present primarily for the purpose of being killed or victimized. Of the main females, 72% were victims or killed, for example, whereas only 48% of main males fell into these two categories. These data are consistent in their overall thrust with findings in the United States. The present study also looked at the context in which violence occurred and analyzed the program tone, time, and location of the events displayed. Results showed that violent programs were mixed in tone (73%) rather than just comic (12%) or serious (15%), heavily accentuated the present (81%) rather than the future (7%) or past (12%), and took place largely in urban (51%) rather than rural (23%) settings.

Although the level of violence reported in this study is relatively low compared to data from some countries, the frequency of violent episodes indicates the presence of substantial violence on Australian television. If nonfictional programs are excluded—and these programs are relatively unpopular with children—the number of violent episodes per broadcasting hour rises from 5.4 to 7.4. Thus television provides children with a large number of violent models to observe. Moreover, Pingree and Hawkins (1981) suggest that there are cumulative effects. Australian children who were heavy TV viewers tended to shift their views of the world toward reality as portrayed on television.

Limitations in this analysis of content must be acknowledged. Particular features, such as the level of violence or the type of aggressive behavior portrayed, have not been linked to children's liking for programs. In addi-

TABLE 6.1

Indices of Perceived Violence for Different Program Categories

Program Category	Number of Programs	Number of Hours	Percent of Programs Violent	Percent of Hours of Programs Containing Violence	Number of Violent Episodes per Program	Number of Violent Episodes per Hour
CARTOONS	7	3.5	85.7	78.6	5.1	10.2
FICTION	51	38.5	66.7	72.6	5.4	7.2
Crime	15	14.0	96.7	96.4	8.5	9.2
Western	1	1.0	50.0	50.0	3.5	3.5
Action	19	14.5	73.7	75.9	6.4	8.4
Comedy	16	9.0	31.3	30.6	1.5	2.7
NON-FICTION	22	17.0	4.6	4.4	0.3	0.4
Variety	13	9.0	3.9	2.3	0.2	0.3
Documentary	5	5.0	10.0	10.0	0.7	0.7
Educational	4	3.0	0.0	0.0	0.0	0.0
TOTAL	80	59.0	51.3	53.0	4.0	5.4

Note: Statistics included in this table are taken from McCann and Sheehan (1985).

tion, research of this kind entirely begs the question of how aspects of content are connected with the viewers' actual behavior. Although the literature tells us that negative effects of television watching are not uniform, such effects nevertheless exist. Data reported here indicate sufficiently high levels of violence on Australian television to justify examining the nature of the association between television watching and aggression. Further, it is important to note that the methodology for analyzing television content adopted in this chapter seems likely to yield an upper limit for what might be considered (physically) "violent programs" in Australia. When aggregate ratings are taken, however, the estimate of aggression for Australian television is much lower (see chapter 2).

METHOD

Subjects

Three State primary schools in the metropolitan area of Brisbane (Australia's third most populous city) participated in the research. In each of these schools, children were tested in 1979, 1980, and 1981 and participated in the study in two cohorts. In 1979 one cohort was enrolled in grade 1 and the other in grade 3. By testing these two cohorts, data were collected from grades 1 through 5. In summary, 137 grade 1 children, 122 grade 2 children, and 106 grade 3 children (the younger cohort) were tested in 1979, 1980, and 1981, respectively; and 159 grade 3 children, 141 grade 4 children, and 120 grade 5 children (the older cohort) were tested in the same 3 years, respectively. Samples consisted of virtually every first and third-grader for whom permission could be obtained. By 1981, the younger cohort contained 54 boys and 52 girls and the older cohort held 63 boys and 57 girls. The 70 children who dropped out of the study from 1979–1981 did so largely because their parents moved away from the school district. A small number of children (approximately six) deliberately chose not to continue with testing or were withdrawn from the study by either parents or teachers.

The average age of children in the younger cohort at the commencement of testing was 6.1 years and the average age of children in the older cohort at the same time was 8.2 years. All three schools could be classified as upper middle class. As many parents of the participating children as possible were interviewed in 1979 ($n = 569$) and 1981 ($n = 426$). Analyses of results focus for the most part on the chidren, though the relation between parent variables and the pattern of aggressiveness in children is also considered. Where parent data are reported, however, data from the first testing is cited because not all countries in this international project tested parents twice.

Measuring Periods for Child Testing

With the exception of grade 1 children in the younger cohort, all children were tested at approximately the same time, the mid-year of the school term (July–August). Testing was delayed for 2 months for the grade 1 children as extra time was needed to ensure that these young children fully understood the nature of the test materials.

Procedures of Testing and Variables Measured

Consistent with the testing program adopted by the other countries, each first and second-grade child was initially tested in class. In this session, testing was conducted in small groups and children were given a fantasy questionnaire, a sex-role questionnaire, and were assessed for identification with aggressor or victim. In a second session, conducted individually, children judged their peers for aggression (defined as an act that physically injures or irritates another person) and answered questions about television programs they were viewing currently at home. For the third, fourth, and fifth-grade children, both sessions were conducted in groups in the classroom.

Television viewing was studied in relation to the ratings children gave specifically named programs. Eighty television shows were chosen each year by the author as likely to be popular for children aged 6–11 and included most of the available programs. These shows were then divided into eight lists of 10 programs each. As far as possible, the lists were equated for violence, types of shows, gender of central characters, and time of the week in which the programs were shown. Movies, current affairs programs, and news reports were not used, but cartoons and serialized documentaries were listed. Table 6.2 illustrates a TV program list selected for inclusion in the 1981 testing session and highlights the average violence rating and gender of the main character for the different types of programs included.

Each year of the study two graduate students independently rated these 80 programs for the amount of visually portrayed physical aggression depicted. Ratings were made on a 5-point scale ranging from "not violent" to "very violent." The average interrater reliability for a comparable measure used by the author (see Sheehan, 1983, for details) in this study for each year of the testing program was .69 (averaged across the 3 years). The child's TV violence scores were based on the sum of the violence ratings of the eight shows the child indicated he or she watched and corrected for the frequency with which the child reported watching each program according to procedures outlined earlier (see chapter 2).

Full details for child and parent measures are provided elsewhere (see chapter 2), and only the main variables that were adopted in this study are

TABLE 6.2
Examples of TV Programs Included in the Study

Title of Program	Type of Program	Sex of Main Character	Overall Violence Rating by Judges (Scale, 0–4)
Grange Hill	Drama	Male/Female	3.0
Breakfast with Jacki Mac	Variety	Female	0.5
Incredible Hulk	Crime	Male	4.0
Countdown	Variety	Male	0.0
Inventors	Panel/Educ	Male/Female	0.0
Circus	Drama	Male	3.5
Laff-A-Olympics	Fantasy	Male	3.5
I Can Jump Puddles	Drama	Male	1.5
Kingswood Country	Comedy	Male	0.0
Prisoner	Crime	Female	2.0

Note: This list is one of the eight sets of 10 programs presented to children in both cohorts in the 1981 round of testing. The table is reprinted from Sheehan (1983) by courtesy of the Australian Psychological Society.

listed here.[3] The major television viewing variables used in the study were (a) the child's regularity of TV viewing, and (b) the child's overall TV violence viewing (determined by multiplying preference for violence by regularity of viewing). The other major child variables selected for investigation were (a) sex-typed behavior; (b) fantasy activity; (c) judged realism of programs being watched; (d) identification with TV characters; and (e) peer-nominated aggression. The major parent variables selected for study were parents' (a) income; (b) rejection; (c) punishment; (d) mobility orientation; and (e) TV violence viewing. Fathers' and mothers' aggression were also studied. The peer-nominated aggression measure for children was the major dependent variable for analysis.

All testing was conducted by teams of researchers who were recruited and trained especially for the study. All child and parent variables were essentially those measured in most of the other countries.

RESULTS

Results are presented according to four major emphases. First, data are presented showing the longitudinal age trends for key variables. Second, the correlates of peer-rated aggression are examined. Third, both child and parent data are analyzed longitudinally to investigate the prediction of aggressive

---

[3]For noting, there were some differences in the scoring of variables used in the study by Sheehan (1983) and those used here, but the differences are minor.

behavior, over time. And finally, the 10 least and 10 most aggressive children tested in the program are compared.

Age-Trend Data and Sex Differences

Six key variables isolated for attention were peer-rated aggression, overall violence viewing, engagement in aggressive fantasy through daydreaming, judged realism of programs, identification with TV characters, and masculine and feminine activities. Results were examined separately for boys and girls and individually for the two cohorts.

For each of the six variables, separate 3 (year of testing) $\times$ 2 (sex of subjects) $\times$ 2 (cohort) ANOVAs were conducted to examine significant effects. The analyses indicated appreciable time trends for the majority of variables. For aggression ($F = 22.12, df = 2,438, p < .001$), television violence viewing ($F = 9.06, df = 2,442, p < .001$), and neutral sex role ($F = 11.31, df = 2,442, p < .001$), there were significant increases over time. Identification with TV characters decreased within each cohort ($F = 31.64, df = 2,442, p < .001$), whereas the judged realism of TV violence increased in the younger cohort and remained relatively constant in the older cohort ($F = 8.48, df = 2,426, p < .002$). Female sex-role identification decreased over time for girls and increased for boys ($F = 16.51, df = 2,442, p < .001$), whereas male sex-role identification decreased over time for boys and increased for girls ($F = 11.05, df = 2,442, p < .001$). Notable also was the extent of gender differences evident across the set of variables. Significant gender differences were present across time for television violence viewing ($F = 27.85, df = 1,221, p < .001$), aggressive fantasy ($F = 22.83, df = 1,221, p < .001$), judged realism ($F = 17.15, df = 1,213, p < .001$), identification with TV characters ($F = 8.49, df = 1,193, p < .01$), and for both male ($F = 1,448.14, df = 1,221, p .001$) and female sex-role activities ($F = 800.97, df = 1,221, p < .001$). Surprisingly, the main effect of gender on peer-nominated aggression only approached significance ($F = 2.69, df = 1,219, p < .15$) with boys scoring substantially higher than girls only in the older cohort. In all other cases except for identification with television characters, boys scored appreciably higher on the measures than girls. Males, especially in the older cohort, engaged in greater violence viewing, fantasized more aggressively, considered the programs they watched more realistic, and engaged in more masculine and less feminine sex-role activities than girls. Also, as previously mentioned, boys increased in feminine activities over time whereas girls increased in masculine activities over time.

Overall, the age-trend data indicated the special importance of considering results for boys and girls separately. Sex differences among Australian children were quite clear cut and more pronounced than in most other countries as well. Australian girls, for example, were lower on preference for male activities than girls tested in any of the other five countries, and (with the exception of Poland) were highest on preference for female activities as well. Sex-role data, then, differentiated girls in Australia from girls tested in other countries and confirmed observations made earlier about sex-role differences.

PEER-RATED AGGRESSION AND ITS CORRELATES

The major concern of this study is how TV habits such as overall violence viewing and regularity of television viewing are related to aggressive behavior. As just mentioned, the data indicate that it is important to analyze the pattern of relations for boys and girls and younger and older cohorts separately. Accordingly, Table 6.3 reports the correlations between TV viewing and aggression separately for boys and girls in grades 1 to 5. To maximize the

TABLE 6.3

The Relation of Overall TV Violence Viewing and Regularity of TV Viewing with Peer-Rated Aggression for Boys, Girls, and the Total Sample of Children as a Function of Cohort and Grade

Cohort and Grade	Variable	Correlation with Aggression		
		Boys	Girls	Total
Younger				
Grade 1 (1979)		$N = 71$	$N = 66$	$N = 137$
	TV Violence Viewing	—	—	—
	Regularity of Viewing	—	—	—
Grade 2 (1980)		$N = 62$	$N = 60$	$N = 122$
	TV Violence Viewing	—	.22[+]	.17[+]
	Regularity of Viewing	—	—	—
Grade 3 (1981)		$N = 54$	$N = 52$	$N = 106$
	TV Violence Viewing	—	—	—
	Regularity of Viewing	—	—	—
Older Cohort				
Grade 3 (1979)		$N = 93$	$N = 66$	$N = 159$
	TV Violence Viewing	.18[+]	.24*	.23**
	Regularity of Viewing	.26**	.22[+]	.26***
Grade 4 (1980)		$N = 79$	$N = 62$	$N = 141$
	TV Violence Viewing	.33**	—	.30***
	Regularity of Viewing	.23*	.21[+]	.25**
Grade 5 (1981)		$N = 63$	$N = 57$	$N = 120$
	TV Violence Viewing	.21[+]	—	.22*
	Regularity of Viewing	—	.24[+]	—

[+]$p < .10$.   *$p < .05$.   **$p < .01$.   ***$p < .001$.
Note: All significance levels are two-tailed.

use of available data, correlational analyses were based on all children who were tested at any time during the study.

This table shows that TV violence viewing and regularity of TV viewing were significantly related to aggressive behavior for children in the older cohort (grades 3 to 5) much more so than for children in the younger cohort (grades 1 to 3). Effects were strongest for male children. Overall violence viewing was significantly related to aggressive behavior for the older cohort in each of grades 3, 4, and 5, but the strongest association in the study was observed for boys in grade 4.

Table 6.4 presents the correlations of the TV variables with peer-nominated aggression and aggressive fantasy for the older cohort alone. In this table, each child's score has been aggregated over all three waves of observations. The correlations between TV violence viewing and peer-nominated aggression are notable for boys and the total sample, but they are less than the correlations between TV habits and fantasy aggression. The correlations between fantasy aggression and the product of TV violence viewing times identification with TV characters were all over .30 and significant. Children who perceive themselves as being similar to TV characters fantasize more about aggressive topics. In the United States data and the data from urban Finland, similar trends were found relating boys' identification with TV characters to their actual aggressive behavior.

Why are the relations between TV habits and aggression much stronger for the older cohort than for the younger? Perhaps the peer nominations of aggression were less valid for the younger cohort. As mentioned earlier, gender differences on this measure only approached significance in the younger cohort, whereas in other countries they were very significant. In addition, detailed observation of the data for children completing all 3 years of testing indicated that stability of peer-rated aggression was greater in the older cohort than in the younger cohort. The data for boys, for instance, yielded a correlation of .72 from 1979 to 1981 in the older cohort and the data for girls yielded an estimate of .82. The comparable estimates for the younger cohort were significant but lower (.64 for males and .49 for females). Another factor may have been the age trends in television viewing. In grade 4, where the relations were strongest, overall violence viewing peaked and peer-rated aggression was still strong. Television viewing was also most regular at this time (again, especially for boys). At grade 4, fantasy activity began to decline for boys as compared with girls whose aggressive fantasies began to increase at this stage.

Table 6.5 lists the major variables that were appreciably related to peer aggression among the children in the older cohort. It considers separately the results for boys, girls, and the total sample of children at each of the three grade levels tested. As in Tables 6.3 and 6.4, all available data are considered.

TABLE 6.4

Correlations of Older Children's Aggression and Aggressive Fantasy with Their TV Habits Averaged over 3 Years

TV Variables	Peer-Nominated Aggression			Aggressive Fantasy		
	Boys (N = 62)	Girls (N = 56)	Total (N = 118)	Boys (N = 63)	Girls (N = 56)	Total (N = 119)
Regularity of TV Viewing	.14	.18	.17+	—	.27*	.20*
TV Violence Viewing	.22+	—	.21*	.18	.30*	.30***
Judged Realism of TV Violence	—	—	—	—	.20	.14
Identification with TV Characters	—	—	—	.34**	.32*	.25**
TV Violence × Identification	.17	—	.12	.31*	.33**	.32***
Peer-Nominated Aggression	—	—	—	.23+	.27*	.28**

+$p < .10$.   *$p < .05$.   **$p < .01$.   ***$p < .001$.

Note: All significance levels are two-tailed.

TABLE 6.5
Child Variables Associated with Peer-Rated Aggression
for the Older Cohort (Grades 3 to 5)

Variable	Boys	Girls	Total Sample
GRADE 3 (1979)	$N = 93$	$N = 66$	$N = 159$
Preference for male activities			+
Aggressive fantasy		**	*
TV violence viewing	+	*	**
Regularity of TV viewing	**	+	***
Judged realism of TV violence	+		**
Identification with TV chars.		*	+
Peer-nominated popularity	*** (−)	*** (−)	*** (−)
Peer-nominated avoidance of agg.	** (−)	** (−)	*** (−)
GRADE 4 (1980)	$N = 79$	$N = 62$	$N = 141$
Identification with aggressor	***	+	***
Preference for male activities			+
Preference for neutral activities			* (−)
Aggressive fantasy	***	*	***
Frequency of fantasy	*	*	*
Active-heroic fantasy	**		***
TV violence viewing	**		***
Regularity of TV viewing	*	+	**
Judged realism of TV violence		+	+
Identification with TV chars.	+	+	+
Peer-nominated popularity	*** (−)		*** (−)
Peer-nominated avoidance of agg.	*** (−)	*** (−)	*** (−)
GRADE 5 (1981)	$N = 63$	$N = 57$	$N = 120$
Identification with aggressor	**		***
Preference for male activities	*		+
Aggressive fantasy	+		*
Active-heroic fantasy			+ (−)
TV violence viewing	+		*
Regularity of TV viewing		+	
Peer-nominated popularity			+ (−)
Peer-nominated avoidance of agg.	*** (−)	** (−)	*** (−)

+$p<.10.$ *$p<.05.$ **$p<.01.$ ***$p<.001.$
(−) denotes an inverse relation
Note: All significance levels are two-tailed.

Table 6.5 indicates a considerable range of corelates that were significantly associated with aggression at different age levels.

Data in Table 6.5 (and Table 6.4) indicate that more aggressive children fantasized or daydreamed more. These results appear to contradict the catharsis model that predicts that subjects who fantasize about aggression more will be less aggressive. Such findings seem to relate as Huesmann and Eron (1984) claim, to a fantasy-aggression cycle that may implicate television viewing. It seems plausible to argue that the more a child watches television and identifies with TV characters, the more the child will fantasize about aggression. Accordingly, longitudinal regressions were calculated on the Australian data in an attempt to ascertain the nature of the ordering between aggressive fantasy and behavioral aggression. The results of those analyses indicated comparable effects for fantasy on aggression as for aggression on fantasy. Collectively, data are consistent with the model that postulates that aggression stimulates aggressive fantasies, which, in turn, may serve as rehearsals for later aggression.

So far, aggressiveness in a child has been shown to correlate with a number of child characteristics including exposure to TV violence. Is the child's aggressiveness also related to characteristics and behaviors of the child's parents? In Table 6.6, selected parent variables (for definitions, see chapter 2) are correlated with children's peer-nominated aggression, the major TV viewing variables, and family social status.[4] Table 6.6 reveals significant relations of children's aggression and TV habits to their parents' social status, aggression, TV habits, and child-rearing styles. The relations are generally somewhat stronger for boys than for girls. In particular, more aggressive boys have lower status parents, who are more aggressive, who fantasize more about aggression, who watch more TV in general and prefer more violent programs, who use harsher punishments with their sons, and who reject their sons more. More aggressive girls also have more aggressive parents who prefer more violent television, who use harsher punishments, and who reject their daughters more. As is discussed later, rejection and punishment by the parents could be responses to aggression as well as instigators of aggression. However, as Table 6.6 shows, rejecting parents also have sons and daughters who watch more TV violence, and have sons who believe that violent programs are more realistic and who watch TV more regularly. Parents' aggression also relates in much the same way as rejection to a son's TV habits. One key difference between daughters and sons, however, is that lower social status is predictive of greater rejection of sons but predictive of harsher punishment of daughters. The nature of these correlations suggest that parent characteristics may be more important determinants of child aggression than the child characteristics that were measured.

The Prediction of Aggression

Although previous longitudinal research (Lefkowitz, Eron, Walder, & Huesmann, 1977) has utilized cross-lagged correlational analyses to corroborate cause and effect relations, these techniques have been heavily critiqued

---

[4]The selection of parent variables was influenced by the pattern of variables that emerged as significant in regression analyses examining the prediction of aggression over time (see next section and discussion of Table 6.7).

TABLE 6.6
The Relation of Selected Parent Variables to A Child's Aggression and TV Habits in the First Year of the Study

	Parent Variables							
Children's Variables	Occupational Status	Education	Aggression (MMPI F49)	Aggress. Fantasy	TV Violence	TV Frequency	Rejection of Child	Punishment of Child
Boys (N = 161)								
Peer-nominated aggression	-.21**	-.19*	.24**	.28***	.18*	.26***	.43***	.29***
Regularity of TV viewing	-.14+	—	.14+	—	—	.17*	.26***	.13+
TV violence viewing	—	—	.18*	—	—	—	.18*	.13+
Identification with TV chars.	-.16*	-.14+	—	—	—	—	—	—
Judged realism of TV violence	-.20**	-.21**	.24**	—	.19**	.17*	.21**	.19**
Father's Occupational Status	1.00	.48***	-.27**	—	—	-.25**	-.22*	—
Girls (N = 129)								
Peer-nominated aggression	—	—	.20*	—	.17*	—	.38***	.19*
Regularity of TV viewing	—	-.24**	—	—	—	-.21*	—	—
TV violence viewing	—	-.28***	—	—	—	.28**	.18*	—
Identification with TV chars.	—	—	—	—	—	—	—	—
Judged realism of TV violence	-.26**	-.21*	—	—	—	—	—	—
Father's occupational status	1.00	.53***	-.33***	—	-.15	-.23*	—	-.21*

+ $p < .10$.   * $p < .05$.   ** $p < .01$.   *** $p < .001$.
Note: All significance levels are two-tailed.

(see Rogosa, 1980) because of the difficulty of sustaining the assumptions that underlie the methodology. Multiple regression analysis thus was used for examining the contribution of TV viewing (and other) variables to the prediction of aggression. A series of regression analyses were conducted on the older cohort's data in which the prediction of later aggression from earlier TV habits and early aggression was compared with the prediction of later TV habits from earlier TV habits and aggression. These longitudinal regressions examined the effect of TV violence viewing, regularity of television watching, and identification with TV characters. However, no analysis for boys or girls indicated significant regression coefficients for early TV viewing on later aggression. The coefficients were positive but insignificant. Consistently, the best predictor of later aggression was the initial level of aggression of the child. The television viewing variables did not add appreciably to the prediction for either of the two genders. Similarly, early TV habits were the best predictors of later TV habits. None of the regressions provided results that would by themselves allow one to conclude that TV violence viewing causes aggression among Australian children. Neither do the analyses provide support for alternative explanations of the obtained correlations between violence viewing and aggression. In fact, further regression analyses revealed that none of the child variables measured in the first year predicted aggression in the final wave after initial aggression was partialed out. Variables such as sex-role preferences, aggressive fantasy, and TV habits were correlated with aggression, but they did not predict changes in aggression over time in 6- to 11-year old Australian children.

In Table 6.7, child aggression in the last year of the study is predicted from TV violence viewing and parent variables measured in the first year. The results of these regressions suggest that parental characteristics and behaviors are indeed better predictors of aggression in Australian children than the child's own characteristics (other than previous aggression). The more aggressive child had parents who punished and rejected the child more, who viewed more television (boys) or television violence (girls), who fantasized more about aggression, and who were from lower social strata (boys).

Though the parents' rejection and punishment of the child are the best predictors of later aggression, it is possible that punishment and rejection of the child could simply be a response to the child's earlier aggressiveness as was the case in the United States (see chapter 3). Causal regressions similar to the ones done for TV viewing and aggression were computed to test this hypothesis. They showed that for girls neither rejection nor punishment was a significant predictor of later aggression once early aggression was controlled. When early rejection and punishment were controlled, aggression predicted later rejection for girls but not later punishment. For boys, however, early rejection was a significant predictor of later aggression even when early aggression was controlled. When early rejection and punishment were controlled,

TABLE 6.7

Multiple Regressions Showing Effects of Socio-Economic Variables, Parent Behaviors, and Parent Child-Rearing Practices on the Relations Between TV Violence Viewing and Aggression in Australia

Dependent Variable	Predictors	Standardized Regression Coefficients		
		Boys (N = 115)	Girls (N = 108)	All (N = 223)
3rd Wave Aggression				
	Gender (Male = +)			.12$^+$
	Cohort	—	—	—
	TV Violence Viewing in 1st & 2nd Waves	—	—	—
	Father's Occupational Status	−.14	—	−.11
	Parents' Educational Status	—	−.15	—
	Parents' Aggression from MMPI Scales 4 + 9	—	—	—
	Parents' Aggressive Fantasy	.12	−.18$^+$	—
	Parents' TV Violence Viewing	—	.36***	.20**
	Parents' TV Frequency	.13	—	.10
	Parents' Nurturance of Child	—	—	—
	Parents' Rejection of Child	.29**	.17$^+$	.24***
	Parents' Punishment of Child	.22*	—	.11$^+$
	Parents' Social Mobility Orientation	.13	—	—
	R2 =	.26	.27	.22
	df =	12,102	12,95	13,209
	F =	2.97***	2.95**	4.57***

$^+p<.10.$ $*p<.05.$ $**p<.01.$ $***p<.001.$
Note: All significance levels are two-tailed.

aggression predicted later punishment for boys but not later rejection. These analyses suggest that parents' punishment of their sons and rejection of their daughters were mainly responses to the child's aggression. However, greater parental rejection of a son seems to have instigated later aggressive behavior by the boy regardless of his initial aggressiveness.

Most Versus Least Aggressive Children

Table 6.3 indicates that the relation between violent television viewing and peer-rated aggression was stronger in the older cohort than in the younger cohort and appears to be concentrated around grades 3 and 4. Accordingly, scores for the 10 most and least aggressive boys and girls in grade 4 were isolated for closer scrutiny of major variables. Instances were examined in which scores on the set of six selected variables exceeded the mean score for the group. Data were considered separately for the most and least aggressive children. Scores for the main set of six measures were calculated following the definition of scoring procedures set out in Sheehan (1983). A seventh variable, popularity, was calculated following scoring procedures outlined by Eron and Huesmann (this volume). In grade 4 (1980 testing), the total number of boys was 79 and the total number of girls was 60.

On inspection, data demonstrated considerable variation among all of the measures for the four samples of children selected for observation. There was some consistency, however, for data associated with the TV violence and aggressive fantasy measures across samples. For the most aggressive boys, 7 of the 10 children showed high TV violence viewing and high aggressive fantasy. This trend was only partially evident for girls. For the sample of least aggressive children, only 3 of the 10 boys showed high violence viewing and only 1 showed high aggressive fantasy. This trend was apparent for girls, but not as strong for girls as it was for boys. The only other measure demonstrating obvious consistency was the popularity scores—aggressive children were unpopular children (a result common to some other countries such as the United States (chapter 3) and Israel (chapter 7), but not all—e.g., Finland (chapter 4). Analyses for individual children confirm previous findings that a positive relation between TV violence viewing and aggression exists for children at this grade level and that the effect is more apparent for boys than for girls. The pattern of relation among the set of measures as a whole, however, was quite variable and not strong.

Summary of the Data

Results collected in the 3-year longitudinal study indicated a significant relation between television viewing and level of aggressive behavior among children. The effects observed in the study were small, as in other field studies in this general area of research. Nevertheless, the Australian results were statistically significant and comparable in size to effects obtained in the other countries. Both regularity of television watching and the extent of violence expressed in children's preferred programs were related to aggressive behavior as judged by the children's peers. Considering the sample of children as a whole, the relation was stronger for boys than for girls. The peaking of the effect for boys in grade 4 suggests perhaps that during this period of cognitive and social development, male children are particularly sensitive to the influence of television.

The relation between violent television watching and aggression in children would appear to be multiply determined. Engagement in aggressive fantasy, for example, is clearly relevant. Television violence viewing correlated with peer-nominated aggression, but aggressive fantasies or daydreams correlated appreciably with both violence viewing and peer nominated aggression. Results from the Australian data thus contradict the notion that fantasy works cathartically to reduce the level of children's aggressive play.

Earlier patterns of television watching may be associated with later aggressive behavior, but the Australian data bearing on this issue in the present study yielded no proof of a causal connection. Child variables analyzed in this study did not facilitate the prediction of aggression in children 3 years later. However, parent variables did significantly predict aggression for both boys and girls. Rejection and punishment were especially strongly correlated with aggression, and for boys rejection was a significant predictor of later aggression even when the initial level of aggression was controlled. While parental rejection and punishment are also associated with child aggressiveness in other countries, they were especially prominent in Australia where child variables had little predictive power.

DISCUSSION

Four major issues are raised by the Australian findings. The first relates to the question of why effects for children in this country occurred relatively late. Little effect was evident in the younger cohort and peaking of the effect occurred in the fourth grade as opposed to the third grade in the United States, for example. The second issue concerns the strong gender differences that were observed. The third issue relates to how well aggression actually can be predicted from variables adopted in this study. In particular, what evidence exists in the Australian data to support a causal connection between violent television viewing and aggressive behavior? The fourth issue concerns the influence parents exert in the network of mediating variables. What might explain the fact that in Australia parents' violent television viewing was related to later aggression, whereas children's violent television viewing was not. Finally, this section canvasses some of the methodological difficulties faced in the study and attempts to draw a number of broad policy implications from the data.

The Occurrence of Effects Over Time

The fact that the association between violence viewing and peer-rated aggression comes late in time for Australian children, points to the possibility of a sensitive "stage of development" in the cognitive and social development of children tested in this study. Major theories of sex-role development including social learning theory (Mischel, 1966) and cognitive-developmental theory (e.g., Kohlberg & Ullian, 1974) argue that same-sex modeling is a crucial process, but there is considerable debate in the literature concerning the timing of this process. Gender constancy theory (see Ruble, Balaban, &

Cooper, 1981) argues that children become interested in same-sex models and perceive sex-appropriate behavior as reinforcing because of an acquired sense of the inevitability of their gender. The child's gender becomes constant with time, however, and where in time that development process is placed might be important in determining the perception of what is appropriate behavior for one's sex. Gender constancy occurs relatively early in development, but the emergence of effects observed in the Australian data could reflect the appearance of the progression of the inevitability of gender over time. Here, for example, one might be observing heightened attention to same-sex models during the later stages of development. In addition, what might be linked with this hypothesis is the degree of preference for male activities that was sustained over time. It could be that the relevance of male activities is especially heightened by the aggression associated with characters on TV. The impact of this aggression is felt "late," as it were, in terms of characters' modeling influence. Girls also show effects in the older cohort. For the older cohort in which observing aggressive characters on TV was associated statistically with peer-nominated aggression, it was male aggressors that were implicated for both boys and girls just as in the United States and Finland. The average correlation between peer-nominated aggression and observing male characters was .22 ($N = 118, p < .02$) but between peer-nominated aggression and observing female aggressive characters was only .08 (n.s.).

One of the attractions of this mode of theorizing is that one expects the child to shift from being relatively passively influenced by sex-role reinforcement and information to actively seeking out such stimulation. The question remains, however, whether heightened attention to same-gender models during later stages of development reliably translates into heightened behavioral responsiveness at the same time. Whatever the explanation of effects, there seems to be some connection between a child's cognitive developmental level and the impact of aggressive content displayed on television. Content analysis of television programs in this study showed the extent to which the aggressive content on TV is gender-related. Males are both perpetrators of violence and victims of it, and it seems that male aggressors are influential as models for boys and girls alike.

Gender Differences in Aggression and Violence Viewing

The issue of relations occurring that are more evident for one gender than for the other focuses directly on the meaning of gender differences for Australian culture, especially because different television effects have occurred in other cultural groups. Sex-role differentiation emerges as predictably strong among Australian children.

The pattern of sex differences found for the relation between violent television viewing and child aggression in Australia is consistent with those found by Lefkowitz et al. (1977) in their earlier longitudinal study in which effects were also more evident for boys than for girls. Lefkowitz et al. interpreted their gender differences as resulting from different expectations for aggressive behavior considered appropriate for boys and girls in America. Present findings for the United States indicate that this pattern has now changed in the direction of more comparable effects occurring for the two sexes. In the current set of United States data, for example, the relation between violent television viewing and aggression is as strong for girls as it is for boys. In the present set of Australian data, boys and girls showed violence viewing effects, but there are some indications that Australian children lie closer to the United States children of the 1960s than to the United States children of the present. These gender differences were observed in Finland (see chapter 4) as well.

Sociologists and psychologists have written much at a theoretical level about changes in sex-role socialization in Western European societies including both Australia and the United States. General trends indicate that differences between the sex roles of boys and girls are diminishing as women generally become more assertive. There is evidence, for example, of changing sex roles for females within the Australian family as women take a more important position in the work force (Bryson, 1974). Thus, women are presenting more aggressive and competitive female role models for their children. Such modeling influences may help to explain the data. But another possibility that should be checked empirically is that American television as a whole may actually be supplying more aggressive female role models for girls in the United States than in Australia.

The final point to be made here relates to the interpretation of effects found for both sexes in Australia. It appears that Australian society is not as violent as American society (see chapter 1). Australian males are reported to be encouraged to behave aggressively and are socialized in ways that facilitate risk-taking, which may lead to aggression (Grabosky, 1983), but crimes against persons are not compellingly on the increase though criminal offences are generally rising. Further, crimes involving aggression against others are increasing more for males than they are for females. Interpreting these data in relation to the content shown on TV, it seems clear that Australian television presents a level of aggression to viewers that is considerably out of phase, as it were, with viewers' real-life environments. The association between TV violence and aggression that is evident may not be strong for boys, and especially not for girls, because the external world of Australian children does not match the reality constructed on television. Even in the United States the level of aggression presented on the TV screen is an over-exaggeration of most viewers' real-life environment (Gerbner et al., 1980) but probably less so than in Australia.

The Prediction of Aggression

It is very difficult in an observational field study to produce conclusive evidence to confirm a causal connection between related events. Television is selectively used by people who hold certain types of beliefs and the possibility of a causal connection between violent television viewing and aggression depends integrally on isolation of the relevant variables which mediate that relationship. Present data did not indicate that a relation exists in Australia between children's early television violence viewing and the level of their aggression 3 years later. Regression analyses applied to the Australian data failed to provide evidence for a causal connection over time. Results in this respect were quite different from the data collected from the United States children, Finnish children, Polish children, and Israeli (city) children. Generally speaking, data from these other countries suggest the association is bidirectional, with higher TV violence viewers behaving more aggressively and more aggressive children watching more TV violence. On the other hand, the weak longitudinal relations in Australia are similar to the pattern reported by Wiegman, Baarda, and Kuttschreuter (1984) for a parallel study in The Netherlands. It is perhaps important in this respect to note the relatively close association between violence viewing and aggression that occurred for the 10 most aggressive Australian boys. Australian culture may not be a sufficiently aggressive culture to reinforce the impact of television violence viewing among the general child population over a considerable period of time. This is not to say that changes in Australian society cannot occur that would facilitate more enduring effects. At the moment, however, effects appear to illustrate influences that are temporary, not permanent in their nature. Correlations for Australian children exist only at synchronous points in time.

One of the most salient features of the Australian data is the relatively high contribution of parent variables as opposed to child variables to the prediction of aggression 3 years later. Tables 6.6 and 6.7 illustrate these effects. As in most other countries, parents' use of physical punishment and/or rejection of the child was reliably linked to child aggression. However, these effects were stronger in Australia and subsumed any effects of the measured child variables. That rejection and punishment are predictors of aggression is entirely consistent with findings in the general literature. Sears, Maccoby, and Levin (1957), Eron, Walder, and Lefkowitz (1971), Lefkowitz et al. (1977), McCord, McCord, and Howard (1961), and Olweus (1980), for example, highlight the same finding. Severe parental rejection and punishment are important aspects of child-rearing practice that are both a response to child aggression and a promoter of the development of aggression. The current data suggested that in Australia punishment is more a response to aggression whereas rejection (at least for boys) is more an instigator of aggression.

The link between parental violence viewing and later aggression in children is a result requiring closer scrutiny. More research into the variables associated with parental violence viewing is needed before the issue can be clarified. Nevertheless, some comment seems possible. In the Lefkowitz et al. (1977) study, young adults (18 year olds) who viewed high levels of television violence saw this violence as more realistic than those who viewed low levels. This lends some support to the notion that adults with high levels of television violence viewing may be more accepting of violence as a legitimate means of attaining social ends and thus may be more accepting of their children's aggression toward peers than parents with low levels of television violence viewing. Also relevant is the evidence reviewed by Lagerspetz and Viemero (this volume). Data show that parents of children who are aggressive watch more TV than the parents of children who are non-aggressive. Further, parents who become absorbed and influenced by the world on television may develop unrealistic expectations of their children, and their interactions with them may suffer as a result.

One can only speculate at this stage about the influence of parent variables in mediating television violence effects for children. Nevertheless, it would seem fruitful in future work to concentrate on characteristics of the child's environment such as parents' interactions with their chidren. Definite outcomes may be triggered by particular parent behavior in association with specific child characteristics. Moreover, there are clear implications in these data (see Table 6.6) that parent influences are different for the two sexes.

Methodological Limitations

The validity of any set of data critically depends on the accuracy of the methods used to study the phenomena. It is instructive, therefore, to comment briefly on some of the methodological factors that may have limited the present study. (A more comprehensive discussion of this issue appears in chapter 8.)

Young children in Australia had some difficulty with the testing materials, especially in grade 1 where testing was delayed for a short period of time until the author was confident that the protocols were understood (see Procedures description). Data showed that effects were not as pronounced in the younger cohort. Differences in the comprehension of material, therefore, might have been a relevant factor. Also, results indicated there was an appreciable cohort effect. Grade 3 overlapped in the current design for both cohorts. Though the testings were separated by 2 years, data for grade 3 in the younger cohort ought to have been comparable with data for grade 3 in the older cohort. But findings indicated there were substantial differences in results for the two samples. Similar effects occurred in other countries as well (e.g., Finland) although in the United States data, there was no evidence of a cohort effect. The reasons for these differences in the Australian data are not clear and probably relate to the lowered incidence of significant associations among variables for the younger cohort of children.

The longitudinal design used in this study had special strengths. It tracked children developmentally through time, and the advantage of this feature is illustrated by the association found between time of testing and strength of effects. Such a design, however, can suffer from instability in its measures. Aggression in this study was relatively stable, but other variables such as television violence viewing were not as reliable. For example, the correlation between aggression in grade 3 and grade 5 was .72 but the correlation between violence viewing in the two grades was only .24.

There are other difficulties that characterize studies relying heavily on the self-reports of parents and children. Data collected in Australia (ABT, 1979a) have shown that results gathered from parents and children do not necessarily agree even when parents and children are asked the same questions. This raises the possibility that artifacts could be determining, in part, the nature of children's and/or parents' reports. The reasons for the discrepancy may relate to the social desirability of particular responses or perhaps to lack of knowledge on the parents' part about what their children do. Factors such as these may have influenced the nature of parents' reports in this study. Recall, however, that there was moderate agreement between parent and child reports in the United States (see chapter 3).

Finally, measurement of television violence in this study might have underestimated the extent of aggression portrayed on Australian television. Verbal aggression, for example, was not tapped at all. Emphasis was placed entirely on physical injury. The samples tested were relatively high in socioeconomic status, and high status was appreciably associated with lower aggression ratings for the male children who were tested ($r = -.21, N = 161, p < .01$). In a study that measured all aspects of aggression and that tapped samples from a broader range of socioeconomic strata, the nature of effects might well have been different. Any statement about the ideal research situation, however, must recognize the practical difficulty of realizing one's well founded aims. No clear objective measure exists, for instance, to measure verbal assault on television.

CONCLUSION AND POLICY IMPLICATIONS

In conclusion, results indicate that there is a relationship between television violence viewing and child aggression among Australian children, but the association seems to involve a range of child variables including age, sex, aggressive fantasy, judged realism, identification with TV characters (especially male), and preference for male activities. All these variables, for example, were appreciably related not only to peer-nominated aggression but to TV violence viewing as well. The pattern of correlates is similar to those found in many of the countries participating in this study. However, in Australia parent variables including parent TV habits seem to play a more important role in determining child aggression than child variables. Aside from earlier aggression, the best predictors of later aggression in Australian children were parent–child rearing behaviors.

In one other major respect, the results in Australia are somewhat distinct. Unlike the United States, Finland, Poland, and Israel, future aggression could not be predicted from children's TV violence viewing 3 years earlier in Australia. Thus, the correlation between TV violence viewing and aggression clearly does not seem to be due to any direct causal effect as far as Australian children are concerned. Data imply a definite role for fantasy in encouraging or facilitating aggressive response. Evidence is not inconsistent with the view that observing aggression stimulates aggressive fantasy and may, in turn, serve as a rehearsal for aggression. Certainly, data offer very little support for the catharsis view in which fantasy is said to alleviate tension and reduce aggressiveness (see also Milavsky, Kessler, Stipp, & Rubens, 1982).

Australian society does not appear to be an especially aggressive society, though some would argue to the contrary. Thus it is difficult to know whether the time-dependent association between television violence viewing and aggression observed in Australia implies a sensitive stage in the child's development or a relative impermanence of effect in a country where reality fails to match the aggressive world portrayed on the television screen. It seems plausible, however, to argue that Australia may arrive at a point in time where the impact of televised aggression on children will be more enduring because its rising crime rate and recorded instances of aggression may make the world on TV more akin to the world they know away from the television screen. The family unit is strong in Australia (Royal Commission on Human Relationships, 1977) and it seems plausible to suggest that parent variables will continue to play an important role in mediating effects more strongly in this country than in others where the family unit may be weaker. Further research in Australia should take care to focus on both child and parent influences.

It is often difficult to draw policy recommendations from research data. Nevertheless, sufficient data are in hand on TV viewing and it is enough of a general pastime in Australia to suggest that some policy guidelines should be contemplated. This is particularly important because children's aggression was as strongly related to regularity of viewing as it was to violence viewing alone. Outright censorship is not a viable option, but it is possible to envisage some reduction in the amount of violence that is portrayed on this country's television screens. Constructive programming seems the most tenable course of action. Television producers ought to be expected to adopt self-restraint in their depiction of violence and aggression, to refrain from exploiting viewers by irresponsible portrayal of actual aggression, and to develop a broader range of programs that will both entertain and facilitate the adoption of constructive values and attitudes. Researchers can play an important role in achieving these objectives. Social scientists, for example, can consult with media professionals to develop programs that are especially suited for viewing by children and that reinforce less sex-role stereotyped behavior. Detailed content analysis of aggression depicted in current programming also ought to be conducted regularly (as it is now in New Zealand) so that the level of violence viewing can be monitored closely. That some of these goals and objectives are being recognized and pursued is indicated by the fact that the Australian Broadcasting Tribunal has instituted a special committee to develop policy recommendations that relate to children's television programming (see ABT Report, 1979b). The formation of such a committee represents a constructive and useful attempt to come to grips with the potential impact of the medium. Ultimately, the aim of the Children's Program Committee (1979) is to foster the creation of television programs that "speak specifically and significantly to the real needs and interests of children at different developmental stages" (p. 1). As argued elsewhere (Sheehan, 1983), data from the present study indicate that the cognitive and social developmental stage a child has reached may well be important in determining some of the more negative effects of television viewing.

ACKNOWLEDGMENT

This research was supported by funds made available by the Australian Research Grants Scheme through a grant to the author, and by the National Institute of Mental Health (USA) through grant MH-31886 to L. R. Huesmann at the University of Illinois at Chicago. Special thanks are due to the parents and children participating in the project who gave generously of their time over the 3 years of testing, and to all the principals and teachers who also gave their support and encouragement. The author wishes to thank Valerie Burns, Edna Crassini, Graham Jamieson, Kevin McConkey, Judith Minto, and Barbara Rigsby for their valued help. Thanks are further due to the Werner Reimers Stifftung, Bad Homburg, Germany for its support in the final drafting of this chapter.

REFERENCES

Australian Broadcasting Tribunal. (1979a). *Research report. Television and children—Australia 1977/1978.* Canberra: Australian Government Publishing Service.

Australian Broadcasting Tribunal. (1979b). *Annual report: 1978-1979.* Canberra: Australian Government Publishing Service.

Australian Broadcasting Tribunal. (1980). *Television in Australia: Its history through the ratings. Research report.* Canberra: Australian Government Publishing Service.

Australian Broadcasting Tribunal. (1983). *Annual Report: 1982-1983.* Canberra: Australian Government Publishing Service.

Australian Broadcasting Tribunal. (1984). *Annual report: 1983-1984.* Canberra: Australian Government Publishing Service.

Biles, D. (Ed.). (1977). *Crime and justice in Australia.* Canberra: Australian Institute of Criminology.

Broom, L., & Lancaster-Jones, F. (1976). *Opportunity and attainment in Australia.* Canberra: Australian National University Press.

Bryson, L. (1974). Men's work and women's work: Occupation and family orientation. In M. Dawson (Ed.), *Families: Australian studies of changing relationships within the family and between the family and society* (pp. 19-23). Canberra: Australian and New Zealand Association for the Advancement of Science.

Children's Program Committee. (1979). *Recommendations to the Australian Broadcasting Tribunal on children's programs.* Communication of Australian Broadcasting Tribunal, North Sydney.

Comstock, G., Chaffee, S., Katzman, N., McCombs, M., & Roberts, D. (1978). *Television and human behavior.* New York: Columbia University Press.

Conway, B. (1978). *Land of the long weekend.* Melbourne: Sun Books.

Dixon, M. (1976). *The real Matilda: Woman and identity in Australia, 1788 to 1975.* Ringwood, Vic.: Penguin Press.

Edgar, P. (1975). *Growing up feminine: The part played by schools and the mass media.* Woden, ACT: Curriculum Development Centre.

Edgar, P. (1977a). *Children and screen violence.* St. Lucia: University of Queensland Press.

Edgar, P. (1977b). Families without television. *Journal of Communication, 27,* 73-77.

Edgar, P. (1983). *Children and television policy implications.* Melbourne, Vic.: Australian Children's Television Foundation.

Eron, L. D., Walder, L. O., & Lefkowitz, M. M. (1971). *Learning of aggression in children.* Boston: Little, Brown.

Evatt, P. (1980). *Parental communication style as related to children's television behavior.* Honours Dissertation, University of Queensland.

Gerbner, G. (1972). Violence in television drama: Trends and symbolic functions. In G. A. Comstock, & E. A. Rubinstein (Eds.), *Television and social behavior. Vol. 1. Media content and control* (pp. 28-187). Washington, DC: U.S. Government Printing Office.

Gerbner, G., Gross, L., Morgan, M., & Signorielli, N. (1980). *Violence Profile No. 11: Trends in network television drama and viewer conceptions of social reality, 1967-1979.* University of Pennsylvania, Philadelphia.

Goldstein, A. P., & Segall, M. H. (1983). *Aggression in global perspective.* New York: Pergamon.

Grabosky, P. (1983). How violent is Australia? *Australian Society, 2,* 38-41.

Greenberg, B. S., & Reeves, B. (1976). Children and the perceived reality of television. *Journal of Social Issues, 32,* 86-97.

Haines, H. (1983). *Violence on television: A report on the Mental Health Foundation's Media Watch Survey.* Auckland, New Zealand: Mental Health Foundation.

Halloran, J. D., & Croll, P. (1972). Television programs in Great Britain: Content and control. In G. A. Comstock & E. A. Rubinstein (Eds.), *Television and social behavior, Vol. 1. Media content and control* (pp. 415-492). Washington, DC: U.S. Government Printing Office.

Henderson, R. F., Harcourt, A., & Harper, R. J. A. (1970). *People in poverty: A Melbourne survey.* Melbourne, Vic.: Cheshire.

Holman, J., & Braithwaite, V. A. (1982). Parental lifestyles and children's television viewing. *Australian Journal of Psychology, 34,* 375-382.

Horne, D. (1965). *The lucky country: Australia today.* Baltimore, MD: Penguin Books.

Huesmann, L. R. (1982). Television violence and aggressive behavior. In D. Pearl, L. Bouthilet, & J. Lazar (Eds.), *Television and behavior: Ten years of scientific progress and implications for the eighties* (pp. 126-137). Rockville, MD: U.S. Department of Health and Human Services.

Huesmann, L. R., & Eron, L. D. (1984). Cognitive processes and the persistence of aggressive behavior. *Aggressive Behavior, 10,* 243-251.

Iwao,S., de Soola Pool, I., & Hajiwana, S. (1981). Japanese and US Media: Some cross cultural insights into TV violence, *Journal of Communication, 35,* 28-36.

Kippax, S., & Murray, J. P. (1977). Using television programme content and need gratification. *Politics, 12,* 56-69.

Kippax, S., & Murray, J. P. (1980). Using the mass media: Need gratification and perceived utility. *Communication Research, 7,* 335-360.

King, J. (1978). *Waltzing materialism.* Sydney: Harper & Row.

Kohlberg, L., & Ullian, D. Z. (1974). Stages in the development of psychosexual concepts and attitudes. In R. C. Friedman, R. M., Richart, & R. L. Van de Wiele, (Eds.), *Sex differences in behavior.* New York: Wiley.

Langham, J., & Stewart, W. (1981). Television viewing habits and other characteristics of normally aggressive and nonaggressive children. *Australian Psychologist, 16,* 123-133.

Lefkowitz, M. M., Eron, L. D., Walder, L. O., & Huesmann, L. R. (1977). *Growing up to be violent: A longitudinal study of the development of aggression.* New York: Pergamon Press.

Lovibond, S. H. (1967). The effects of media stressing crime and violence upon children's attitudes. *Social Problems, 15,* 91-100.

McCann, T. E., & Sheehan, P. W. (1985). Violence content in Australian television. *Australian Psychologist, 20,* 33-42.

McCord, W., McCord, J. & Howard, A. (1961). Family correlates of aggression in nondelinquent male children. *Journal of Abnormal Psychology, 62,* 79-93.

McGregor, C. (1966). *Profile of Australia.* Ringwood, Vic.: Penguin Books.

Milavsky, J. R., Kessler, R. C., Stipp, H. H., & Rubens, W. S. (1982). *Television and aggression: A panel study.* New York: Academic Press.

Mischel, W. (1966). A social learning view of sex differences in behavior. In E. E. Maccoby (Ed.), *The development of sex differences.* (pp. 56-82). Stanford, CA: Stanford University Press.

Mukherjee, S. K. (1981). *Crime trends in twentieth-century Australia.* Sydney: George Allen & Unwin.

Murray, J. P. (1980). *Television and youth: 25 years of research and controversy.* Stanford, WA: Boy's Town Center for the Study of Youth Development.

Murray, J. P., & Kippax, S. (1979). From the early window to the late night show: International trends in the study of television's impact on children and adults. In L. Berkowitz (Ed.), *Advances in experimental social psychology* (pp. 253-320). New York: Academic Press.

Naffin, N. (1981). Theorizing about female crime. In S. K. Mukherjee, & J. A. Scutt (Eds.), *Women and crime* (pp. 70-91). Sydney: George Allen & Unwin.

Noble, G. (1975). *Children in front of the small screen.* London: Constable.

Noble, G., & Sinclair, J. (1983). Normal and autistic children's interactions with Playschool and Sesame Street. *Regional Journal of Social Issues, 12,* 39-43.

Oeser, O. A., & Hammond, S. B. (1954). *Social structure and personality in a city.* London: Routledge, Kegan Paul.

Olweus, D. (1980). Familial determinants of aggressive behavior in adolescent boys: A causal analysis. *Developmental Psychology, 16,* 644-660.

Pingree, S., & Hawkins, R. (1981). US programs on Australian television. The cultivation effect, *Journal of Communication, 35,* 97–105.

Robinson, J. P., & Bachman, J. G. (1972). Television viewing habits and aggression. In G. A. Comstock, & E. A. Rubinstein (Eds.), *Television and social behavior. Vol. 3. Television and adolescent aggressiveness* (pp.372–382). Washington, DC: U.S. Government Printing Office.

Rogosa, D. (1980). A critique of cross-lagged correlation. *Psychological Bulletin, 88,* 245–258.

Royal Commission on Human Relationships. (1977). Volumes 1–5. Canberra: Australian Government Publishing Service.

Rubinstein, E. A. (1976). Television and the young viewer. *The American Scientist, 66,* 685–693.

Ruble, D. N., Balaban, T., & Cooper, J. (1981). Gender constancy and the effects of sex-typed televised toy commercials. *Child Development, 52,* 667–673.

Schramm, W., Lyle, J., & Parker, E. G. (1961). *Television in the lives of our children.* Stanford: Stanford University Press.

Sears, R. B., Maccoby, E. E., & Levin, H. (1957). *Patterns of childrearing.* New York: Harper & Rowe.

Senate Standing Committee on Education and the Arts. (1978). *Inquiry into the impact of television on the development and learning behavior of children.* Canberra: Australian Government Publishing Service.

Sheehan, P. W. (1983). Age trends and the correlates of children's television viewing. *Australian Journal of Psychology, 35,* 417–431.

Stewart, D. E. (1983). *The television family: A content analysis of the portrayal of family life in prime time television.* Melbourne, Vic.: Institute of Family Studies.

Tindall, K., & Reid, D. (1975). *Television's children.* Sydney: Sydney Teachers College.

Tindall, K., Reid, D., & Goodwin, N. (1977). *Television: 20th century cyclops.* Sydney: Sydney Teachers College.

Wiegman, O., Baarda, B., & Kuttschreuter, M. (1984). *The Dutch contribution to the cross-national study on television and aggression as well as prosocial behavior.* Paper presented at Conference on Role of Culture and the Media for the Development of Aggression, Bad Homburg, West Germany.

Wilson, P. R., & Brown, J. W. (1973). *Crime and the community.* St. Lucia: University of Queensland Press.

7 The Differential Effect of Observation of Violence on Kibbutz and City Children in Israel

Riva S. Bachrach
Kibbutz Child and Family Clinic, Tel-Aviv

INTRODUCTION

Aggression is a social act and as such is carried out within a group setting. Groups can either facilitate aggression or inhibit the expression of aggression. Regardless of which of the dominant theories of aggression is better in explaining human aggression, one must study the relation of group culture and structure to the incidence of aggression within the group. In particular, to understand the process through which interpersonal violence on television might stimulate violent behavior, one must understand how group structure promotes or inhibits the imitation of media violence.

The groups to which an individual belongs may affect both intragroup and intergroup aggression by that individual. War is a rather remarkable example of intergroup aggression where the group acts as a facilitator for an individual's aggression. Another social situation in which the group facilitates and stimulates aggression by releasing the individual from normative inhibition is the mob situation (e.g., Zimbardo, 1969). If one considers a crowd of anonymous or relatively anonymous people as a group, then the density of the crowd or group itself can be viewed as a stimulus to aggression (e.g., Freedman, Levy, Bachanan, & Price, 1972; Milgram & Toch, 1969). However, the theoretical explanation and the findings in regard to the crowding effect are not clear cut. Another theoretical mechanism by which the group may affect individual aggression involves diffusion of responsibility (e.g., Darley & Latane, 1968; Jaffe & Yinon, 1979; Jaffe, Shapir, & Yinon, 1981). Though they were conducted by several different researchers with various research paradigms, these studies are rather impressive in their unanimity of results.

When an individual is part of a group, that individual's perceived responsibility for group aggression is lower and that individual's aggression becomes greater and escalates faster than when that individual is alone.

The group can also act as an inhibitor of aggressive behavior. The group's power to inhibit, rather than facilitate aggression, lies in the power of the group to establish norms of behavior and enforce sanctions against deviate acts. National and ethnic groups are known to differ in the prescription of norms and in the reinforcement and punishment of aggressive acts. Jaffe et al. (1981) found rather remarkable differences among four ethnic groups in Israel in their tendency to react aggressively to a given situation. Although the differences in aggression machine scores obtained in individual settings were minimal, the differences in group settings were much larger. In the group settings, for example, Israelis of Georgian ethnic background behaved much more aggressively and felt much less responsible for their acts than Israelis of most other ethnic backgrounds.

Because groups can have such an important influence on human aggression, it is important to examine how the development of aggression in children differs from group to group. In this chapter, I examine the development of aggression in Israeli children living in two distinctly different environments, the kibbutz and the city. I particularly examine how development of aggression is related to social factors, cognitive factors, and the observation of violent behavior either in the child's actual daily environment or in the media to which the child is exposed.

Aggression in Israel

Israel as a society has been dealing with the phenomenon of aggression throughout its history, and, indeed, even before it came into existence as a state. Israel came into existence as a state because of a massive act of group aggression—the holocaust conducted against the Jewish people before and during World War II. Unfortunately, the establishment of the state of Israel did not terminate the necessity for the Israeli citizen to be concerned about group aggression. Over a period of years the people of Israel have had to fight desperately for the existence of their newly established state. For most Israelis, concerns about being aggressed against by other groups or aggressing as a group against others remain a part of daily life. As a matter of fact, during parts of the current study Israel was involved in a war in Lebanon. Thus, the basic existence of most people in Israel includes dealing with aggression daily both as victims and aggressors.

Landau and Beit-Hallahmi (1983) in their extensive chapter on the psycho-historical perspective of aggression in Israel suggest at least two possible ways in which the war situation in Israel affects internal aggression. "It may serve as a legitimized outlet for aggression, turning it outside the group, or it may serve as a stimulus or stressor, creating more internal aggression in the group, or both. It may reduce internal aggression by providing an outlet outside the system. It may increase aggression by making it more habitual or legitimate or by providing aggressive stimuli. It may increase aggression by affecting the whole social system negatively" (p. 263). In their historical, macro-level analysis of aggressive acts in the Jewish population in Israel during the period 1950–1980, they show (via various measures of crime statistics) first, that there has been a steady increase in violence and second, that there has been an increase in the public concern about aggression. However, with regard to the specific relation between war and internal aggression they found that "the high points of the continuing conflict, namely outright war, are followed by high levels of aggression within Israeli society" (p. 279). Thus, it does not seem as if external conflict serves an outlet or "catharsis" for aggression but rather as an instigator of individual aggression.

In another study, Landau (1984) compared crime statistics in several countries in the period between the mid 1960s and the end of the 70s. The findings are quite indicative of the fact that in all the countries (except India and Japan) there was an increase in the rate of offenses in the last decade, and in most countries this increase was of a large magnitude. Israel was one of the countries with the largest increases. Landau's explanation for this increase of violence and aggression is that it followed from increases in social stressors (as measured by inflation rate and the war situation) and from the parallel weakening of the family as a social support system. The importance of cultural factors in violence statistics is apparent in the case of Japan. Unlike Israel and the other western countries where social stress and weakening of the family social support system were followed by increases in crime rates, in Japan most measures of aggression showed a decrease over the same period. This decrease occurred in spite of increasing inflation and weakening of the family support system. Landau concludes that cultural norms, values, and standards, as well as the level of homogeneity and cohesiveness of the society, are significant mediating factors in the relation between social stress and expressions of violence.

The Kibbutz Society in Israel

The case of Japan leads us to expect similar cultural and group control over the expression of violence in the kibbutz society in Israel. The kibbutz setting, its history and ideology have been very well described by Leon (1969). The kibbutz is a cooperative organization in which the whole community is a central economic unit. All real property is community property. The kibbutz provides or pays for each individual's basic needs including food, housing, clothing, health care, education, and recreation. Disposable income beyond basic needs is equivalent for each kibbutz member. Each member works at whatever jobs best match his or her personal preferences and the kibbutz's needs. Until the 1960s most of the output of the kibbutzim were agricultural products. More recently they have developed light industries. The size of kibbutzim ranges from perhaps 40 families to 200 families. Children born into a kibbutz almost automatically become members; however, others must be accepted by a vote of the membership. In 1980 there were 253 kibbutz communities in Israel with a population of 110,000 or about 3.3% of the Israeli population. These kibbutzim hold 33% of all cultivated land and produce 40% of the food supplies in Israel.

The members of the kibbutz community live in close proximity both physically and psychologically. They form a homogeneous group with great intradependency among its members. Most kibbutzim in Israel have reached a heightened standard of living in terms of quality of life and level of education of their members. Demographically, they are considered to be parallel to the upper middle class in western urban societies. Within the context of Israeli society, which is remarkably heterogenous in its ethnic background, the kibbutzim are rather homogeneous. Most kibbutz members are of East European decent, or are Israeli born. Most kibbutzim were formed and developed by socialistic political parties. Hence, the attitudes and political ideology of most kibbutz members are also relatively homogeneous.

Child Rearing in the Kibbutz

Kibbutz structure and life, particularly as it pertains to the development and socialization of children, have been well documented in several books (e.g., Bettelheim, 1969; Rabin & Beit-Hallahmi, 1982; Spiro, 1958). The kibbutzim from which samples of children were studied in the current investigation belong to the most conservative, leftist group of kibbutzim (*Hashomer-Ha'tza'ir*). By conservative I mean that there is more emphasis on the communal sharing of property and more emphasis on ideology and remaining true to the original kibbutz concept. Thus, in these kibbutzim all children sleep communally, whereas in some other kibbutzim children now sleep in their parents' family quarters.

For the child, the central factor of kibbutz life is the domination of the peer group. Beginning in infancy, the baby is placed in the "infant house" until it is about 1-year-old. The house is large with several sleeping rooms and communal areas. In each room there are two to four babies. In the first 9 months the mother comes to feed her baby and take care of it according to its needs. However, many of the babies' needs are taken care of by a specialist child caretaker called the *metapelet*. Thus, from the beginning of its life the baby is placed in a peer-group setting and other significant figures besides its parents are very much involved with him or her. At about 12 months, groups of four to six children are formed and are moved to the "toddler" house. There, the mother's involvement is reduced greatly, and the metapelet takes over most responsibilities for the socialization of the child (self-feeding, toilet training, etc.). The child remains in this toddler group until the age of 3 or 4. Then, several toddler groups are joined together into a pre-kindergarten unit. Its size depends on the size of the kibbutz and the rate of birth during the relevant years. The kindergarten group generally consists of 10 to 20 children. They have both a teacher and one or two metapelet. They share with their peers learning activities, recreation, eating, sleeping, and all other parts of their lives except for 4 hours during the afternoon in which they visit with their parents. During the kindergarten years there is an emphasis on group activities, working habits, mutual aid, discipline, and social interaction with the group. After kindergarten, at the age of 6 or 7, they enter elementary school, which is called the "children's society." During elementary school, each age group lives in its own house that also contains its classroom. Again, two to four children share a sleeping room, and all activities are done communally. The group thus develops an entity of its own that Rabin and Beit-Hallahmi (1982) termed the *group conscience*. "Any deviation of the individual from proper behavior and any neglected duty, whether work or academic, comes immediately to the attention of the rest of the group . . . the very knowledge of accountability becomes a strong deterrent to deviant behavior" (p. 29). Several researchers (e.g., Devereux, Shouval, Bronfenbrenner, Rodgers, Kav-vanaki, Kiely, & Karson, 1974) have pointed out that both the peer group and the metapelet are perceived by the children as agents of discipline and disapproval rather than supportive figures.

Daily Life for the Kibbutz and City Child

Child rearing in urban areas in Israel is very similar to child rearing in the western societies from which the Israeli population has emigrated. The extensive differences between the structure of the lives of kibbutz-raised and city-raised children in Israel have been well documented elsewhere (Kaffman, 1972; Rabin & Beit-Hallahmi, 1982) and are only briefly summarized here.

The city children typically attend school 6 days a week from 8 a.m. to noon or 1 p.m. The rest of their time is spent at home or in activities with their peers. In the majority of Israeli homes, women work outside the home, and the child is often supervised in the afternoon by an older sibling, neighbor, or hired caretaker. However, because the main meal of the day is generally taken at noontime in Israel, many working mothers do come home and see the child at that time. In the evening, the family will eat a small meal, generally after 7 p.m. when the shops have closed. City schools usually have relatively large classes (e.g., 40 children) with a substantial turnover from year to year of both children and teachers. Although children may form strong bonds with individual peers, there is by no means the general group cohesiveness and tightly knit peer bonds that exist among kibbutz children.

A kibbutz-raised child will live mostly with the same peers from birth through the end of high school. The size of the same-age peer group or class is likely to be closer to 15 than 40. Because children are constantly taught that one must always consider the good of the group, it is not surprising that a closely bonded peer group emerges in which prosocial behavior is emphasized. The kibbutz-raised child's daily schedule during the elementary school years will be somewhat different from the city child's. After waking at about 6:30 a.m. the children immediately go to the classroom that is in the same building as the sleeping and dining rooms. After about an hour of instruction, breakfast will be taken. Formal classroom instruction generally ends by noon when the main meal is eaten, again as a group. Often a break from classes will be taken during the morning for the children to work on kibbutz projects. After the mid-day meal, the children will spend time in smaller groups on sports, crafts, and other extracurricular activities as well as resting in their sleeping rooms. About 4:30 p.m., the children go to their parents' quarters where they may eat snacks, do homework, watch television, talk, and play with their parents, siblings, and friends. Around 7 p.m. the children would eat the evening meal with their parents either in the kibbutz dining hall or in the parents' quarters. After dinner they return to their children's house where they may do homework, read, or have group meetings and activities. Once or twice a week they may watch TV as a group at this time. By 9 p.m. they would be going to sleep.

Aggression in the City and Kibbutz Environments

Although violence in Israel is an ever-present daily threat for most people, children seldom see violent acts in person. Terrorism and war affect everyone, but more often indirectly rather than directly. Still, crime and concern about crime have generally been increasing in Israel over the last decade (Landau & Beit-Hallahmi, 1982). However, the crime rates in kibbutz society remain much lower than in the city environment. For example, between 1969 and 1975 over 34,500 juveniles earned police records. Of these, only 250 or about 0.7% were kibbutz children, though kibbutz children comprise about 3% of the population (Landau, personal communication, March 1984). According to clinical archives (Kaffman, 1965), the rates of cases of psychopathic behavior are also significantly lower in the kibbutz population than in the city population. Thus, it seems fair to conclude that kibbutz children are exposed to less interpersonal violence in their environment than are city children. In the next section we argue that the same can be said about exposure to violence in the media. At the same time there has been increased concern among kibbutz members as among other members of Israeli society about the possibility of becoming a victim of a crime. One of the factors contributing to this concern may be due to the expansion of kibbutz society. In the last decade many more non-kibbutz people visit the kibbutz daily, and thus there is the increased possibility for the kibbutz member to be a victim of a crime by a non-kibbutz member. Thus, the concerns of kibbutz members about crime are almost entirely externally directed.

Although little data exist comparing aggressive behavior in kibbutz and city children, clinical observations and case studies suggest that aggressive behavior is less frequent among kibbutz children. Personal observations during 6 years of clinical work with kibbutz and city children have led me to adopt the following assumptions. Up to the first or second grade (e.g., 7 to 8 years of age) there seems to be an equal or perhaps a heightened level of interpersonal aggression in the kibbutz youngsters compared with the city children. However, from the second grade on, one must be impressed with the striking differences between the level of interpersonal aggression one can observe in the city schoolyard and the kibbutz play areas. This difference is apparent even when one compares the kibbutz children with children from urban schools having comparable socioeconomic composition. Similarly, to the visiting observer, the classroom behavior is distinctly different in the two environments in terms of noise level, hitting, speaking up rudely, and other types of inappropriate and at least partially aggressive behaviors. Of course, a confounding factor in this last observation must be the differential size of the two classrooms. The size of a kibbutz class is likely to be closer to 15 than the 40 typically found in the city classroom. In addition, the kibbutz classroom is generally much larger in space than the city classroom; so crowding is not a problem at all. Thus, from elementary school on, the visitor must be impressesd with the rather increased level of aggression and acting out behavior observed in city schools in contrast with a marked reduction in interpersonal aggression observed in kibbutz schools.

Comparative research of psychopathology among kibbutz and city children also supports the thesis that deviant and predictably aggressive behavior are less frequent among kibbutz children. In two separate studies Kaffman (1965, 1972) found that in spite of similar trends and distributions of diagnosis of psychopathology in city and kibbutz children, one striking difference existed — there was an extremely low incidence of antisocial personality disorders among kibbutz children. Moreover, a clinical survey of referred kibbutz children (Kaffman, 1972) showed that among the unsocial type of reactive behavior disorders, a gradual decline occurs in the frequency and intensity of aggressive symptoms as age increases in kibbutz children. "The significant difference in the incidence of psychopathic disturbances appears to be determined by diverse factors, the most important of them being the kibbutz child's identification with the heightened . . . groups standards regarding adequate social behavior, mutual help and moral values" (Kaffman, 1965, p. 519). Antisocial behavior and antisocial ideas are rejected by the kibbutz social group. The small size of the children's peer group and the intensified community concern about the children provide for closer control of antisocial behavior than in the overcrowded urban schools. Moreover, there are no socially deprived adult or juvenile groups in the kibbutz with whom the child can identify, and there is no practical possibility of the child joining an "external" gang.

Because of the structure of kibbutz life, peers tend to replace parents and educators as interpreters and enforcers of the kibbutz moral code. Parents tend to be rather permissive and tolerant of "normal" impulsive behavior, including aggression. After all, when one can only interact with one's child 3–4 hours a day during what is called the "pleasure time" in the afternoon, it is difficult for a parent to be other than permissive. These parental attitudes are most apparent with younger children. Kaffman (1972) points to another important factor in the daily activity of the kibbutz youngster that could explain why aggression might decrease as a child grows older. The kibbutz child is assigned productive work for the kibbutz at a very early age (e.g., from first grade on). These work assignments increase gradually both in allocated time and in involvement with various branches of the kibbutz as the child grows older. The work experience provides a very important channel for achievement that enables a child to obtain social prestige. This is important because it provides an alternative mode of achievement as a legitimate activity for children who are having difficulty achieving in classrooms and have become frustrated.

Numerous studies have investigated social behavior and personality factors in kibbutz and city children. However, some are more relevant than others to the development of aggression and how the observation of violence in the environment or the media may affect the development of aggression. Perhaps the most salient finding is that the similarities among the kibbutz born, *moshav*[1] born, and city children are more numerous than the differences (e.g., Kaffman, 1965; Nevo, 1977: Rabin & Beit-Hallahmi, 1982). Few researchers talk seriously any more about the "kibbutznick personality." However, among the numerous personality characteristics and behaviors that have been studied, some differences between the kibbutz and city populations that seem relevant have been found. Rabin, in his early study (1965) using paper and pencil measures, found some differences among adolescents of kibbutz and moshav environments. Kibbutz adolescents showed greater

---

[1]*Moshav* is another form of rural settlement in Israel that is a cooperative organization with limited liability for members. There is considerable amount of mutual solidarity as well as cooperative economic enterprise, but the family is the basic economic and social unit as in the cities. However, in terms of population size, the moshav is similar to the kibbutz.

control and sublimation of primitive drives. Moshav adolescents tended to fantasize about aggression more often and assume the role of aggressor whereas the kibbutz adolescents saw themselves more often as victims of aggression. Shapira (1976) found that children ages 4 to 11 were less competitive in the kibbutz than in the city environment. Competitive behavior can be seen as a sublimated form of aggressive behavior. Excessive competitive behavior is also incompatible with cooperative behavior. In a different study comparing 7 to 9 year olds from four cultural settings, the United States, West Germany, an Israeli city, and Israeli kibbutz (Madsen & Shapira, 1977), Israeli kibbutz children were found to be significantly less competitive than any of the other children. In a still different study using the same experimental paradigm, Shapira and Madsen (1974) found that not only were kibbutz children more cooperative, but they were also more influenced by their peer group. They gave more to the group even under conditions in which the group-oriented response was detrimental to them.

Altruistic behavior is also incompatible with aggressive behavior (Eron & Huesmann, 1984). Bizman, Yinon, Mivtzari, and Shavit (1978) studied verbal and behavioral altruism in kindergarteners. However, they found no difference between city and kibbutz children. Also, Bar-Tal, Raviv, and Shavit (1981) found no difference between 6- to 11-year-old children of the kibbutz and city in helping behavior or motives for helping behavior. Moral development and especially internality may also be associated with the development of aggression. Ziv, Shulman, and Schleifer (1979) found that in spite of the same moral judgment level, kibbutz children expressed less fear and were less punitive toward a transgression than were city children. They suggest that this difference is due to the permissiveness of kibbutz parents. A previous study (Devereux et al., 1974) confirmed that kibbutz children generally expect a more positive relation with their parents and view them as more permissive and less punitive than do city children.

To summarize, it appears that the level of interpersonal aggression in kibbutz children is somewhat less than in city children particularly after the early elementary grades. Also, alternative behaviors that are incompatible with aggression such as cooperation, joint projects and work habits seem to be greater in kibbutz children and to increase with age.

Aggression and the Observation of Violence in Israel

The role of group structure in the child's social environment may be particularly important in explaining the effect of media and environmental violence on the development of aggression in the child. As described in the introduction to this book, it is by now well established that in most western countries children who view more violence (either through the media or in person) are more aggressive. The reasons for this relation are more controversial. Observational learning in which the child encodes aggressive strategies viewed in the media and later imitates them may be an important process. So may attitude change engendered by continuous observation of aggression. So may arousal and desensitization of arousal caused by continuous viewing of highly stimulating television. Regardless of the process, however, it seems likely that group structure and social environment may exacerbate or mitigate the effect. For example, Huesmann, Lagerspetz, and Eron (1984) have suggested that changes in the effects of media violence on girls in the United States over the past 10 years have resulted from changing norms about the appropriateness of aggressive behavior in females. Similarly, one explanation offered in other chapters in this book for differences between countries (e.g., Finland and the United States) has involved the differing socialization practices and norms that females are subjected to in the different countries.

Although in Israel there may be numerous occurrences of interpersonal violence in the general society, the opportunities for children to observe such violence are very limited, particularly in the kibbutz society. We have already documented that the occurrence of interpersonal violence between adults in the kibbutz society is rare. We have also suggested that systematized violence by "gangs" of children or other types of group violence with which a child could identify do not occur, particularly in the kibbutz society. Thus, a child's major opportunities for the observation of aggression both in the city environment and in the kibbutz may be through the medium of television.

Television Programming in Israel

Television programming in Israel is controlled by the government just as it is in Poland and Finland, and its introduction is relatively recent, having started in 1968. There is only one channel, with a limited selection of programs (partially because of government controls). About 60% of the programs are of foreign origin, mostly from the United States and the United Kingdom. As in Finland, the foreign programs are shown with the original soundtrack and subtitles in Hebrew rather than having the soundtrack dubbed. Many Israeli households can also receive Jordanian TV. However, the programming on Jordanian TV is also censored and contains many similar imported programs. Furthermore, because the subtitles are in Arabic and most young Israeli children cannot read them, it is doubtful that Jordanian TV has much impact on Israeli children.

Israeli television broadcasting is highly structured according to the time of day. Throughout the morning, educational programs (e.g., math, English, arts, and early education programs) are broadcast. These shows are intended mostly for children. Then from noon until 3 p.m. television is devoted entirely to "the open university" programs. Some days there may be no television at this time. From 3 p.m. to 6:30 p.m. mainly children's programs are broadcast. These may include educational programs similar to *Sesame Street*, children's entertainment programs, including cartoons which may be violent, or adult programs considered particularly appropriate for children (e.g., *Different Strokes*). From 6:30 p.m. to 8 p.m. Arabic speaking programs are broadcast. Any children's shows, broadcast during this time, have subtitles in Hebrew. Generally, none of these shows will contain dramatic violence. From 8 to 9 p.m. family-oriented programs such as quiz shows, documentaries, family dramas (e.g., *Upstairs Downstairs*) or comedies (e.g., *Love Boat*) are shown. At 9 p.m. the national news is broadcast, consisting mostly of visuals of the newscasters and seldom containing visual portrayals of violence. Of course, in content the news on Israeli television often contains reports of severe violence. After the news, from 9:30 to 10 or 10:30 the typical program would be a documentary, either political or scientific and educational. Finally, from 10 or 10:30 until midnight adult dramas are broadcast that may at times include extensive violence. For example, the *Professionals* and *Charlies Angels* were shown in this time period during the course of the study. More typical and frequent are other dramas with less explicit violence such as *Dallas*, which is also shown in this time period. The broadcasting day closes with the final news shortly after midnight. On Saturdays in Israel there is no broadcasting at all before sunset, and on Friday afternoons broadcasting is reduced with no programming from 3 to 6:30 p.m.

Children's Responses to War Movies

When studying the relation between television violence and the development of aggression in a country such as Israel one cannot limit oneself to regular programs. In particular, one must consider the effect of televised war films on children. In the most important study in Israel of the effect of war films on children, Adoni and Cohen (1979) exposed third, fifth, and seventh grade children to war films from the TV archives 2 years after the 1983 Yom Kippur war. Two findings are particularly relevant to the current study. First, although war movies stimulate emotional arousal in all children, the arousal was less among children who had discussed the movies with their parents. Second, children who were exposed to the war movie with the soundtrack of battle sounds experienced more fear and arousal than those children who were exposed to the movie with the soundtrack consisting of an explanation by a narrator. These results are consistent with some previous studies that have shown that television viewing with a parent present reduces the effects of television (Hicks, 1968) and intervention studies that have shown that explanations of television violence reduces effects on children (Huesmann, Eron, Klein, Brice, & Fischer, 1983).

Exposure to television is quite different for children living in the city and those raised on the kibbutz. The differing structure of their daily lives, as previously documented, strongly affects their access to television. Whereas the city child has his or her afternoons relatively free of required activities and therefore can spend that time watching television, the kibbutz child is occupied until the parental visiting time at 4:30 p.m. During the kibbutz child's visit with his or her parents, the child may watch television. However, when the child returns to his or her peer group after the evening meal, it would be only rarely that more television would be watched. For the city child, television viewing all evening is possible if the parents' consent. Because most seriously violent programs are on late at night, the kibbutz child's access to such programs is far more limited than the city child's. Furthermore, it is much more likely that the kibbutz child would observe any such program with a group of his or her peers and the metapelet. This substantial difference between the potential exposure to television violence of kibbutz and city children coupled with the strong group structure and social bonds of the kibbutz child's society lead to the hypothesis that the usual relation between television violence viewing and the development of aggression in children should not pertain among kibbutz raised children.

In the current study, the development of aggressive behavior is compared between kibbutz and city children in Israel with particular attention directed at how any relation between the observation of media violence and overt aggression emerges in the kibbutz population. Specifically, attention is paid to how the group's structure and the social relations of the kibbutz society affect the media violence — aggression relation and affect the development of aggression in general.

METHOD

Subjects

The subjects in the city sample were children in the first and third grades at two public schools in Ra'anana, Israel. Ra'anana is a small town in the Sharon District — 15 kilometers north of Tel-Aviv. The population consists mostly of upper middle-class families, and many of the fathers and mothers work in Tel-Aviv. The sample consisted of one class of third-graders in both schools and one class of first-graders in one school. This gave us 39 first-graders (19 boys and 20 girls) and 73 third-graders (37 boys and 36 girls) in the original city sample.

The children in the kibbutz sample were residents of two kibbutzim located also north of Tel-Aviv in the Sharon District (Ma'abarot and Ein-Ha'Horesh). Both of these kibbutzim had been in existence for over 40 years, and both were established by the same socialistic political movement

(*Hashomer Hatzair*). The entire first and third grade in both kibbutzim were used, giving us a sample of 38 first-graders (16 boys and 22 girls) and 26 third-graders (12 boys and 14 girls). In addition, in one of the kibbutzim 10 second-graders were also studied (4 boys and 6 girls) because they were in the same class with the third-graders. It is common to split classes in kibbutz schools due to the small number of children in each settlement. Thus, a total of 186 children were studied in the original sample — 74 from kibbutz schools and 112 from city schools.

During the course of the study a number of children dropped out of the city sample; however, only one child (a girl) was lost from the kibbutz sample. Because it was easier to test entire classes, a substantial number of new subjects were added to the city sample in the second and third years. The first-grade classes in the city school were broken up after the first year, and the students were redistributed into two second-grade classes. Some were transferred to another school where they could not be tested. This was the greatest single cause of subject attrition in the city sample. For most analyses only the subjects who were present for all 3 years were used. Out of the 256 subjects on whom some data were obtained, 158 were interviewed in all three waves. This constituted 85% of the original sample of 186; so the overall mortality rate was only 15%. However, among city children the mortality rate was 24% compared to 1% among kibbutz children. The complete breakdown of the subject sample is shown in Table 7.1.

TABLE 7.1
The Distribution of Subjects in the Kibbutz and City Samples

Original Sample	Kibbutz		City		
	Girls	Boys	Girls	Boys	
Cohort 1	22	16	20	19	
Cohort 2	20	16	36	37	
	—	—	—	—	
	42	32	56	56	
		74		112	186

Complete Interview Sample	Kibbutz		City		
	Girls	Boys	Girls	Boys	
Cohort 1	22	16	9	13	
Cohort 2	19	16	30	33	
	—	—	—	—	
	41	32	39	46	
		73		85	158

Procedure

The children were interviewed three times at 1-year intervals, giving us an overlapping longitudinal design with data on first through fifth-graders. The younger cohort was in the third grade in the final year (third) of the study whereas the older cohort was in the third grade in the first year of the study. Each year, the children were interviewed in the spring in two group sessions lasting about 1 hour each. In addition, some information was obtained about each child from school records and teacher interviews. There were no parent interviews.

Measures

As described in chapter 2 of this volume the primary measure of overt aggression was a modified version of the widely used peer-nominated index of aggression (Eron, Walder, & Lefkowitz, 1971) in which each subject in the sample names all the subjects in his or her class who have displayed 10 specific aggressive behaviors during the last school year (e.g., "Who starts a fight over nothing"). This measure has been used in many countries and is both highly reliable (Coefficient Alpha > .95) and valid. In the final wave of the study, the children also completed self-ratings of aggression to provide some concurrent validation in the Israeli population. This scale was based on four self-descriptive items and has also been described in chapter 2. The reliabilities of all the measures used in Israel were computed and are compared in Appendix II with the reliabilities from other countries.

Three additional peer-nomination scales were also used — one for popularity consisting of two items, one for avoidance of aggression consisting of one time ("who never fights even when picked on"), and a single "affiliation" item ("who often lends his/her belongings to other children").

A child's TV violence viewing score was based on the child's self-report of the shows he or she watched most often. In Israel, three lists of nine (1981), seven (1982), or six (1983) programs each were presented to a child. Because there were so few suitable programs available for the lists in Israel, a slightly different choice procedure was used than in the other countries. From each list the child chose the two programs he or she watched most often and then rated how often he or she watched them on a 3-point scale. Each list contained popular violent and non-violent programs, child or adult oriented. The violence of each show was rated by 5 independent raters (interrater reliability was above .70). Their average rating was the program's score. Two violence viewing scores were computed for each child. One was the simple mean of the violence ratings for the six programs the child selected. For the other score each violence rating was weighted by the frequency of viewing that show as reported by the child. A separate frequency of viewing score was also computed representing how "regularly" the child watched his or her favorite shows.

Besides measuring violence viewing and frequency we asked each child questions about his or her beliefs in the realism of certain violent television programs and questions about the extent to which the child identified with various TV characters as described in chapter 2. The child's use of aggressive fantasy was evaluated with part of the Children's Fantasy Inventory (Rosenfeld, Huesmann, Eron, & Torney-Purta, 1982). On this inventory the child answers a number of questions about how often he or she daydreams about or imagines acting in certain ways. From these self-ratings, two scale scores—aggressive fantasy and fanciful fantasy—were derived. The children's preferences for sex-typed activities were measured through their selection of favorite games and activities as described in chapter 2.

To evaluate the role of possible social class differences between the kibbutz and city samples, measures were taken in a teacher's interview and from school records as to ethnic background, place of birth, parents' education (number of years of schooling), and parents' occupation. Finally, each child completed a Draw-a-Person that was scored for intellectual development (Harris, 1963).

RESULTS

Before examining the aggression of the kibbutz and city samples, we consider how they differ on demographic variables. The differential attrition rate in the two samples (described in the Methods section and Table 7.1) is in itself an important demographic difference. This difference indicates the rather closed and static nature of kibbutz life in which low mobility is the norm. In a number of various studies in western countries, higher family mobility has been associated with higher levels of child aggression (Eron, Huesmann, Dubow, Romanoff, & Yarmel, in press; Lefkowitz, Eron, Walder, & Huesmann, 1977). Thus, attrition in the city sample might have selectively eliminated the higher aggression children, but of course, not in the kibbutz sample where there was no attrition.

The ethnic background of the kibbutz and city children also differs significantly as Table 7.2 indicates. The major difference is that the parents of kibbutz children were more likely to be native born (*sabras*) than were the parents of city children. Because ethnic background was only measured in terms of the parents' origins, there is no way of knowing the original ethnicity of the Israeli born parents.

The number of years of education of the parents in the two samples was about the same: both mothers and fathers averaged about 1.5 years of education beyond high school. Similarly, kibbutz and city fathers did not differ in

TABLE 7.2
The Distribution of the Subjects' Ethnic Background

| | Father's Ethnic Background | | | |
	Israeli Born	Middle East	European or American	No Data
Kibbutz	58	7	6	4
City	48	28	29	76

Chi-Square = 20.7, $df = 2, p < .0001$

| | Mother's Ethnic Background | | | |
	Israeli Born	Middle East	European or American	No Data
Kibbutz	53	8	9	5
City	43	37	24	22

Chi-Square = 22.9, $df = 2, p < .0001$

their average occupational status as measured by the Hartman Occupational Status Scale (1975). However, the standard deviation of occupational status scores was about 21% higher for the city fathers. Although there were a few city fathers who were doctors and lawyers and a few with low-status occupations, the statuses of most kibbutz fathers' occupations were homogeneous and in the middle range.

The one substantial difference between kibbutz and city families on traditional socioeconomic variables was that kibbutz mothers all work and on the average have lower status occupations than working city mothers [$F(1,109) = 6.4, p < .013$]. Only 64% of city mothers worked.

In conclusion, although both populations are apparently within the upper middle range of socioeconomic status, as represented by level of occupation and years of education, the kibbutz group is far more homogenous than the city group.

Aggression in Kibbutz and City Children

The mean peer-nominated aggression scores for the different cohorts of boys and girls are shown in Fig. 7.1. Apparent are a number of substantial differences whose significance were confirmed by analyses of variance. As one would expect, boys were consistently rated as more aggressive than girls [$F(1,148) = 16.76, p < .0001$]. The cohort and time effects were marginal [$F(1,148) = 3.35, p < .07$ and $F(2,296) = 2.91, p < .06$ respectively] suggesting only a slight overall increase in aggressiveness with age. To our surprise, however, the peer-nominated aggression scores of kibbutz children were much higher than the scores for the city children [$F(1,148) = 22.1, p < .0001$]. This robust finding seems to contradict the a priori expectation that kibbutz children are less aggressive. Therefore several alternative explanations must be considered before such a conclusion is accepted.

One possibility is that kibbutz children are simply more willing to nominate their peers on any characteristic, and the higher peer-nominated aggression scores are an artifact of this willingness to nominate. The data do support the contention that kibbutz children nominate their peers more readily

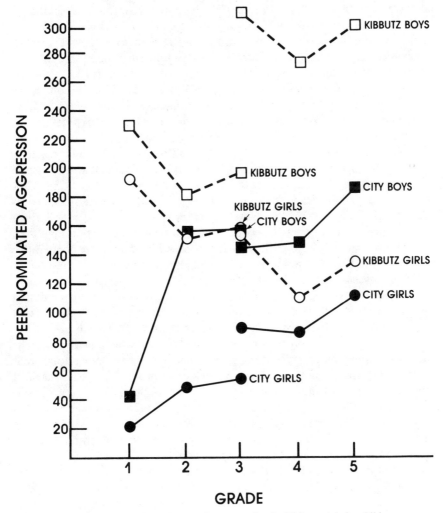

FIG. 7.1 Mean peer-nominated aggression scores for the kibbutz and city children as a function of grade.

on other questions besides aggression [$F(1,148) = 33.2, p < .001$]. If one divides each child's nominations on aggression questions by the average number of nominations within his or her class on all questions, the significant difference between kibbutz and city children disappears [$F(1,148) = 1.54$, n.s.]. Nevertheless, a closer examination of the data suggests that more than a difference in tendencies to nominate is involved.

First, if one divides peer-nominated aggression scores only by the peer nominations on avoidance of aggression, the resulting ratio is still significantly higher among kibbutz children [$F(1,148) = 29.1, p < .0001$]. In fact, average nominations on avoidance of aggression were lower among kibbutz children than city children [$F(1,148) = 4.13, p < .05$]. Thus, the kibbutz children nominated their peers more on aggression questions relative to aggression-avoidance questions than did city children. Second, the kibbutz children scored significantly higher on the self-ratings of aggression obtained in the last year of the study [$F(1,203) = 10.1, p < .002$] and higher on the ratio of these self-ratings to self-ratings of nonaggressiveness [$F(1,203) = 4.92, p < .03$]. Although these self-ratings only correlated .30, ($p < .01$) with concurrent peer-nominations and were only moderately reliable (Coefficient Alpha = .60); still this result makes it difficult to dismiss the higher aggression scores among kibbutz children as artifactual. Kibbutz children perceive more aggressive behavior among themselves and their peers than do city children. Whether this perception is accurate or not cannot be determined without unbiased observational measures of aggression. These were not obtained in this study nor in any previous controlled study. However, kibbutz children have been found to be significantly less competitive and more cooperative than city children in a series of studies (Madsen & Shapira, 1977; Shapira, 1976; Shapira & Madsen, 1974). Also, clinical data suggest that kibbutz children are, if anything, socialized to be less aggressive than city children (Kaffman, 1965, 1972). Finally, some fantasy data obtained in the current study support this view that kibbutz children are actually less aggressive.

The fantasy-aggression scale measures the extent to which the child admits to daydreaming about aggression against someone else or having done other bad things. Admitting such fantasy aggression appears to be easier for most children than admitting comparable overt aggressive behavior. Yet from our perspective such fantasy serves as a cognitive rehearsal of overt aggressive behavior, and such fantasy has been found to correlate positively with overt aggression in several countries (See chapters on United States and Finland; Huesmann & Eron, 1984). In the current study, aggressive fantasy is substantially higher in city children than in kibbutz children [$F(1,139) = 12.14, p < .0007$]. The difference between kibbutz and city children on peer-nominated aggression, peer-nominated aggression avoidance, self-rated aggression, and fantasy aggression are summarized in Fig. 7.2. Perhaps the most plausible conclusion to explain these results is that kibbutz children are

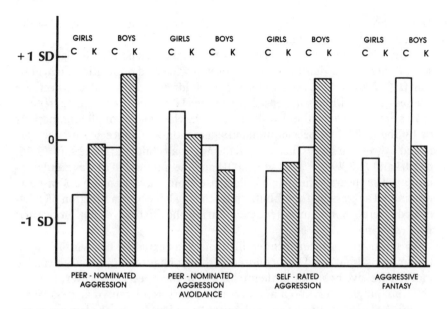

FIG. 7.2 Mean scores on four aggression measures for kibbutz and city children.

more cognizant of aggressive acts and more willing to admit them but per-haps commit no more interpersonal aggression (or possibly even less) than city children. Kibbutz children are taught that confessing and naming others is all right. Furthermore, kibbutz children typically present themselves in a more negative light than city children. In fact, in their follow-up comparison of kibbutz and moshav raised children, Rabin and Beit-Hallahmi (1982) con-cluded that negative self-presentation among kibbutz born was the most sali-ent difference between them and moshav born.

If it is true that the higher peer and self-ratings of aggression in kibbutz children do not reflect highter absolute levels of aggression but rather low-ered inhibitions about confessing or naming others along with a greater sensi-tivity to overt interpersonal aggression, one would expect to find less accept-ance of aggression among kibbutz children. Such appears to be the case as peer-nominated popularity is very significantly inversely related to aggres-siveness among kibbutz children ($r = -.44, N = 40, p < .005$ for girls; $r = -.61, N = 31, p < .0005$ for boys) but not among city children ($r = .01, N = 39$, n.s. and $r = -.19, N = 46$, n.s. respectively). Of the 25% of children who were most aggressive in the kibbutz sample, not one scored in the upper quartile on popularity. Of the city children in the upper quartile on aggres-sion, 18% scored in the upper quartile on popularity. Such a result cannot be attributed to differential affiliative behavior among aggressive kibbutz and city children since affiliation was inversely related to aggression in both pop-ulations ($r = -.34, N = 40, p < .03$ and $r = -.45, N = 31, p < .01$ for kibbutz boys and girls; $r = -.40$, $N = 39$, $p < .01$ and $r = -.38$, $N = 46$, $p < .01$ for city boys and girls).

Although there was no main effect of wave on peer-nominated aggression scores, there was a significant interaction of wave and population on aggression [$F(2,296) = 18.1$, $p < .001$]. Kibbutz children's scores tended to decrease whereas city children's increased over time. However, when the aggression scores are corrected either by dividing by the class means of all nominations or by the individual peer-nominated aggression avoidance scores, the corrected aggression scores increase over time for all children [$F(2,296) = 3.76$, $p < .03$ and $F(2,296) = 9.42$, $p < .0001$] and the interaction of wave and population disappears. The original decrease from wave 1 to wave 3 in peer-nominated aggression for kibbutz children may have been a function of an elevated overall nomination tendency during the first wave that moderated with retesting.

To summarize, age and gender differences in aggressive behavior are similar among kibbutz and city children. Kibbutz children apparently perceive more aggressive behavior in themseles and in their peers. However, kibbutz children fantasize less about aggression and are less tolerant of aggressive behavior that exceeds the norm. This is evidenced by the much stronger negative relation between popularity and aggressiveness found in kibbutz children.

Demographic Factors and Aggression

Because kibbutz and city families vary on certain demographic variables, it is particularly important to consider the relation between these variables and child aggression in Israel. Differences in ethnic origin as measured in this study do not generally relate significantly to aggression once they are separated from kibbutz–city status. The only significant effect was an interaction between child gender and father's ethnic background so that girls from middle-eastern families were the least aggressive whereas boys from such backgrounds were the most aggressive [$F(2,127) = 3.41$, $p < .04$]. However, ethnic origin was only measured for one generation, is skewed toward Israeli born, and is heavily confounded with kibbutz status. Moreover, we don't know what the distribution of the second generation is in terms of ethnic background. Thus, the "Israeli-born" group includes both European and middle-eastern backgrounds. Another possible explanation is that socioeconomic variables are more dominant in terms of norms of aggression than ethnic background. Thus, it is really impossible to determine from these data whether ethnic background does affect aggression in these populations.

Parents' education was strongly negatively related to aggression among city boys ($r = -.52$, $p < .001$ for aggression with combined parent education). Surprisingly, though, as Table 7.4 reveals, there was no such relation for city girls or kibbutz boys and only a marginal one for kibbutz girls. Similarly, the effect of a family's social status on aggression was quite weak. The one exception was city boys. For them, a marginal correlation existed between father's status and aggression. However, the key factor was whether or not the chld's mother worked. The sons of working mothers were less aggressive. Interestingly, the result is the opposite of a trend found in the United States (see chapter 3) where working mothers have somewhat more aggressive children. Again, however, no such results were obtained among the kibbutz children. The probable explanation is that the better educated women in this city (Ra'anana), which is predominately upper middle class, are the ones who are working ($r = .52, p .001$), and mother's education was negatively related to son's aggression in the city. On a kibbutz every woman has an occupation; so there is no confounding of working and education. In summary, higher educational and socioeconomic status in Israel significantly predict non-aggressiveness only among city boys.

Demographic Factors and TV Viewing

As with aggression, TV violence viewing did not vary significantly with the family's ethnic origin. However, the same reservations apply about the interpretation of this result—namely ethnicity is much too confounded with kibbutz–city status to permit a clear interpretation.

TV viewing habits do relate significantly to parents' educational and occupational status among both populations of children but in different ways. For city boys frequency of viewing favorite programs and violence viewing are inversely related to parents' education ($r = -.42, p < .01$ and $r = -.22$, n.s. respectively). This result is comparable to what has been reported from other countries. However, unlike some other countries, the sons of working mothers in the city sample watched less TV ($r = -.38, p < .05$) and less TV violence ($r = -.37, p < .05$) than the sons of non-working mothers. Again, this latter result may be a function of the fact that in the suburban community in which the study was conducted more highly educated mothers are more likely to be working ($r = .52, p < .001$). For city girls and the kibbutz children, the relations between TV viewing habits and parental status were quite different than those for city boys. More educated and higher status parents had children who watched their favorite programs more and watched more TV violence. This effect was strongest for city girls ($r = .47, p < .01$ between education and violence viewing; $r = .39, p < .05$ between father's occupational status and violence viewing). However, there were significant effects for both kibbutz boys and kibbutz girls as well ($r = .33$ for boys, $p < .10$ and $r = .27$ for girls, $p < .10$ between parents' education and TV frequency; $r = .27$ for boys, n.s., and $r = .36$ for girls, $p < .05$ between father's occupation and TV violence viewing). Because most of the kibbutz child's TV viewing is done in the parents' quarters, it is not surprising that these parent variables affect the kibbutz child's TV habits. However, the direction of effect is surprising. Perhaps, the more highly educated and higher status parents spend less time with their children during the "children's hour."

Television Habits in Kibbutz and City Children

The mean scores on the major television variables are compared for kibbutz and city children in Fig. 7.3 One can see that city children on the average watched their favorite programs more regularly [$F (1,139) = 12.36$, $p < .001$], were exposed to more television violence [frequency weighted violence, $F (1,139) = 4.13, p < .05$], and perceived television violence as marginally more like real life than did kibbutz children [$F (1,137) = 3.33, p < .07$]. City boys also identified more with TV characters in general [$F (1,94) = 5.40$, $p < .025$]. However, kibbutz children's preferred shows were just as violent [$F (1,139) = 0.10$, n.s.], and they identified just as much with violent characters [$F (1,108) = 1.97$, n.s.]. All these findings are consistent with the picture of kibbutz children living in an environment with far fewer opportunities to observe media violence but being similar to city children in their reaction to television.

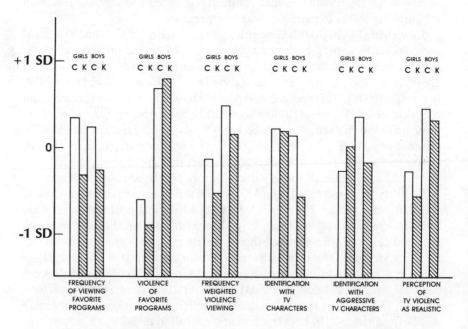

FIG. 7.3 Mean scores on the television variables for kibbutz and city children.

Correcting Aggression Scores for Nomination Biases

The large differences in mean peer-nomination scores in different class-rooms presents two obstacles for correlational analyses. First, the kibbutz and city children must be analyzed separately because part of any overall cor-relation would reflect the different mean aggression scores of the two groups. Second, the high level of nominating observed in some groups may obscure relations between aggression and other variables. The peer-nominated ag-gression scores obtained in Israel are not only higher on an absolute scale than in other countries, they are higher relative to the observed variance. For example, among boys in the United States, the standard deviation was slightly higher than the mean aggression score (105% of the mean). Among kibbutz boys the standard deviation was only 64% of the mean. This suggests that the high aggression scores observed in Israel are approaching a practical ceiling. Although the mean score of .27 for kibbutz boys is well below the the-oretical maximum of 1.00, a mean score this high could only be obtained if, on the average, every child was nominating over 25% of the boys in the class on every aggression question. Considering the time constraints placed on the children during testing, such a score may indeed be close to a practical ceiling.

The solution we have adopted is to use as our dependent variable the ratio of peer-nominated aggression to peer-nominated aggression avoidance plus 1 (to avoid infinite ratios). Thus, a boy who scored zero on the old aggression measure will still score zero on this ratio. A boy who scored high on aggres-sion and low on aggression avoidance will have a higher score on the new measure. However, a boy who was nominated many times on both aggres-sion and aggression avoidance will have a lower score on the new measure. The end result is that the standard deviation will be smaller relative to the mean, and the effective ceiling will be raised. For example, for kibbutz boys the standard deviation of this ratio is 155% of its mean compared with 64% of the old measure.

Television Habits and Aggression

Table 7.3 contains the correlations between this ratio measure of aggression and the various television variables averaged over the 3 years of the study for each gender and population group. The results are very clear cut. Television violence viewing is very significantly correlated with aggressiveness among both city boys and girls but not among kibbutz children. These significant correlations among city children are quite substantial, in fact, much higher than has been found in any of the other countries in this cross-national re-search. Interestingly, among kibbutz children, there is not the least indica-

TABLE 7.3

The Correlations of Average Aggressiveness Over All Three Waves With
Average Television Viewing

| | Correlations with Aggression | | | |
| | Girls | | Boys | |
Television Viewing Variables	City	Kibbutz	City	Kibbutz
Regularity of Viewing Favorite	.28	–	.42**	–
Programs	($N = 34$)		($N = 42$)	
Violence of Favorite Programs	.42**	–	.24	–
	($N = 34$)		($N = 42$)	
TV Violence Viewing	.48**	–	.45**	–
(Regularity × Violence)	($N = 34$)		($N = 42$)	
Identification with All	–	.66**	.34*	.33
Characters		($N = 15$)	($N = 35$)	($N = 17$)
Identification with Violent	–	.68***	.29⁺	–
Characters		($N = 24$)		
Perceived Realism of Violent	–	–	–	–
Programs				

$^+p < .10.$ $^*p < .05.$ $^{**}p < .01.$ $^{***}p < .001.$

Note: Aggression was measured as the ratio of peer nominations on aggressive items to nominations on the aggression avoidance items.

tion of a correlation between aggression and violence viewing, but those boys (to a slight extent) and those girls (to a great extent) who perceive themselves as being like TV characters are the more aggressive children. The relation between TV violence viewing and aggression among city children is illustrated in Fig. 7.4.

City children were divided into the lower 25%, middle 50%, and upper 25% on TV violence viewing, and their mean aggression scores were plotted.

Before examining the causal ordering of aggression and TV habits with longitudinal analyses, one must ask if the observed correlations might be spurious and due to the effect of a third variable. In particular, can the parent's education, socioeconomic status, the child's IQ or the child's age be generating the relation? For example, IQ in the United States data (see chapter 3) and social class in the Milavsky, Kessler, Stipp, and Rubens (1982) study have been found to be relevant third variables. In the current study, there were no significant correlations between the child's IQ and either TV habits or aggression. Unfortunately, the IQ scores had to be derived from Draw-a-Person tests given in group settings. Thus, the IQ's have questionable validity, and their failure to correlate with either TV habits or aggression should not be given much credence. In most other countries and many previous studies, IQ has consistently correlated with both aggression and TV habits.

As Table 7.4 reveals, parent's education correlated positively with violence viewing and aggression among city girls, negatively among city boys, and not at all among kibbutz children. Father's occupational status displayed similar relations. The child's age also correlated differentially with violence viewing, depending on the population. Older kibbutz children view TV violence less regularly perhaps because their structured life allows less time for it. Despite these relations, when parent's education, father's occupational status, child's IQ, and child's age were all partialed out of the relation between violence viewing and aggression among city children, these latter variables remained very significantly correlated (.39 for girls and .42 for boys). Thus, the relation between violence viewing and aggression cannot be attributed to these variables. More is said later about the independent effects of these social class variables on aggression.

The causal relation between violence viewing and aggression in the city population can best be examined by the multiple regressions shown in Table 7.5. From Table 7.5 one can see that a city child's average TV violence viewing over the first two waves of the study was a significant predictor of that child's aggression in the last year relative to his or her avoidance of aggression. This was true even when initial level of aggression and avoidance of

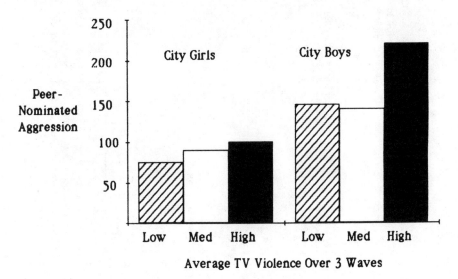

FIG. 7.4 Mean peer-nominated aggression scores for children in the lower quartile, middle 50%, or upper quartile on TV violence viewing.

TABLE 7.4

The Relations of Childrens' Aggression and TV Violence Viewing to Intellectual Development and Their Parents' Social Status

Population	Aggression	Parents Education	Fathers Occupational Status	Does Mother Work? (0 = No, 1 = Yes)	Childs Age	Childs IQ
City Girls						
TV Violence Viewing	.52** (.38*)	.47**	.39*	—	.29$^+$	—
Aggression		—	—	—	.28$^+$	.28
Kibbutz Girls						
TV Violence Viewing	—	.23	.36*	—	-.46**	—
Aggression		-.24	—	—	—	—
City Boys						
TV Violence Viewing	.46** (.46**)	-.22	—	-.37*	.24$^+$	—
Aggression		-.52***	-.21	-.43**	—	—
Kibbutz Boys						
TV Violence Viewing	—	.33$^+$	.30	—	—	—
Aggression		—	—	—	—	—

$^+ p < .10.$ $* p < .05.$ $** p < .01.$ $*** p < .001.$

Note: The aggression measure is peer-nominated aggression divided by peer-nominated aggression avoidance. Discrepancies between this table and Table 7.3 are due to slight reductions in sample size necessitated by partial correlation analysis. Partial correlations controlling for all other variables are shown in parentheses.

TABLE 7.5
Multiple Regressions Predicting City Children's Aggression From Earlier TV Violence
Viewing Controlling for Initial Levels of Aggression and Aggression Avoidance

Criterion Variable	Predictor Variable	Standardized Regression Coefficients	
		City Girls	City Boys
Ratio of Aggression to Aggression Avoidance in Third Wave			
Grade		$-.21$	$-.31*$
Peer-Aggression Wave 1		$.55**$	$.58***$
Peer-Aggression Avoidance Wave 1		$-.08$	$-.03$
TV Violence Viewing Waves 1 and 2		$.52**$	$.29*$
		$R^2 = .46, F(4,29) = 6.13, p < .001$	$R^2 = .44, F(4,37) = 7.3, p < .001$

$*p < .05.$ $**p < .01.$ $***p < .001.$

aggression were partialed out by adding those variables to the regressions,[2] and it was true for both boys and girls. In other words, greater violence viewing was predictive of greater later aggressiveness independently of initial aggression.

In Table 7.6 regressions are presented designed to make the opposite prediction—later TV violence viewing stemming from early aggression and aggression-avoidance. However, when initial level of violence viewing was partialed out, there was no significant effect of either of these variables on later violence viewing. In conjunction, these results suggest that among both city boys and city girls, extensive exposure to media violence is causing increased displays of aggression (particularly physical aggression) in schools.

Having established that in city but not kibbutz children television violence viewing seems to engender aggressive behavior, one must ask what factors produce the difference between these populations and what these factors suggest about the psychological processes that are involved. The most obvious difference, of course, is that city children have more control over their TV viewing and watch more TV violence. Most violence, in fact, is shown after 9 p.m. when kibbutz children have few opportunities to observe it. This time factor may also partially explain why the correlations within the city sample are more substantial than those found in other countries. The children who see more violence must be the ones who are staying up later; so violence

---

[2]These analyses were repeated partialing out the initial ratio of aggression to aggression-avoidance. The results remained the same except that the initial ratio was not as good a predictor of the final ratio as were peer-aggression and peer-aggression-avoidance separately.

TABLE 7.6
Multiple Regressions Predicting TV Violence Viewing From Aggression and
Aggression Avoidance While Controlling for Initial Levels of Violence Viewing

Criterion Variable	Predictor Variable	Standardized Regression Coefficients	
		City Girls	City Boys
TV Violence Viewing in Third Wave			
Grade		−.24	−.04
TV Violence Viewing			
Wave 1 Peer-Aggression		.31	.45**
Waves 1 and 2		.38	.10
Peer-Aggression Avoidance		.39	−.15
Waves 1 and 2			
		$R^2 = .21, F(4,29) =$ 1.89, n.s.	$R^2 = .26, F(4,37) =$ 3.25, $p < .03$

$^+p < .10.$ $*p < .05.$ $**p < .01.$ $***p < .001.$

viewing is confounded with age and parental attitudes and child-rearing practices. Nevertheless, one cannot simply dismiss the effect as an artifact of
child's age and parental attitudes. The partial correlations in Table 7.4
controlling for age and parents' socioeconomic status make such an explanation implausible.

Aside from overall exposure to violence, it is difficult to find relevant differences between kibbutz and city children on TV habits or attitudes. Kibbutz children "like" violent shows no less than city children and identify no
less with aggressive characters. Kibbutz children do identify less with TV
characters in general, but such lack of identification relates inversely to aggression within the kibbutz sample as well as within city boys. In Finland and
the United States boys' identification with TV characters (see chapters on
United States and Finland; Huesmann, Lagerspetz, & Eron, 1984) exacerbates the effect of violence viewing on aggression, but that could not be demonstrated among Israeli children. Finally, kibbutz children did perceive television violence as less realistic than did city children, but judgments of
realism were not correlated with aggression in any sample.

In their analysis of the effects of media violence on children's aggression in
Finland and the United States, Huesmann, Lagerspetz, and Eron (1984) have
emphasized the role of social norms for aggression as exacerbating or
mitigating factors. For example, they suggest that the reason why females are
now susceptible to media violence in the United States but were not susceptible 20 years ago and are not now in Finland is because of the current emphasis
on female assertiveness and aggressiveness in the United States. The data on
the relation between popularity and aggression in Israel suggest that a similar
difference in attitudes about aggression between kibbutz and city children

may be contributing to the differential effect of media violence. As described earlier, aggression is an unpopular behavior among kibbutz children but is not related to popularity among city children. This suggests that the imitation of specific interpersonal aggressive acts observed on a TV show or in a movie may be met with far more reprobation when committed by a kibbutz child than when committed by a city child. Because kibbutz children believe that the violence shown on TV is not representative of the real world and, because they identify less with TV characters (perhaps because they see less TV), they are less likely to accept aggressive behavior as the norm. Thus, the combination of children having substantially decreased opportunities to observe violence, coupled with peer attitudes that are less tolerant of aggression and more skeptical about the reality of TV violence, makes it less likely that the aggressive strategies observed on TV will be encoded for later use and makes it less likely that such strategies will be retrieved when a child is faced with a social problem.

Sex-Role Orientation, TV Viewing, and Aggression

Although most of the analyses described thus far have been reported separately for boys and girls, one must realize that broad differences exist within the genders themselves. Some girls may have more "masculine" attitudes and values than some boys or vice-versa. To measure such differences and how they relate to aggression, data were collected on each child's preferences for stereotypic male, female, or neutral games and activities. The relation between these scores and aggression and violence viewing are shown in Table 7.7.

For kibbutz boys and girls a preference for stereotypic male activities is positively correlated with aggression or violence viewing. But a preference for neutral activities relates inversely as does a preference for female activities among kibbutz boys. However, the picture does not remain completely consistent for city children. Although the more aggressive city girls prefer more "male" and less "female" activities, they also prefer more neutral activities. Equally puzzling, among city boys a preference for female activities is associated with more aggression.

It is difficult to put these results together. For kibbutz children the pattern partially fits the thesis developed elsewhere (Huesmann, Lagerspetz, & Eron, 1984) that less rigid preferences for sex-typed activities predict lower aggression and lower TV viewing. Greater preferences for neutral activities may reflect a greater cognitive flexibility that makes violent TV shows less appealing and also leads the child to learn many alternative social behaviors besides aggression. However, why did similar results not obtain for city children?

Kibbutz children score lower than city children on preferences for stereotypically male and female activities but higher on preferences for females on preference for neutral activities [$F (1,74) = 5.40, p < .025$] and for females

TABLE 7.7

The Correlations of TV Violence Viewing and Aggression With Self-Reported
Preferences for Sex-Typed Activities

| | Kind of Sex Typed Activity | | |
Population	Male	Female	Neutral
Girls			
City			
TV Violence Viewing	.32 +	− .46**	.35*
Aggression	.24	− .26*	.27*
Kibbutz			
TV Violence Viewing	−	−	− .22*
Aggression	.43**	−	− .45**
Boys			
City			
TV Violence Viewing	−	−	−
Aggression	−	.27 +	− .28 +
Kibbutz			
TV Violence Viewing	.46**	− .45**	− .21*
Aggression	−	−	−

$^+p<.10.$ $^*p<.05.$ $^{**}p<.01.$ $^{***}p<.001.$
Note: The aggression measure is peer-nominated aggression divided by peer-nominated aggression avoidance.

on preference for male activities $[F(1,74) = 3.90, p<.05]$ were statistically significant, it still seems fair to say that kibbutz children are substantially less rigidly sex-typed than their city counterparts. Also, for city girls, there was a significant effect of ethnic background on sex role such that recent immigrant families have daughters who scored higher on female preferences and lower on male and neutral. Such relations may obscure the direct effect of sex role on other variables. The fact that parental background predicts sex-typed preferences only in city girls is more evidence of the power of the kibbutz environment in socializing the child.

In summary, although sex-role preferences do relate to TV habits and aggression, the relations are too weak to account for the effect. Nevertheless, the less rigid sex-typing of kibbutz children may be one of the mitigating factors that eliminated the TV violence − aggression relation among kibbutz children

Fantasy, TV Violence Viewing, and Aggression

As reported earlier, kibbutz children fantasize less about aggression than do city children. Yet, from Table 7.8 one can see that both aggressive fantasy and immature-fanciful fantasy are correlated with aggressive behavior in kibbutz children. For kibbutz girls such fantasizing is also significantly related to TV violence viewing. The TV viewing may stimulate the fantasy. If the fantasy is aggressive, it will serve as a cognitive rehearsal of the aggressive behavior and enhance its probability of being emitted. However, why should immature-fanciful fantasy be related to aggression? This type of fantasy may serve as a marker of the emotional immaturity of the child and the child's failure to face reality. The child scoring high on immature-fanciful fantasy is one who is perhaps frustrated by failure and seeking gratification in fantasy.

In order to examine the effects of these several predictors of aggression relatively independently of each other, two multiple regression equations were calculated for each subsample. In the first, aggressiveness is predicted from parent demographic and child cognitive variables excluding early aggression. In the second, early aggression and aggression avoidance are added as predictors and then child behaviors are tested. The regressions for boys in Table 7.9 reveal, first, that aggression is much more predictable in kibbutz boys than in city boys. The multiple correlation is much higher for kibbutz boys than it is for city boys. However, for city boys, TV violence viewing predicts later aggression even when early aggression is added to the prediction equation. The regressions for girls in Table 7.10 reveal similar patterns. Aggression is more predictable among kibbutz girls, but TV violence only affects aggression significantly among city girls. In other words, for city children in Israel, substantial exposure to TV violence is predictive of increases in aggression even when the effects of these other variables are taken into account.

TABLE 7.8
The Correlations of a Child's TV Violence Viewing and Aggression with the
Child's Self-Reported Frequency of Aggressive and Fanciful Daydreaming

Population	Aggressive Fantasy	Immature-Fanciful Fantasy
Girls		
City		
TV Violence Viewing	—	—
Aggression	—	—
Kibbutz		
TV Violence Viewing	.39**	.41**
Aggression	.25	.29+
Boys		
City		
TV Violence Viewing	.21	—
Aggression	.24	—
Kibbutz		
TV Violence Viewing	—	− .25
Aggression	.52***	.33+

$+p<.10.$ $*p<.01.$ $**p<.01.$ $***p<.001.$
Note: The aggression measure is peer-nominated aggression divided by peer-nominated aggression avoidance.

TABLE 7.9
Predictions of a Boy's Aggressiveness in the Third Year of the Study from His Parents' and His Own Characteristics in the First 2 Years

| | Standardized Regression Coefficients | | | | | |
| | City Boys (N = 41) | | | Kibbutz Boys (N = 24) | | |
Predictor Variables	First	Second	Third	First	Second	Third
Demographic and Cognitive Characteristics						
Child's grade	-.25	-.52**	-.46**	—	—	—
Child's IQ	—	—	—	—	—	—
Parents' Education	-.26	—	—	.45	.28	.37*
Father's Occupational Status	—	—	-.19	—	—	—
Child's initial aggressiveness						
Peer-nominated aggression	—	.73***	.69***	—	.72***	.55**
Peer-nominated avoidance of aggression	—	—	—	—	—	—
Child's behaviors in first 2 years						
Preference for male sex-typed activities			—			—
Preference for neutral sex-typed activities			—			—
Aggressive fantasy			—			.30+
Immature-Fanciful fantasy			.28*			—
TV violence viewing			—			—
Peer-nominated affiliation			—			-.25+
Peer-nominated popularity			—			—
Squared Multiple Correlation	.14	.45***	.52***	.21	.70***	.78***

+ $p < .10$.   * $p < .05$.   ** $p < .01$.   *** $p < .001$.

Note: The dependent variable was the ratio of the child's peer-nominated aggression to the child's avoidance of aggression. The only variables added in the third regression were those that would be significant at less than the .20 level.

TABLE 7.10
Predictions of a Girl's Aggressiveness in the Third Year of the Study from Her Parents' and Her Own Characteristics in the First 2 Years

	Standardized Regression Coefficients					
	City Girls (N = 32)			Kibbutz Girls (N = 34)		
Predictor Variables	First	Second	Third	First	Second	Third
Demographic and Cognitive Characteristics						
Child's grade	—	—	—	—	—	—
Child's IQ	—	—	—	—	—	—
Parents' Education	—	—	—	—	—	—
Father's Occupational Status	—	—	—	—	—	—
Child's initial aggressiveness						
Peer-nominated aggression	—	.51*	.65**	—	.80***	.70***
Peer-nominated avoidance of aggression		—	—		—	—
Child's behaviors in first 2 years						
Preference for male sex-typed activities			—			—
Preference for neutral sex-typed activities			—			−.29*
Aggressive fantasy			—			—
Immature-Fanciful fantasy			.55**			—
TV violence viewing			—			—
Peer-nominated affiliation			—			—
Peer-nominated popularity			—			—
Squared Multiple Correlation	.13	.31	.49**	.03	.57***	.64***

*p < .05.   **p < .01.   ***p < .001.

Note: The dependent variable was the ratio of the child's peer-nominated aggression to the child's avoidance of aggression. The only variables added in the third regression were those that would be significant at less than the .20 level.

233

DISCUSSION AND CONCLUSION

The Israeli study reported in this chapter is unique for this book in that the subjects come from two distinctly different cultural environments — city and kibbutz — with quite different opportunities to observe TV. In all the other countries in this cross-national research a positive relation between amount of exposure to violent TV programs and aggression was discovered for at least some children. In Israel the situation is the same. Among city children, a significant positive relation was found between television violence viewing and amount of aggressive behavior. In fact, the magnitude of the correlation was higher for Israeli city children than for children in any other country. Furthermore, the longitudinal effects seemed to be more from violence viewing to aggression than from aggression to violence viewing. City children who viewed violence more often appeared to become more aggressive relative to the rest of the children over the course of the study. It is surprising to this author that such results should occur in a country in which only a few violent programs are broadcast late at night each week and in which the environment contains regular examples of real salient violence to which the child is exposed. However, the most important finding in this study is that these relations between exposure to media violence and aggression were not obtained for children raised on a kibbutz. More aggressive kibbutz children do identify more with aggressive TV characters, but there is no detectable relation between amount of exposure to TV or TV violence and aggression in kibbutz children.

What are the essential factors associated with growing up on a kibbutz that mitigate the effect of TV violence viewing on the development of aggressive behavior? The most obvious and direct factor is the different patterns of TV viewing observed among kibbutz children. Because of their daily schedule, kibbutz children are exposed less to television, particularly during the evening hours. This fact minimizes their opportunities to watch violent programs since these (with a few exceptions, e.g., cartoons) are broadcast late at night. Like city children and children in other countries, they "like" action shows containing violence, but these programs are rarely accessible for kibbutz youngsters.

Another characteristic of kibbutz TV and film exposure that may mitigate against any behavioral effects is group viewing. As described in chapter 1 and the introduction to this chapter, a number of studies (e.g., Adoni & Cohen, 1979; Hicks, 1968) have suggested that the presence of co-observers, and particularly adult co-observers who comment on the material, may mitigate against imitation of the material by the child. The kibbutz child is most likely to watch television with other people. They either watch in the family quarters during the "afternoon family hour" when the parents are always there, or they watch in the evening with their peer group and adult caretaker. Moreover, sitting alone in front of a TV would generally not be accepted as an appropriate behavior for a kibbutz child. Associated with the kibbutz style of life is a continuous stream of organized group activities for children. For older children especially, there are always alternative modes of entertainment to sitting in front of a TV. Thus, it is not suprising that for kibbutz children in Israel, unlike children in some other countries in this study, TV viewing declined with age.

In addition to the natural constraints on TV viewing, though, there are other powerful characteristics of the kibbutz environment that probably minimize the impact of TV violence on the development of aggression. Most important, perhaps, is the power of the peer group. From infancy onward the peer group prescribes acceptable norms of behavior and establishes intragroup sanctions against deviations from these norms. For children, peer-group prescriptions for certain prosocial behaviors and sanctions against aggressive behavior are undoubtedly more powerful factors in social learning than infrequent exposures to television models. Of course, the peer group's prescriptions are molded by the adult community of the kibbutz through the caretakers and teachers. However, even the parent's views and behaviors seem to be less important to the kibbutz child than the collective norms. Thus, several parental and demographic variables that were discovered to be related to aggressiveness in city children (ethnic background, parents' education, parents' occupations) were not related to aggressiveness in kibbutz children. At the same time, individual differences in the patterns of TV viewing of kibbutz children were correlated with individual differences in their parents' patterns. Such a result is to be expected because almost the only opportunity that a kibbutz child has for differential viewing is at home during the family hour.

Aggressiveness in general is less acceptable among kibbutz children than city children. Unpopularity was very significantly related to aggressiveness among kibbutz children but not among city children. Of the upper quartile of children who were most aggressive in the kibbutz sample, not one scored in the upper quartile on popularity. Yet of the city children in the upper quartile on aggression, 18% scored in the upper quartile on popularity. Kibbutz children also fantasize less about being aggressive. In short, the powerful group norms against aggression prevalent in the kibbutz society seem to be the most important factor in mitigating the effect of what little media violence the kibbutz child observes. The power of cultural norms to influence aggression has been documented in a number of countries and cultures (Landau, 1982).

Given these results it seems most likely that the higher average scores obtained for kibbutz children on peer-nominated and self-rated aggressive behavior reflect their lower tolerance for aggression. Because of their group consciousness, their experience with group criticism of the individual and their training in accountability to the group, kibbutz children are more cognizant of aggressive acts and more willing to admit them either within themselves or within their peers.

In conclusion, in a children's society in which values and norms of behavior are clear, where accountability to the society is emphasized, where interpersonal aggression is explicitly criticized, and where solo TV and film viewing are infrequent, the children's aggressive behavior is influenced very little, if at all, by what media violence they do observe.

ACKNOWLEDGMENTS

This research was supported in part by Grants MH-31886 and MH-38683 from the USA NIMH to Rowell Huesmann. The research was also facilitated by the support of the Kibbutz Child and Family Clinic and its director, M. Kaffman. Zvia Zilberman, Sara Rosen, and Rowell Huesmann assisted in the collection of the data in Israel. The data were analyzed at the University of Illinois at Chicago under the direction of Rowell Huesmann. Pat Brice, Eric Dubow, Evelynne Seebauer, and Patty Yarmel assisted in the data analyses.

REFERENCES

Adoni, H., & Cohen, A. (1979). Children's responses to televised war news films. *Megamot Behavioral Sciences Quarterly, 25*(1), 49–64.

Bar-Tal, D., Raviv, A., & Shavit, N. (1981). Motives for helping behaviors: Kibbutz and city children in kindergarten and school. *Developmental Psychology, 17*(6), 766–772.

Bettelheim, B. (1969). *The children of the dream.* New York: Macmillan.

Bizman, A., Yinon, Y., Mivtzari, E., & Shavit, R. (1978). Effects on the age structure of the kindergarten on altruistic behavior. *Journal of School Psychology, 16*(2), 154–160.

Darley, J., & Latane, B. (1968). Bystander intervention in emergencies: Diffusion of responsibility. *Journal of Personality and Social Psychology, 8,* 377–383.

Devereux, E. C., Shouval, R., Bronfenbrenner, U., Rodgers, R. R., Kav-Vanaki, S., Kiely, E., & Karson, E. (1974). Socialization practices of parents, teachers and peers in Israel: The kibbutz versus the city. *Child Development, 45,* 269–281.

Eron, L. D., & Huesmann, L. R. (1984). The relation between aggression and prosocial behavior. *Aggressive Behavior, 10,* 201–211.

Eron, L. D., Huesmann, L. R., Lefkowitz, M. M., & Walder, L. O. (1972). Does television violence cause aggression? *American Psychologist, 27,* 253–263.

Eron, L. D., Huesmann, L. R., Dubow, E., Romanoff, R., & Yarmel, P. W. (in press). Aggression and its correlates over 22 years. In D. H. Crowell, R. J. Blanchard, I. Evans & C. R. O'Donnel (Eds.), *Childhood aggression and violence: Sources of influence, prevention and control.* New York: Academic Press.

Eron, L. D., Walder, L. O., & Lefkowitz, M. M. (1971). *Learning of aggression in children.* Boston: Little-Brown.

Freedman, J. L., Levy, A. S., Bachanan, R. W., & Price, J. (1972). Crowding and human aggressiveness. *Journal of Experimental Social Psychology, 8,* 528–548.

Harris, D. B. (1963). *Children's drawings as measures of intellectual maturity: A revision and extension of the Goodenough Draw-a-Man Test.* New York: Harcourt, Brace & World.

Hartman, M. (1975). *Occupation as a parameter of social status in Israeli society*. Unpublished manuscript. The Institute for Research on Work and Society, Tel-Aviv University, (Hebrew).

Hicks, D. J. (1968). Effects of co-observer's sanctions and adult presence on imitative aggression. *Child Development, 38,* 303–304.

Huesmann, L. R. (1982). Television violence and aggressive behavior. In D. Pearl, L. Bouthilet, & J. Lazar (Eds.), *Television and Behavior: Ten years of scientific progress and implications for the eighties* (pp. 126–137). Washington, DC: U.S. Government Printing Office.

Huesmann, L. R., & Eron, L. D. (1984). Cognitive processes and the persistence of aggressive behavior. *Aggressive Behavior, 10,* 243–251.

Huesmann, L. R., Eron, L. D., Klein, R., Brice, P., & Fischer, P. (1983). Mitigating the imitation of aggressive behaviors by changing children's attitudes about media violence. *Journal of Personality and Social Psychology, 44,* 899–910.

Huesmann, L. R., Lagerspetz, K., & Eron, L. D. (1984). Intervening variables in the television violence-aggression relation: Evidence from two countries. *Developmental Psychology, 20,* 746–775.

Jaffe, Y., & Yinon, Y., (1979). Retaliatory aggression in individuals and groups. *European Journal of Social Psychology, 9,* 177–186.

Jaffe, Y., Shapir, N., & Yinon, Y. (1981). Aggression and its escalation. *Journal of Cross-cultural Psychology, 12,* 91–36.

Kaffman, M. (1965). A comparison of psychopathology; Israeli children from kibbutz and from urban surroundings. *American Journal of Orthopsychiatry, 35*(3), 509–520.

Kaffman, M. (1972). Characteristics of the emotional pathology of the kibbutz children. *American Journal of Orthopsychiatry, 41*(4), 692–709.

Landau, S. F. (1984). Trends in violence and aggression: A cross cultural analysis. *International Journal of Comparative Sociology, 25,* 133–158.

Landau, S. F., & Beit-Hallahmi, B. (1983). Israel: Aggression in psychohistorical perspective. In A. P. Goldstein & M. H. Segall (Eds.), *Aggression in global perspective* (pp. 261–286). New York: Pergamon Press.

Lefkowitz, M. M., Eron, L. D., Walder, L. O., & Huesmann, L. R. (1977). *Growing up to be violent: A longitudinal study of the development of aggression.* New York: Pergamon Press.

Lefkowitz, M. M., & Huesmann, L. R. (1980). Concomitants of television violence viewing in children. In E. L. Palmer & A. Dorr (Eds.), *Children and the faces of television: Teaching violence, selling.* New York: Academic Press.

Leon, D. (1969). *The kibbutz: Portrait from within.* London: Pergamon Press.

Madsen, M. C., & Shapira, A. (1977). Cooperation and challenge in four cultures. *The Journal of Social Psychology, 102,* 189–195.

Milavsky, J. R., Kessler, R. C., Stipp, H. H., & Rubens, W. S. (1982). *Television and aggression: A panel study.* New York: Academic Press.

Milgram, S., & Toch, H. (1969). Collective behavior: Grounds and social movements. In G. Lindzey & E. Aronson (Eds.), *The handbook of social psychology,* (Vol. 4, pp. 507–610). Reading, MA: Addison-Wesley.

Nevo, B. (1977). Personality differences between kibbutz born and city born adults. *The Journal of Psychology, 96,* 303–308.

Rabin, A. I. (1965). *Growing Up in the Kibbutz.* New York: Springer.

Rabin, A. I., & Beit-Hallahmi, B. (1982). *Twenty years later — Kibbutz children grown up,* New York: Springer.

Rosenfeld, E., Huesmann, L. R., Eron, L. D., & Torney-Purta, J. V. (1982). Measuring patterns of fantasy behavior in children. *Journal of Personality and Social Psychology, 42,* 347–366.

Shapira, A. (1976). Developmental differences in competitive behavior of kibbutz and city children from Israel. *Journal of Social Psychology, 98*(1), 19–26.

Shapira, A., & Madsen, M. C. (1974). Between and within group cooperation and competition among kibbutz and nonkibbutz children. *Developmental psychology, 10,* 140–145.

Spiro, M. E. (1958). *Children of the kibbutz.* Cambridge: Harvard University Press.

Zimbardo, P. G. (1969). The human choice: Individuation, reason and order versus deindividuation, impulse and chaos. In W. J. Arnold & D. Levine (Eds.), *Nebraska Symposium on Motivation* (pp. 237–307). Lincoln, NE: University of Nebraska Press.

Ziv, A., Shulman, S., & Schleifer, H. (1979). Moral development: Parental and peer group influence in kibbutz and city children. *The Journal of Genetic Psychology, 134,* 233–240.

8 Cross-National Communalities in the Learning of Aggression from Media Violence

L. Rowell Huesmann
University of Illinois at Chicago

At the beginning of this book, it was noted that serious antisocial behavior seldom seems to develop in children unless there is a convergence of a number of predisposing and precipitating factors. Constitutional factors may predispose the individual to respond aggressively, but children's interactions with their environment during their development and the lessons they learn from these interactions are probably more important determinants of human aggressiveness. No one can expect any one factor by itself to explain which child becomes a very aggressive adult and which child does not. However, when certain cognitive, familial, and environmental characteristics occur in conjunction, aggressive behavior becomes much more likely in a child.

One cannot understand and integrate the results presented in the various chapters of this book without adopting a model for the development of aggression. Accepting the fact that serious aggression requires the convergence of many factors, the model we adopt is primarily an information-processing, learning model. According to this model, the aggressiveness of a child is determined most by the extent to which a child's environment frustrates and victimizes the child, provides aggressive models, and reinforces aggression. However, different children are affected differently by these instigators because of differences in their cognitive functioning. Of course, many of these cognitive, information-processing differences in turn are probably to a great extent learned from their environment.

As described in chapter 1, we believe that social behavior is controlled largely by programs for behavior (scripts) that a child acquires during a sensitive period in his or her development. If a child has only acquired aggressive scripts for behavior, he or she can only behave aggressively. Scripts are memory structures that are encoded through the same processes as any other material in memory. Many scripts are cue specific, being retrieved only when a particular cue is present. However, more general scripts for behavior may be inferred as abstractions of several cue specific scripts; so an overall disinhibition of aggression can occur. Faced with a social problem, a child searches memory for an appropriate script for behaving. Salient cues in the situation (e.g., smiles, frowns, or a gun or other weapon) may activate particular scripts that are then used as guides for behavior. The more aggressive individual quite probably has not only stored more cue specific scripts for aggressive behavior but probably also has stored fewer cue specific prosocial scripts and may have abstracted a general script for aggressive responding.

How does a child learn aggressive scripts? One way is by observing others' behaviors and encoding their behaviors in conjunction with the stimulus situation and the outcome. Children are probably more likely to encode observed strategies for behaving if they perceive the strategies as realistic and they result in a desirable outcome. Of course, an initial encoding does not guarantee that a strategy or script will be available for retrieval later on or, if available, will be retrieved. The availability of a script will be enhanced if the child rehearses it and elaborates on the observed script. The chances of the script being retrieved when the child faces a particular social problem will also depend on the extent to which the cues in the child's environment resemble the salient cues present when the script was encoded.

Media violence plays multiple roles in this hypothesized model. It provides examples of violence from which aggressive scripts can be learned by children through the processes described. It cues the retrieval of already learned scripts for aggressive behavior. Finally, it serves as a source of vicarious gratification and justification to which the aggressive child can turn when faced with the consequences of aggressive behavior. Under this cyclical process model violence viewing and aggression mutually stimulate each other.

Results From the Five Countries

The data from the five countries investigated in the current study clearly indicate that more aggressive children watch more television, prefer more violent programs, identify more with TV characters, and perceive violence as more like real life than do less aggressive children. Table 8.1 summarizes the relations found in the five countries. There is substantial variation from country to country, but at least some variable relates in each country. It is clear that the relation between TV habits and aggression is not limited to countries with large amounts of programming and is not limited to boys.

Of course, the correlations obtained are small in terms of variance explained. They account for between 1% and 23% of the variance in aggression. Yet "variance explained" is not necessarily a reasonable measure of the

TABLE 8.1
Correlations of Average Aggression and Average TV Viewing Scores in All Countries over the Three Waves

TV Variables	Country		ISRAEL		
	AUS	USA	FINN	CITY	POL
	(N = 107)	(N = 221)	(N = 85)	(N = 39)	(N = 96)
			Girls		
Regularity of TV Viewing	.22*	.35***	.14	.28	–
Violence of Preferred Programs	–	A	.23*	.42*	.16
Overall TV Violence Viewing	.16+	.29***	.16	.48**	.17+
Identification with all TV Characters	.11	–	.28*	–	.23*
Identification with Aggressive TV Characters	–	.11	.27*	–	.25*
Perceived Realism of Violent Programs	–	–	.22+	–	–
	(N = 116)	(N = 200)	(N = 93)	(N = 46)	(N = 107)
			Boys		
Regularity of TV Viewing	.10	.21**	.14	.42**	–
Violence of Preferred Programs	–	A	.18+	.24	.26**
Overall TV Violence Viewing	.13	.25***	.22*	.45**	.17+
Identification with all TV Characters	–	.24***	.43***	.34*	.31**
Identification with Aggressive TV Characters	–	.22**	.35**	.29+	.35***
Perceived Realism of Violent Programs	–	.22***	–	–	.14

$+p < .10.$ $*p < .05.$ $**p < .01.$ $***p < .001.$
Notes: A – Data not available.

potential importance of these variables. As Abelson (1984) and Rosenthal (in press) have argued, the calculation of "variance explained" may grossly misrepresent the practical and social significance of a variable. According to the developmental model that we have adopted, children in the age range covered in this study are learning scripts for behaviors that will last into adulthood. Small effects on concurrent behavior can accumulate through a cyclical reinforcing process in which TV violence teaches aggressive behavior and aggressive behavior stimulates violence viewing. Furthermore, because aggression is affected by so many uncontrolled situational and characterological factors in naturalistic settings, one should be skeptical if large portions of variance are explained by single variables. The statistical significance of the correlations must be given more importance than the "variance explained."

Nevertheless, in two groups of subjects, the effects were particularly weak: Israeli kibbutz children and Australian children. Among kibbutz children, the reasons for small relations between TV habits and aggression seem clear. Such children view TV violence much less frequently. When they do see violent programs, the observation is often followed by a discussion of the social implications of the violence. In addition, the kibbutz child's society is one designed to rebuke children for any within-society aggressive behavior. Given such an environment, the lack of a relation between TV violence and aggression is not surprising.

The Australian results are harder to explain. One possibility is that the peer-nominations were not as valid as measures of aggression within Australia as in other countries. Pointing to this explanation is the fact that boys did not score significantly higher on aggression than girls did in Australia. As far as we know, boys have scored higher than girls in every previous application of this technique.

Given that TV habits are related to concurrent aggression in most countries, we can then ask whether the longitudinal patterns of relations suggest the hypothesized cyclical process by which TV viewing stimulates aggression and aggression leads to more exposure to violent TV. To test this hypothesis, each investigator compared the regression prediction of later aggression from early TV habits and early aggression with the prediction of later TV habits from early TV habits and early aggression. Again, there was substantial variation across countries as to which TV habits related most strongly, but a common pattern emerged. As Table 8.2 illustrates, in the United States, Poland, Finland, and among Israeli city children, early TV habits significantly predicted the aggressiveness of children at the end of the study even when the children's initial aggressiveness was statistically controlled. Depending on the country, TV viewing, TV violence viewing, or TV violence viewing coupled with identification with TV characters best predicted changes in aggression. This was true for boys and girls in the United States,

TABLE 8.2

A Comparison of Regression Coefficients for Predicting Later Aggression from Early TV Habits with Predicting Later TV Habits from Early Aggression and TV Habits

Regression Model	Country				
	AUS	USA	FINN	ISRAEL CITY	POL
	Girls				
	(N = 107)	(N = 221)	(N = 85)	(N = 39)	(N = 84)
AGG(3) = AGG(1)	.66***	.53***	.65***	.55**	.72***
+ TV(12)	.00	.14**	.01	.52**	.14+
TV(3) = TV(1)	.19+	.29***	.41***	.31	.00
+ AGG(12)	.08	.26***	.15	.38	.03
	Boys				
	(N = 116)	(N = 200)	(N = 93)	(N = 46)	(N = 95)
AGG(3) = AGG(1)	.71***	.68***	.75***	.58***	.82***
+ TV(12)	.08	.15**	.21***	.29*	.14*
TV(3) = TV(1)	.12	.38***	.32***	.45**	.08
+ AGG(12)	.10	.10	.18	.10	−.02

$+p<.10.$ $*p<.05.$ $**p<.01.$ $***p<.001.$

Poland, and Israel cities, but only for boys in Finland. In Australia, there were no significant longitudinal effects.

In the United States, early aggression also significantly predicted increases in later violence viewing for boys and girls. There were trends in the same direction among city girls in Israel and among both boys and girls in Finland. However, there was no such trend in Poland. In summary, longitudinal effects were obtained to some extent in every country except Australia. There was substantial evidence of influences in both directions, but the most significant effects appeared to be from early TV habits to later aggressive behavior.

These results suggest that the correlation between exposure to media violence and aggression is a consequence first of exposure promoting aggressive acts and second of aggressive acts stimulating exposure. Furthermore, for many subjects, the degree of identification with TV characters seems to be as important as the amount of exposure. Such results are consistent with the proposed model in which children acquire aggressive scripts from observations of media violence and in which the emission of aggressive behavior generates consequences leading the child to watch more media violence.

Were girls more susceptible to learning aggressive scripts performed by female actresses? Not particularly! As Table 8.3 shows, boy's and girl's aggres-

TABLE 8.3

Correlation of Average Aggression with Gender Specific TV Viewing Scores in All Countries over the Three Waves

	Country				
				ISRAEL	
TV Variables	AUS	USA	FINN	CITY	POL
	(N = 107)	(N = 221)	(N = 85)	(N = 39)	(N = 96)
			Girls		
Viewing of Male Actor Violence	.17+	.30***	.16	A	.18+
Viewing of Female Actor Violence	.15	.23***	—	A	.15
Identification with Male Actors	—	.12+	.32**	—	.29**
Identification with Female Actors	—	—	.19	—	—
	(N = 116)	(N = 200)	(N = 93)	(N = 46)	(N = 107)
			Boys		
Viewing of Male Actor Violence	.13	.26***	.23*	A	.19*
Viewing of Female Actor Violence	—	.26***	—	A	—
Identification with Male Actors	—	.20**	.34***	.32*	.30**
Identification with Female Actors	—	.22**	.46***	—	.24**

+ $p < .10$. * $p < .05$. ** $p < .01$. *** $p < .001$.
Notes: A – Data not available.

siveness relate about equally strongly to male and female actor violence. Male actor violence seems to have a stronger influence on both sexes perhaps because of the more heroic character of much of the male actor violence on television. Aggressive children are more likely to identify with TV characters regardless of sex and may be more likely to store in their memories scripts for heroic violent behavior.

According to our model, once a script for aggressive behavior is stored, whether or not it is ever retrieved may depend on whether it is rehearsed. One form of rehearsal is daydreaming. As Table 8.4 shows, greater aggressive behavior and more TV violence viewing were associated with more frequent aggressive and heroic daydreams in most countries. The strength of the relation varied greatly across samples, but overall the results are consistent with the theory that violent TV (and violent behavior) may stimulate violent fantasies, and violent fantasies may increase the likelihood of violent behavior. Certainly, these data contradict the theory that aggressive fantasies stimulated by aggressive TV might act as a catharsis and reduce the likelihood of aggressive behavior.

What about the possibility that social class or IQ are responsible for the relation between aggression and TV violence viewing? Perhaps less intellectually competent, lower class children behave more aggressively (out of frustration or because they cannot learn non-aggressive scripts) and watch more TV (to obtain the rewards vicariously they are missing in their own life)? It is true that, in most of our samples, aggression and TV habits were related to the social status of the family and the intellectual competence of the child. However, as the regression analyses in each chapter demonstrated, early TV habits remained a significant predictor of changes in aggression in most samples even when social class and intellectual competence were controlled statistically. Among boys and girls in the United States and in the Israeli city samples, and among boys in Finland, partialing out these third variables did not change the results noticeably. In Poland, the impact of TV habits on a boy's aggressiveness appeared greater when IQ and social status were controlled whereas the impact on a girl's aggressiveness appeared less. These results provide little support for the concept that the observed relations between TV violence viewing and aggression are entirely due to social class and intelligence factors.

Low intelligence was correlated with higher TV viewing in most countries, perhaps because less able children may find TV an anxiety reducing substitute for the more intellectually demanding tasks they find difficult. In addition, they may obtain rewards vicariously from viewing such programs that are difficult for them to obtain in other ways. A positive relation between IQ and violence viewing was found only in Poland. Perhaps in that social milieu, viewing the mostly imported violent programs provides a vicarious satisfaction for the more intellectually able children that they are otherwise denied.

TABLE 8.4
Correlations of Average Aggression and TV Violence Viewing with Fantasy Behavior

	Aggression					TV Violence Viewing				
	AUS	USA	FINN	ISRAEL CITY	POL	AUS	USA	FINN	ISRAEL CITY	POL
Girls	(N = 107)	(N = 219)	(N = 85)	(N = 35)	(N = 95)	(N = 108)	(N = 218)	(N = 85)	(N = 35)	(N = 95)
Aggressive Fantasy	.26**	.27***	–	–	.20*	.28**	–.11	–	.23*	–
Active-Heroic Fantasy	–	.15*	–	A	.20*	.43***	.25***	–	A	–
Boys	(N = 116)	(N = 190)	(N = 93)	(N = 42)	(N = 108)	(N = 117)	(N = 189)	(N = 93)	(N = 42)	(N = 107)
Aggressive Fantasy	.27**	.18**	–	.24$^+$	–	–	–	.21*	.21	–
Active-Heroic Fantasy	–	–	.20*	A	–	.12	.13$^+$	.16	A	–

$^+p < .10.$ $*p < .05.$ $**p < .01.$ $***p < .001.$

Note: A – Data not available.

Increased TV viewing by the low IQ child will generally increase the chances of that child observing and storing scripts for aggressive behavior. Also, the easy aggressive solutions to social problems promoted so often by the mass media may particularly appeal to the less intellectually able viewer. In this way in most countries, low IQ can be seen as a factor that exacerbates the effect of media violence on the development of aggressive behavior. However, as the regression analyses previously described demonstrate, IQ does not *account* for the relation. It is worthwhile reiterating at this point an important finding from Huesmann, Eron, and Yarmel's (in press) analyses of the relation between childhood and adult aggression and intellectual competence. On the basis of data spanning the 22 years from age 8 to age 30, they concluded that childhood aggression interferes with adult intellectual development more than childhood intellectual failure stimulates adult aggression. The implication is clear. A side effect of a child's learning aggressive behavior from violent TV shows may be diminished intellectual achievement by adulthood.

Among United States and Australian children, the lower the family's social status the more aggressive the children and the more TV violence they watched. This was particularly true for boys. In Israel, it was also true of city boys, but for kibbutz boys and all girls, the relations reversed. Higher status children were more aggressive and watched more violence. In Poland, family income was inversely related to a child's aggression, and girls whose fathers had higher status jobs watched less TV violence. In Finland, there was little direct relation between social status or income and aggression, but in conjunction with other parent variables, higher social status was predictive of greater aggression in boys and lesser aggression in girls. These results are puzzling. Part of the problem undoubtedly is that social status was very difficult to measure in Finland, Poland, and Israel. Traditional rankings based on the English-speaking, free-enterprise societies of the United States and Australia did not apply very well. However, the differences may go deeper. In the United States and Australia, lower socioeconomic status may both stimulate aggressiveness and be a product of aggression. In societies with greater homogeneity, such effects may not obtain.

On the average, more aggressive children and children who watched more TV violence had more aggressive parents. Their parents were also more dissatisfied with them (i.e., rejected them more) and punished them more severely. This was especially true of boys, though there were many variations across countries as Table 8.5 reveals. In every country in which it was measured, rejection of the child, a measure of the parents' dissatisfaction with the child, was significantly related to the child's concurrent aggression. Furthermore, early rejection was one of the best predictors of later aggression in the longitudinal multiple regression predictions (particularly for boys). Although longitudinal regressions predicting TV violence viewing from paren-

TABLE 8.5
Correlations of Average Aggression and TV Violence Viewing with Parent's Child-Rearing Behaviors

	Aggression					TV Violence Viewing				
	AUS	USA	FINN	ISRAEL CITY	POL	AUS	USA	FINN	ISRAEL CITY	POL
Parent Behavior	(N = 129)	(N = 303)	(N = 100)	(N = 0)	(N = 90)	(N = 130)	(N = 296)	(N = 100)	(N = 0)	(N = 90)
					Girls					
Rejection of Child	.38***	.30***	.24*	A	.37***	.37***	.18	.14	A	—
Punishment of Child	.19*	—	.28**	A	.35***	—	—	—	A	—
Aggression (MMPI49)	.19*	—	—	A	—	—	—	—	A	—
	(N = 161)	(N = 281)	(N = 93)	(N = 0)	(N = 107)	(N = 161)	(N = 278)	(N = 92)	(N = 0)	(N = 107)
					Boys					
Rejection of Child	.43***	.27***	.37***	A	.43***	.19*	.31***	—	A	—
Punishment of Child	.29***	.31***	.22*	A	—	.13+	.16*	—	A	—
Aggression (MMPI49)	.24**	.19*	—	A	.18+	.18*	—	.21*	A	—
Physical Aggression	—	—	—	A	—	—	—	.18+	A	.29**

+ p < .10.   * p < .0.   ** p < .0.   *** p < .001.

Note: A – Data not available.

tal rejection did not yield significant positive coefficients for any of the three samples on which complete rejection data were available, all the coefficients for boys and two of three for girls were positive.

Parental rejection of a boy might cause him to be more aggressive because of frustration. However, before one concludes that parental rejection stimulates a boy's aggression, one must examine the longitudinal relation between rejection and aggression with the effects of early aggression partialed out. When this is done, the longitudinal relation between rejection and aggression disappears completely in the United States and Finland. Only in Australia is there any evidence of an effect of rejection on change in aggression. In the other two countries where there were two waves of parent interviews necessary to test the hypothesis (the United States and Finland), longitudinal regression analyses showed that the correlation between rejection and aggression was due more to aggressive behavior by the child stimulating rejection of the child by the parent than vice-versa. For punishment the findings were similar. More aggressive children seem to have been punished more severely as a response to their aggression. The longitudinal analyses did not provide much evidence in support of the view that harsher parental punishment stimulated more aggressive behavior by the child. It may be that aggression by the child stimulates rejection and punishment by the parents which in turn, although not directly stimulating aggression, isolates the child more and drives the child to watch more TV and more violent programs. The child can justify his or her aggressive behavior on the basis of what he or she observes on these shows, and the punishment and rejection have little effect except to diminish the parents' influence.

Finally, let us examine the role of popularity as a mediator. Elsewhere, Eron and Huesmann (1984) have argued that prosocial skills play an important role in preventing childhood aggression from developing into adult criminality. In their 22-year study they obtained evidence that aggressive children who are popular and have some prosocial skills are less likely to become aggressive adults (Eron & Huesmann, 1984). Prosocial skills provide the child with a viable alternative to solving social problems with aggressive responses. According to this view, children with greater prosocial skills should be more popular and less aggressive. On the other hand, aggressive behavior would make a child less popular. If the child withdraws from social contacts as a result of this unpopularity and turns to watching more television, unpopularity may exacerbate the relation between television violence and aggression.

The correlations obtained in each country between aggression, popularity, and TV viewing are summarized in Table 8.6. In every sample (except perhaps Israel city children) the more aggressive children are less popular (and among Israel kibbutz children this is also true). However, only in the United States was there evidence that the less popular children watched more TV violence. Among boys and girls in the United States and Australia, and among

TABLE 8.6

The Correlations of Average Popularity with Average Aggression and Average TV Violence Viewing Over 3 Years

| | Aggression | | | | | TV Violence Viewing | | | | |
	AUS	USA	FINN	ISRAEL CITY	POL	AUS	USA	FINN	ISRAEL CITY	POL
					Girls					
Popularity	−.38***	−.44***	−.17	—	−.42***	—	−.18**	—	.21	—
					Boys					
	−.32***	−.51***	−.32**	−.19	−.46***	—	−.16*	—	−.24	—

*p < .05.   **p < .01.   ***p < .001.

250

boys in Poland and Israel, early aggression also predicted decreases in popularity over time. But again, only in the United States, was there evidence that unpopularity increased TV violence viewing. Thus, an hypothesized involvement of unpopularity in the television violence aggression cycle only seems plausible in the United States.

As was argued in chapter 2, it is much more difficult to explain differences in results across countries than it is to explain similarities. Fortunately, as this chapter illustrates, there seem to be many more communalities in the results across countries than there are serious discrepancies. Let us now examine two other very similar recent studies and see how their results compare with ours.

The Parallel Study in The Netherlands

At the same time as the current study was being conducted in Australia, Finland, Israel, Poland and the United States, a similar study was being performed in The Netherlands by Wiegman, Baarda, and Kuttschreuter (1984). As described in the Preface, their longitudinal field study was originally intended to duplicate the investigations being conducted in the other countries included in this volume. However, for a variety of reasons, the procedures Wiegman et al. eventually adopted deviated very substantially from the procedures used elsewhere. As a consequence, the comparison of exact results is problematic. Nevertheless, an overall evaluation of their study in the light of the results reported in the book is possible.

The Netherlands group's methodology was influenced strongly by a number of questionable assumptions about Dutch society for which little supporting data exist. For example, it was assumed that in The Netherlands "the relation between parents and children is less based on authority and more on friendship" (p. 1). As a consequence, questions about harsh punishments (such as beating with a belt) were deleted from The Netherlands questionnaire because it was felt that "parents were shocked by these questions" (p. 18). In addition, The Netherlands investigators rejected the theoretical assumptions underlying many of the psychological tests employed, and invented new measures of their own. For example, again with regard to punishment, the Dutch investigators assumed "there is a wide difference between a parent who strikes his child in the heat of the moment and a parent who strikes his child in the conviction it is the right thing to do" (p. 17). Therefore, they altered the response form of the punishment questions.

Almost every measure employed in The Netherlands was redesigned on the basis of similar new assumptions about Dutch society or psychological theory. In the child interview, the TV viewing measures, the judged realism of TV measure, the identification with TV characters measures, the fantasy measures, and the sex-role orientation measures were all changed so substantially that an exact comparison of results would be impossible. The peer-nominated aggression questions remained unchanged, although unvalidated prosocial behavior questions were added as filler items. In addition to these scale changes, The Netherlands researchers used different age subjects. Although first graders successfully handled the procedures in every other country, The Netherlands researchers felt that even their revised measures were too complex for first graders in their country, and they began with second and fourth graders. In the parent interviews, equally substantial changes were made. The rejection, nurturance, mobility, and fantasy scales were not used nor was the MMPI given. The scales that were used were altered substantially. Only mothers were interviewed, and they were only interviewed once, during the second wave.

The methodological deviations of The Netherlands researchers present a number of problems for interpreting their data and particularly for comparing their results with the results from other countries. Although many variables are called by the same names (e.g., TV realism, punishment) they are by no means the same variables. Nevertheless, in many respects, the results of The Netherlands study are consistent with the results reported in this book and with the explanatory model proposed in this chapter.

Very significant positive correlations were obtained between TV violence viewing and aggression for both boys and girls. As in the United States, these correlations were, if anything stronger for girls (average $r = .25$) than for boys (average $r = .20$). These correlations obtained despite the fact that TV violence was measured in a quite different fashion (which nevertheless correlated .92 with our measure). However, as in Australia, there were no significant longitudinal regression effects either from early TV viewing to later aggression or from early aggression to later TV violence viewing. Still, for both boys and girls, all the causal coefficients were positive, and the longitudinal correlations were significant. TV violence viewing and aggression may be affecting each other in a reciprocal fashion, but the stability of each behavior may be too great over the years in question for significant coefficients to obtain. It is worth noting that the stability of TV violence viewing over 3 years in The Netherlands (as measured by their methodology) was higher than in the United States.

The Netherlands researchers suggest as an alternative explanation that low intelligence may account for the relation between TV violence and aggression. We have seen that in most countries, as our reciprocal action model predicts, low IQ and low academic achievement are associated with increased aggression and increased TV viewing. However, the theory that poor intellectual functioning is the only cause of the relation does not hold up in the countries we studied. Neither does it withstand scrutiny in The Netherland's data. IQ was only measured for the older subjects and only measured in the third wave. When it was partialed out, the correlations between TV violence viewing and aggression were reduced (as in most countries) but remained mostly significant. Thus, IQ cannot be the only cause of the relation. The Netherlands researchers have also reported a path analysis that seems to suggest that low IQ is the major cause of the relation. However, the structural model on which that analysis is based is seriously flawed. It used IQ as a precursor variable to first and second wave aggression even though IQ was not measured until the third wave.

One final piece of data from The Netherlands study deserves comment. In addition to everything else, the researchers attempted to measure both prosocial behavior and viewing of prosocial TV. They found no evidence of a relation between viewing prosocial TV and prosocial behavior. However, both their measures of prosocial behavor and their measure of prosocial TV have no established validity. In particular, the TV measure was questionnable. Any prosocial act was given an equal weight even if it was coupled with a highly violent act by the same person. Not surprisingly, with this definition, prosocial viewing was found to correlate .90 with violence viewing.

In summary, The Netherlands data generally are consistent with the data from the countries in the current study. More aggressive children consistently watch more TV and more violent TV. Lontitudinal correlations and regression coefficients are positive in both directions though the longitudinal regression coefficients were not significant. The other findings must be viewed skeptically because of the methodological issues raised earlier.

The NBC Study

In the early 1970s, another longitudinal study, using a very similar design to the current one, was conducted by Milavsky and his associates at NBC. Analysis of the data from that field study took many years, and the results were not published until 1982 (Milavsky, Kessler, Stipp, & Rubens, 1982). To some, the results from this NBC study may seem quite discrepant with the results reported in this book. In reality, the results are quite similar and only the researchers' interpretation of the results is different.

Milavsky et al. collected data on a substantial sample of elementary school children in the United States at repeated intervals. The lags between observations ranged from a few months to several years. The major measure of aggression by the children was again peer nominations of aggressive behaviors.

Like most other researchers, Milavsky et al. discovered that more aggressive children were watching more television violence. As in the cross-national study, the correlations between TV violence viewing and aggressive behavior were uniformly positive and mostly significant (rangeing from .13 to .23). Furthermore, as in our own United States study and in The Netherlands study just described, Milavsky et al. found a somewhat stronger relation for girls than for boys and found almost as strong a relation between total viewing time and aggression as between violence viewing and aggression.

To examine the longitudinal relations between TV habits and aggression, Milavsky et al. (1982) used the same type of regression analyses we employed in the cross-national study. For each different lag, they constructed a different regression equation yielding a total of 15 different analyses. In each analysis, aggression in one wave was predicted from TV violence viewing and aggression in a previous wave. Of course, as one would expect from other research, previous aggression is a very strong predictor of subsequent aggression. The question is whether earlier TV violence viewing predicts later aggression once the effect of early aggression is statistically controlled in the regression analysis. Among boys and girls in the United States, Poland, and Israel cities, and among boys in Finland, we reported that early TV habits did significantly predict later aggression under these conditions. In Australia, no such effect could be detected. In the parallel study in The Netherlands, positive coefficients were reported though they were not significant. Similarly, although Milavsky et al. found mostly positive coefficients (12 of 15) in the critical analyses, only a few were significant on their own. Still, if there were really no effect of violence viewing on later aggression, the chances of obtaining 12 positive coefficients in 15 analyses would be less than 1 in 1000. These results seem reasonably consistent with all other results reported in this volume and consistent with the proposed model through which exposure to TV violence increases aggressive behavior. In this regard, it is important to note that the "causal" coefficients Milavsky et al. obtain increase almost monotonically with the duration of the lag between observations. Although they are very small for short lags, they are not so small for longer lags. This is what one would expect from a cumulative effect, bidirectional model.

Milavsky et al. do not believe that their data provide support for the theory that TV violence viewing increases the likelihood of aggression behavior in children. They do not believe the small positive coefficients are sufficient to justify such a conclusion. Furthermore, they argue that the observed correlations between TV violence viewing and aggression are enhanced by a number of artifacts and are really even smaller than they seem.

The authors argue that these cross-sectional correlations exaggerate the relation because (a) high aggressive boys exaggerate their violence viewing, and (b) both violence viewing and aggression are correlated with social class. The corrected estimates are much lower and mostly nonsignificant. It is certainly to be expected that data from more aggressive boys (who generally are poorer readers and have lower IQs) will be least valid. The question is whether it is appropriate to remove these subjects from the analyses either physically or statistically. One should at least first ask why these subjects are behaving this way and what psychological processes this behavior represents. Furthermore, it is not clear that an aggressive boy who underreported his TV viewing would have been detected and have been removed. The drop in correlations when social class is partialed out is also much higher than that reported in most other studies. The measure of social class used differs from most others in that it includes mother's occupation (or lack of occupation). This may be critical because, as our own recent studies have indicated, children of working mothers with relatively low-status jobs tend to be more aggressive and watch more television. But again, before partialing out such a variable, one should ask what psychological processes are involved and whether partialing is appropriate. For example, the mother's presence in the house may serve as a control that limits the extent to which violence viewing could influence aggression. Finally, though the role of social class and invalid responding in artificially raising correlations is given prominent display, the role of unreliability in lowering correlations is given only secondary play.

Milavsky et al.'s (1982) conception of the potential universe of psychological processes for explaining the relation between television violence viewing and aggression seems to be that either "television exposure leads to increased aggressiveness; or aggressive children tend to select violent television programs; or some third variables . . . lead (to) both" (p. 114). These are not psychological process theories; they are simply descriptive statements. Furthermore, they are not even mutually exclusive descriptive statements. By neglecting psychological theory and particularly developmental theory, Milavsky et al. are forced into summarizing their results solely in terms of descriptive relations between variables. Thus, their conclusions seem quite different from the conclusions derived from the current study. Yet, in fact, their results are not inconsistent with the results from most countries in the current study and with the developmental, reciprocal influence model described in this chapter.

SUMMARY

As was expected, there were many discrepancies in the results from the different countries in the current study. Some defy easy explanations. Nevertheless, on the whole, the results were remarkably consistent, especially when one considers the vastly different television and social environments in the participating countries. The findings were also generally consistent with the results of other recent similar investigations.

More aggressive children watch more violence in the media in almost every country. Of that, there can be no doubt. The common covariation of TV habits and aggression with social class, gender, age, IQ, and cultural factors contributes to this relation but does not explain it. Although there is much less consistency across countries in the longitudinal data suggesting causal relations, substantial evidence was derived that supports a bidirectional learning model. The child learns aggressive scripts for behavior from observing media violence, and aggressive behavior on the part of the child produces environmental and cognitive reactions that make it more probable the child will watch more violence. Unpopularity and poor school achievement are two examples of such intervening variables. Other cognitive characteristics appear to increase the likelihood that the child will encode, retain, and later employ observed aggressive scripts. For example, identifying more with TV actors appears to have such an effect. Aggressive fantasies may increase the probability of aggressive scripts being retained because the fantasies serve as rehearsals of the scripts. Aggressive fantasies are more prevalent in children who behave more aggresssively and watch more media violence.

Children's scripts for social behavior seem to be learned at quite an early age, and, once established, are very resistant to change. As described in Chapter 1, the more aggressive child becomes the more aggressive adult (Huesmann, Eron, Lefkowitz, & Walder, 1984; Olweus, 1979). Aggressiveness is even transmitted across generations (Huesmann et al., 1984). The children of more aggressive parents seem to form more aggressive scripts for behavior. The disattenuated correlation from child to adult aggression has been estimated at 0.46 (Huesmann et al., 1984). In the current study, 3-year observed stabilities of peer-nominated aggression ranged from 0.62 in Australia to 0.75 in Poland.

In reaching a final conclusion about the role of media violence in promoting aggressive behavior, one must deal with two additional issues. First, if at least part of the relation between TV violence and aggression is due to the fact that more aggressive children turn to watching more violence, does one need to be concerned about the violence? If the proposed process model is even partially accurate, the answer must be yes. TV viewing that occurs after an aggressive act can still make the act easier to commit. Children may justify their aggressive acts after the fact or may obtain vicarious rewards from the TV that would not normally follow aggressive behavior. The real question one must ask is what would have happened to the child if the media violence had not been available. The second issue concerns the magnitude of the observed relations between TV violence viewing and aggression. By traditional standards of measurement, correlations of .15 to .30 are not large even if they are statistically significant. One might argue that media violence represents only 2% to 9% (the correlations squared) of the variance in individual differences in aggression. There are several answers to this argument. First, as Abelson (1984) and Rosenthal (in press) have argued, equating importance with percentage of variance explained can be quite misleading. Small differences (e.g., less than 1%) in variance explained can have major effects on performance in such areas as sports and clinical diagnosis, for example. Second, by the standards of personality measurement and prediction of behavior, .20 is not a small correlation. Aggression is a multiply determined behavior with many different factors causing it. To expect any one factor to explain even 10% of its variance is unrealistic. Third, aggression is a quite stable behavior, whereas TV viewing is not. Early aggression is the best predictor of later aggression even by age 6. Therefore, a substantial portion of the variance in aggression will never be predictable by other variables because it is predicted by previous aggression. Finally, one must realize that if even 1% of the variation in homicide rates between the United States and many other countries could be attributed to media violence, one would be talking about at least 200 homicides per year in the United States. This is not a small effect.

ACKNOWLEDGMENT

Preparation of this chapter was supported in part from grant MH38683 from the National Institute of Mental Health.

REFERENCES

Abelson, R. P. (1984). A variance explanation paradox: When a little is a lot. *Psychological Bulletin, 97,* 129–133.

Eron, L. D., & Huesmann, L. R. (1984). The relation of prosocial behavior to the development of aggression and psychopathology. *Aggressive Behavior, 10,* 201–211.

Huesmann, L. R., Eron, L. D., Lefkowitz, M. M., & Walder, L. O. (1984). The stability of aggression over time and generations. *Developmental Psychology, 20,* 1120–1134.

Huesmann, L. R., Eron, L. D., & Yarmel, P. W. (in press). Intellectual functioning and the development of aggression. *Journal of Personality and Social Psychology: Personality Processes and Individual Differences.*

Olweus, D. (1979). The stability of aggressive reaction patterns in human males: A review. *Psychological Bulletin, 85,* 852–875.

Milavsky, J. R., Kessler, R. C., Stipp, H. H., & Rubens, W. S. (1982). *Television and aggression: A panel study.* New York: Academic Press.

Rosenthal, R. (in press). The social consequences of small effects. *Journal of Social Issues.*

Wiegman, O., Baarda, B., & Kuttschreuter, M. (1984). *The Dutch contribution to the cross-national study.* Paper presented at the conference on The Role of Culture and the Media in the Development of Aggressive Behavior, Werner-Reimers Stifting, Bad Hornburg, West Germany.

9 International Research on Television Violence: Synopsis and Critique

Jo Groebel
Educational University Rheinland-Pfalz

Does TV violence have an effect on aggression? Most of the studies conducted over the past 25 years have supported the hypothesis that there is a positive relation between TV violence viewing and aggressive behavior (see Eron & Huesmann, 1985; Huesmann, 1982).

Many of the studies, however, are not comparable: Some deal with short-term effects; others with long-term effects. They have been conducted with different social groups. They have been developed in differing cultural backgrounds. One major problem has been the different definitions and operationalizations of the concept of aggression. These differences have made it easy for some public media to talk of contradictory results (Eron, 1986; Groebel, 1986). Even if the results of the studies are comparable, the interpretations have often differed. One of the most prominent examples is a panel study conducted by Milavsky, Kessler, Stipp, and Rubens (1982) that found results as to the relation between TV violence and aggression similar to what was found by Huesmann & Eron (this volume), Krebs (1981), and Groebel (1983). However, although the last mentioned authors interpreted their data as not falsifying the "TV has an effect" hypothesis and suggesting a complex system of relations between TV and aggression, Milavsky et al. denied any causal relation.

These differences in interpretation can partly be traced back to the lack of a more general integrative framework. Causal analyses — as is claimed by most psychometricians — only make sense if they are strictly applied within a model-testing or confirmatory framework. It therefore is difficult to follow all of Milavsky et al.'s conclusions — despite the finesse of their methodology—because they did not formulate an explicit theory to be tested by their analyses.

Until recently, there have been insufficient theoretical models for the explanation of TV violence effects in a more complex personal and situational context. The numerous experimental studies on TV and aggression—important as they have been for testing short-term effects—only added one situational or personal moderating variable to another without being able to determine the interactive qualities of the whole network of contributing variables. It is one of the major advantages of the study reported in this volume that it attempts to validate a more global—and supercultural—theory to explain long-term effects of TV violence.

MEDIA RESEARCH IN INTERNATIONAL PERSPECTIVE

We seem to approach what some are calling a global media culture. "J.R." or "Krystle Carrington," "Magnum" or "Kojak" probably are just as famous all over the world as Coca Cola or Mercedes-Benz. With an increasing distribution of the electronic media in even the poorest countries, there is an increasing demand for knowing what the specific cross-cultural effects of the mass media and especially television are. This cross-cultural or international perspective can be treated under several aspects:

- Do the media aid in increasing mutual understanding of the different cultures?
- Do the media lead to a homogenization of cultures because of similar content? . . . Is this homogenization identical to an Americanization?
- Is it possible to generalize research findings from one nation to another nation when one studies media effects?

Definitely, United States studies have influenced the international debate on the effects of media violence to the highest extent. The results of Bandura (1977), Berkowitz (1962), Feshbach (1961), and Eron, Huesmann, Lefkowitz, and Walder (1972) were transferred to the TV violence debate in other countries—mostly without adequately testing them again in the new settings. And though it seems logical to import the American research findings along with the violent American TV programs, one must question whether TV effects are a priori the same in different cultural contexts.

Here, the study under consideration fills a gap that has been open for too long: For the first time, the effects of violent TV programs were studied simultaneously under comparable conditions in five different countries. In addition, a Dutch group of researchers analyzed the problem with a similar but not identical approach (Wiegman, Kuttschreuter & Baarda, 1984; Wiegman

& Baarda, in preparation), nevertheless offering the chance to integrate their results into the cross-national research frame.

A study like this, however, faces some strong difficulties: One of the major problems of cross-cultural research is the comparability of the concepts used and of the operationalization of these concepts. Aggression especially is a very complex phenomenon with numerous definitions, numerous theories about its origins, and an internal structure hard to determine (see Goldstein & Segall, 1983). Instead of diving too deeply into the theoretical considerations of the concept of aggression, the authors of the present study chose to define *aggression* as an "antisocial act, an act that injures or irritates another." This approach seems to be legitimate as a more differentiated treatment of all the possible facets of aggression probably would have been too sophisticated for the children investigated in this study. Here, aggression is treated on a commonsense basis, or — as one might argue according to a cognitive theory — on the level of a basic category (see Rosch, 1978). Developmental cognitive theories also show that in younger ages there are no representations of more sophisticated concepts.

Three problems remain even when considering the "basic" definition of aggression:

1. The structural comparability between media content and the viewers' reactions,

2. the question whether the "common-sense" definitions are really identical for all nations or whether these definitions have to be controlled for the "over-all" level of aggression in the respective cultures,

3. the similarity/dissimilarity between *intranational* subcultures compared to the *international* cultures.

Although the second mentioned problem has been one of the issues studied in this research program, the first one demands a process theory as to the effects of violent — and general — TV programs.

Had there been another data basis, one could have applied a direct structural comparison between the content-related categories of the TV programs (e.g., on the basis of content analyses or viewers' ratings) and the — latent — categories of the viewers' reaction patterns. However, as these data were not available because of reasons presented elsewhere in this book, the authors had to use a process theory that could not directly be tested using these specific data but that has been relatively well confirmed in recent studies by the authors themselves and by other researchers. In a later section, we offer some additional comments in regard to constructing an integrative theory of media effects on aggressive habits.

The third of the aforementioned problems touches a classical question of cross-cultural research: The homogeneity of the respective cultures under consideration. Two groups of lower class people in two different nations may be more similar with respect to certain behavior patterns than a group of lower class people and a group of upper class people within the same nation. It is plausible to expect a similar phenomenon when analyzing aggression. Here the study in general offers some interesting results: It appears that — summarizing what the authors are reporting — there is a continuum of cultural homogeneity for the different nations. Finland seems to be a relatively homogeneous country, whereas Israel and the United States seem to be more heterogeneous, with Poland and Australia somewhere in the middle of this continuum. Israel's heterogeneity becomes immediately apparent from the results: There is a strong dichotomy separating the behavioral habits of kibbutz inhabitants from those of non-kibbutz children. Although Israel's society is two-fold, the United States situation is more complex with so many possible subgroups that it is difficult to clearly identify each of them.

One could offer a hypothesis on the basis of the data described in this volume: The continuum of TV homogeneity is the reverse of the continuum of cultural homogeneity. The United States has the most homogeneous structure of TV programs (talking of the "biggies," the commercial broadcasting stations) with mostly stable, even stereotyped, dramaturgical, and content-related program patterns whereas Finland — probably due to a certain import rate of different nations — presents a wide range of very different programs.

How these specific patterns interact in moderating TV effects on aggression is reviewed in some of the following sections.

METHODS OF CROSS-CULTURAL RESEARCH

Operationalizations of Aggression

The specific difficulties of cross-cultural methodology cannot be discussed extensively here (for further details of the respective methods see, Triandis & Berry, 1980). However, one dilemma is inherent in nearly all cross-national research: The determination of a common reference point when measuring psychological concepts. This of course also applies when dealing with aggression. As already mentioned, the authors of this particular study decided to use a definition of aggression with a high probability of cross-cultural concurrence — intentional, mostly physical injury. Yet, this definition also means that the whole range of possible aggression phenomena is only partly covered. For the age group investigated in this research program, it seemed to be plausible to limit the respective aggression concept. For future research, however, it definitely will be interesting to analyze more subtle ways of possibly modelling aggressive TV (e.g., denigration of minorities, verbally aggressive family interactions, etc.). This would demand exceptional effort in determining the specific structural and dimensional characteristics of the aggression concepts in the respective cultures. These specific patterns then could be tested with respect to a possible overlapping (e.g., by means of MDS procedures).

The Design of the Study

One of the basic conditions for testing causal effects in field studies, was met in this research program, applying a panel design. Actually, the American authors belong to the pioneer representatives of this particular research paradigm (Eron, 1963; Eron et al., 1972; Huesmann, 1982). A problem in the context of longitudinal field studies is the mostly missing possibility of systematic experimental treatment variation. In a quasi-experimental design, this problem can be compensated by applying causal data analyses, like multiple regression, path analysis, or structural modeling. Still, one difficulty may remain: control for measurement effects. With longitudinal designs, the specific problem of repeated-measurement effects arises. Subjects develop hypotheses about the goals of the study, they may communicate with each other on the assumed intentions between waves, they probably try to remember how they responded during the last wave, and try to give consistent responses. This may lead to an overestimation of the stability on the one hand – due to a consistency tendency – or to overrated differences on the other. At best, these two opposite trends will neutralize each other. With a large sample of subjects, as in this particular study, one can assume such a neutralization of effects.

Another possibility, however, is to control for repeated-measurement effects systematically as in the application of a complete Baltes–Schaie design (Baltes, 1968; Schaie, 1973). However, this probably means a significant increase in sample sizes. Here the already large-scale investigation certainly would have met temporal and financial limits.

Yet, a somewhat sophisticated longitudinal design was partly realized in this cross-cultural study. The consideration of two entry levels of age at the beginning allowed to control for cohort effects. The respective analyses demonstrated that there were no significant cohort differences. This also means that the slight shift in age groups between the different national samples can be discounted.

The Measures

The problem of comparability of measures when applying them in different cultures has been stated previously. The authors decided for a simple translation of the original American scales into their respective languages. This may reduce the specific cultural adequacy of the measures; and certain specific aspects — only predominant in an American population — may be over-represented whereas others — more relevant to a non-American culture — may not be covered. At the same time, however, the confinement to *one* standardized instrument allows a maximum direct comparability of the data. One could also argue, that due to the fact that most international violent TV content is of American origin, a measure based on "American" items can capture possible TV violence effects best.

There is at least one delicate aspect when using peer nominations as aggression measures: The implications of attribution processes and implicit theories. It is often the outward appearance or teacher labelling rather than the actual behavior that affects peer ratings. By recording actual behaviors and not general impressions of the classmates, this possible bias probably was avoided here. Another problem in this context may be the existence of response tendencies and threshold effects. One student tends to name as many peers as possible, another as few as possible. For one student, the criterion of "hitting" is only fulfilled when the victim actually is hurt, for another the threatening gesture already meets the criterion. These tendencies are hard to control. High validity should be an indication of a minor impact of these effects. The authors report recent studies where both criterion and construct validity were tested and turned out to be in accordance with the usual test-theoretical standards. The same applies to the other instruments used (chapter 2, this volume). Thus, one can conclude that the measures were not highly biased.

Data Analysis

With a large number of possible relations between variables at least three strategies for data analyses are possible:

1. Analyzing the data on an iterative basis and collecting many single correlations, cross-tabulations, ANOVAS etc.

The advantages of such a procedure are relatively simple and clear-cut single results. The disadvantages are isolated, not generalizable, and "artificial" outcomes. In addition, and this condition often is the case, with an increase of single analyses, the application of significance testing becomes obsolete. One out of 20 results would be — following the logic of the procedure — significant by chance ($p = .05$). This, as a consequence, could lead to an overestimation of single effects. Also in this cross-cultural study, some results may be biased by a too-extensive use of significance testing without corrections. On the other hand, the investigators were very scrupulous in only interpreting findings that had been double-checked by the use of different procedures (see the multi-trait-multi-method paradigm, Campbell & Fiske, 1959; and others).

2. Applying data-reduction procedures, like factor analysis, cluster analysis, then following the aforementioned strategy.

When applied on a confirmatory basis, factor analysis may be a useful means to determine latent structures of variables. The usual catch-as-catch-can procedure, however, has yet to prove its justification (see the scholarly critique by Schonemann & Steiger, 1978).

3. Following a multivariate strategy of data analysis.

One of the major advantages of the study, as compared to previous projects, was the application of multivariate causal analyses. This led to a more generalizable representation of the media variables, the environmental and personal factors, at the same time fitting better with the interactive theory of reciprocal-cognitive-processes as advocated by the authors.

Multiple regression analysis was the major means of identifying the status of TV in the whole network of variables having a possible impact on aggression.

A remark as to the applied data procedures: A correction for the respective reliability scores would have added to the precision of the multivariate results. However, in at least two countries, the USA (chapter 3, this volume) and Finland (chapter 4, this volume) a comparison of corrected and uncorrected coefficients showed no remarkable differences in the overall outcomes of the respective analyses.

For a cross-cultural comparison of relations between single variables it might have been interesting, in principle, to determine the un-standardized regression coefficients as well as the standardized coefficients within the multiple analyses. But one can easily follow the authors' arguments (see chapter 2, this volume) that the differing populations did not allow *direct* statistical comparison of means and coefficients.

One problem difficult to solve is that of possible spurious correlations. It could be plausible that some supposedly causally interrelated variables in fact are facets of a common latent structure without any clear-cut one-way impacts. The reciprocal patterns that were found support this hypothesis and they are the integrative elements of the cognitive process theory described in this volume.

The Individual National Studies

United States.   To start the reviews of the individual national studies with the United States seems plausible because of two reasons: (a) the whole study was in its origins more or less based on the American investigators' paradigm and initiated by these authors, and (b) American programs influence the global TV culture far more than do any other national programs. For many nations, American TV already represents today what they will be facing in the future. Thus, TV effects found in the United States can serve as signals for other cultures.

Methodological remarks have already been presented in a previous section. Here, we concentrate on the results as described and interpreted by Huesmann and Eron in their chapter.

When checking the lists of programs presented to the American subjects it is obvious that many of the stimuli correspond to the ones that also can be found in other national TV broadcasts due to the imports of American programs. Hence, although restricted to the pure single TV stimuli, one can expect similar effects in all nations. Differences then can be explained by the differing cultural backgrounds. However, it is not only the surrounding culture that contributes to the specifity of TV effects but also the amount of viewing and especially the embedding of the single programs in the overall broadcast. Here, *Starsky and Hutch* on an American screen, may actually differ from the same *Starsky and Hutch* on an European screen. In the United States, the show is interrupted by commercials. In Europe, it is not. In the United States, most of the other programs follow a similar dramaturgy, if the viewer does not watch Public Broadcasting Channels. In Europe, *Starsky and Hutch* contrasts with many documentary and political programs. In addition, the perceived environment within this or similar programs may correspond more closely to the actual environment of the American viewers. This is probably less the case with a European viewer. Accordingly, we would expect greater correspondence between violent TV and aggression in the United States compared to most of the other nations.

The American results demonstrate the positive correlation between TV violence and aggressive behavior. Although in many studies, such a correlation probably can be traced back to a certain (semantic) response tendency when only using self-report data, thus creating an artifact, the design of this particular study excludes such an interpretation: The correlation was based on self-reports and peer nominations. The advantage of this procedure in our opinion outweighs any possible criticism of biased aggression ratings by other children.

Despite the usual gender differences in the aggression measures, American girls displayed a higher positive correlation between TV violence and aggression than boys, at the same time identifying more with male aggressive TV characters than with female models. This result could be an indicator of an increasing homogenization between originally differing role orientations and cultures due to media influences. In fact, this probably will turn out to be one of the research areas more systematically investigated in the future (see Groebel, in press b).

The importance of role orientation becomes obvious in the result that for American boys the combination of high identification with TV models and excessive violent TV viewing is most strongly related to aggressive behavior.

Together with the finding that unpopularity is related to a TV diet of more violence, there is a perfect correspondence to other, super-cultural conclusions: In a German study with a design similar to the project under consideration here (Groebel, 1981b; Groebel & Krebs, 1983; Krebs, 1981), the data showed that boys with difficulties in their actual social surrounding and low self-esteem were the ones with the highest amount of TV viewing that, in turn, reinforced their social fear and, as an indirect effect, their tendency to act aggressively (Groebel, 1984). From a cognitive point of view this supports the following interpretation. Violent TV serves an escapism function. It offers vicarious positive experiences with "strong" aggressive models with whom a socially insecure viewer can identify. At the same time, the contrast to the viewer's own actual position is increased leading to even higher social instability. Aggression then can be the result of two overlapping processes: (a) the belief that only aggressive means lead to a solution of problems (learned from the TV characters), and (b) the frustration of actual isolation and unpopularity.

The resulting aggressive behavior causes more difficulties with peers and parents (see rejection and punishment) and increases the escapism tendency, TV viewing. These interpretations are consistent with the American, and other, data. The relation between TV and aggression is most adequately described by the authors in the context of a reciprocal process. Actually, the majority of longitudinal studies on violence and television support the conclusion that there is less evidence for a unidirectional relationship than for some kind of a closed control loop. Within this process, there still may be clear-cut "one-way" effects, at certain stages. Huesmann and Eron (this volume) point to the different probabilities of specific TV effects during different ages. However, in general, these single effects are integrated in a self-reinforcing process system that, with a cumulation of TV diet over time, seems to be increasingly hard to alter. This system is characterized by environmental and personal, stable and unstable, cognitive and emotional elements: social popularity, intellectual achievement, parental influences, perceived TV realism, and fantasy behavior. In most studies, especially academic achievement and the parents' socioeconomic status, together with the already described factors turn out to be the major moderators for TV effects (Milavsky et al., 1982; Singer & Singer, 1981). This study is no exception.

Three additional single findings seem to bear a certain importance for those countries with an increasing similarity to the American TV structure:

1. Adults with higher socioeconomic status watch less TV in general but watch slightly more aggressive shows compared to other programs. This result probably supports the uses-and-gratifications approach and the Berlyne-hypothesis. Single programs are selected and used for relaxation without having a necessary antisocial effect. This clearly would be an indicator for the

operation of different habits and individual approaches when using TV. Thus, TV for some persons can serve as short-term entertainment without far-reaching consequences; but for others, it can lead to cumulative long-term escapism, with an increasing probability of antisocial effects. The American data demonstrate the evidence for the last-mentioned effect on young children.

2. Not only aggressively pre-disposed children are affected by violent TV. Thus, even in a little aggression-oriented culture, the introduction of a high amount of aggressive TV may lead to the already described processes. This particularly seems to be relevant for American TV imports in other countries.

3. In the United States, regular TV viewing in general is equivalent to regular violent TV viewing. The percentage of violence in the overall programming is so high that one can hardly escape from being confronted with aggression on the screen, especially — as Huesmann and Eron (this volume) state — as TV violence can be produced with relatively little financial and dramaturgical effort and, at the same time, guarantees high viewer attention and high viewer percentages. In the 1980s, the United States still seem to set trends for violence in the media.

Australia. What about the "second generation" media cultures? A "naive" European might have the stereotype of Australia as some kind of a small scale United States. Both countries were colonized by European emigrants some centuries ago. Both countries' cultures are mainly of Anglosaxon origin. Most of all, it is hard for a European to tell whether a certain adventure drama shown on TV is an Australian or an American production; both mostly follow a similar dramaturgy.

This study, however, reveals some remarkable differences. Unlike the United States, Australian society appears to be relatively homogeneous. And although TV watching for Australian children is the major leisure time activity as it is in America, the respective effects differ to a certain extent from those found in the United States: Sheehan (this volume) reports no clear-cut causal relation between TV viewing and aggression over time. There are only time-synchronous correlations at certain stages of the longitudinal study, nevertheless supporting the hypothesis that, depending on age, a specific proneness to violent TV effects exists. This particular result corresponds to the American findings.

Which factors account for the differences? It becomes obvious from the data that Australian society seems to have a relatively stable normative system with a strong sex-role orientation, rejection of aggressive behavior, a probably above-average sanctioning school system, and official regulation of TV content. This, together with a rather low actual aggression level, may inhibit the development of long-term aggressive habits as a consequence of TV violence. That this inhibition is not merely the result of external norms, but probably is inherent in the children themselves becomes apparent from the result that aggressive peers turned out to be the most unpopular ones.

The particular consequences of effective norms do not lead the author to plead for more censorship. However, the impact of official efforts to put more energy in the production of prosocial and non-violent programs and in the regulation of the program-structure may be contributing to the relatively low relation between violent TV and aggression; especially when considering that the level of significance in the respective ANOVA equals $p = .10$. With the number of ANOVAs reported, this can be interpreted as no more than a random result.

Still, a small significant cross-sectional correlation between TV violence and aggression remains. This finding can be integrated into the cognitive theory of media effects: At certain age stages (see also the American results) aggression as a behavioral and cognitive category is more probable than at other stages, especially for boys. At these stages, aggressive behavior and aggressive media preferences are indicators of a common situational cognitive pattern rather than of a continuing interaction. A long-term interaction, as is more obviously the case in the United States, would only start, if two conditions are met:

1. The social and cultural environment facilitates or at least does not inhibit the development of aggression (e.g., the impact of different gun laws, Goldstein & Segall, 1983; The New Yorker, 1984; and the treatment of the Bernhard Goetz case in the American media).

2. The actual environment is perceived to be similar to what can be seen on the TV screen.

In Australia, the perceived (imported violent) TV reality matches the actual reality much less than it does in the United States. Here, cultural factors like architecture, language, lifestyle, will be important cues for a perceived similarity. However, a long-term homogenization (Americanization) of cultures may also create a higher identity between TV and actual reality. This will be especially true for heavy viewers, who are so distracted from their actual environment, that they probably won't have the means to check reality in an adequate way.

Another relevant issue is raised by Sheehan (this volume): The uses of TV. The same program can serve very different functions for the viewer. It can be used to be informed, to be entertained, to escape from actual problems, or to offer role models. Especially for boys, TV seems to meet the last-mentioned function: The Australian data also demonstrate that identification with aggressive male TV characters is a necessary condition for the development of aggressive habits.

There is perhaps one special bias in the Australian results: With the particularly strong gender differences one would have expected a higher relation between TV violence and male aggression. The normative context in Australia may, in fact, be an effective inhibitor of actual aggressive preferences. It is also possible, however, that due to the perceived norms high social desirability creates a response set that leads to an underestimation of aggressive trends. But also, social desirability can be an indicator for stable aggression control.

As a conclusion, it is interesting to note that in Australia, official institutions monitor the TV programs on a regular basis to prevent a higher percentage of screen violence. Yet, the emphasis is not so much on censorship but rather, as Sheehan reports, on "constructive programming." If we consider the Australian data, these actions seem to contribute to a reduced influence of media violence.

Finland.   The Finnish results again demonstrate the influence of violent American TV imports. No Finnish production contains significant aggressive acts, whereas most of the American programs presented on Finnish screens have a high percentage of violence.

These imports meet a society that differs from the American one: It is more homogeneous and has lower crime rates. The broadcasting system is under official control with only 20% of TV broadcasting time covered by commercial network companies. Overall, this also means a relatively low percentage of TV violence — and lower viewing rates.

Using the cross-cultural data from this study for a "simulated" experimental design, Finland would fit well under the condition "dramaturgical effects on perceived realism." Not only does the content of violent shows on Finnish screens differ to a high extent from the actual environmental reality, but it is also the specific dramaturgy of these shows that contributes to a low probability of a transfer from the media to the everyday life situation: The imported films are not dubbed. So, the viewing children likely do not immediately understand what is going on. In several studies, it was demonstrated how important a synchronous comprehension is for information processing as well as emotional responses. Especially dramaturgical asynchronity heavily interferes with an adequate understanding of media content (Sturm, 1982) and prevents the establishment of respective cognitive categories. When not dubbed, most information with regard to the plot is presented visually (image plus captions). The sound only contributes to the dramaturgical effects. In other non-American countries, it is primarily the actual environment that inhibits a more dramatical increase of aggression as a consequence of TV violence. In Finland, it probably is also the characteristics inherent in the media presentation itself.

Yet, there is another relevant impact of these shows at the same time that is symptomatic of possible intercultural media effects. Finnish children believe to a high extent that the imported shows present life as it really is in America, thus creating a typical media stereotype of another nation. These kinds of effects could turn out to be as important as media violence.

Media belong to the major sources of information about the world (Schulz, 1982). If not for direct attitude formation, they have at least the power to create topics, to create images of the world mostly hard to test in reality (see the debate about the adequacy of "Docu-Dramas"). One possibly fatal consequence of these particular media effects is the fact that, in the long run, even purely fictitious programs can contribute to the establishment of cognitive categories of "world-facts." Applying MDS-procedures, Groebel (1981a) demonstrated the increasing cognitive overlapping of actual and fictitious information over time. With Finnish children, these "reality" categories about America—in fact mostly based on fictitious dramas—seem to apply. In this case, the mentioned dramaturgical qualities, non-dubbing, may even add to the perceived authenticity of the programs.

Despite the environmental and media-specific limitations to TV violence effects in Finland, a noticeable result remains. Again, the significance of boys' identification with male TV models for the development of aggression is demonstrated. In addition, Lagerspetz and Viemero (this volume) offer an interesting conclusion for gender differences in the level of aggression. For boys, TV contributes to the establishment of stable aggressive traits, for girls, the TV aggression relation is primarily characterized by situational responses not persisting over time.

Israel.   Could most American or European children imagine watching TV only once or twice a week for an hour together with many other children? This particular TV watching behavior still exists in the Israeli kibbutz. Kibbutz children have nearly no access to violent TV. Almost all violent shows are on after 10:30 p.m. when kibbutz children already have gone to sleep.

Again, we find a natural "experimental" setting: The Israeli city children fit mostly into the usual standards of Western TV viewing behavior, whereas the kibbutz children are subject to a strict collectively determined daily routine with fixed limited hours of TV diet. The two kibbutzim investigated in this study (both members of the conservative *Hashomer - Ha'tza'ir*) show an especially high domination of the peer group and relatively little influence of the individual parents. This also means that there is strong control of aggression and high rejection of antisocial acts, combined with the development of alternative behaviors, incompatible with aggression. The resulting near-zero correlation between aggression and TV violence for kibbutz children therefore is not surprising.

However, kibbutz children score higher on peer-nominated aggression than do non-kibbutzim, whereas these last mentioned have the highest synchronous correlation between TV violence and aggression of all nations under consideration. Bachrach (this volume) offers a plausible explanation for this phenomenon: Kibbutz children have such a high sensibility toward aggression—due to their strong normative surrounding—that already slight cues of a respective behavior are rated as antisocial (an alternative interpretation is that the normative restrictions through strong peer control create frustration and, as a consequence, higher aggression). This effect points to a more general problem of the methodology used to obtain the aggression scores through peer ratings, i.e., the dependence on the individual reference point of the aggression rater. (In terms of scaling theory, the effect of the position of the rater on the latent common aggression scale.) If the kibbutz rater him- or herself has a low position on the respective scale, he or she probably will perceive acts, relatively low on the scale but higher than his or her own position, as aggressive, whereas an outside rater with an average or high position would not call these acts aggressive. This is especially effective when a whole group—in this case the kibbutzim—is "systematically biased" by a low position on the scale. A possible solution could be a modified version of "joint scaling" (Coombs, 1964), where both raters and rated, would be represented on a common scale, with a respective determination of weighted ratings. But again, this procedure probably would have exceeded the economic and especially temporal capacity of the project.

A remarkable issue in this cross-cultural context is the different meaning of aggression in everyday life. The foundation of the state of Israel was, and still is, determined by a permanent presence of external aggressive conflict (Holocaust, war) that seems to have a strong impact on the place of internal aggression (Landau & Beit-Hallahmi, 1983). Here, special attention should be directed to the relation between perceived reality and media content. TV violence in Israel may not be perceived as coming from a fictitious or an outside world but it may only reinforce what children already know from their own experience or at least from discussions with family and friends. This would explain the high synchronous correlation between violent TV viewing and aggression for Israeli city children despite the relatively low percentage of violence on TV. The more that information on external threat is added, the more aggression seems to be appropriate. This hypothesis is supported by the fact that for non-kibbutzim children high aggression scores did not diminish popularity with classmates.

Poland.   Whereas Israel has been facing external conflicts over a long period of time, the situation in Poland has been characterized by repeated internal conflicts since World War II. In recent years, reports on tensions related to the occurrence of the "Solidarity" movement can be found in the international press. Nevertheless, as Fraczek (this volume) reports, the overall level of aggression in Poland is rather low compared to other countries and the specific results of the study indicate a decrease in the aggression level of children.

Again, we find a well-functioning normative system in this country. Of this mostly homogeneous population, 86% are active Catholics; at the same time, an official Committee for Radio and TV controls the content of TV. And although one can wonder whether a centralized organizational structure of TV as in Poland is desirable, it seems at least to prevent a high percentage of TV violence that accounts for "only" 6.8% of all program and is not readily available to children.

With this combination of a strong normative frame and low rates of TV violence, it is not surprising to find that there are primarily other factors that determine the level of aggression of Polish children (see Fraczek, this volume). Yet, even with this low a priori possibility of a TV violence impact, the results demonstrate a certain causal effect of violent TV together with identification on aggressive behavior especially for boys. As already mentioned (see chapter 3), identification with male TV characters seems to be a major facilitator of the TV aggression relation. We deal with this particular result in a later section.

The influence of the normative frame also becomes obvious with the finding that aggression is related to unpopularity. Thus, unlike Israel city society, for example, Poland has a social system where aggression mostly is negatively reinforced. Fraczek (this volume) accordingly attributes the stabilization of aggression mainly to motivational and trait factors, and postulates two complementary mechanisms based on personal experiences: (a) the arousal of aggressive tendencies, and (b) the inhibition of aggressive tendencies. In this context, TV can be regarded as one of the aggression facilitating factors as has been previously described.

The Polish family is an example of the direct social impact on the development of aggression: It may be a culturally specific result that, unlike the United States, parent rejection constitutes one of the origins of child aggression in Poland and not vice versa.

The Parallel Dutch Study

Parallel to the already described studies, a group of Dutch scientists investigated second and fourth graders applying a similar but not identical research design (for details see Wiegman & Baarda, in preparation; Wiegman et al., 1984).

Somewhat modified measures were used to determine the relation between TV violence and aggression; in addition, special emphasis was put on the influence of intelligence and the role of prosocial programs and prosocial behavior. A number of variables were also omitted from the design because they were deemed inappropriate by the Dutch investigators.

Some of the results, based on correlations and LISREL analyses were as follows:

1. Violent *and* prosocial TV viewing showed a high correlation with over-all viewing frequency.
2. The correlation between TV and aggression was similar to the relations found in the other countries.
3. There was no evidence for bi-directionality.
4. TV violence influenced later aggression.
5. For *general* TV viewing the result was completely the same.
6. Most of the common variance between viewing frequency and aggres-sion was explained by the inclusion of IQ scores.

The fact that overall viewing frequency had exactly the same effect on ag-gression as violent TV viewing frequency probably can be interpreted on the basis of generalized viewing behavior: Experimental studies have demon-strated the high impact of TV dramaturgy on both, the formation of rela-tively stable cognitive categories (Sturm, 1982) and especially aggression (Huston & Wright, in press). So, if one agrees that usual TV programs, at least dramas and serials, frequently follow a similar dramaturgy — regardless of aggressive content — it can be postulated that (a) dramaturgy itself has an effect on short-term aggressive reactions (short cuts, zooms, soundtracks: physiological arousal), and (b) reactions to aggressive content are generalized for "neutral" even prosocial programs with similar dramaturgy and consti-tute a common cognitive category.

The application of a similarity model (Tversky & Gati, 1978) could aug-ment the evidence of a respective hypothesis. For example, Groebel (1981a), applying MDS procedures, demonstrated that very different experiences with TV- and not-TV-related threat information became elements of the same cognitive category in the long run.

For the strong moderating effect of intelligence, the Dutch authors them-selves offer the explanation that intelligence probably is one indicator of a certain cultural and educational climate. Less intelligent children have prob-lems coping with normal social situations and spend more time watching TV, which in turn influences their aggressive behavior (see previous section). Ger-man results support this postulate (see next section).

Some Additional German Results

A study of TV violence similar to the one under consideration here was con-ducted in West Germany with other age groups. It is described in detail else-where (Groebel, 1981b; Krebs, 1981). In a longitudinal Baltes–Schaie design around 2,500 11- to 15- year-old students were investigated over a period of 2 years with three waves. The results were evaluated with path analyses. Ag-gression was measured along three, empirically confirmed dimensions: Re-active ("instrumental"), legitimated, and destructive ("spontaneous") aggres-sion. The reactive aggression showed a reciprocal interaction with TV as was the case in the United States.

An additional analysis, however, revealed some effects that could contribute to an explanation of the underlying processes in the TV aggression relation (Groebel, 1984). Boys with low self-esteem and high social fear more frequently had higher TV viewing frequency scores compared to the other groups. This tendency can be interpreted in terms of an *escapism function* of TV. The high amount of aggressive — or threatening — content presented on the screen in the long run probably reinforced social fear, as the results would indicate.

Adding "destructive aggression" to the respective analysis resulted in findings that can be regarded as indicators for different processes intervening between TV and aggression for the different dimensions of aggression. The previously mentioned interaction between TV and reactive aggression most probably results from a modelling process. For "destructive aggression," however, there was no direct relation with TV. Yet, boys with high social fear as facilitated by TV viewing frequency, at the same time had significantly higher destructive aggression scores ($p < .01$). In this case, destructive aggression probably is the reaction to frustrating difficulties with the actual surrounding (see also the Finnish and Dutch results). These difficulties are reinforced by TV content, which usually presents direct threat of actors and vivid reality. This vividness could increase the viewer's social fear, due to the perceived gap between the actors' and one's own behavior.

Thus, for reactive aggression (i.e., aggressive reaction to an attack), we would assume a modelling process:

TV → aggression

Probably as a reciprocal process:

TV → aggression → TV → aggression

For destructive aggression (i.e., aggressive acts without any clearly identifiable reasons), we could assume a more complex process moderated by frustration:

Social difficulties → escapism → TV → social difficulties → frustration → aggression

Both processes may be interlocked.

CROSS-NATIONAL COMPARISON AND INTEGRATION OF THE RESULTS

A review of all the individual national results, taken together, demonstrates that it is mainly the impact of cultural/environmental/parental norms on the one hand and TV on the other that inhibits or facilitates the occurrence and manifestation of aggression. In addition, there seem to be direct personal characteristics that contribute to aggressive habits (e.g., self-esteem and the ability to cope with the social surrounding).

Some interesting differences regarding the culture-specific normative frames within society and also for TV content become obvious when comparing the different nations. These norms also are related to the homogeneity/nonhomogeneity of the respective cultures (see Table 9.1).

Nations with a high homogeneity seem to have a relatively effective (informal) normative system that limits the occurrence of aggression (Australia, Finland, Ireland, Poland, The Netherlands, and West Germany). At the same time, as already mentioned in a previous section, the heterogeneous TV content in these countries prevents a too consistent impact of the different programs on aggressive behavior through a generalized dramaturgy. Yet, even with these inhibiting factors a — situational — causal effect of TV on aggression is evident.

With its low homogeneity, its relatively high level of actual aggression and crime, and its high homogeneity of TV content, it is no surprise that the most consistent relation between TV and aggression has been found in the United States. Here, TV facilitates the adoption of aggressive habits; the actual environment is not necessarily a falsification of what is presented on the screen; the overall normative frame is no consistent inhibitor of aggression (see gun laws). The result is a reciprocal process whereby TV violence and aggression affect each other.

Israel, with its societal dichotomy, to a certain extent combines both aspects: On the one hand, we have a group with very strong norms, the kibbutzim, where due to the nearly total absence of TV violence, no respective effect can be found. On the other hand, despite a relatively low percentage of violent programs, TV has a significant impact on non-kibbutzim children who are not necessarily subject to negative sanctions as reactions to aggressive behavior.

All in all, the results demonstrate that TV violence, regardless of the cultural context, at least has the power to facilitate or even to engender children's aggression. This may be the case on a situational basis (Australia, Finnish girls), on the basis of a one-way impact (Israel, Poland, The Netherlands), or on the basis of a reciprocal process (Finnish boys, United States, West Germany). The underlying mechanisms may be different and more or less complex, but there is no evidence for a zero or even negative — statistical — relation between TV violence and aggression. Still, the cultural and normative environment is a powerful agent for the development of antisocial, but also prosocial behavior. In a recent study, Huesmann et al., (1983) could show that there is a chance in the actual environment to mitigate the impact of violent TV when applying direct social intervention. However, low levels of societal aggression and low television violence still seem to be the best general predictors of low aggressive behavior.

TABLE 9.1
Survey of Some Remarkable Results From the Different National Studies

	Culture			TV		Results
	Homogeneity	Level of Aggression	Availability of Programs, Relative Importance	Account of Aggressive Content		
AUS	High homogeneity, Small minorities	Relatively low, though slightly increasing	Medium to high	Medium		Time-synchronous correlation between TV-violence and aggression; no clear-cut causal relationship
FIN	High homogeneity	Low	Medium	Low		Aggression-violent TV viewing: Reciprocal process (boys); girls only situational relation
ISR	Dichotomous society: Kibbutzim, non-Kibbutzim (plus minorities)	Medium; increasing aggression level (less with Kibbutzim)	Low	Medium (mostly night time programs)		TV violence has impact on aggression (non-Kibbutzim); little impact on Kibbutzim
POL	Relatively high homogeneity	Low	Medium	Relatively low		Slight impact of TV violence on later aggression
U.S.A.	Low homogeneity	High; increasing crime rates	High	High		Aggression-violent TV viewing: Reciprocal process
NL	High homogeneity	Relatively low	Medium	Medium		Viewing frequency-aggression moderated by intelligence
FRG	High homogeneity	Relatively low; slightly increasing	Medium; increasing	Medium		TV-Reactive aggression: Reciprocal Process TV-Destructive aggression: Moderated by social fear

A COGNITIVE MODEL OF TV VIOLENCE EFFECTS

The cross-cultural study described in this volume clarified for the first time the role of the different cultures and the media in the development of aggression. It now seems to be interesting to integrate the relations that were discovered into a more general — cognitive — model of TV violence effects. Each of the authors of the respective studies offered bases for such a model. Huesmann and Eron postulate a reciprocal process where elements of cognitive and developmental theory are combined. Sheehan stresses the perceived uses of TV for the viewer. Lagerspetz regards the occurrence of aggression as a reaction to actual social stress. For Bachrach, group processes and group control play an important role. Fraczek describes the motivational elements for the development of aggression. Of course, as the authors indicate, these factors do overlap.

A hypothetical model including the already mentioned variables plus additional ones identified in other studies on media violence conclude this chapter. Although this model seems to be quite complicated at first sight, it actually tries to integrate the different findings of this cross-cultural study as well as additional studies on the underlying processes intervening between TV and aggression (see Fig. 9.1).

As becomes apparent, the respective processes either may be independent or they may be interlocked: On the physiological level, the motivation to watch violent TV is probably determined by an arousal need (see Berlyne, 1967). On a short-term basis, this need is satisfied by two characteristics of the medium, content and dramaturgy. However, given a specific situation, this arousal already can be associated with aggressive reactions (Zillmann, 1971). In addition, perceived discrepancies within the dramaturgy (e.g., picture–sound discrepancies), can also lead to arousal and anger reactions (Sturm, 1982). In the long run, the physiological stimulation through "normal" media violence seems to suffer from a wear-out effect. The occurrence of slasher films and their high viewing rates may be an indicator of the shift of arousal level over time (see Donnerstein, 1984). At the same time, absence of positive experience in the actual environment or even negative experiences increase the probability of media use. TV then serves a vicarious experience and escapism function (Groebel, 1981). TV content reinforces this tendency and may finally lead to aggressive reactions as the consequence of frustration in the actual social environment (Berkowitz, 1982). Identification with TV characters is a strong indicator, especially for boys, of the respective processes (see the studies reported in this volume). But girls also increasingly seem to show a similar pattern (Huesmann & Eron, this volume). A major role for the acquisition of aggression through TV is played by the surrounding cultural and normative framework. It either may facilitate or inhibit (Feshbach, 1984) the occurrence of aggressive reactions. Imitation processes help in the

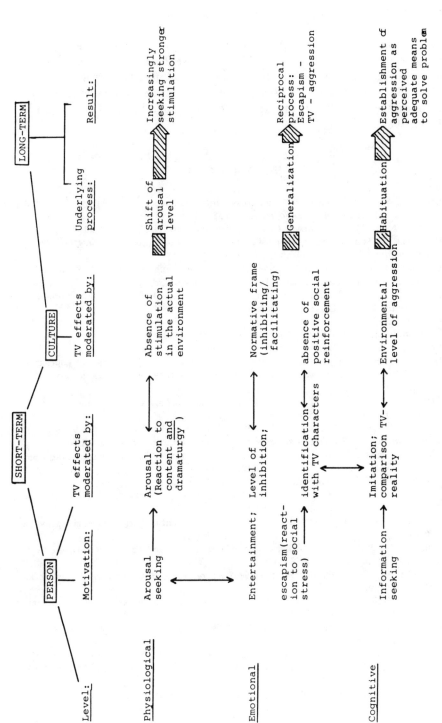

FIG. 1 A model of the different effects of TV violence.

acquisition of antisocial behavior. A facilitating normative framework and positive reinforcement (Bandura, 1977) increase the probability that aggression is perceived as an adequate and appropriate means of reaching one's goals. Such short-term acquisition, however, can determine the establishment of aggressive habits through a life-long period of time (Huesmann & Eron, 1984).

REFERENCES

Baltes, P. B. (1968). Longitudinal and cross-sectional sequences in the study of age and generation effects. *Human Development, 11,* 258–268.

Bandura, A. (1977). *Social learning theory.* Englewood Cliffs, NJ: Prentice-Hall.

Berkowitz, L. (1962). Violence in the mass media. In W. Schramm (Ed.), *Paris-Stanford Studies in Communication.* Stanford University.

Berkowitz, L. (1983). Aversively stimulated aggression: some parallels and differences in research with animals and humans. *American Psychologist, 38,* 1135–1144.

Berlyne, D. E. (1967). Arousal and reinforcement. In D. Levine (Ed.), *Nebraska symposium on motivation.* Lincoln: University of Nebraska Press.

Campbell, D. T., & Fiske, D. W. (1959). Convergent and discriminant validation by the multitrait-multimethod matrix. *Psychological Bulletin, 56,* 81–105.

Coombs, C. (1964). *A theory of data.* New York: Wiley.

Donnerstein, E. (1984). *Massive exposure to media violence and desensitization.* Paper presented at the 6th Biennial Meeting of the International Society for Research on Aggression. Turku, Finland.

Eron, L. D. (1963). The relationship of TV viewing habits and aggressive behavior of children. *Journal of Abnormal and Social Psychology, 67,* 193–196.

Eron, L. D. (1986). The social responsibility of the researcher. In J. H. Goldstein (Ed.), *Reporting science: The case of aggression.* Hillsdale, NJ: Lawrence Erlbaum Associates.

Eron, L. D., & Huesmann, L. R. (1985). The role of television in the development of prosocial and antisocial behavior. In D. Olweus, J. Block, & M. Radke-Yarrow (Eds.), *Development of antisocial and prosocial behavior* (pp. 285–313). New York: Academic Press.

Eron, L. D., Huesmann, L. R., Lefkowitz, M. M., & Walder, L. O. (1972). Does television violence cause aggression? *American Psychologist, 27,* 253–263.

Feshbach, S. (1961). The stimulating versus cathartic effects of a vicarious aggressive activity. *Journal of Abnormal and Social Psychology, 63,* 381–385.

Feshbach, S. (1984). The catharsis hypothesis, aggressive drive, and the reduction of aggression. *Aggressive Behavior, 10,* 91–101.

Goldstein, A. P., & Segall, M. H. (Eds.) (1983). *Aggression in global perspective.* New York, Oxford: Pergamon Press.

Groebel, J. (1981a). *Cognitive dimensions of environmental threat.* Paper presented at the University of California, Los Angeles.

Groebel, J. (1981b). Vielseher und Angst. Theoretische Uberlegungen und einige Langsschnittergebnisse. *Fernsehen und Bildung, 15,* 114–136.

Groebel, J. (1983). Federal Republic of Germany: Aggression and aggression research. In A. P. Goldstein & M. H. Segall (Eds.), *Aggression in global perspective.* New York, Oxford: Pergamon Press.

Groebel, J. (1984). Mediengewalt: Sich andernde Perspektiven, neue Fragestellungen. In *Gewalt im Fernsehen - Gewalt des Fernsehens.* Sindelfingen:Expert-Verlag.

Groebel, J. (1986). Determinants of science reporting in Europe. In J. H. Goldstein (Ed.), *Reporting science: The case of aggression.* Hillsdale, NJ: Lawrence Erlbaum Associates.

Groebel, J. (in press b). Homogenisierung durch Massenmedien? Ein Beitrag zur Diskussion um internationale Massenkommunikation. In M. Grewe-Partsch and J. Groebel (Eds.), *Mensch und Medien*. Fur Hertha Sturm. Munchen: Saur Verlag.

Groebel, J., & Krebs, D. (1983). A study of the effects of television on anxiety. In C. D. Spielberger & R. Diaz-Guerrero (Eds.), *Cross-cultural anxiety* (Vol. 2). Washington, New York: Hemisphere/McGraw Hill.

Huesmann, L. R. (1982). Television violence and aggressive behavior. In D. Pearl, L. Bouthilet, & J. Lazar (Eds.), *Television and behavior: Ten years of scientific progress and implications for the eighties* (Vol. 2, pp. 126-137). Washington, DC: U.S. Government Printing Office.

Huesmann, L. R., & Eron, L. D. (1984). *Television viewing habits in childhood and adult aggression.* Paper presented at the 6th Biennial Meeting of the International Society for Research on Aggression. Turku, Finland.

Huesmann, L. R., Eron, L. D., Klein, R., Brice, P., & Fischer, P. (1983). Mitigating the imitation of aggressive behavior by changing children's attitudes about media violence. *Journal of Personality and Social Psychology, 44,* 899-910.

Huston, A. C., & Wright, J. C. (in press). Eine Formsache: Die Einwirkungsmoglichkeiten des Fernsehens auf Kinder. In M. Grewe-Partsch and J. Groebel (Eds.), *Mensch und Medien*. Fur Hertha Sturm. Munchen: Saur Verlag.

Krebs, D. (1981). Gewaltdarstellungen im Fernsehen und die Einstellungen zu aggressiven Handlungen bei 12- bis 15- jahrigen Kindern - Bericht uber eine Langsschnittstudie. *Zeitschrift fur Sozialpsychologie, 12,* 381-302.

Landau, S. F., & Beit-Hallahmi, B. (1983). Israel: Aggression in psychohistorical perspective. In A. P. Goldstein & M. H. Segall (Eds.), *Aggression in global perspective* (pp. 261-286). New York, Oxford: Pergamon Press.

Milavsky, J. R., Kessler, R. C., Stipp, H. H., & Rubens, W. S. (1982). *Television and aggression, a panel study.* New York: Academic Press.

The New Yorker (1984, November 12). A reporter at large: An extraordinary people. *The New Yorker,* pp. 109-173.

Rosch, E. (1978). Principles of categorization. In E. Rosch & B. B. Lloyd (Eds.), *Cognition and categorization*. Hillsdale, NJ: Lawrence Erlbaum Associates.

Schaie, K. W. (1973). Methodological problems in descriptive developmental research on adulthood and aging. In J. R. Nesselroade & H. W. Reese (Eds.), *Life-span developmental psychology. Methodological issues.* New York, London: Academic Press.

Schonemann, P. H., & Steiger, J. H. (1978). On the validity of indeterminate factor scores. *Bulletin of the Psychonomic Society, 12,* 287-290.

Schulz, W. (1982, September). *News structure and people's awareness of political events.* Paper presented at the Joint Congress of the World Association for Public Opinion Research and the International Association for Mass Communication Research. Paris.

Singer, J. L., & Singer, D. G. (1981). *Television, imagination and aggression: A study of preschoolers' play.* Hillsdale, NJ: Lawrence Erlbaum Associates.

Sturm, H. (1982). Neue Medien - Programmausweitungen: Das Problem sind die Kinder. *Fernsehen und Bildung, 16,* 235-245.

Triandis, H. C., & Berry, J. W. (Eds.). (1980). *Handbook of cross-cultural psychology, Vol. 2, Methodology.* Boston: Allyn & Bacon.

Tversky, A., & Gati, I. (1978). Studies of similarity. In E. Rosch & B. B. Lloyds (Eds.), *Cognition and categorization*. New York: Wiley.

Wiegman, O., Kuttschreuter, M., & Baarda, B. (1984). *The Dutch contribution to the cross-national study on television and aggression as well as prosocial behavior.* Paper presented at the Conference on "The Role of Culture and the Media for the Development of Aggression." Bad Homburg, West Germany.

Wiegman, O., & Baarda, B. (in preparation). *A Dutch panel study on television and aggression.*

Zillmann, D. (1971). Excitation transfer in communication-mediated aggressive behavior. *Journal of Experimental Social Psychology, 7,* 419-434.

Appendix I:
Instructions for Classroom
Procedures

It is important that before a class list is prepared, it is verified with the school secretary for sex of each child. Several days before going out to the school, contact the teacher. You can usually reach the teacher by calling the principal's office between 8:30 and 9:00 a.m. or at noon.

Tell the teacher that you and several assistants would like to come out (give the day, time) to test his or her class in connection with the TV viewing project. Explain that the testing needs to be done in the classroom without the teacher being present. Then, if there are children for whom we do not have permission, explain that there are several children who cannot participate in the testing because we do not have permission for them to do so. Ask if it would be possible for them to go with him or her, or would he or she prefer that you bring along an assistant to occupy these children.

Also, before going to the school, get the names of all the children who have permission and fill in the face sheet of a booklet for each child (name, identification, etc.).

Note to assistants: Familiarize yourself with these instructions so that you know what you must watch for (e.g., on questions 2–15 on the peer nomination, children are not to cross out their own name, and they must pick out at least one boy and one girl or NO BOY, NO GIRL, for each item). Also, find those children who are slowest and concentrate on helping them and on getting them to make their choices in a reasonably short time.

Materials to take for testing include the following:

1. A set of instructions for each E and assistants. (There should be no fewer than three of you for classroom testing, and if one is needed to tend to the non-permission children, you will need four individuals going along.)

2. A prize for each child.

3. A response booklet for each child, plus several extras. (Be sure these are the response booklets for the appropriate classroom testing session, that the peer-nomination class lists in each booklet are for the appropriate class, and that all face sheets are filled in before arriving at school).

4. Pencils.

5. First page of peer-nomination response sheets, to read to class during administration of peer-nomination.

6. A list of those children in the class who do not have permission to participate.

After testing is completed, pick up all booklets and pencils you handed out. Thank the children for their help and pass out the treats.

Get the teacher and thank him or her for the help and cooperation. As soon as possible, enter code # for each child on each page of his or her booklet, and code any responses for keypunching that need to be coded. Remove the face sheet from the rest of the booklet after coding has been completed. Treat the booklets as highly confidential documents. Until the face sheet has been removed, do not let anyone see them, including the project staff or the principal investigator. Even after the face sheet has been removed, do not leave the booklets in any place where an unauthorized person might see them. Turn in the face sheets as soon as possible and note in the card files that the testing has been completed.

APPENDIX I.1

After teacher and non-permission children are gone, introduce yourself and assistants by name to the class. Then reseat the class, in alternate rows of boys and girls. Then say:

"We are going to ask you to do a number of things for us today. These things are not tests. We just want to know how you feel about some things. All of the answers you give us today will be a secret between you and us. You will know your answers, and we will know your answers, but no one else in your class will know, not even the teacher.

"Now, there are some rules we have for today, and if you follow these rules you get a prize. The first rule is:

Don't talk to other children while you are doing these things.

Second rule:

Don't shout out your answers; we don't want you to tell anyone your answer.

Third rule:

Don't look at other children's papers or answers.

Fourth rule:

Don't turn any pages until we tell you to.

Once again, the rules are (repeat them). You get a prize if you follow these rules.

"We are going to pass out some papers to you now. Just leave the papers on your desk and don't make any marks or write on them yet. Remember that one of the rules is that you don't turn any pages until we tell you to."

(Pass out booklets to each child according to name on face sheets, being certain each child has a pencil.)

"Now we are going to ask you some questions about the boys and girls in your class, and things they have done since school started *this year, since you have been in the third grade.* Turn to the first page. You should have a blue page in front of you. Does everybody have a blue front page?" (Pause and check to be sure children are on the blue page of this measure.) Look at the bottom of this blue page. There's a number at the bottom. "Does everybody have a number one on the blue front page?" (Pause). "I'll read the question that goes with the number one blue page:

1. *Who are you? Who are you?*

"On the front page there are two lists of names (demonstrate where on the page the names are – down right-hand side). Don't pay attention to the numbers down the other side of the page. Your name is in one of the two lists. The first list has girls' names; the second list has boys' names. I'll read the names in the list for you. First the girls' list. (Read the names in the order in which they appear in the list on the top half of the page. When you read NO BOY and NO GIRL, say "Remember, NO BOY (GIRL) is a name.").

"Now the boys' list." (Read the names in the order in which they appear in the list on the bottom half of the page.) "Now look for your own name. Find your name and put your finger on your own name. Put your finger on your own name."

"Keep your finger on your own name and watch what I do at the blackboard." (Write your own name on the board.) "Here is my name, Ms. xxxxxxxxxx . I'm going to draw a line through my name like this. Now you draw a line through your own name. Remember, you have a first and a last name, so make sure you draw a line through your whole name, your first name and your last name." (E and assistants go to every child and read the crossed-out name aloud). "If you want to change your mark, make a wavy line through it like this." (Demonstrate).

"Now go on to the next page; fold back the first page like this." (Demonstrate). "The next page is yellow. Does everybody have a yellow page?" (Pause). "The number of this page is 2. It's a yellow two. Soon I will read you the question that goes with yellow two. Listen, from now on, do not draw a line through your own name. Remember, it's against the rules of the game to mark your own name. "Now I will read you the yellow question, the number two question:

Who would you like to sit next to in class? (Repeat).

"Look through the names in both lists and find the children who you would like to sit next to in class. Draw a line through the names of the children who you would like to sit next to. Make sure you find the names in both lists. First look at the names in the first list and draw a line through the names of all the children in that list who you would like to sit next to. Then look at the second list and draw a line through the names of all the children in that list who you would like to sit next to." (Pause). "Remember, NO BOY and NO GIRL are names, so if there is no boy that you would like to sit next to, cross out the name NO BOY, and if there is no girl that you would like to sit next to, cross out the name NO GIRL. You must pick at least one name from each list; NO GIRL and NO BOY are names."

(If child marks only one name in either of the lists, ask:) "Aren't there any other boys (girls) who you would like to sit next to?"

"We'll play this game the same way from now on. I'll read you the question for each page. You find the names in both lists that you think are right for the question. First look at all the names in the first list and draw a line through all the names that fit. Then look at all the names in the second list and draw a line through all the names in that list that fit. Here is how the game is played: First, make a line through at least one name in each list. Do not make a line through your own name. Second, look only at your own game. Never look at your neighbor's game. Third, if you want to change your mark, make a wavy line through it. Fourth, do not answer out loud. Mark names in each list, don't mark your own name, don't answer out loud, don't look at your neighbor's game.

"Remember, for every question make sure that you look at every name in the two lists and make sure that you draw a line through any name that fits the question. Remember to look at the person's first name and last name. Do not mark your own name.

"In question number two, the yellow question, not everybody made lines through the same names. This is because the answer depends on who you would like to sit next to. So, what was the right answer for you was not the right answer for somebody else. On the other questions, I'll ask you, different children draw lines through different names because there are no answers that are the same for everybody. On each page, you will have to decide for yourself what names to make a line through. Do not cross out your own name. When we get finished, we will take the papers and we won't show them to anybody else.

"Now turn the page so that the pink page is on top. What number is it? That's right, number three. I'll read the question that goes with the pink three and you be sure to draw a line through names in the two lists—all the names that fit the question.

(You may find it necessary to repeat the NO BOY/NO GIRL instruction if they don't pick someone from each list. Also, you can repeat several times, "Draw a line through each name that fits the question.").

pink 3—"Who does not obey the teacher?" (Repeat).

green 4—"Who often says, "Give me that"?" (asked with emphasis) (Repeat).

gold 5—"Who gives dirty looks or sticks out their tongue at other children?" (Repeat).

blue 6—"Who makes up stories and lies to get other children into trouble?" (Repeat).

yellow 7—"Who does things that bother others?" (Repeat).

pink 8—"Who starts a fight over nothing?" (Repeat).

green 9—"Who pushes or shoves children?" (Repeat).

gold 10—"Who is always getting into trouble?" (Repeat).

blue 11—"Who says mean things?" (Repeat).

yellow 12—"Who takes other children's things without asking?" (Repeat).

pink 13—"Who says, 'Excuse me," even when they have not done anything bad?" (Repeat).

green 14—"Who will never fight even when picked on?" (Repeat).

gold 15—"Who are the children you would like to have for your best friends?" (Repeat).

"Now turn the page; the next page tells you to stop and not turn any more pages." (Pause).

APPENDIX I.2

"The next questions we would like to ask you are about how much you are like some other children. Now you can turn the page. This is a pink page. Put your finger on the triangle #1. We use these symbols because they help us to see if everyone is on the right question." (Draw the symbol on the board, with the boxes next to it. Check all children to be sure they're on the right page on the right symbol). "Suppose I told you that Sally can run faster than any other girl in school and Harold can run faster than any other boy. Now, if you are *just like* Sally or *just like* Harold, put an X in the big box next to triangle #1 (demonstrate). This means you can run faster than any other girl or any other boy in school. If you are a *little bit like* Sally or a little bit like Harold, put an X in the medium-size box on the line with triangle #1 (demonstrate). This means you can run fast, but not faster than any other girl or any other boy in the school. If you are not at all like Harold or not at all like Sally, put an X in the little box (demonstrate). This means that you can't run very fast."

(Pause. Check all papers to be sure they have marked an X by item #1).

"Now put your finger on circle #2. Suppose I told you that Mary is a big, strong girl who fights with other kids and that Peter is a big, strong boy who fights with other kids. Are you just like Mary or Peter, a little bit like Mary or Peter, or not at all like Mary or Peter? Put an X in the box that tells how much you are like Mary or Peter."

(Read each of the following items, repeating the questions "Are you just like or a little bit like or, not at all like" for the first several items. For the remaining items, just ask "Are you just like _____, a little bit like _____, or not at all like _____." Be certain to mention the names in each item; this is to be sure they don't see themselves as like one of the "kids" mentioned in some items).

Star #3:	Joe is a leader and all the kids do what he tells them, and Karen is a leader and all the kids do what she tells them. Are you just like . . . ?
Diamond #4:	Nancy and Timmy are never the first one in line. Are you . . . ?
Flower #5:	Kids sometimes take things away from Bobby and Lisa. Are you . . . ?
Apple #6:	Gail and Allan will grab away any toy that they want.
Heart #7:	Walter and Barbara lend their pencils to other kids even though they have not always gotten them back.
House #8:	Debbie and Steven often get angry and punch other kids.
Candle #9:	Kids are always picking on Johnny and Ann.

"Now turn the page; the next page tells you to stop and wait." (Pause).

APPENDIX I.3

"Now we are going to ask you about TV shows. Turn to the next page, which is blue." (Check to be sure all are on blue page.)

"This is a list of 10 TV shows. I'm going to read the list, and you follow along with me. (Read first 10 shows—lists follow).

"Read the whole list again to yourself and circle the show you watch the most. You can only pick one show you watch the most on the blue page." (Check to be sure all have circled one show.)

"At the bottom of the page are 3 boxes. Now think about the show you just circled. If you watch that show *every time it's on*, put an X in the big box; if you watch the show *a lot, but not always,* put an X in the medium size box; if you watch the show only *once in a while*, put an X in the little box."

(Repeat this format for next 7 lists on following page. If a child insists she or he cannot pick one, you can say, "if they were all on at once, which one would you watch.")

(After finishing 8th list: "Turn the page and STOP." (Pause).

TV VIEWING – 8 LISTS

List 1 (blue)
Most Wanted
Six Million Dollar Man
Land of the Lost
Clue Club
Carol Burnett
I Love Lucy
Archies
Barnaby Jones
Welcome Back Kotter
Dynomutt

List 2 (yellow)
Star Trek Cartoons
Scooby Doo
Happy Days
I Dream of Jeannie
All in the Family
Chico and the Man
Big Blue Marble
Isis
Busting Loose
Hawaii Five-O

List 3 (pink)
Sylvester and Tweety
Muppets
Gilligan's Island
Blansky's Beauties
Zoom
Rockford Files
Mash
Little House on the Prairie
Streets of San Francisco
Emergency One

List 4 (green)
Dick Van Dyke
Big John/Little John
Odd Couple
Speed Buggy
Switch
Wonder Woman
Life and Times of Grizzly Adams
Hazel
Captain and Tennille
Baa Baa Black Sheep

List 5 (gold)
What's Happening
Shazam
Partridge Family
Electric Company
Three Stooges
Charlie's Angels
Kojak
Rhoda
New Adventures of Batman
Fish

List 6 (blue)
Andy Griffith
Brady Bunch
Phyllis
Sonny and Cher
Krofft's Supershow
Starsky and Hutch
Hogan's Heroes
One Day at a Time
Superfriends
Delvecchio

List 7 (yellow)
Tarzan, Lord of the Jungle
Bionic Woman
Flipper
Donny and Marie
Pink Panther
Space Ghost/Frankenstein Jr.
My Favorite Martian
Alice
Jeffersons
Barney Miller

List 8 (pink)
Police Woman
Rocket Robin Hood
Waltons
Laverne and Shirley
Bugs Bunny/Road Runner
Baretta
Munsters
Maude
Jabberjaw
Bob Newhart

APPENDIX I.4

"Next we are going to ask you about some things, and we want to know how true you think these things are in telling what life is really like. Now you can turn the page. This page is yellow. (Pause and check to be sure all are on proper page). We want to know first, how true do you think the stories *Jack in the Beanstalk* and *Goldilocks and the 3 Bears* are in telling what life is really like? If they tell it just like it is in real life, circle *Just like it is.* If it is a little bit like it is in real life, circle *A little bit like it is.* If it is not at all like it is in real life, circle *Not at all like it is.* If you don't know the stories, and you don't know how true they are to real life, circle *I don't know.* Do you have any questions? (Pause).

"The #2 question is about newspapers. Next to #2, circle how true you think newspapers are in telling what life is really like, or circle that you don't know if you don't know.

"The next questions, #3 through #12, are about TV shows. For #3, circle how true you think *Six Million Dollar Man* is in telling what life is really like. (Repeat). If you don't know or don't watch the show, circle *Don't know.*" (Repeat this format for following shows):

    #4 — *Charlie's Angels*
    #5 — *Bionic Woman*
    #6 — *Krofft's Supershow*
    #7 — *Pink Panther*
    #8 — *Starsky and Hutch*
    #9 — *Wonder Woman*
    #10 — *Bugs Bunny/Road Runner*
    #11 — *Three Stooges*
    #12 — *Star Trek Cartoons*

"Now turn the page and stop."

APPENDIX I.5

"The next questions we will ask you are more questions about television shows. What we want to know next is how much you act like or do things like some of the people from TV shows. Turn to the next page, which is blue. (Pause and check to be sure all are on blue page.)"

"For question #1, we want to know how much you act like the *Six Million Dollar Man* from the *Six Million Dollar Man*? How much do you do the things he does? A lot, a little, or not at all? If you act like the *Six Million Dollar Man* a lot or do the things he does a lot, circle the words *A lot*. If you do the things he does a little or act like him a little, circle *A little*. If you don't ever act like him or if you don't ever do the things he does, circle *Not at all*. If you don't watch the show, circle *Don't know*."

(Repeat this format for the following items 2–8.)

#2 — The bionic woman from *Bionic Woman*
#3 — "Gilligan" from *Gilligan's Island*
#4 — Mary Tyler Moore from *The Mary Tyler Moore Show*
#5 — "Kojak" from *Kojak*
#6 — "Shirley" from *Laverne and Shirley*
#7 — "Kotter" from *Welcome Back Kotter*
#8 — The police woman from *Police Woman*

APPENDIX I.6

"Next, we have some different kinds of questions to ask you. There are no right or wrong answers to these questions. We just want to find out about you and the things you like. We want to know which things *you* like best, so remember the rules and don't look at what someone else has put down and don't call out either, because sometimes when you call out, you make someone else change their mind about which ones they like best. Another reason I don't want you to call out is because your answers to all the questions that we'll be asking will be a secret. You will know and we will know how you answered, but no one else in your class will know, not even your teacher.

"Now you can turn the page. You should all have a green page, with some pictures on it. Do you all have a green page in front of you?"

(Pause; check all children to be sure they have proper page.) "There are 6 pictures on this page. First, listen while I read out the names of these things. On the first line of the green page you see pictures of playing baseball and working a jigsaw puzzle. On the second line, owning a train set and using a wading pool. On the third line, giving a tea party and using lipstick. Now, I want you to choose the *two* you like best. The way that you pick the two you

like best is by putting an X (demonstrate on sample page held up in front of class) just like this through the two boxes on the page that you like the best. Everything in one box counts as one choice. Make your choices, but don't turn the page until I tell you to. Are there any questions?"
(Pause. Assistants should be certain *2 boxes* are checked off on each page.)

"Remember that from now on, first I read the names of the things on the page, then you choose the *two* boxes you like best. Don't pick your choices until after I read them all. Don't turn the pages until I tell you to." (Pause).

"Now turn to the next page, which is gold. Is everyone on the gold page? (Pause). On the top line you see pictures of using a dumptruck and dressing a dolly. On the second line, wearing jewelry and riding a bicycle. And on the last line playing football and playing checkers. Now I want you to choose the two you like best of these by making an X through two of the boxes. (Pause. Check all papers).

"Turn to the blue page. (Pause). Is everyone on the blue page? (Pause). On the top line is using a water colors set and baking cupcakes. On the second line is using a sewing machine and working a crane. On the third line is using swings and slides and driving a motorcycle.

"Now I want you to choose the two you like best of these. Don't turn the page until I tell you." (Pause).

"Turn to the yellow page."

"Is everybody on the yellow page? On the top line is using crayons and building model airplanes. On the second line is owning a tool set and wheeling a baby buggy. On the third line is playing skipping rope and playing a board game like Candyland. I want you to choose the two you like best of these. When you are finished, turn back to the first page and leave the booklet on your desk."

APPENDIX I.7

"We are going to ask you to do a number of things for us today. These things are not tests. We just want to know how you feel about some things. All of the answers you give us today will be a secret between you and us. You will know your answers, and we will know your answers, but no one else in your class will know, not even the teacher.

"Now, we had some rules when we were here (the other day.) We have the same rules today. If you follow these rules you get a prize. The first rule is:

Don't talk to other children while you are doing these things.
Second rule:

Don't shout out your answer; we don't want you to tell anyone your answer.
Third rule:

Don't look at other children's papers or answers.

Fourth rule:

Don't turn any pages until we tell you to.

Once again, the rules are (repeat them). You get a prize if you follow these rules.

"We are going to pass out some papers to you now. Just leave the papers on your desk and don't make any marks or write on them yet. Remember that one of the rules is that you don't turn any pages until we tell you to.

(Pass out booklets to each child according to name on face sheets, being certain each child has a pencil.)

"We would like to ask you all some questions because we really want to know what boys and girls your age think about and what kinds of things you play. Your answers will be very helpful to us and will make it possible for us to help other boys and girls. So we really want to thank you for helping us.

"You know how sometimes when you're by yourself, or before you fall asleep at night, or when you're just not doing anything special, you start to think about something just for fun or because it just pops into your head? Well, this happens to everybody — adults as well as boys and girls. Sometimes these thoughts are big, long, make-believe stories, and sometimes they are just quick little thoughts. We call these make-believe thoughts "daydreams." You know, also, how sometimes you play (by yourself, or with friends) and you pretend that you're somebody or something else? Or you pretend that a toy is really something besides the toy? Well, I would like very much to know about your daydreams and about the pretend games that you play.

"I am going to ask you some questions. Some of the things I ask you about you will say yes to and some things you will say no to. Everybody has daydreams, but we all think about different kinds of things. There are no right or wrong answers. This is not a test. Try to remember which things you did think about *a lot,* which things you did think about *a little,* and which things you *never* thought about.

"Now you can turn to the first page."

"Look at the first page in front of you. It's a blue page. Does everybody have a blue front page?" (Pause). "Do you see the boxes on the blue page?" (Draw the boxes on the board.) "Now, what we want you to do is, after I ask you a question, put an X in the big box if your answer is *a lot* (demonstrate on board). Put an X in the middle-size box if your answer to a question is *a little* (demonstrate) and put an X in the little box (demonstrate) if your answer is *no.* The pictures next to the boxes tell you which question we are on. So, when I say put your finger on the flower, everyone will know that they should mark the boxes next the the flower, and we will be able to see that you are all on the right question. What you mark down will be just between you and me. I won't tell anyone — not your teacher or your parents or the other kids. Do you have any questions? Do you think you know what a daydream is?"

(Pause). If you change your mind after marking a box, put a wavy line through it like this (demonstrate) and then pick another box.

"Now (read item 1 from list on next page). If your answer to this question is *a lot,* put an X in the big box; if your answer is *a little,* put an X in the medium-size box; if your answer is *no,* put an X in the little box."

(Read off symbol, symbol number, and item up to #39, using above format. Read each item twice. You should repeat instructions about finger on the symbols only a few times, then drop it. Check to be sure all children are on proper page and have fingers on proper symbol. Be sure to tell them when to turn the page.)

Fantasy Items	*Scale*
1. Did you ever have a whole special pretend world with lots of people or animals that you thought about or played with?	Intellectual
2. Did you ever have a make-believe friend who you talked to and who went places with you?	Fanciful
3. Do you have a special daydream that you like to think about over and over?	Absorption
4. When you are by yourself, do you like to sit and just be very quiet?	Absorption
5. Do you keep right on playing or reading, even when it's noisy in the room?	Absorption
6. Do you sometimes dream about falling or getting hurt?	Dysphoric
7. Do you find that even if you try real hard to pay attention to what you're doing or to your teacher, that you sometimes start to think of something else?	Absorption
8. Do you sometimes dream about someone in your family getting hurt?	Dysphoric
9. Do your daydreams sometimes seem so real to you that you almost forgot it is just pretend and really think that it happened?	Vividness
10. Have you ever wondered about things like how a bird can fly or how a fish can live in water?	Intellectual
11. When you get mad sometimes, do you think about the things you would like to	Aggressive

do to the person you're mad at — like hitting, or breaking his toys or telling on him?

12. When you are daydreaming, do you think about being the winner in a game that you like to play?   Active-Heroic

13. Are your daydreams about things and people that could never really happen, like monsters or fairies or men from outer space?   Scary

14. When you're daydreaming, do you think about how to make or build something or how to put together a real hard puzzle?   Intellectual

15. Do you sometimes daydream about what would happen if you did real bad in school — even when this didn't really happen?   Aggressive, Dysphoric

16. Do you have daydreams about how the world will be and what you are going to be many years from now when you're all grown up?   Intellectual, Absorption

17. Do the people and things that you daydream about sometimes seem so real that you think you can almost see or hear them in front of you?   Vividness

18. When you are daydreaming, do you think about being a great astronaut, or scientist, or singer, or somebody like that who is very famous?   Intellectual, Active-Heroic

19. Do you sometimes have daydreams about hitting or hurting somebody that you don't like?   Aggressive

20. Do you sometimes have daydreams or nightdreams about running away from somebody who is trying to catch you and punish you — even when you weren't really bad?   Aggressive, Dysphoric

21. Do you have daydreams about people in other far away countries — where they live, what they wear and eat, or what they do every day?   Intellectual

22. Do you have daydreams about things that can work by magic and have all kinds of magic wishes?   Intellectual

23. Do you sometimes think about something bad that you did, that nobody knows about but you?   Aggressive, Dysphoric

24. Does your Mother or Father or someone else read fairy tales to you (3rd grade: do you read . . .)–like Hansel and Gretel or Snow White?   Fanciful

25. When you play pretend games, do you feel like you can really see the pretend places and people in the room with you?   Vividness

26. Do you play pretend games about how things used to be when you were much younger — before you started going to school?   Fanciful

27. Do you sometimes pretend that you are a brave hero who saves somebody or who captures a bad guy?   Active-Heroic

28. Do you play games where you pretend to fight with somebody?   Aggressive, Active-Heroic

29. Do you play pretend games about things that don't ever really happen in real life?   Intellectual, Vividness

30. Do you play scary pretend games — like ghost or monsters or something like that?   Scary, Active-Heroic

31. Sometimes when you play pretend things, do you feel so happy that you don't ever want the game to end?   Vividness, Fanciful

32. When you are playing checkers or cards or other games like that, do your friends sometimes have to tell you that it's your turn because you were thinking about something else?   Absorption

33. Do you sometimes feel like you don't want to think about anything and wish that someone would tell you a story or that you could turn on the TV?   Scary, Vividness

34. Are your daydreams sometimes so scary that you try real hard not to think about them anymore?   Scary

35. Do you daydream about very happy things?   Fanciful

36. If someone asks what you're thinking or   Dysphoric
    doing when you're daydreaming, does it
    make you feel silly?
37. Do you sometimes think about very sad   Scary, Dysphoric
    things when you are daydreaming?
38. Do you sometimes dream about acci-   Dysphoric, Active-Heroic
    dents or fires or crashes?
39. Do you get real scared because of some-   Scary
    thing that you daydream about?

(After Question 39 say)

"The rest of the questions are just a little different. You see four boxes instead of three after each question. I will read what it says under each box after
I ask the question and you put an X in the box which is the best answer for
you."
"Let's try bird number 4. (read question).
If you do that every night, put an X in the first box; if you do that almost every night, put an X in the 2nd box; if you do that some nights, put an X in the
3rd box; and if you never do that, put an X in the last box.

(Repeat for next 5 questions)

Fantasy Items   *Scale*

40. How often do you dream about things   Frequency
    that you see on television?
41. Counting all the different kinds of pre-   Frequency
    tend games-when you are by yourself,
    how much do you daydream?
42. Counting all the different kinds of   Frequency
    daydreams-when you are sitting in the
    classroom, how much do you daydream?
43. Counting all the different kinds of pre-   Frequency
    tend games-when you are alone, how
    much do you play pretend games?
44. Counting all the different kinds of pre-   Frequency
    tend games-when you are with your
    friends, how much do you play pretend
    games?
45. Do you have dreams at night or early in   Frequency
    the morning just before you get up?

"The next page tells you to stop. Don't turn the page yet. (Pause).

Appendix II:
Coefficient Alphas for Selected Variables in Each Country

	Country				
VARIABLES	USA	POLAND	FINLAND	ISRAEL	AUSTRALIA
Child Variables					
Identification with Aggressor	.35	.22	.35[a]	.34[a]	.34
Male Sex Role	.87	.89	.86	.84	.88
Female Sex Role	.81	.86	.77	.79	.85
Neutral Sex Role	.48[a]	.34	.38[a]	.54	.38
Aggressive Fantasy	.64	.66	.62	.57[a]	.59
Fanciful Fantasy	.59	.52	.61[a]	.41	.55[a]
Active-Heroic Fantasy	.61	.70	.64	—	.62
Frequency of TV Viewing	.72	.55[a]	.68	.75	.67
Perceived Realism of Violent Programs	.86	.72	.87	.88	.88
Identification with All Characters	.78	.67	.80	.61	.81
Identification with Violent Characters	.71	.77	.85[a]	.42	.77
Peer-Nominated Aggression	.97	.96	.96	.96	.97
Peer-Nominated Popularity	.87	.85	.92	.83	.92
Peer-Nominated Aggression Avoidance	.67	.84	.60[a]	—	.76
Parent Variables					
Rejection	.62	.73	.60	—	.65
Nurturance	.29	.53	.77	—	.31
Punishment	.44	.55	.43	—	.38
Mobility Orientation	.63	.65	.59	—	.73
Self-Rated Aggression (MMPI 4 + 9)	.78	.72	.73	—	.79

[a]Coefficient alpha computed for third wave of data

Epilogue

L. Rowell Huesmann
Leonard D. Eron
University of Illinois at Chicago

When we embarked on this research project 10 years ago, we were naive enough to believe that anyone who examined our findings up to that time would come away convinced that media violence plays an important role in the development of aggression. However, such a conclusion has not found universal acceptance. Debate has remained vociferous for many reasons including that the topic is fraught with far-reaching social and economic implications. In a polarized atmosphere certain research, however well conceived and executed, will find its detractors, and other research that is poorly conducted will find its advocates, insofar as the findings of either one support a particular point of view. Since completion of the present study, but before its publication, a review article that already has been widely cited because of its appearance in a prestigious journal, (Freedman, 1984), concluded that there was no evidence for a significant effect of television violence on behavior. To many of us, (Huesmann, Eron, Berkowitz & Chaffee, 1985) that review, written by someone who has never conducted research in the area, seemed unfair in its presentation of the evidence, distorting the findings of some researchers and neglecting to mention others. Yet, it is widely cited.

The approach taken by the participants in this cross-national study essentially by-passed this controversy. Our objective was aimed at determining the psychological processes through which exposure to media violence and aggressive behavior become associated, not to prove or disprove whether increases in media violence increase aggressive behavior. The process models that have emerged stress the role of social and cognitive factors as intervening variables. They emphasize reciprocal effects of media viewing behaviors on social behavior and of social behavior on media viewing behavior. Although there are substantial differences in results across countries, there are even more communalities. We leave it to each reader to draw his or her own conclusion about whether the amount of interpersonal violence in the world would be any less if children had not been exposed to so much television and film violence over the past 20 years. However, there can be little doubt that childrens' (and adults') aggressive behavior *can* be influenced by their exposure to TV and films and that the extent of this influence depends on numerous social and cognitive factors that differ among subjects.

REFERENCES

Freedman, J. (1984). Effect of television violence on aggressiveness. *Psychological Bulletin, 96,* 227–246.
Huesmann, L. R., Eron, L. D., Berkowitz, L., & Chaffee, S. (1985). *Effect of television violence on aggression: A reply to Freedman* (Technical Report). Chicago: Department of Psychology, University of Illinois at Chicago.

Author Index

A

Abelson , R. P., 16, *27,* 31, *44,* 242, *257*
Andison, F. S., 5, *23*
Aromaa, K., , 82, 83, 84, *115*
Australian Broadcasting Tribunal, 162, 163, 170, 172, 194, *196, 197*

B

Baarda, B., 35, *44,* 192, *199,* 251, *257,* 260, 273, *281*
Bachanan, R. W., 201, *236*
Bachman, J. G., 168, *199*
Bailyn, L., 22, *23*
Balaban, T., 189, *199*
Baltes, P. B., 263, *280*
Bandura, A., 6, 9, 10, 11, 22, *23, 24,* 36, *42,* 151, *157,* 260, 280, *280*
Banta, T. J., 31, *44*
Baron, R. A., 14, *24*
Bar-Tal, D., 209, *236*
Beit-Hallahmi, B., 202, 203, 204, 205, 206, 208, 219, *237,* 272, *281*
Belson, W., 6, 17, *24*
Bem, S. L., 37, *42*
Berkowitz, L, 6, 9, 11, 15, 17, *24, 26,* 154, 155, *157,* 260, 278, *280*
Berlyne, D. E., 278, *280*
Berndt, T. J., 10, *24*

Berry, J. W., 262, *281*
Berts, M., 104, *116*
Bettelheim, B., 204, *236*
Biles, D., 165, 166, *197*
Birnbacher, D., 156, *157*
Bizman, A., 209, *236*
Björkqvist, K., 94, 104, *115, 116*
Black, J. B., 16, *24*
Block, J., 41, *42,* 94, *115*
Bogunia, L., 123, *157*
Bower, G. H., 16, *24*
Braithwaite, V. A., 170, *198*
Brice, P., 9, 10, 13, 15, *24, 25,* 52, 53, 58, *79,* 99, *115,* 211, *237,* 276, *281*
Bronfenbrenner, U., 156, *157,* 205, 209, *236*
Broom, L., 164, *197*
Brown, J. W., 167, *199*
Bryson, L., 191, *197*
Buki, H., 32, *43*

C

Calder, B. J., 6, *25*
Calvert, S. L., 15, *24*
Camino, L., 6, *26*
Campbell, D. T., 264, *280*
Cantell, I., 82, 83, *115*
Carroll, J. C., 107, *115*
Cerro, D. S., 84, *117*
Chaffee, S. H., 5, *24,* 34, *42,* 46, *79,* 168, *197*

Chauvin -Faures, C., 32, *43*
Choynowski, M., 129, *157*
Clark, W. W., 67, *80*
Clevitt, A. S., 12, *25*
Cline, V. B., 13, *25*
Cohen, A., 211, 234, *236*
Cole, A. M., 84, *117*
Collins, W. A., 9, 10, 16, *24*
Comstock, G. A., 5, 6, *24,* 46, *79,* 168, *197*
Connel, R. H., 12, *27*
Conway, B., 164, *197*
Cook, T. D., 6, 7, *24, 25*
Coombs, C., 272, *280*
Cooper, J., 190, *199*
Crains, B. D., 149, *157*
Crains, R. B., 149, *157*
Croft, R. G., 13, *25*
Croll, P., 174, *197*
Courrier, S., 13, *25*
Cumberbatch, G., 11, *25*

D

Darczewska, K., 124, *157*
Darley, J., 201, *236*
Del Rosario, M. L., 6, *25*
deSoola Pool, I., 174, *198*
Devereux, E. C., 205, 209, *236*
Dixon, M., 165, *197*
Dollard, J., 154, *157*
Dominick, J. R., 11, *24*
Donnerstein, E., 278, *280*
Doob, A. N., 12, *24,* 154, *157*
Dorr, A., 156, *157*
Drabman, R. S., 12, 14, *24, 27*
Dubow, E., 215, *236*
Duval, E. M., 123, *157*

E

Eagly, A. H., 143, *157*
Edgar, P., 165, 169, 170, 172, *197*
Edwards, C. P., 94, *117*
Eels, K., 39, *44*
Ekman, K., 94, *115*
Emery-Hauzeur, C., 32, *43*
Eron, L. D., 2, 4, 6, 8, 9, 10, 11, 13, 15, 16, 22,
    23, *24, 25, 26,* 31, 32, 33, 34, 35, 36, 37, 38,
    39, 40, 41, *42, 43, 44,* 52, 53, 54, 56, 57, 58,
    67, 68, 76, *79,* 84, 94, 97, 99, 100, 106, 107,
    110, *115, 116,* 132, 143, 145, 149, 151, 154,
    155, 156, *157, 158, 159,* 183, 184, 191, 192,

193, *197, 198,* 209, 210, 211, 214, 215, 218,
    228, 229, *236, 237,* 240, 247, 249, *257,* 259,
    260, 263, 267, 276, 280, *280, 281*
Evatt, P., 170, *197*
Eysenck, H. J., 5, *25*

F

Fenn, M. R., 9, 15, *27*
Feshbach, S., 16, *25,* 32, 35, 37, *43,* 102, *115,*
    143, 145, 152, *157,* 260, 278, *280*
Fischer, P., 9, 10, 13, 15, *24, 25,* 52, 53, 58, *79,*
    99, *115,* 211, *237,* 276, *281*
Fiske, D. W., 264, *280*
Fraczek, A., 123, 128, 143, 154, 155, 156, *157,*
    158, 159
Frasure-Smith, N., 18, *26*
Freedman, J. L., 201, *236*
Friedrich-Cofer, L. K., 6, 12, *25, 27*
Froddi, A., 143, *158*

G

Gati, I., 274, *281*
Geen, R. G., 14, *25,* 156, *158*
Geller, S., 155, *158*
George, C., 107, *115*
Gerbner, G., 11, 21, *25,* 47, *79,* 86, 105, *115,*
    126, *158,* 169, 172, 173, 192, *197*
Goldstein, A., 17, *25,* 167, *197,* 261, 269, *280*
Gorney, R., 6, *26*
Goodwin, N., 170, *199*
Gottfredson, M. R., 2, *25*
Grabosky, P., 191, *197*
Granzberg, G., 6, 17, *25*
Greenberg, B. S., 11, *24,* 168, *197*
Groebel, J., 17, *26,* 97, *115,* 259, 267, 271,
    274, 275, 278, *281*
Gross, J., 35, *43*
Gross, L. P., 11, 21, *25,* 46, 47, 53, *79, 80,* 86,
    115, 126, *158,* 172, 173, 192, *197*
Grusec, J. E., 12, *25*

H

Haavio-Mannila, E., 82, 83, 84, *115, 116*
Haines, H., 172, 174, *197*
Hajiwana, S., 174, *198*
Halloran, J. D., 174, *197*
Halpern, W. I., 14, *25*
Hamers, J. F., 18, *26*
Hammond, S. B., 163, 164, 165, *198*

Harcourt, A., 164, *197*
Harper, R. J. A., 164, *197*
Harris, D. B., 215, *236*
Hartman, M., 216, *237*
Hawkins, R., 174, *199*
Hayes, S. C., 10, 14, *25*
Hearold, S. L., 5, 10, *25*
Heath, L., 6, *25*
Heckel, R. V., 11, *26*
Helmreich, R., 37, *43*
Henderson, R. F., 164, *197*
Hennigan, K. M., 6, *25*
Hess, V. L., 10, *24*
Hicks, D. J., 11, 12, 22, *25,* 96, *115,* 211, 234, *237*
Hirschi, T., 2, *25*
Hoffman, H. R., 46, *80*
Holaday, P., 15, *25*
Holman, J., 170, *198*
Horne, D., 163, 164, *198*
Horton, R. W., 14, *27*
Howard, A., 107, *116,* 192, *198*
Howitt, D., 11, *25*
Huesmann, L. R., 5, 6, 7, 8, 9, 10, 11, 13, 15, 16, 22, 23, *24, 25, 26,* 32, 33, 34, 35, 36, 37, 38, 39, 40, 41, 42, *42, 43,* 52, 53, 54, 56, 58, 67, 68, 76, *79,* 84, 94, 97, 99, 100, *115, 116,* 132, 143, 145, 149, 154, 155, 156, *158, 159,* 167, 168, 183, 184, 191, 192, 193, *197, 198,* 209, 210, 211, 215, 218, 228, 229, *236, 237,* 240, 247, 249, *257,* 259, 260, 263, 267, 276, 280, *280, 281*
Huston, A. C., 274, *281*
Huston-Stein, A., 12, *25*

I

Iwao, S., 174, *198*

J

Jaakkola, R., 82, 83, *115*
Jacklin, C. N., 93, 103, *116*
Jaffe, Y., 201, 202, *237*
Jallinoja, R., 82, 84, *116*
Jarosz, M., 120, 122, *158*
Jasinski, J., 122, *158*
Joreskog, K. D., 42, *43*

K

Kaffman, M., 205, 206, 207, 208, 218, *237*
Kagan, J., 7, *26,* 94, *116*

Karson, E., 205, 209, *236*
Katzman, N., 46, *79,* 168, *197*
Kavanaugh, R. D., 10, *26*
Kav-Vanaki, S., 205, 209, *236*
Kendzierski, D. A., 7, *24*
Kent, G. H., 129, *158*
Kessler, R., 6, *26,* 195, *198,* 224, *237,* 253, 254, 255, *257,* 259, 267, *281*
Kiely, E., 205, 209, *236*
King, E., 104, *116*
King, J., 163, 164, 165, *198*
Kintsch, W., 15, 26
Kipnes, D., 12, *25*
Kippax, S., 17, *26,* 162, 167, 168, 170, *198*
Kirwil, L., 143, *158*
Klein, R., 9, 13, 15, *25,* 99, *115,* 211, *237,* 276, *281*
Kohlberg, L., 189, *198*
Kornadt, H. J., 154, 155, *158*
Krebs, D., 17, *26,* 97, *115,* 259, 267, 274, *281*
Kurczewski, J., 122, *159*
Kuttschreuter, M., 35, *44,* 192, *199,* 251, *257,* 260, 273, *281*
Kwasniewski, J., 122, *158*

L

Lagerspetz, K., 32, *43,* 68, *79,* 94, 104, *115,* 123, 132, *158, 159,* 210, 228, 229, *237*
Lambert, W. E., 18, *26*
Lancaster-Jones, F., 164, *197*
Landau, S. F., 19, *26,* 202, 203, 206, 235, *237,* 272, *281*
Langham, J., 170, *198*
Latane, B., 201, *236*
Laulicht, J. H., 31, *44*
Lefkowitz, M. M., 2, 5, 6, 8, 9, 10, 11, 22, 23, *24, 25, 26,* 32, 33, 34, 35, 36, 39, 40, 41, *43,* 54, 56, 58, 67, 68, *79,* 84, 94, 97, 100, 106, 107, 110, *115, 116,* 143, 145, 149, 151, 154, 155, *157, 158, 159,* 184, 191, 192, 193, *197, 198,* 214, 215, *236, 237,* 240, *257,* 260, 263, 280
Leichtman, H. M., 11, *26*
Leon, D., 203, *237*
Lesser, G., 47, *79*
Levin, H., 107, *116,* 145, 152, 155, *159,* 192, *199*
Levy, A. S., 201, *236*
Leyens, J. P., 6, *26,* 155, *157*
Lindgren, J., 82, *116*
Lippincott, E. C., 14, *27*

Los, M., 122, *159*
Loye, D., 6, *26*
Lovibond, S. H., 169, *198*
Lyle, J., 46, *80, 168, 199*

M

Macauley, J., 143, *158*
Maccoby, E. E., 93, 96, 103, 107, *116,* 145, 152, 155, *159,* 192, *199*
MacDonald, G. E., 12, *24*
Madsen, M. C., 209, 218, *237, 238*
Main, M., 107, *115*
Malak, B., 154, 156, *159*
Markowska, D., 123, *159*
Marshall, H. M., 10, *26*
McCall, R. B., 10, *26*
McCann, T. E., 173, *198*
McCarter, R. E., 11, *26*
McCombs, M., 46, *79,* 168, *197*
McCord, J., 107, *116,* 192, *198*
McCord, W., 107, *116,* 192, *198*
McGregor, C., 163, *198*
Meeker, M., 39, *44*
Mermelstein, R., 10, *24,* 52, 53, 58, *79*
Meyer, T. P., 12, *26*
Milavsky, J. R., 6, *26,* 195, *198,* 224, *237,* 253, 254, 255, *257,* 259, 267, *281*
Milgram, S., 201, *237*
Miller, N., 154, *157*
Miller, R. S., 10, *26*
Mischel, W., 189, *198*
Mivtzari, E., 209, *236*
Morgan, M., 35, *43,* 46, 53, *80,* 172, 173, 192, *197*
Morris, W. N., 10, *26*
Moss, H. A., 7, *26,* 94, *116*
Mowrer, O., 154, *157*
Mukherjee, S. K., 166, 167, *198*
Murray, J. P., 17, *26,* 162, 167, 168, 170, *198*

N

Nadelman, L., 37, *43*
Naffin, N., 166, *198*
Naisten tutkijanuran ongelmat ja esteet, 83, *116*
Neely, J. J., 11, *26*
Nettler, G., 19, *26*
Nevo, B., 208, *237*
Newcomb, A. M., 10, 17, *26*
Newman, G., 3, *26*

The New Yorker, 269, *281*
Nichols, K. B., 11, *26*
Nias, D. K., 5, *25*
Noble, G., 168, 169, *198*

O

Oeser, O. A., 163, 164, 165, *198*
Olweus, D., 7, *26,* 32, *43,* 104, 106, 107, 109, *116,* 145, 149, 152, 154, 155, *159,* 192, *198,* 240, *257*
O'Neal, E. C., 14, *25*

P

Parke, R. D., 6, 10, 17, *26, 27,* 154, *159*
Parker, E. G., 168, *199*
Penttinen, H., 83, *116*
Pingree, S., 174, *199*
Pitkänen-Pulkkinen, L., 6, *26,* 32, *43,* 94, 105, 107, *116,* 155, *159*
Podgorecki, A., 122, *159*
Price, J., 143, *157,* 201, *236*
Pulkkinen, A., 82, 83, *116*
Pulkkinen, L., 84, 94, *116*

R

Rabin, A. I., 204, 205, 208, 219, *237*
Reykowski, J., 154, *159*
Raviv, A., 209, *236*
Reeves, B., 168, *197*
Reid, D., 170, *199*
Reszke, J., 131, *159*
Riihinen, O., 83, *116*
Rincover, A., 10, 14, *25*
Ritamies, M., 83, *116*
Roberts, D., 46, *80,* 168, *197*
Robinson, J. P., 168, *199*
Rodgers, R. R., 205, 209, *236*
Roff, J. D., 7, *27*
Rogosa, D., 42, *43,* 186, *199*
Rosch, E., 261, *281*
Rosekrans, M. A., 11, *27*
Rosenthal, R., 242, *257*
Ross, D., 6, 9, 10, 11, 22, *24,* 36, *42*
Ross, S. A., 6, 9, 10, 11, 22, *24,* 36, *42*
Rogers, C., 33, *43*
Romanoff, R., 215, *236*
Rosenfeld, E., 37, 40, *43,* 215, *237*
Royal Commission on Human Relationships, 163, 164, 165, 166, 195, *199*

Rubens, W. S., 6, *26*, 195, *198*, 224, *237*, 253, 254, 255, *257*, 259, 267, *281*
Rubinstein, E. A., 168, *199*
Ruble, D. N., 189, *199*
Ruusala, R., 85, *116*
Ryback, D., 12, *27*

S

Sagi, P. C., 2, *27*
Sand, E. A., 32, *43*
Sand-Ghilain, J., 32, *43*
Santti, R., 83, *116*
Sarkkinen, R., 85, *116*
Schaie, K. W., 263, *281*
Schank, R., 16, *27*
Schleifer, H., 209, *238*
Schonemann, P. H., 265, *281*
Schramm, W., 168, *199*
Schulz, W., 271, *281*
Sears, R. B., 107, *116*, 145, 152, 154, 155, *157, 159*, 192, *199*
Sebastian, R. S., 6, 17, *26*
Segal, M., 17, *25*, 167, *197*, 261, 269, *280*
Shapir, N., 201, 202, *237*
Shapira, A., 209, 218, *237, 238*
Shavit, N., 209, *236*
Shavit, R., 209, *236*
Sheehan, P. W., 173, 177, 183, *198, 199*
Shouval, R., 205, 209, *236*
Shulman, S., 209, *238*
Signorelli, N., 35, *43*, 46, 53, *80*, 172, 173, 192, *197*
Singer, D. G., 6, 12, 16, *27*, 54, *80*, 267, *281*
Singer, J. L., 6, 12, 16, *27*, 54, *80*, 267, *281*
Singer, R. D., 32, *43*
Sinkko, R., 85, *116*
Slaby, R. G., 154, *159*
Smets, P., 32, *43*
Sonesson, I., 104, *116*
Sorbom, D., 42, *43*
Spence, J. T., 37, *43*
Spiro, M. E., 204, *238*
Stapp, J., 37, *43*
Steele, G., 6, *26*
Steiger, J. H., 265, *281*
Stein, A. H., 6, *27*
Steinbring, J., 6, 17, *25*
Stewart, D. E., 162, 167, 170, 171, *199*
Stewart, W., 170, *198*
Stipp, H., 6, *26*, 195, *198*, 224, *237*, 253, 254,

255, *257*, 259, 267, *281*
Stoddard, G., 15, *25*
Stroo, A. A., 32, *43*
Sturm, H., 270, 274, 278, *281*
Susman, E. J., 12, *25*
Szustrowa, T., 128, *158*

T

Takala, M., 82, 83, 105, *117*
Tannenbaum, P. H., 14, *27*
Thomas, M. H., 12, 14, *24, 27*
Thomas, S. V., 7, *24*
Thome, P., 143, *158*
Tiegs, E. W., 67, *80*
Tindall, K., 170, *199*
Toch, H., 201, 237
Torney-Purta, J. V., 37, 40, *43*, 215, *237*
Triandis, H. C., 262, *281*
Turner, C. W., 9, 11, 15, *27*, 84, *117*
Turner, T. J., 16, *24*
Tversky, A., 274, *281*
Tymowski, A., 125, *159*
Tyszka, Z., 123, 124, *159*

U

Ullian, D. Z., 189, *198*
U.S. Bureau of Census, 19, *27*, 46, *80*

V

Valiaho, H., 83, *116*
Verkko, V., 84, *117*
Volosin, D., 10, 14, *25*

W

Walder, L. O., 2, 6, 8, 9, 10, 11, 22, 23, *24, 25, 26*, 31, 32, 33, 34, 35, 36, 39, 40, 41, *43, 44*, 54, 56, 58, 67, *79*, 84, 94, 97, 100, 106, 107, 110, *115, 116*, 143, 145, 149, 151, 154, 155, *157, 158, 159*, 184, 191, 192, 193, *198*, 214, 215, *236, 237*, 240, *257*, 260, 263, *280*
Walters, R. H., 10, *27*, 151, *157*
Warner, W. L., 38, *44*
Watkins, B. A., 15, *24*
Wellford, C. F., 2, *27*
West, S., 6, 17, *26*
Westman, M., 123, *159*
Wharton, J. D., 6, *25*
Whiting, B. B., 94, *117*

Wiegman, O., 35, *44,* 192, *199,* 251, *257,* 260, 273, *281*
Williams, T. M., 6, 17, *27*
Wilson, P. R., 167, *199*
Wilson, W., 96, *115*
Winn, M., 14, *27*
Wirt, R. D., 7, *26*
Wright, J. C., 274, *281*

Y

Yarmel, P. W., 38, *43,* 76, *79,* 143, *158,* 215, *236,* 247, *257*

Yearbook of Population Research in Finland, XXII, 83, *117*
Yinon, Y., 201, 202, 209, *236, 237*

Z

Zillmann, D., 14, *27,* 278, *281*
Zajonc, R. B., 14, *27*
Zeckman, P., 19, *27*
Zimbardo, P. G., 201, *238*
Ziv, A., 209, *238*
Zumkley, H., 155, *159*

Subject Index

A

Academic achievement and aggression, 66, 67, 72, 73, 76, 77, 78, 111, 252, 256; *see also* Intelligence
  in selected countries, 67, 72, 73, 76, 111
    Finland, 111
    United States, 67, 72, 73, 76
Age and aggression, 7, 10, 12, 17, 22, 51–54, 55–57, 76, 92–93, 108, 132, 134, 135, 136, 137, 138, 139, 140, 179–181, 186, 189, 195, 220, 224, 225, 228, 255, 269
  in selected countries, 51–54, 55–57, 76, 92, 93, 132, 134, 135, 136, 137, 138, 139, 140, 179–181, 186, 189, 195, 220, 224, 269
    Australia, 179–181, 186, 189, 195, 269
    Finland, 92, 93
    Israel, 220, 224
    Poland, 132, 134, 135, 136, 137, 138, 139, 140
    United States, 51–54, 55–57, 76
Aggression, anxiety about, *See* Prosocial behavior, measures of
Aggression, avoidance of, *See* Prosocial behavior, measures of
Aggression, concern with, 2–4, 206, *See also* Crime
Aggression, definitions of, 2, 261, 262
Aggression, field studies on, 5, 6, 8, 37, 167, *See also* selected countries

Aggression, in selected countries, *See* Crime, in selected countries
Aggression, laboratory studies on, 5, 6, 14, 22, 36, 167, *See also* selected countries
Aggression, learning processes, 9–17, 22, 23, 36, 37, 61, 62, 65, 77, 155, 210, 229, 231, 239, 240, 245, 256, 278, 280
  arousal processes, 13–14
  attitude change, 11–13
    "mitigation" and "enhancement" studies on, 12
  information-processing model, 14–17, 37, 61, 239
    encoding and retrieval in, *See* Cognitive processes
    scripts, schemas as guides, *See* Cognitive processes
  observational learning, 9–11, 22, 36, 62, 210
Aggression, longitudinal studies of: *See* Longitudinal studies of aggression
Aggression, measures of, 31–38
Aggression, mediating variables in, *See* Mediating variables in aggression
Aggression, predispositions, 64
Aggression, reduction of, 6
Aggression, stability of, 7–9, 41, 62, 93, 94, 98, 107, 149, 152, 155, 181, 185–187, 189, 192–193, 252
  predictive quality of early behavior, 7–9,

94, 98, 154, 185–187, 189, 192, 193, 194
Altruistic behavior, 209, *See also* Prosocial
    behavior
Ancient Rome, 1
Australia, 5, 19, 21, 23, 31, 46, 47, 48, 84, 97,
    108, 109, 132, 152, 161–196, 240, 242,
    243, 247, 249, 252, 254, 262, 268–270,
    276
  broadcasting tribunal in, 162, 170, 171, 172,
    194, 196
  prior research on aggression in, 168–171
  Royal Commission on Human
    Relationships, 163, 164, 166, 195

C

California Achievement Text, 67
Cartoons, 35, 87, 130, 162, 172, 174, 175, 177,
    211
Catharsis through fantasy, *See* Fantasy as
    catharsis
Causal relation, violence viewing and
    aggression, 5–6, 60–64, 77, 113,
    148–152, 189, 192–193, 195, 224–225
Censorship, government of TV, 21, 47, 210,
    269, 270, 273
Child measures, 31–38; *see also* Appendix I
Children's Fantasy Inventory, 37, 177, 215,
    218, 251, 252
Cognitive processes, 14–17, 22, 23, 37, 61, 65,
    77, 155, 229, 231, 239, 240, 242, 245,
    256, 278–280
  encoding, 15, 77, 229, 240, 256
  rehearsal, 15, 16, 65, 231, 240, 245
  retrieval, 15, 16, 229, 240, 245
  scripts and schemas, 15, 16, 77, 239, 242,
    245, 256
  storage, 15, 16, 77, 245
Cohort effects, 30, 54, 93, 103, 193
Constitutional factors and aggression, 4, 239
Crime, 2–3, 15, 19–20, 23, 45, 84, 85, 120–123,
    163, 165, 166, 167, 191, 203, 206, 256,
    270
  alcohol and, 84, 122, 163, 166, 167
  homicide, 18, 19, 20, 84, 120, 121, 122, 165,
    166, 256
  in selected countries, 2, 3, 18, 19, 20, 45,
    84, 85, 120–123, 165–166, 167, 191,
    203, 206, 256
    Australia, 19, 20, 165, 166, 167, 191
    Finland, 19, 20, 84, 85
    Israel, 19, 20, 203, 206

Netherlands, 19, 20
Poland, 18, 19, 20, 120–123
United States, 2, 3, 18, 19, 20, 45, 256
reasons for increase and decline, 2–3, 45
statistics, 2, 19, 120, 121, 203
Cross-national study, 5, 17–19, 23, 29, 30,
    31–42, 260–265, 275–277
  aims of, 23
  data analysis techniques, 40–42, 264, 265
  methodological issues, 18, 29–30, 193, 194,
    261, 265
  research design, 30–40, 263, 264
    measures used in, 31–40, 129, 176–178,
    214, 215
Culture and aggression, 17–19, 48, 103, 113,
    123–125, 154–156, 202, 220, 255, 262
  in selected countries, 48, 123–125, 154–156,
    202, 220, 262
    Australia, 202, 262
    Israel, 220, 262
    Poland, 123–125, 154–156, 262
    United States, 48, 262

D,E,F

Data analysis techniques, *see* Cross-national
    study
Demographic characteristics and aggression,
    2–4, 19, 38, 84, 125, 168, 215, 216, 220,
    221, 235
Desensitization, viewer, 12, 13–14
  physiological, *See* Aggression, learning
    processes
Disinhibition, 10, 12, 16, 17, 240
Economic value of media violence, 47, 49
Encoding, *See* Cognitive processes
Family structure, 82–84, 123–125, 144,
    163–164, 170, 191, 195, 203, 273
  in selected countries, 82–84, 123–125, 144,
    163–164, 170, 191, 195, 203, 273
    Australia, 163–164, 170, 191, 195
    Finland, 82–84
    Israel, 203
    Poland, 123–125, 144, 273
Fantasy, 16, 37, 40, 57, 65, 66, 76, 78, 93, 108,
    132, 134, 135, 138, 139, 144, 148, 152,
    153, 154, 169, 177, 178, 179, 181, 183,
    184, 186, 188, 189, 195, 209, 215, 218,
    220, 230–234, 235, 245, 246, 251, 252,
    256, 267
  as catharsis, 16, 37, 65, 108, 169, 183, 189,
    195, 245

as cognitive rehearsal, 16, 37, 65, 218, 256
in selected countries, 65, 76, 78, 93, 132,
    138, 139, 152, 153, 178, 179, 181, 183,
    184, 186, 188, 195, 215, 218, 230–234,
    235, 246, 267
    Australia, 178, 179, 181, 183, 184, 186,
        188, 195, 246
    Finland, 93, 246
    Israel, 215, 218, 230, 231, 232, 233, 234,
        235, 246
    Poland, 132, 138, 139, 152, 153, 246
    United States, 65, 76, 78, 246, 276
Finland, 5, 6, 19, 20, 21, 23, 31, 39, 41, 46, 47,
    48, 81–117, 123, 128, 132, 136, 169,
    181, 188, 190, 191, 192, 194, 195, 210,
    218, 228, 242, 243, 245, 247, 249, 251,
    254, 262, 270, 271, 275, 276

G,H,I

Gender and aggression, 8, 11, 17, 22, 36, 54,
    55–57, 58–59, 61, 62, 63, 64, 65, 70, 71,
    74, 75, 76, 92–95, 97–100, 102, 105,
    106, 107, 110–114, 132, 133, 134,
    135–140, 142–153, 179–195, 216, 217,
    220, 221, 255, 266, 271, See also Sex
    roles and aggression
in selected countries, 8, 9, 51–54, 55–57,
    58–59, 61, 62, 63, 64, 65, 70, 71, 74, 75,
    76, 92–95, 97–100, 102, 105, 106, 107,
    110–114, 132–133, 134, 135–140,
    142–144, 145–153, 179–193, 195, 216,
    217, 220–236, 266, 271
    Australia, 179–193, 195
    Finland, 92–95, 97–100, 102, 105, 106,
        107, 110–114, 271
    Israel, 216, 217, 220–236
    Poland, 132, 133, 134, 135–140, 142–144,
        145–153
    United States, 8, 9, 51–54, 55–57, 58–59,
        61, 62, 63, 64, 65, 70, 71, 74, 75, 76, 266
Habituation to violence, 14
Identification with television characters, 11,
    36, 55, 57–58, 63, 68, 71, 74, 76, 77, 78,
    93, 95, 96, 97, 99, 102, 105, 111, 112,
    113, 114, 132, 134, 135, 140, 141, 145,
    154, 177, 178, 179, 181, 182, 183, 185,
    186, 195, 215, 224, 228, 229, 240, 241,
    242, 243, 245, 251, 256, 266, 269, 271,
    273, 278
in selected countries, 36, 55, 57–58, 63, 74,
    76, 77, 78, 93, 95, 96, 97, 99, 102, 105,

111, 112, 113, 114, 134, 135, 177, 178,
    179, 181, 182, 183, 185, 186, 195, 215,
    224, 228, 229, 241, 242, 243, 269, 271
    Australia, 177, 178, 179, 181, 182, 183,
        185, 186, 195, 241, 242, 243, 269
    Finland, 93, 95, 96, 97, 99, 102, 105, 111,
        112, 113, 114, 241, 242, 243, 271
    Israel, 215, 224, 228, 229, 241, 242, 243
    Poland, 134, 135, 241, 242, 243
    United States, 36, 55, 57–58, 63, 74, 76,
        77, 78, 241, 242, 243
Imaginative play and daydreams, 16; see also
    Fantasy
Institutionalized aggression, 2
Intelligence (IQ), 38, 67, 72, 76–77, 110, 142,
    143, 224, 225, 232, 233, 245, 247, 252,
    253, 254, 255, 267; see also Academic
    achievement and aggression
in selected countries, 38, 110, 142, 143, 224,
    225, 232, 233, 245, 267
    Finland, 110, 245
    Israel, 224, 225, 245
    Poland, 142, 143, 245
    United States, 245, 267
Israel, 5, 19, 20, 38, 41, 46, 48, 100, 103, 132,
    141, 188, 192, 195, 201–238, 242, 243,
    245, 247, 249, 254, 262, 271, 272, 273,
    276
    city life in, 205–209
    kibbutz society in, 203–209

L,M,N

Longitudinal studies of aggression, 5, 6, 8, 9,
    13, 17, 22, 30, 50–79, 88–114, 129–156,
    164, 177–196
Measures; see Child measures; see also Parent
    measures
Mediating variables in aggression, 35, 76–77,
    143, 170, 224, 249, 267, 301
    fantasizing, See Fantasy
    identification, See Identification with TV
        characters
    intellectual achievement, See Intelligence;
        See also Academic achievement and
        aggression
    social popularity, See Popularity
Message System Analysis, 172
Method of study, 5, 30–42, 49–51, 88–92,
    127–131, 176–178, 212–215
in selected countries, 5, 30–42, 49–51,

88–92, 127–131, 176–178, 212–215
Australia, 31, 176–178
Finland, 31, 41, 88–92
Israel, 212–215
Poland, 31, 41, 127–131
United States, 31, 38, 39, 49–51
Methodological issues, *See* Cross-national
study
"Mitigation" studies, 12, 13
MMPI, 40, 51, 68, 69, 91, 147, 187, 248, 252
NBC (Milavsky) study, 6–7, 195, 224,
253–255, 259–260, 267
The Netherlands, 5, 19, 29, 35, 48, 192,
251–253, 254, 260, 273, 274, 275, 276
Nurturance, *See* Parental influences on
aggression

O,P

Observational learning, *See* Aggression,
learning processes
Parental influences on aggression, 38–40,
67–76, 78, 90, 104–110, 113, 145, 148,
149, 151, 152, 153, 154, 155, 156, 163,
178, 184, 186, 189, 192, 193, 195, 220,
221, 222, 224, 225, 228, 232, 233, 247,
248, 249, 267
child-rearing styles, 72–76, 90, 106–108,
113, 145, 146, 148, 151, 152, 153, 154,
155, 156, 163, 178, 184, 186, 187, 189,
192, 195, 228, 247, 248, 249
nurturance, 90, 108, 145, 146, 187
punishment and rejection, 72–76, 90,
106–108, 113, 145, 148, 151, 152, 153,
154, 156, 163, 178, 184, 186, 187, 189,
192, 247, 248, 249
education and social status, 70–72, 78, 90,
109, 110, 113, 145, 146, 184, 186, 187,
220, 221, 222, 224, 225, 232, 233, 267
fantasy behavior, 40
in selected countries, 38–40, 67–76, 82–84,
90, 104–109, 111, 112, 113, 114,
144–152, 153, 154, 155, 156, 163–164,
178, 184, 186, 187, 189, 192, 193, 195,
220, 221, 222, 224, 225, 232, 233, 248,
249, 267
Australia, 163, 164, 165, 178, 184, 186,
187, 189, 192, 193, 195, 248, 249
Finland, 39, 82–84, 90, 104–109, 111,
112, 113, 114, 248, 249
Israel, 38, 220, 221, 222, 224, 225, 232,
233, 248

Poland, 39, 144–152, 153–156, 248
United States, 39, 67–76, 248, 249, 267
mobility orientation, 39, 72, 145, 187
parents' aggression, 38–40, 68–70, 90, 108,
109, 147, 178, 184, 186, 187
parents' television viewing, 40, 70, 90,
104–105, 113, 178, 184, 186, 187, 193,
195
Parent measures, 38–42
Peer-nominated index of aggression, 31–33,
41, 50, 52, 54, 89, 93, 214, 252 (index
itself, 283–285)
reliability and validity of, 32
Poland, 5, 18, 19, 21, 23, 31, 39, 41, 47, 48, 84,
97, 100, 108, 109, 119–156, 169, 192,
195, 210, 240, 243, 245, 247, 249, 251,
254, 262, 272, 273, 276
Popularity, 65, 66–68, 76, 77, 78, 93, 104, 141,
143, 165, 168, 183, 188, 214, 218, 220,
228, 229, 235, 249, 251, 256, 267, 269,
272
in selected countries, 65, 66, 67, 76, 77,
78, 93, 104, 141, 143, 165, 183, 188,
214, 218, 220, 228, 229, 235, 249, 251,
267, 272
Australia, 165, 183, 188, 249
Finland, 93, 104
Israel, 214, 218, 220, 228, 229, 235, 251,
272
Poland, 141, 143, 251
United States, 65, 66, 67, 76, 77, 78, 249,
251, 267
Popularity of violent TV content, 47
Prosocial behavior, 6, 10, 12, 16, 33, 235,
249, 252, 253, 273, 276; *see also*
Popularity
measures of, 33
modeling of, 6, 12
rehearsal of, 16
Punishment, *See* Parental influences on
aggression

R,S

Race of models, 11
Realism of television, 13, 35, 36, 41, 55,
58–60, 66–67, 68, 71, 74, 78, 93,
100–103, 113, 132, 134, 144, 145, 168,
169, 178, 179, 182, 183, 185, 193, 195,
215, 222, 224, 228, 229, 240, 241, 251,
252, 267, 270, 271
in selected countries, 35–36, 41, 55, 58–60,

67, 71, 74, 78, 93, 100–103, 113, 132, 134, 169, 178, 179, 182, 183, 185, 195, 215, 222, 224, 228, 229, 241, 267, 269, 270, 271
  Australia, 169, 178, 179, 182, 183, 185, 195, 241, 269
  Finland, 41, 93, 100–103, 113, 241, 270, 271
  Israel, 215, 222, 224, 228, 229, 241
  Poland, 132, 134, 241
  United States, 35–36, 41, 55, 58–60, 67, 71, 74, 77, 78, 241, 267
Reciprocal action model, 76–79, 252, 267, 275, 276, 278, 301
Regularity of television viewing, 33, 55, 64, 66, 71, 95, 96, 105, 106, 135, 180, 182, 183, 185, 186, 188, 224, 241, 268
  in selected countries, 33–35, 55, 64, 71, 95, 96, 105, 106, 113, 135, 180, 182, 183, 185, 186, 188, 224, 241, 268
  Australia, 180, 182, 183, 185, 186, 188, 241
  Finland, 95, 96, 105, 106, 113, 241
  Israel, 224, 241
  Poland, 135, 241
  United States, 33–35, 55, 64, 71, 241, 268
Rehearsal, *See* Cognitive processes
Rejection, *See* Parental influences on aggression
Reliability of measures, 32–40; *see also* Appendix II
Retrieval, *See* Cognitive processes
Rogers Adjustment Inventory, 33
Roots, broadcast of, 12
Samples, 49, 50, 88, 89, 128, 130–131, 176, 212–213
  in selected countries, 49, 50, 88, 89, 128, 130, 131, 176, 212–213
  Australia, 176
  Finland, 88, 89
  Israel, 212–213
  Poland, 128, 130, 131
  United States, 49, 50
Scripts and schemas, *See* Cognitive processes
Sensitive period for learning aggression, 10, 54, 76
Sex of models, 11, 56, 96, 190
Sex roles, 11, 36–37, 56, 78, 83, 89, 96, 103, 104, 143, 144, 177, 179, 183, 186, 190–192, 195, 210, 215, 229, 230, 251, 266, 268; *See also* Gender and aggression

in selected countries, 36–37, 78, 83, 89, 96, 103, 104, 143, 144, 177, 179, 183, 186, 190, 195, 215, 229, 230, 266, 268
  Australia, 177, 179, 183, 186, 190, 195, 268
  Finland, 83, 89, 96, 103, 104
  Israel, 215, 229, 230
  Poland, 143–144
  United States, 37, 78, 266
Short Intelligence Scale, 129
Social class and aggression, 38, 67, 70, 71, 72, 73, 75, 78, 108, 109, 110, 113, 114, 145, 184, 220, 247
Surgeon General's report, 45

T,U

Technology and aggression, 4
Television characters, 86, *see also* Identification with television characters
Television commercials, 47, 126
Television programming, 20, 21, 46–48, 85–86, 125–127, 162–163, 171–176, 196, 210, 211, 234
  in selected countries, 20, 21, 46–48, 85–86, 125–127, 162, 163, 171–176, 196, 210, 211, 234
  Australia, 21, 162, 163, 171–176, 196
  Finland, 21, 47, 85–86
  Israel, 21, 47, 210, 211, 234
  Poland, 221, 47, 125–127
  United States, 21, 46–48
Television usage, 20–22, 33–36, 46–48, 54, 77, 85–86, 95, 97, 105, 111, 112, 125–127, 132–133, 139–141, 156, 161–162, 164, 171, 192–193, 234, 241, 242
  in selected countries, 20–22, 33–36, 46–48, 85–86, 95, 97, 105, 111, 112, 125–127, 132–133, 139–141, 161–162, 164, 234, 241, 242
  Australia, 21, 46, 161, 162, 164, 241
  Finland, 21, 46, 85–86, 95, 97, 105, 111, 112, 241
  Israel, 21, 46, 234, 241, 242
  Poland, 21, 46, 125–127, 132–133, 139–141, 241
  United States, 20–22, 46–48, 421
  measures of, 33–36; *see also* Appendix I
Television viewing, *see* Television usage; *see also* Regularity of television viewing
Television violence, 33–35, 51; *see also*

Television usage; *see also* Violence in television programming

measures of, 33–35, 51; *see also* Appendix I

United States, 5, 13, 17, 18, 19, 20, 21, 23, 31, 32, 33, 34, 36, 37, 38, 39, 41, 45–80, 84, 88, 89, 95, 96, 97, 100, 101, 102, 103, 106, 107, 108, 109, 114, 126, 127, 129, 130, 131, 132, 136, 137, 144, 152, 154, 162, 163, 167, 171, 172, 173, 174, 181, 186, 188, 189, 190, 191, 192, 194, 195, 209, 210, 218, 221, 223, 224, 228, 242, 243, 245, 247, 249, 251, 252, 253, 254, 256, 260, 265–268, 269, 273, 274, 276

V,W

Violence in television programming, 21, 34, 35, 46, 47, 51, 53, 85, 86, 87, 88, 161, 130, 171–176, 241

Visual cues and aggression, 15

WISC, 38, 129

World War II, 2, 20, 45, 82, 202